KNOWLEDGE GRAPHS FOR EXPLAINABLE ARTIFICIAL INTELLIGENCE:
FOUNDATIONS, APPLICATIONS AND CHALLENGES

Studies on the Semantic Web

Semantic Web has grown into a mature field of research. Its methods find innovative applications on and off the World Wide Web. Its underlying technologies have significant impact on adjacent fields of research and on industrial applications. This book series reports on the state of the art in foundations, methods, and applications of Semantic Web and its underlying technologies. It is a central forum for the communication of recent developments and comprises research monographs, textbooks and edited volumes on all topics related to the Semantic Web.

Volume 047

Previously published in this series:

ISSN 1868-1158 (print)
ISSN 2215-0870 (online)

KNOWLEDGE GRAPHS FOR EXPLAINABLE ARTIFICIAL INTELLIGENCE: FOUNDATIONS, APPLICATIONS AND CHALLENGES

Edited by

Ilaria Tiddi

Vrije Universiteit Amsterdam, Amsterdam, The Netherlands

Freddy Lécué

Thales, Montreal, Canada & Inria, Sophia Antipolis, France

and

Pascal Hitzler

Kansas State University, Manhattan, Kansas, USA

ISBN 978-3-89838-754-5 (AKA, print)
ISBN 978-1-64368-080-4 (IOS Press, print)
ISBN 978-1-64368-081-1 (IOS Press, online)
doi: 10.3233/SSW47

Bibliographic information available from the Katalog der Deutschen Nationalbibliothek (German National Library Catalogue) at https://www.dnb.de

Publisher
Akademische Verlagsgesellschaft AKA GmbH, Berlin

Represented by Co-Publisher IOS Press
IOS Press BV
Nieuwe Hemweg 6B
1013 BG Amsterdam
The Netherlands
Tel: +31 20 688 3355
Fax: +31 20 687 0019
email: order@iospress.nl

Preface

Explanations have been the subject of study in a variety of fields for a long time, and are experiencing a new wave of popularity due to the latest advancements in Artificial Intelligence (AI). While machine and deep learning systems are now widely adopted for decision making, they also revealed a major drawback, namely the inability to explain their decisions in a way that humans can easily understand them. As a result, eXplainable AI (XAI) rapidly became an active area of research in response to the need of improving the understandability and trustworthiness of modern AI systems – a crucial aspect for their adoption at large scale, and particularly in life-critical contexts.

The field of Knowledge Representation and Reasoning (KRR), on the other hand, has a long standing tradition in managing structured knowledge, i.e. modeling, creating, standardising, publishing and sharing information in symbolic form. KRR methods and technologies developed over the years result by now in large amounts of structured knowledge (in the form of ontologies, knowledge graphs, and other structured representations), that are not only machine-readable and in standard formats, but also openly available, and covering a variety domains at large scale. These structured sources, designed to capture causation as opposed to correlation in Machine Learning methods, could therefore be exploited as sources of background knowledge by eXplainable AI methods in order to build more insightful, trustworthy explanations.

This book provides the very first comprehensive collection of research contributions on the role of knowledge graphs for eXplainable AI (KG4XAI). We gather studies using KRR as a framework to enable intelligent systems to explain their decisions in a more understandable way, presenting academic and industrial research focused on the theory, methods and implementations of AI systems that use structured knowledge to generate reliable explanations.

We include both introductory material on knowledge graphs for readers with only a minimal background in the field, and advanced specific chapters devoted to methods, applications and case-studies using knowledge graphs as a part of knowledge-based, explainable systems (KBX-systems). The final chapters convey current challenges and future directions of research in the area of knowledge graphs for eXplainable AI.

Our goal is not only to provide a scholarly, state-of-the-art overview of research in this field, but also to foster the hybrid combination of symbolic and and subsymbolic AI methods, motivated by the complementary strengths and limitations of both the field of KRR and Machine Learning.

The editors would like to thank all contributing authors for their efforts in making this book possible.

March 2020

Ilaria Tiddi
Freddy Lécué
Pascal Hitzler

Contents

Part 3. Challenges for Knowledge-Based eXplainable Systems

Part 1

Foundations of Knowledge-Based eXplainable Systems

Knowledge Graphs for eXplainable Artificial Intelligence: Foundations, Applications and Challenges   3
I. Tiddi et al. (Eds.)
IOS Press, 2020
doi:10.3233/SSW200009

Knowledge Graphs on the Web – An Overview

Nicolas HEIST, Sven HERTLING, Daniel RINGLER, and Heiko PAULHEIM

Data and Web Science Group, University of Mannheim, Germany

Abstract. Knowledge Graphs are an emerging form of knowledge representation. While Google coined the term *Knowledge Graph* first and promoted it as a means to improve their search results, they are used in many applications today. In a knowledge graph, entities in the real world and/or a business domain (e.g., people, places, or events) are represented as nodes, which are connected by edges representing the relations between those entities. While companies such as Google, Microsoft, and Facebook have their own, non-public knowledge graphs, there is also a larger body of publicly available knowledge graphs, such as DBpedia or Wikidata. In this chapter, we provide an overview and comparison of those publicly available knowledge graphs, and given insights into their contents, size, coverage, and overlap.

Keywords. Knowledge Graphs, Linked Data, Semantic Web, Dataset Profiling

1. Introduction

Knowledge Graphs are increasingly used as means to represent knowledge. Due to their versatile means of representation, they can be used to integrate different heterogeneous data sources, both within as well as across organizations [8,9].

Besides such domain-specific knowledge graphs which are typically developed for specific domains and/or use cases, there are also public, cross-domain knowledge graphs encoding common knowledge, such as DBpedia, Wikidata, or YAGO [33]. Such knowledge graphs may be used, e.g., for automatically enriching data with background knowledge to be used in knowledge-intensive downstream applications [34]. In particular for the case of eXplainable AI, knowledge graphs can be used as additional input to the AI algorithm, as a means to support interpretation of the results, or both [18].

Since Google coined the term *Knowledge Graph* for marketing purposes, it has subsequently been used in the scientific literature as well. The slogan by which Google announced KGs was *Things, not Strings*[1]. The idea of that slogan is: while strings are often ambiguous, knowledge graphs consist of disambiguated entities, so that entities of the same name can be told apart more easily. Nowadays, almost all companies processing large amounts of heterogeneous data use knowledge graphs as a means of representation, including, but not limited to IBM, Microsoft, Facebook or Ebay [27].

There are quite a few different definitions for knowledge graphs [5]. Typically, a knowledge graph

---

[1]https://www.blog.google/products/search/introducing-knowledge-graph-things-not/

1. mainly describes real world entities and their interrelations, organized in a graph.
2. defines possible classes and relations of entities in a schema.
3. allows for potentially interrelating arbitrary entities with each other.
4. covers various topical domains [29].

In this chapter, we provide an overview of publicly available, cross-domain knowledge graphs on the Web. We discuss the techniques used to create those knowledge graphs and provide an in-depth comparison in terms of size, level of detail, contents, and overlap.

2. Overview

There are different techniques for creating knowledge graphs. The most common ones are (1) manual curation, (2) creation from (semi) structured sources, and (3) creation from unstructured sources. Some knowledge graphs also use a mix of those techniques.

2.1. Manual Curation

Cyc [20] is one of the oldest knowledge graphs; the Cyc project dates back to the 1990s. Cyc was created along with its own language (CycL), which provides a large degree of formalization.

While Cyc was developed by a comparatively small group of experts, the idea of *Freebase* [32] was to establish a large community of volunteers, compared to Wikipedia. To that end, the schema of Freebase was kept fairly simple to lower the entrance barrier as much as possible. Freebase was acquired by Google in 2010 and shut down in 2014.

Wikidata [43] also uses on a crowd editing approach. In contrast to Cyc and Freebase, Wikidata also imports entire whole large datasets, such as several national libraries' bibliographies. Porting the data from Freebase to Wikidata is also a long standing goal [32].

Curating a knowledge graph manually can be a large effort. The total cost of development for Cyc have been estimated as 120 Million USD[2]. This corresponds to a total cost of 2-6 USD per single axiom in Cyc [30].

2.2. Creation from (Semi) Structured Sources

A more efficient way of knowledge graph creation is the use of structured or semi structured sources. Wikipedia is a commonly used starting point for knowledge graphs such as *DBpedia* [19] and *YAGO* [40].

DBpedia mainly uses infoboxes in Wikipedia. Those are manually mapped to a predefined ontology; the mapping is crowd sourced using a Wiki and a community of volunteers. Given those mappings, the DBpedia Extraction Framework creates a graph in which each page in Wikipedia becomes an entity, and all values and links in an infobox become attributes and edges in the graph.

YAGO uses a similar process, but classifies instances based on the category structure and WordNet [24] instead of infoboxes. YAGO integrates various language editions of

---

[2]http://www.ttivanguard.com/conference/Napa2017/4-Lenat.pdf

Wikipedia into a single graph and represents temporal facts with meta-level statements, i.e., RDF reification.

CaLiGraph also uses information in categories, but aims at converting them into formal axioms using DBpedia as supervision [11]. Moreover, instances from Wikipedia list pages are considered for populating the knowledge graph [31]. The result is a knowledge graph which is not only richly populated on the instance level, but also has a large number of defining axioms for classes [12].

A similar approach, i.e., the combination of information in Wikipedia and WordNet, is used by *BabelNet* [25]. The main purpose of BabelNet is the collection of synonyms and translations in various languages, so that this knowledge graph is particularly well suited for supporting multi-language applications. Similarly, *ConceptNet* [38] collects synonyms and translations in various languages, integrating multiple third party knowledge graphs itself.

DBkWik [14] uses the same codebase as DBpedia, but applies it to a multitude of Wikis. This leads to a graph which has a larger coverage and level of detail for many long tail entities, and is highly complementary to DBpedia. However, the absence of a central ontology and mappings, as well as the existence of duplicates across Wikis, which might not be trivial to detect, imposes a number of challenges not present in DBpedia.

Another source of structured data is the structured annotations in Web pages using techniques such as RDFa, Microdata, and Microformats [23]. While the pure collection of those could, in theory, already be considered a knowledge graph, that graph would be rather disconnected and consist of a plethora of small, unconnected components [28] and would require additional cleanup for compensating irregular use of the underlying schemas and shortcomings in the extraction [22]. A consolidated version of this data into a more connected knowledge graph has been published under the name *VoldemortKG* [42].

2.3. Creation from Unstructured Sources

The extraction of a knowledge graph from semi structured sources is considered more easy than from the extraction from unstructured sources. However, there is much more information in unstructured sources (such as text). Therefore, extracting knowledge from unstructured sources has also been proposed.

NELL [4] is an example for extracting a knowledge graph from free text. NELL was originally trained with a few seed examples and continuously runs an iterative coupled learning process. In each iteration, facts are used to learn textual patterns to detect those facts, and patterns learned in previous iterations are used to extract new facts, which serve as training examples in later iterations. To improve the quality, NELL has introduced a feedback loop incorporating occasional human feedback.

WebIsA [37] also extracts facts from free text, but focuses on the creation of a large-scale taxonomy. For each extracted fact, rich metadata are collected, including the sources, the original sentences, and the patterns used in the extraction of a particular fact. Those metadata are exploited for computing a confidence score for each fact [13].

3. Comparison of Knowledge Graphs

Whenever a knowledge graph is to be used in an application, it is important to determine which knowledge graph is best suitable for an application at hand. The knowledge graphs mentioned above differ in their content, their level of detail, etc. Hence, in this chapter, we will discuss several characteristics of knowledge graphs and provide insights into the differences between them.

3.1. General Metrics

The most straightforward metrics to be used consider the mere amount of information contained in a knowledge graph. Measures that may be used include:

- The number of instances in a graph
- The number of assertions (or edges between entities)
- The average and median linkage degree (i.e.: how many assertions per entity does the graph contain?)

As for using a knowledge graph in an XAI system, these metrics hint at the utility – the more information about the domain at hand is present (i.e., the more instances are represented in the knowledge graph and the more detailed that information is), the more can an XAI application benefit in providing better results or better interpretations.

Another set of metrics can be defined for the schema or ontology level of a knowledge graph:

- The number of classes defined in the schema
- The number of relations defined in the schema
- The average depth and width (branching factor) of the class hierarchy[3]
- The complexity of the schema

While the instance-based metrics focus more on the coverage of a domain in a knowledge graph, these schema-level metrics provide information about the richness and formality of that knowledge. They determine which techniques to use – e.g., while more formal, very complex ontologies will call for using ontology reasoning, light-weight, but large-scale ontologies will be better exploited by statistical and distributional approaches.

Table 1 depicts those metrics for some of the knowledge graphs discussed above. ConceptNet and WebIsA are not included, since they do not distinguish a schema and instance level (i.e., there is no specific distinction between a class and an instance), which does not allow for computing those metrics meaningfully. For Cyc, which is only available as a commercial product today, we used the free version OpenCyc, which has been available until 2017.[4]

From those metrics, it can be observed that the KGs differ in size by several orders of magnitude. The sizes range from 50,000 instances (and Voldemort) to 50 million instances (for Wikidata), so the latter is larger by a factor of 1,000. The same holds for assertions. Concerning the linkage degree, YAGO is much richer linked than the other graphs.

---

[3]While this could also be done for the property hierarchy, extensive property hierarchies are rather rare in common knowledge graphs.

[4]It is still available, e.g., at `https://github.com/asanchez75/opencyc`

Table 1. Basic Metrics of Open Knowledge Graphs

	DBpedia	YAGO	Wikidata	BabelNet
# Instances	5,044,223	6,349,359	52,252,549	7,735,436
# Assertions	854,294,312	479,392,870	732,420,508	178,982,397
Avg. linking degree	21.30	48.26	6.38	0.00
Median ingoing edges	0	0	0	0
Median outgoing edges	30	95	10	9
# Classes	760	819,292	2,356,259	6,044,564
# Relations	1355	77	6,236	22
Avg. depth of class tree	3.51	6.61	6.43	4.11
Avg. branching factor of class tree	4.53	8.48	36.48	71.0
Ontology complexity	SHOFD	SHOIF	SOD	SO
	Cyc	NELL	CaLiGraph	Voldemort
# Instances	122,441	5,120,688	7,315,918	55,861
# Assertions	2,229,266	60,594,443	517,099,124	693,428
Avg. linking degree	3.34	6.72	1.48	0
Median ingoing edges	0	0	0	0
Median outgoing edges	3	0	1	5
# Classes	116,821	1,187	755,963	621
# Relations	148	440	271	294
Avg. depth of class tree	5.58	3.13	4.74	3.17
Avg. branching factor of class tree	5.62	6.37	4.81	5.40
Ontology complexity	SHOIFD	SROIF	SHOD	SH

Figure 1 shows an overview of the knowledge graphs considered. We follow the conventions of the Linked Open Data Cloud diagrams[5] [36], which are used to depict linked datasets and their connections. In those diagrams, the size of the circles is proportional to the number of instances, and the strength of the connecting lines is proportional to the number of links.

The knowledge graphs also differ strongly in the characteristics of their schema. DBpedia and NELL have comparably small schemas, while Wikidata and BabelNet build deep and detailed taxonomies. For example, while NELL does not define detailed subclasses for *Scientist*[6], DBpedia defines four subclasses[7], Wikidata has more than 600[8] and CaLiGraph almost 2,000[9], including detailed classes such as *sickle-cell disease researcher* or *loop quantum gravity researcher*. Voldemort, on the other hand, reuses the schema.org ontology, which is comparably small [21].

Looking at the complexity, it is not much of a surprise that Cyc, originating in classic AI research and strongly building on logical rules [3,20], has the highest complexity. Wikidata, BabelNet, and Voldemort have only little complexity, the other graphs are somewhere inbetween.

---

[5]https://www.lod-cloud.net/
[6]http://rtw.ml.cmu.edu/rtw/kbbrowser/pred:scientist
[7]http://dbpedia.org/ontology/Scientist
[8]https://www.wikidata.org/wiki/Q15976092
[9]http://caligraph.org/ontology/Scientist

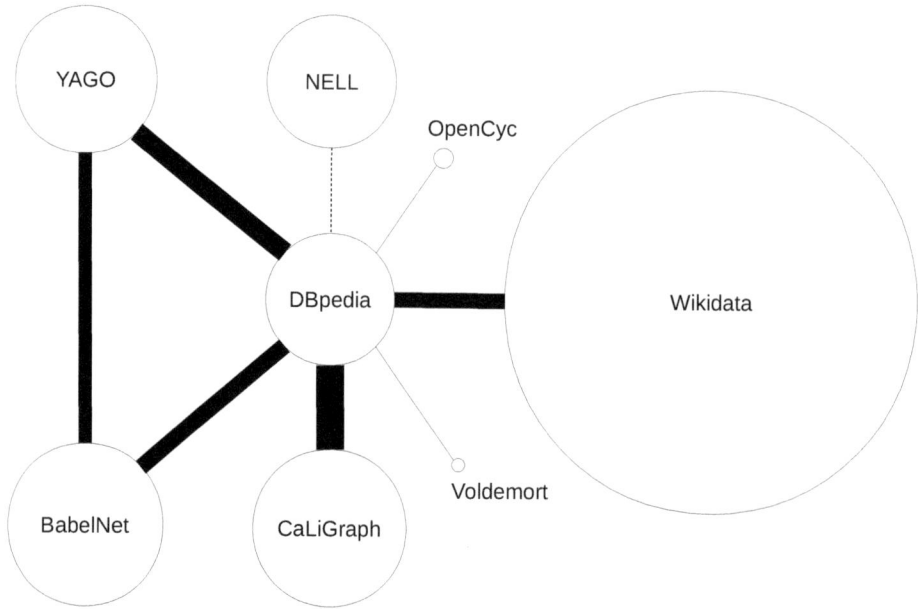

Figure 1. Depiction of the size and linkage degree of publicly available knowledge graphs. Although NELL and DBpedia are not explicitly interlinked, NELL contains links to Wikipedia, which can be trivially translated to DBpedia links.

3.2. Contents

The knowledge graphs do not only differ in their size and level of detail, but also in their contents. The most straightforward way to assess the content focus of a knowledge graph is to look at the size of its classes. Figures 2-9 show graphic depictions of those class sizes. The diagrams were created starting from the most abstract class and following the class hierarchy to the largest respective subclasses.

At first glance, the figures reveal differences in the development of the taxonomies. While Cyc builds a formal ontology with very abstract top level categories such as *partially intangible thing* or *thing that exists in time*, the more pragmatic classification in DBpedia and Voldemort (the latter using schema.org as an ontology) has top level classes such as *Place* or *Person*. The reason for these differences lies in the origins of the respective knowledge graphs: While Cyc's classification was created by AI researchers, the ontology in DBpedia is the result of a crowdsourcing process [30]. The same holds for schema.org, which is a pragmatic effort of a consortium of search engine developers.

Moreover, the diagrams reveal some differences in the contents. The main focus of DBpedia is on persons (and their careers), as well as places, works, and species. Wikidata also has a strong focus on works (mainly due to the import of entire bibliographic datasets), while Cyc, BabelNet and NELL show a more diverse distribution.

3.3. Looking into Details

To obtain deeper insights which classes are more prominent in which KGs, and, ultimately, which KGs are suitable for building eXplainable AI system in a specific domain,

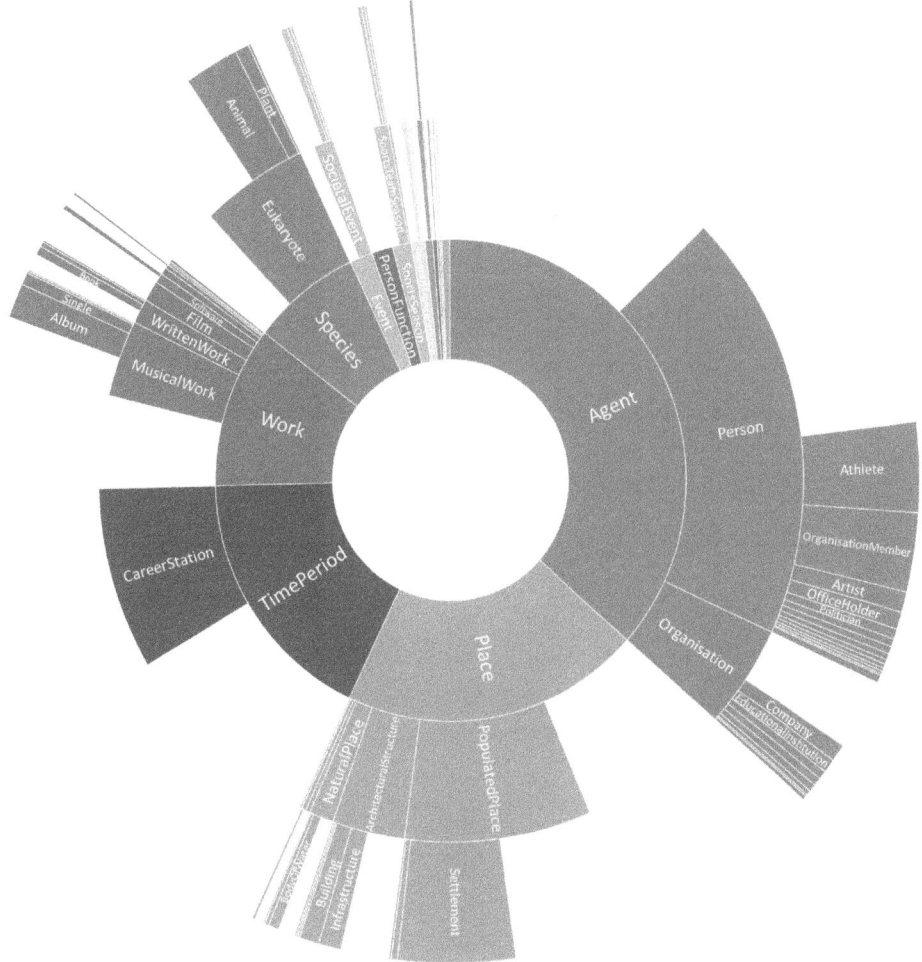

Figure 2. Instances in DBpedia

it is useful to not only look at the number of instances, but also the level of detail in which those instances are represented (i.e., the linkage degree and number of assertions per instance).

Table 2 depicts such a detailed view for ten prominent classes:

- Person
- Organization
- Populated place (city, country, etc.)
- Uninhabited place (mountain, lake, etc.)
- Species
- Work (book, movie, etc.)
- Building
- Gene
- Protein
- Event

Figure 3. Instances in YAGO

The global trend observed in this table is that Wikidata has the largest number of instances in most of the classes, while YAGO has the largest level of detail. However, there are differences from class to class. While Wikidata has a large number of works, YAGO is a good source of events. NELL often has fewer instances, but a larger level of detail, which can be explained by its focus on more prominent instances.

The contrast of the average and the median degree also reveals a few differences. For example, BabelNet contains a similar amount of instances as DBpedia for some classes, e.g., uninhabited places or works. While the average linkage degree is higher in DBpedia, the median is higher in BabelNet. This hints at a more uneven distribution of information in DBpedia, while BabelNet has a more constant distribution of statements per instance.

Table 2.: Detail statistics for selected classes

Class	DBpedia				YAGO				Wikidata			
	Instances	Avg. Deg.	Med-in	Med-out	Instances	Avg. Deg.	Med-in	Med-out	Instances	Avg. Deg.	Med-in	Med-out
Person	1,243,400	1.54	0	5	2,213,431	5.62	0	258	5,250,840	2.41	0	10
Organization	286,482	10.3	0	7	498,750	136.92	0	64	1,665,319	30.98	0	6
Populated place	513,642	7.38	0	8	319,210	219.49	0	138	2,355,559	3.81	1	6
Uninhabited place	67,495	0.91	0	4	160,615	23.67	0	48	1,516,890	0.23	0	6
Species	306,104	2.56	0	7	2,553,369	4.92	0	224	110	21.53	0	5
Work	496,070	0.81	0	8	1,175,125	28.07	0	36	34,585,828	5.91	0	12
Building	197,831	0.41	0	5	274,606	13.44	0	69	2,291,168	0.98	0	6
Gene	4	0.5	0.5	7.5	12,351	0.00	0	8	172,128	1.27	0	8
Protein	2,747	0.03	0	1	10,935	0.01	0	52	84,163	1.15	1	14
Event	76,029	1.91	0	3	562,583	41.23	0	48	579,559	1.76	0	5

Class	BabelNet				Cyc				NELL			
	Instances	Avg. Deg.	Med-in	Med-out	Instances	Avg. Deg.	Med-in	Med-out	Instances	Avg. Deg.	Med-in	Med-out
Person	2,384,065	0.00	0	17	12,784	0.04	0	3	90,601	8.93	0	0
Organization	764,662	0.01	0	12	26,276	5.70	0	5	41,646	6.31	0	0
Populated place	509,257	0.01	0	9	8,596	20.63	0	12	28,359	39.98	0	0
Uninhabited place	70,209	0.02	0	11	64	2.05	1	12	158,879	3.83	0	0
Species	6,536	0.01	0	17	0	-	-	-	3,273	0.88	0	0
Work	491,057	0.00	0	12	19,908	0.91	0	2	27,038	1.09	0	0
Building	520	0.00	0	8	786	0.14	0	4	50,699	4.51	0	0
Gene	522	0.00	0	5	8	0	0	3	0	-	-	-
Protein	10,399	0.00	0	3	0	-	-	-	0	-	-	-
Event	9,904	0.00	0	13	685	0.86	0	2	37,203	0.65	0	0

Class	CaLiGraph				Voldemort			
	Instances	Avg. Deg.	Med-in	Med-out	Instances	Avg. Deg.	Med-in	Med-out
Person	1,967,339	0.34	0	2	36,370	0.00	0	5
Organization	547,728	2.67	0	2	5,984	0.00	0	1
Populated place	700,559	10.12	0	2	1,278	0.00	0	5
Uninhabited place	170,324	1.16	0	2	60	0.00	0	4
Species	552,249	1.04	0	1	0	-	-	-
Work	678,888	0.49	0	1	6,673	0.00	0	3
Building	404,087	0.21	0	1	108	0.00	0	5
Gene	1,106	0.00	0	0	0	-	-	-
Protein	6,138	0.00	0	0	0	-	-	-
Event	148,122	0.49	0	0	198	0.00	0	4

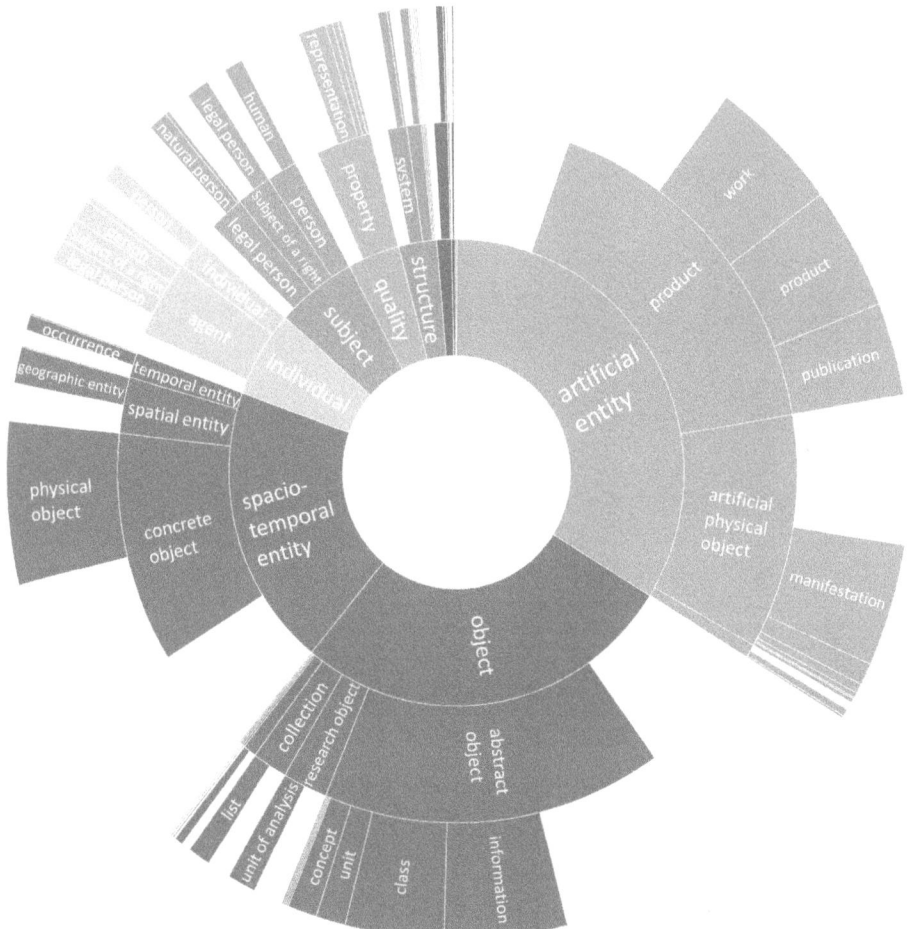

Figure 4. Instances in Wikidata

4. Linkage and Overlap of Knowledge Graphs

Since knowledge graphs differ so strongly in size, coverage, and level of detail, combining information from multiple KGs for implementing one application is often beneficial. To estimate the value of such a combination, we determine the overlap of the knowledge graphs first.

As shown in Fig. 1, many KGs contain explicit interlinks. Those links, usually in the form of `owl:sameAs` links, express that entities in two KGs are the same (or, more precisely: that they refer to the same real world entity) [10]. In other cases, such links can be generated indirectly, e.g., if a knowledge graph contains links to Wikipedia pages, which can be easily mapped to entities in DBpedia and YAGO.

Even if those links provide a first hint at the overlap of KGs, and further links can be found by exploiting the transitivity of the `owl:sameAs` property [1], they do not provide a complete picture. Due to the *open world assumption*, which holds for KG interlinks

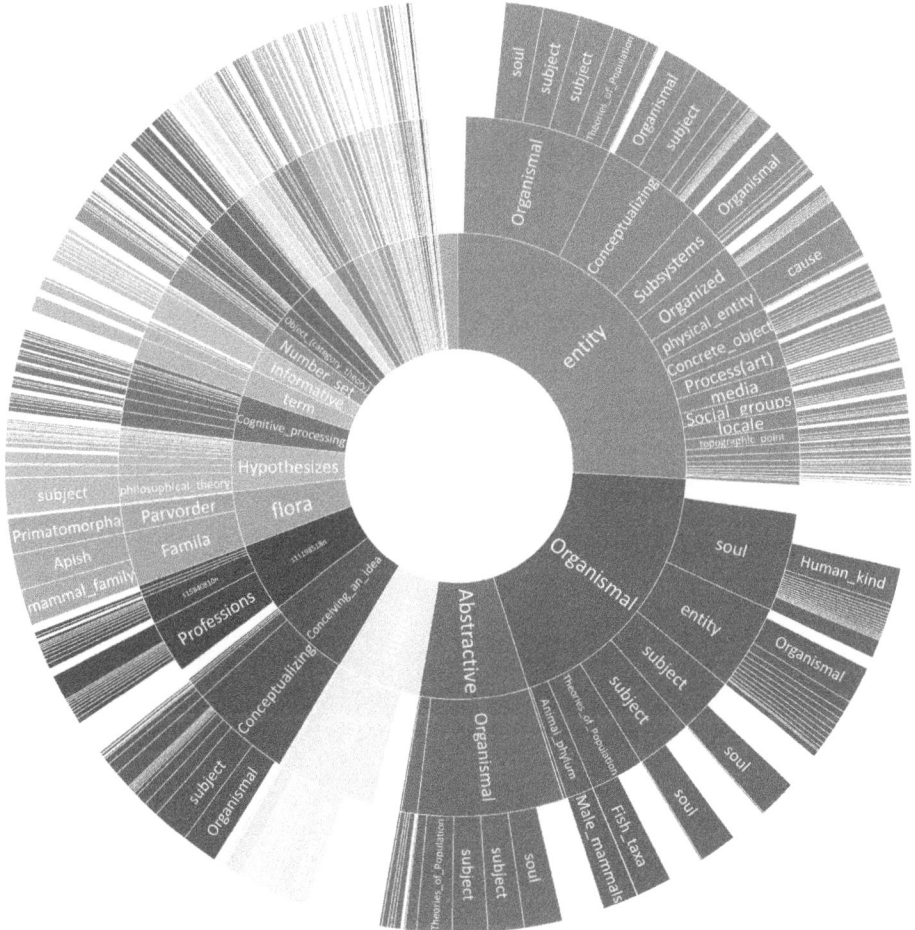

Figure 5. Instances in BabelNet

as well, there might always be more links than the one which are explicitly or implicitly provided by the KGs.

4.1. Method

In order to estimate the actual number of interlinks, we use a method first discussed in [33], which builds on a set of existing links and heuristic link discovery:

1. We use different heuristics to discover links between two KGs automatically, e.g., different string similarity measures [7,26].
2. Based on the existing, incomplete set of interlinks, we measure recall and precision of the individual heuristics [35].
3. With the help of those recall and precision figures, we can estimate the actual number of interlinks. After repeating the procedure with multiple heuristics, we can use the average of those estimations.

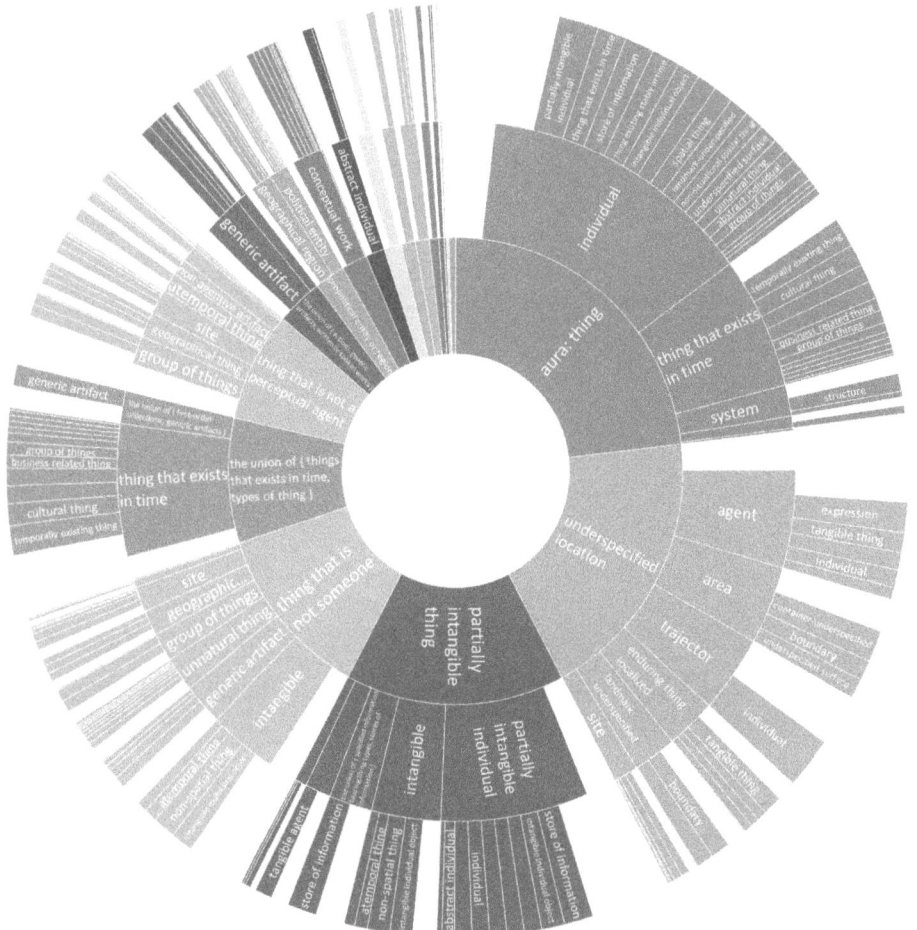

Figure 6. Instances in OpenCyc

Given that the actual number of links is C (which is unknown), the number of links found by a heuristic is F, and that the number of correct links in F is F^+, recall and precision are defined as

$$R := \frac{|F^+|}{|C|} \tag{1}$$

$$P := \frac{|F^+|}{|F|} \tag{2}$$

By resolving both to $|F^+|$ and combining the equations, we can estimate $|C|$ as

$$|C| = |F| \cdot P \cdot \frac{1}{R} \tag{3}$$

Thus, we can obtain an estimate for C given F, R, and P. A more intuitive interpretation of the last equation is that P is a measure of how strongly the heuristic *over*estimates the number of actual interlinks (thus, F is reduced by multiplication with P), and R is

Figure 7. Instances in NELL

a measure of how strongly the heuristic *under*estimates the number of actual interlinks (thus, F is divided by R).

In [33], we have shown that across different heuristics, although F varies a lot, the estimate C is fairly stable. For producing the estimates in this chapter, we have used the following heuristics: string equality, scaled Levenshtein (thresholds 0.8, 0.9, and 1.0), Jaccard (0.6, 0.8, and 1.0), Jaro (0.9, 0.95, and 1.0), JaroWinkler (0.9, 0.95, and 1.0), and MongeElkan (0.9, 0.95, and 1.0). The estimated overlap reported is the average estimate computed using these 16 metrics.

4.2. Findings

To analyze the benefit of the combination of different KGs, we depict the number of estimated links both in relation to (a) the entities existing in the larger of the two KGs (Fig. 10) as well as (b) in relation to the links that exist explicitly or implicitly (Fig. 11). From (a), we can estimate the amount of gain in knowledge of combining two KGs (i.e.,

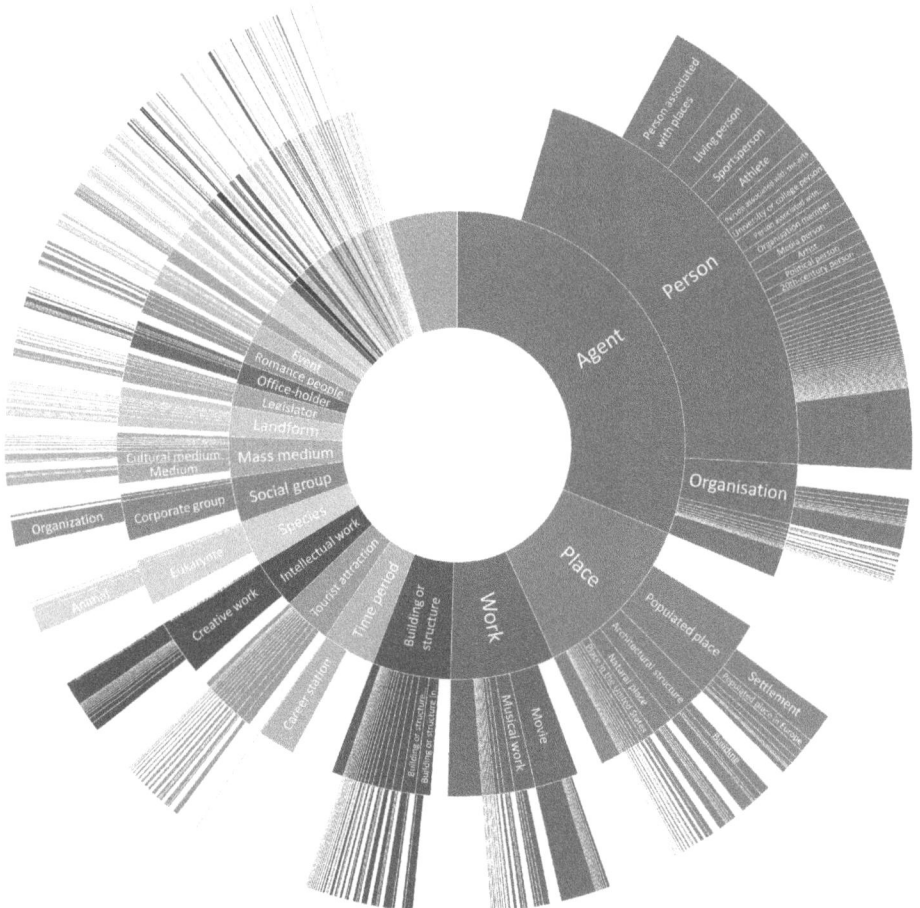

Figure 8. Instances in CaLiGraph

if only a small fraction of one KG is also contained in the other and vice versa, such a combination adds a lot of information). From (b), we can get insights into whether the set of existing links is sufficient for such a combination or not.

Fig. 10 shows that in most cases, the larger of two knowledge graphs contains most of the entities of a smaller one, i.e., its set of entities of a class in larger KG is usually a superset of that set in the smaller one. For example, as depicted in table 2, Wikidata contains about twice as many persons as DBpedia and YAGO. A value close to 0 for the overlap implies that DBpedia and YAGO contain almost no persons which are not contained in Wikidata. In conclusion, combining Wikidata with DBpedia or YAGO for a better coverage of the *Person* class would not be beneficial.

Notable exceptions are BabelNet and CaLiGraph, which often contain complementary instances. For example, DBpedia, BabelNet and CaLiGraph contain 1.2M, 2.4M, and 1.9M instances of the class *Person*, respectively, while DBpedia and BabelNet together are estimated to 2.9M, and all three together are estimated to contain even 3.9M instances of the class *Person*. The reasons for the high complementary of DBpedia/YAGO, BabelNet and CaLiGraph are their sources (only English Wikipedia vs. multiple lan-

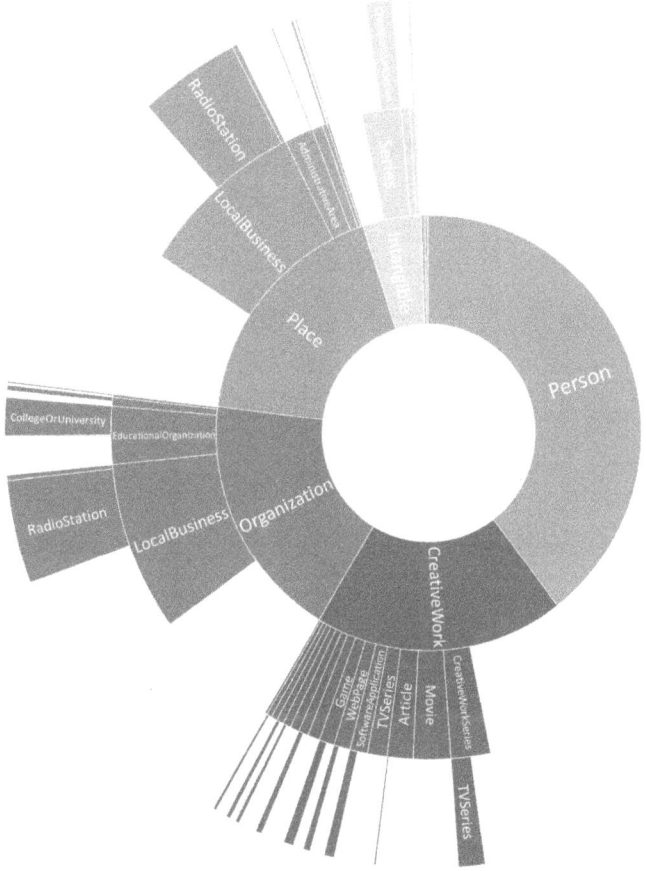

Figure 9. Instances in Voldemort

guage editions) and extraction mechanisms (especially the extraction from list pages in CaLiGraph, which leads to a larger number of instances overall).

Fig. 11 shows that the linkage between DBpedia, YAGO, BabelNet and CaLiGraph is mostly complete (i.e., most of the common instances are also explicitly linked). Since they are all generated from Wikipedia with different means, this is not much surprising. On the other hand, Nell, OpenCyc, and Voldemort have a much lower degree of linkage. This shows that links between KGs are only complete where they are trivial to create, and combining different knowledge graphs otherwise requires efforts in improving the interlinking as a preliminary step.

5. Conclusion and Outlook

In this chapter, we have given an overview of publicly available, cross-domain knowledge graphs on the Web. We have compared them according to different metrics which might be helpful to implement an eXplainable AI project in a given domain.

Besides the metrics used for this comparison, there are quite a few more which help in the selection and assessment of a given KG. For example, data quality in KGs has not

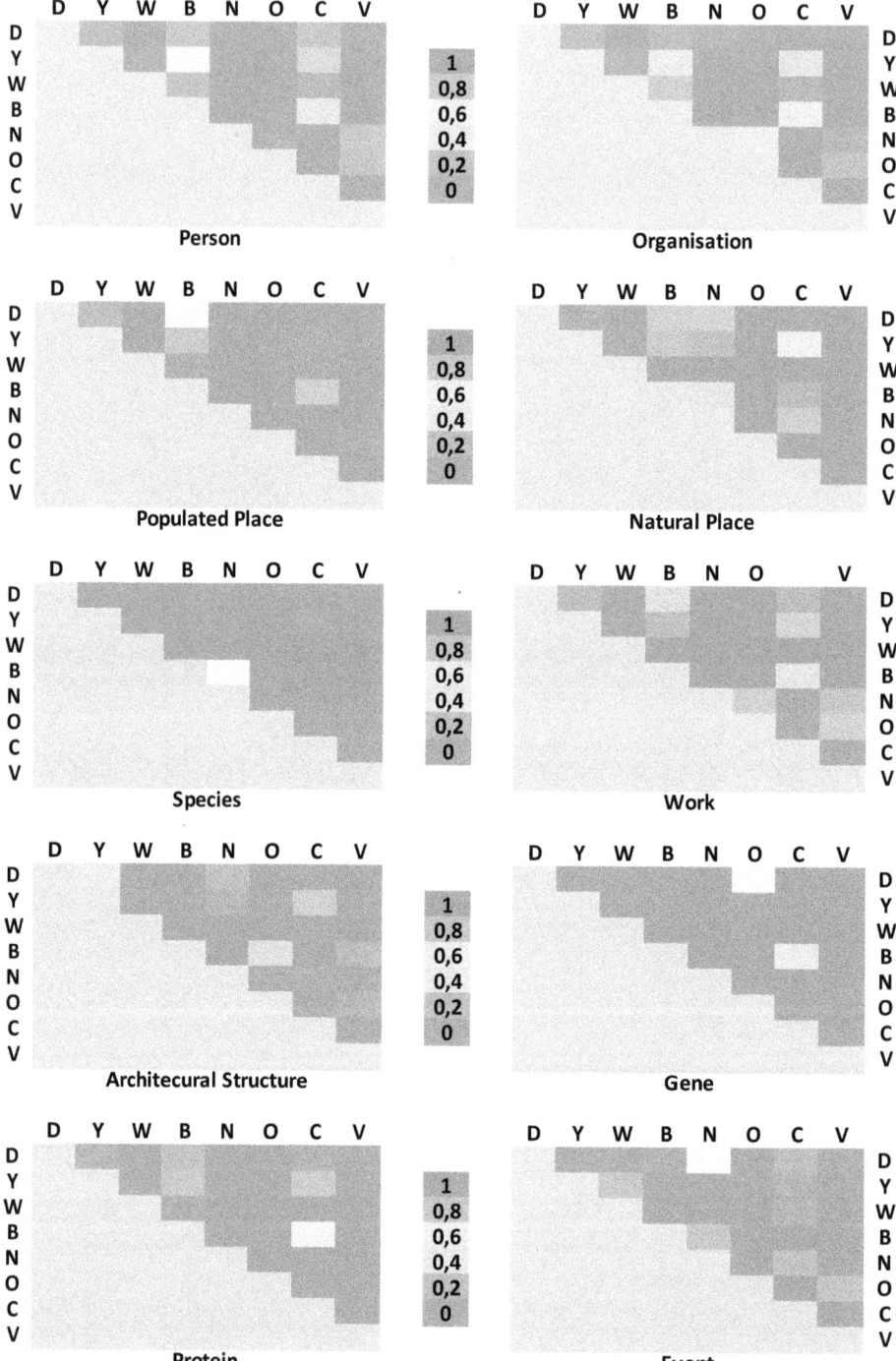

Figure 10. Fraction of entities in a pair of knowledge graphs which is *not* contained in the larger of the two graphs.

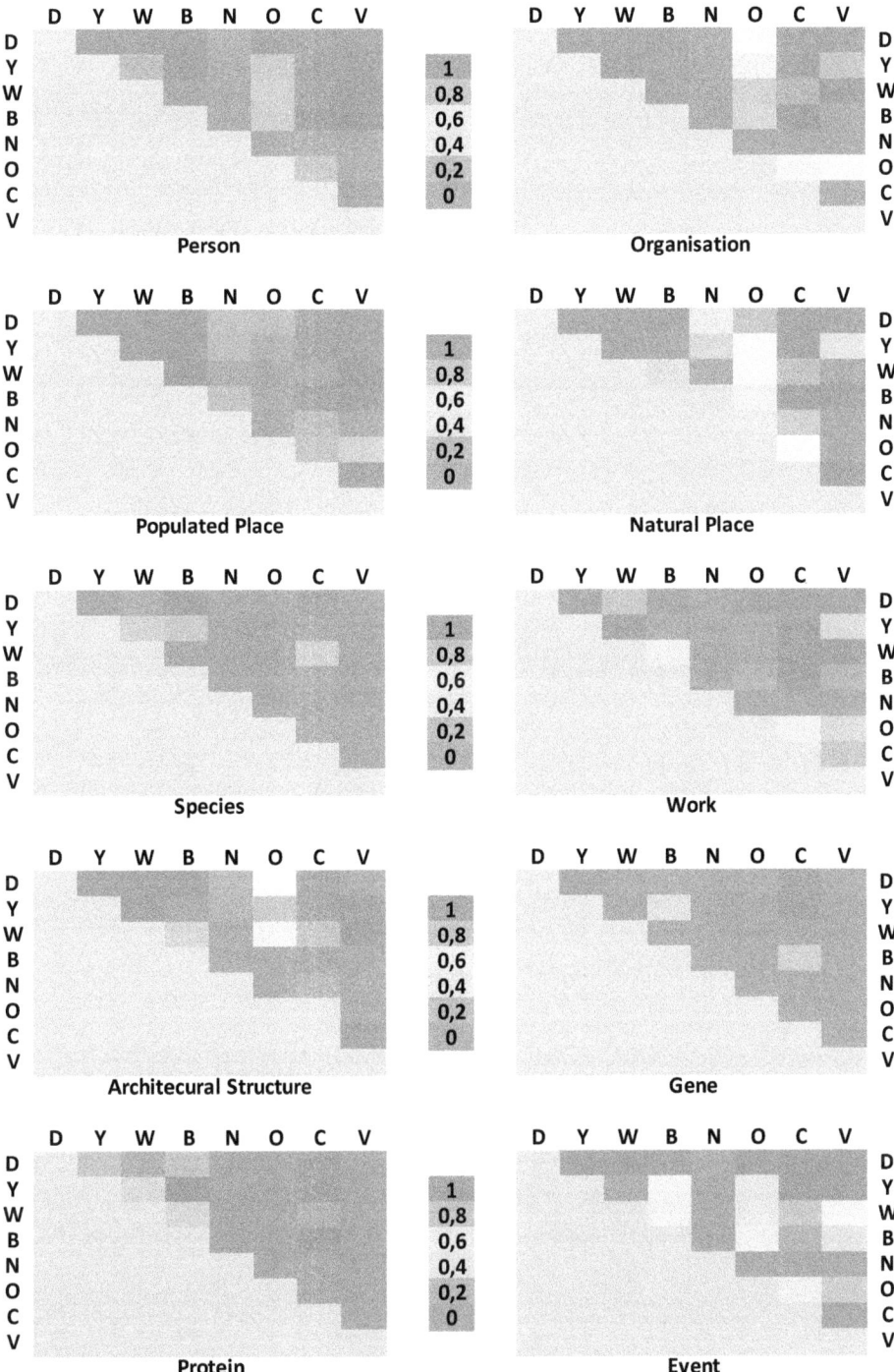

Figure 11. Existing entities in two KGs in relation to the number of links.

been considered in this chapter, since there are already quite elaborate surveys covering this aspect [6,44].

So far, we have measured the overlap of knowledge graphs only based on entities. Another helpful metric would be the overlap on the statement level. Even if two knowledge graphs cover the same entity, the information they contain about that entity might still be complementary. For example, for the entity *University of Mannheim*, DBpedia has the exact number of undergraduate students, PhD students, etc.[10], while Wikidata lists all faculties[11] and can provide a list of researchers employed at the university[12]. The density of information differs as well: while YAGO lists 3 alumni of the University of Mannheim[13], DBpedia lists 11 and Wikidata even 85 alumni[14]. Even contradicting information can be found [2]: for example, DBpedia and Wikidata provide a different number of students and Wikidata and YAGO provide different founding dates of the University of Mannheim.

Developing cross-domain knowledge graphs is an active field of research, and new developments emerge every once in a while. They differ in the data they use and/or the method of extraction:

- *DBkWik* [14,15,16] uses the extraction mechanism of DBpedia and applies it to a multitude of Wikis. The intermediate result is a collection of a few thousand isolated knowledge graphs, which have to be integrated into a coherent joint knowledge graph.
- *Chaudron* [39] uses Wikipedia as a source and focuses on quantifiable values (e.g., sizes, weights, etc.). Besides the mere extraction, Chaudron uses sophisticated methods for recognizing and converting units of measurement.
- The Linked Hypernym Dataset (*LHD*) [17], like the aforementioned WebIsA-LOD, focuses on the extraction of a hypernym graph. It uses a deep linguistic analysis of the first paragraph in Wikipedia.
- *ClaimsKG* [41] extracts claims from fact checking Web pages, such as politifacts, and interlinks them with other knowledge graphs such as DBpedia, which also allows for finding related claims.

The methods discussed in this chapter can be used to assess those emerging knowledge graphs and discuss their added value over existing ones. So, for example, for the above mentioned DBkWik, we have shown that it is highly complimentary to DBpedia: 95% of all entities in DBkWik are not contained in DBpedia and vice versa.

In summary, knowledge graphs are a useful ingredient to XAI systems, as they provide ready-to-use cross-domain knowledge. With this chapter, we have given an overview of existing knowledge graphs on the Web, and some guidelines on picking one or more such graphs to build an application for a task at hand.

---

[10]http://dbpedia.org/page/University_of_Mannheim
[11]https://www.wikidata.org/wiki/Q317070
[12]https://w.wiki/7UU
[13]https://bit.ly/2U4wLOA
[14]https://w.wiki/7UV

References

[1]   Wouter Beek, Joe Raad, Jan Wielemaker, and Frank Van Harmelen. sameas. cc: The closure of 500m
       owl: sameas statements. In *European Semantic Web Conference*, pages 65–80. Springer, 2018.
[2]   Volha Bryl, Christian Bizer, Robert Isele, Mateja Verlic, Soon Gill Hong, Sammy Jang, Mun Yong Yi,
       and Key-Sun Choi. Interlinking and knowledge fusion. In *Linked Open Data–Creating Knowledge Out
       of Interlinked Data*, pages 70–89. Springer, 2014.
[3]   Bruce G Buchanan. A (very) brief history of artificial intelligence. *Ai Magazine*, 26(4):53–53, 2005.
[4]   Andrew Carlson, Justin Betteridge, Richard C Wang, Estevam R Hruschka Jr, and Tom M Mitchell. Cou-
       pled semi-supervised learning for information extraction. In *Proceedings of the third ACM international
       conference on Web search and data mining*, pages 101–110, 2010.
[5]   Lisa Ehrlinger and Wolfram Wöß. Towards a definition of knowledge graphs. *SEMANTiCS (Posters,
       Demos, SuCCESS)*, 48, 2016.
[6]   Michael Färber, Basil Ell, Carsten Menne, Achim Rettinger, and Frederic Bartscherer. Linked data
       quality of dbpedia, freebase, opencyc, wikidata, and yago. *Semantic Web (to appear)*, 2016.
[7]   Alfio Ferrara, Andriy Nikolov, and François Scharffe. Data linking for the semantic web. *International
       Journal on Semantic Web and Information Systems (IJSWIS)*, 7(3):46–76, 2011.
[8]   Mikhail Galkin, Sören Auer, and Simon Scerri. Enterprise knowledge graphs: A backbone of linked
       enterprise data. In *2016 IEEE/WIC/ACM International Conference on Web Intelligence (WI)*, pages
       497–502. IEEE, 2016.
[9]   Jose Manuel Gomez-Perez, Jeff Z Pan, Guido Vetere, and Honghan Wu. Enterprise knowledge graph:
       An introduction. In *Exploiting linked data and knowledge graphs in large organisations*, pages 1–14.
       Springer, 2017.
[10] Harry Halpin, Patrick J Hayes, James P McCusker, Deborah L McGuinness, and Henry S Thompson.
       When owl: sameas isn't the same: An analysis of identity in linked data. In *International semantic web
       conference*, pages 305–320. Springer, 2010.
[11] Nicolas Heist and Heiko Paulheim. Uncovering the semantics of wikipedia categories. In *International
       semantic web conference*, pages 219–236. Springer, 2019.
[12] Nicolas Heist and Heiko Paulheim. Entity extraction from wikipedia list pages. In *Extended Semantic
       Web Conference*, 2020.
[13] Sven Hertling and Heiko Paulheim. Webisalod: providing hypernymy relations extracted from the web
       as linked open data. In *International Semantic Web Conference*, pages 111–119. Springer, 2017.
[14] Sven Hertling and Heiko Paulheim. Dbkwik: A consolidated knowledge graph from thousands of wikis.
       In *2018 IEEE International Conference on Big Knowledge (ICBK)*, pages 17–24. IEEE, 2018.
[15] Sven Hertling and Heiko Paulheim. Dbkwik: extracting and integrating knowledge from thousands of
       wikis. *Knowledge and Information Systems*, pages 1–22, 2019.
[16] Alexandra Hofmann, Samresh Perchani, Jan Portisch, Sven Hertling, and Heiko Paulheim. Dbkwik:
       Towards knowledge graph creation from thousands of wikis. In *International Semantic Web Conference
       (Posters, Demos & Industry Tracks)*, 2017.
[17] Tomáš Kliegr and Ondřej Zamazal. Lhd 2.0: A text mining approach to typing entities in knowledge
       graphs. *Journal of Web Semantics*, 39:47–61, 2016.
[18] Freddy Lecue. On the role of knowledge graphs in explainable ai. *Semantic Web Journal (Forthcoming)*.
       http://www. semantic-web-journal. net/content/role-knowledge-graphs-explainable-ai, 2019.
[19] Jens Lehmann, Robert Isele, Max Jakob, Anja Jentzsch, Dimitris Kontokostas, Pablo N. Mendes, Se-
       bastian Hellmann, Mohamed Morsey, Patrick van Kleef, Sören Auer, and Christian Bizer. DBpedia –
       A Large-scale, Multilingual Knowledge Base Extracted from Wikipedia. *Semantic Web Journal*, 6(2),
       2013.
[20] Douglas B Lenat. CYC: A large-scale investment in knowledge infrastructure. *Communications of the
       ACM*, 38(11):33–38, 1995.
[21] Robert Meusel, Christian Bizer, and Heiko Paulheim. A web-scale study of the adoption and evolution
       of the schema. org vocabulary over time. In *Proceedings of the 5th International Conference on Web
       Intelligence, Mining and Semantics*, page 15. ACM, 2015.
[22] Robert Meusel and Heiko Paulheim. Heuristics for fixing common errors in deployed schema. org
       microdata. In *European Semantic Web Conference*, pages 152–168. Springer, 2015.
[23] Robert Meusel, Petar Petrovski, and Christian Bizer. The webdatacommons microdata, rdfa and micro-
       format dataset series. In *International Semantic Web Conference*, pages 277–292. Springer, 2014.

[24] George A Miller. Wordnet: a lexical database for english. *Communications of the ACM*, 38(11):39–41, 1995.

[25] Roberto Navigli and Simone Paolo Ponzetto. Babelnet: The automatic construction, evaluation and application of a wide-coverage multilingual semantic network. *Artificial Intelligence*, 193:217–250, 2012.

[26] Markus Nentwig, Michael Hartung, Axel-Cyrille Ngonga Ngomo, and Erhard Rahm. A survey of current link discovery frameworks. *Semantic Web*, 8(3):419–436, 2017.

[27] Natasha Noy, Yuqing Gao, Anshu Jain, Anant Narayanan, Alan Patterson, and Jamie Taylor. Industry-scale knowledge graphs: Lessons and challenges. *Communications of the ACM*, 62(8):36–43, 2019.

[28] Heiko Paulheim. What the adoption of schema. org tells about linked open data. In *Joint Proceedings of USEWOD and PROFILES*, 2015.

[29] Heiko Paulheim. Knowledge graph refinement: A survey of approaches and evaluation methods. *Semantic Web*, 8(3):489–508, 2017.

[30] Heiko Paulheim. How much is a triple? estimating the cost of knowledge graph creation. In *ISWC 2018 Posters and Demonstrations, Industry and Blue Sky Ideas Tracks*, 2018.

[31] Heiko Paulheim and Simone Paolo Ponzetto. Extending dbpedia with wikipedia list pages. *NLP-DBPEDIA@ ISWC*, 13, 2013.

[32] Thomas Pellissier Tanon, Denny Vrandečić, Sebastian Schaffert, Thomas Steiner, and Lydia Pintscher. From freebase to wikidata: The great migration. In *Proceedings of the 25th International Conference on World Wide Web*, pages 1419–1428, 2016.

[33] Daniel Ringler and Heiko Paulheim. One knowledge graph to rule them all? analyzing the differences between dbpedia, yago, wikidata & co. In *Joint German/Austrian Conference on Artificial Intelligence (Künstliche Intelligenz)*, pages 366–372. Springer, 2017.

[34] Petar Ristoski and Heiko Paulheim. Semantic web in data mining and knowledge discovery: A comprehensive survey. *Web semantics: science, services and agents on the World Wide Web*, 36:1–22, 2016.

[35] Dominique Ritze and Heiko Paulheim. Towards an automatic parameterization of ontology matching tools based on example mappings. In *Proc. 6th ISWC ontology matching workshop (OM), Bonn (DE)*, pages 37–48, 2011.

[36] Max Schmachtenberg, Christian Bizer, and Heiko Paulheim. Adoption of the linked data best practices in different topical domains. In *International Semantic Web Conference*, pages 245–260. Springer, 2014.

[37] Julian Seitner, Christian Bizer, Kai Eckert, Stefano Faralli, Robert Meusel, Heiko Paulheim, and Simone Paolo Ponzetto. A large database of hypernymy relations extracted from the web. In *Proceedings of the Tenth International Conference on Language Resources and Evaluation (LREC 2016)*, pages 360–367, 2016.

[38] Robert Speer and Catherine Havasi. Representing general relational knowledge in conceptnet 5. In *LREC*, pages 3679–3686, 2012.

[39] Julien Subercaze. Chaudron: extending dbpedia with measurement. In *European Semantic Web Conference*, pages 434–448. Springer, 2017.

[40] Fabian M. Suchanek, Gjergji Kasneci, and Gerhard Weikum. YAGO: A Core of Semantic Knowledge Unifying WordNet and Wikipedia. In *16th international conference on World Wide Web*, pages 697–706, 2007.

[41] Andon Tchechmedjiev, Pavlos Fafalios, Katarina Boland, Malo Gasquet, Matthäus Zloch, Benjamin Zapilko, Stefan Dietze, and Konstantin Todorov. Claimskg: A knowledge graph of fact-checked claims. In *International Semantic Web Conference*, pages 309–324. Springer, 2019.

[42] Alberto Tonon, Victor Felder, Djellel Eddine Difallah, and Philippe Cudré-Mauroux. Voldemortkg: Mapping schema. org and web entities to linked open data. In *International Semantic Web Conference*, pages 220–228. Springer, 2016.

[43] Denny Vrandečić and Markus Krötzsch. Wikidata: a Free Collaborative Knowledge Base. *Communications of the ACM*, 57(10):78–85, 2014.

[44] Amrapali Zaveri, Anisa Rula, Andrea Maurino, Ricardo Pietrobon, Jens Lehmann, and Sören Auer. Quality assessment for linked data: A survey. *Semantic Web*, 7(1):63–93, 2016.

Knowledge Graphs for eXplainable Artificial Intelligence: Foundations, Applications and Challenges   23
I. Tiddi et al. (Eds.)
IOS Press, 2020
doi:10.3233/SSW200010

Foundations of Explainable Knowledge-Enabled Systems

Shruthi CHARI [a], Daniel M. GRUEN [b], Oshani SENEVIRATNE [a], and
Deborah L. MCGUINNESS [a]

[a] *Rensselaer Polytechnic Institute, Troy, NY, USA*
[b] *IBM Research, Cambridge, MA, USA*

Abstract. Explainability has been an important goal since the early days of Artificial Intelligence. Several approaches for producing explanations have been developed. However, many of these approaches were tightly coupled with the capabilities of the artificial intelligence systems at the time. With the proliferation of AI-enabled systems in sometimes critical settings, there is a need for them to be explainable to end-users and decision-makers. We present a historical overview of explainable artificial intelligence systems, with a focus on knowledge-enabled systems, spanning the expert systems, cognitive assistants, semantic applications, and machine learning domains. Additionally, borrowing from the strengths of past approaches and identifying gaps needed to make explanations user- and context-focused, we propose new definitions for explanations and explainable knowledge-enabled systems.

Keywords. Knowledge Graphs, eXplainable AI, Explainable Knowledge-Enabled Systems, Historical Evolution

1. Introduction

The growing incorporation of Artificial Intelligence (AI) capabilities in systems across industries and consumer applications, including those that have significant, even life-or-death implications, has led to an increased demand for explainability. To accept and appropriately apply insights from AI systems, users often require an understanding of how the system arrived at its results.

Such an understanding can include having a model of how the underlying AI system operates, how it was constructed, and how the data used to develop and train it matches the situations in which it was used. It can include information about the specific features of the current situation that contributed to the system's determination. It can also include descriptions of the underlying rationales and reasoning paths the system used to arrive at a conclusion, which in turn can be based on observed statistical regularities, models of underlying mechanisms and causal relationships, and temporal patterns. We draw a distinction, between *transparency*,[1] by which we mean general information about a system's operation, capabilities, underlying training data, and fairness, and *explainability*,

---

[1] In this chapter, we use quotes for terms that we introduce or for direct quotations from publications, and we use italics to either emphasize terminology from papers or highlight important terms.

by which we mean the ability of a system to provide information describing and justifying how a specific result was determined along with the overall context. We build on this notion of explainability and present desired properties for explanations and redefine explanations supporting a user's perspective in Section 2.

By their very nature, explanations are user focused; explanations are needed because they provide information that would otherwise be absent that helps a user trust, apply, and maximally benefit from the AI system's operation. Thus, the need for explanation, and the types of explanations required, are contextual, depending on users, their roles, their prior knowledge, and the situation. For example, a physician recommending a non-standard treatment regimen might want to understand what aspect of the current patient's condition led to an unexpected result, and how the reasoning behind it aligns with scientific knowledge about biological and pharmacological mechanisms. A patient-facing explanation for the same result may need to include more basic information on the condition and what is unique about the patient's situation. An explanation aimed at a hospital administrator or insurance coordinator may need to include information about potential biases that could lead to a lack of fairness in the recommendation.

Explanations can have deeper value beyond the "gating" role they play in helping users determine which results should be trusted and applied. Explanations provided in the above example could contribute to the mental model the physician is constructing of the patient, and of diseases and biological mechanisms in general, that could be valuable in future treatment decisions they make for that patient and others. Explanations also contribute to the model users are creating of the system itself, by exposing the kinds of information and processing mechanisms the system utilizes. Norman famously described how users construct mental models of systems with which they interact across gulfs of execution and interpretation [58]. With AI systems, explanations can help users simultaneously construct models of the system with which they are interacting, and of the underlying domain and situation in which the system is being used.

The importance of explainability is particularly salient with collaborative AI systems meant to work in tandem with human users to augment rather than supplant their skills and capabilities. A "Distributed Cognition" approach [35] is informative here, in which cognition is seen to take place not within the head of any one individual, but rather through the exchange and transformation of representations across multiple actors and artifacts [38]. The ability for a system to provide explanations, and respond to queries that reference other information relevant to the situation, expands the range of ways in which the system and human actors can interact.

1.1. Historical Evolution

Explainability has been a major goal since the early days of AI. In this chapter, we focus on the broad class of knowledge-enabled systems, instead of simply knowledge-based systems. We include rule-based systems as well as hybrid AI systems that may include a wide range of reasoning components including potentially inductive or abductive reasoning as well as the more traditional deductive reasoning. As such, we include historical explanation work (e.g., [13,68,70]) and also explanation work aimed more at evolving hybrid AI systems (e.g., [27,54,66]). The survey includes the domains of expert systems, cognitive assistants, Semantic Web [32], and, more recently, explanations that work with black-box models, i.e., deep learning models [44]. With this background, we will now present a historical perspective on the evolution of explainable AI.

Many early AI systems took a rule-based, expert system approach. Expert systems (e.g., [68,70]) were inherently explainable in that they used a set of rules to come to conclusions, so explanations could be generated that provided a detailed or abstracted collection of the rule executions as an explanation of a conclusion. During the expert system era, much work focused on explaining these systems and their decisions to the end-user. Explanations were broadly intended to address the *Why, What,* and *How* aspects of an AI system that produces a result. Dhaliwal et al. [16] provide an overview of these explanation types and state that the *Why* explanations were populated with the justification for a conclusion, the *How* explanations contained a trace of the mechanistic functioning of the system, and, the *What* explanations exposed the system's decision variables involved in the conclusion. Explanations produced by these systems were mainly focused on introducing the rationale behind a system's decision and the way the system works. Additionally, while trace-based explanations produced by expert systems captured the *why* and *how* aspects, they typically did not account for the context of a user when they generated explanations. There were a wide range of expert systems early on. For example, MYCIN [67] was an early expert system that supported medical diagnosis using a rule-based inference engine and included a trace-based explanation component.

Today, with the availability of vast volumes of data, deep learning algorithms are being widely used. However, these models are largely uninterpretable, and a significant focus of explainable AI research (e.g., DARPA XAI Report 2017 [27]) is focused on explaining the underlying mechanisms of these black-box models. In our opinion, gaining transparency into the black boxes can be useful, and it may decrease the "unintelligibility aspect" [47]. However, it is not enough to provide *personalized, tailored, and trustworthy* [36] explanations to consumers of AI models. Additionally, machine learning (ML) models often output a score or probability as predictions. While the number may be useful to understand some level of confidence, a single number lacks context, and thus is often inadequate without additional information. Semantic Web representation and reasoning work is well suited to help here. Standards for representing terminology, e.g., RDF and OWL [55], as well as representing provenance (e.g., PROV-O [42] and nanopublications [26]), have emerged and can be used to encode information along with its provenance and a system's reasoning provenance, and this may be used to augment explanations. The inclusion of provenance into the underlying representation and thus potentially into the explanations partially addresses the *What* and *Why* aspects of the reasoning behind presenting explanations to consumers.

Recently, researchers have acknowledged an increasing need to include explainability modules into AI systems. As a consequence, several survey papers [10,36,57] have highlighted past noteworthy efforts in explainable AI.[2] These survey papers emphasize the fact that different situations, users, and contexts demand different kinds of explanation [3]. Different AI systems are geared toward addressing an explanation type (or rarely, a combination), e.g., expert systems typically provide trace-based explanations, deep learning models can be leveraged to offer contrasting explanations, etc. We believe that the next-generation AI systems need to go beyond the *Why, What, How* aspects and produce explanations that additionally prioritize issues related to the setting, users' understanding, and contexts. At a minimum, these AI systems need to include a provenance

---

[2]We choose to use the explainable AI phrasing for explainability efforts in AI as XAI has come to be associated with the DARPA eXplainable AI (XAI) program. Our focus is broader than the program's focus on explaining and interpreting black box ML methods from a cognitive perspective.

component to support trust and provide users with tools that can access a reasoning trace to further explore or serve as a means of understanding. In Section 3, we will review a few of these past approaches mentioned in this section.

1.2. Shift and Current Focus of Explainable AI

The evolution of AI systems has been heavily influenced by the availability of resources, computing power and data. As previously stated, AI has moved from primarily using rule-based expert systems to using ML methods, and, sometimes, hybrid methods. With these changes, there has been a shift in the focus of explainability, due to the new challenges of the interpretability of complex ML models. The initial explanation focus on working from system traces to provide a notion of what was done has expanded to including a focus on including a notion of interpretability of an underlying ML model. This *interpretable* ML work may be a first generation of explanation of ML, but as we will expand on below, more is needed. Additionally, in the Semantic Web [32], and more generally, in knowledge representation-based applications, the focus has expanded from traditional *What* explanations to include explanations addressing information attribution and provenance aspects. The motivations for those expansions include improving the trustworthiness of information being represented in knowledge graphs (KGs), and further, to provide more context for users as they are deciding how to use the information in analysis applications. Further, AI models are now being employed in user-facing settings where there is a need for personalized conclusions. Hence, there is a need to rethink explanations produced by AI systems from a user perspective and include components to educate users, align with their cognitive model, help them trust the system, provide relevant information, and tailor suggestions to a user's contexts [10,57]. Borrowing strengths from explanations provided by past approaches, we will attempt to present, synthesize, and refine a definition of explanation and explainable knowledge-enabled systems with an acknowledgment of desired explanation properties that fit today's settings.

2. Terminology

Several researchers have proposed comprehensive definitions of explanations [18,23,54, 71] and have presented explanation components that they deem necessary to satisfy either their work or the domains where they hope the explanations will be useful. However, with a shift of focus in AI we feel the need to revisit the work on defining explanation as we consider what is desirable in next-generation "explainable knowledge-enabled systems." In this section, we list desirable properties (Section 2.1) for both explanations and explainable knowledge-enabled systems that generate these explanations, and use these properties as a basis to provide definitions.

2.1. Desirable Properties

2.1.1. Explanations

As a part of our list of desirable properties for explanations, we present properties, such as, *improving user appeal, and achieving user understandability*, that have been explored as explanation components in the past, and that will be useful in designing explanations suitable for the end-user. In addition, we propose including a higher priority on the inclusion of features, such as, *provenance* and *adapting to user's context* that will have a renewed focus in making explanations user-centric and in mitigating the unintelligibility aspect of current ML methods. We are aligning with others who have called for a greater user focus in explanations [45,56,64].

- **Be understandable:** Borrowing from desired properties of explanations stated by Swartout and Moore [71], we highlight that for explanations to be *understandable* by the user, the explanations should use terminology familiar to the user. If terminology is potentially unfamiliar, then we also suggest that capabilities be included for obtaining definitions of terms, thereby *educating* users. Understandability has the potential to be significantly increased if the AI system incorporates *user feedback* and a model of *user context*.

- **Include provenance:** *Provenance* is a property of explanations that has either been absent in some past descriptions of explanations [71], or has not had the emphasis that it deserves now. As systems expand to include more diverse content the need for capturing provenance increases. Explanations need to include *provenance* that includes information about the domain knowledge utilized by the system, along with the methods used to obtain that knowledge. We borrow from the "counterfactual faithfulness" idea proposed by [18], and argue that, as part of the *provenance* components, explanations need to carry *causal information* about the conclusion, if present in domain literature or supported by expert knowledge.

- **Appeal to user:** Paraphrasing Swartout and Moore [71], we note that explanations need to be *rich, coherent, and appeal to the user.* We propose that explanations need to expose facts that the user finds *resourceful and sufficient for further exploration*. A *resourceful* explanation contains enough granular content and evidence to appeal to the user's mental cognition and current needs. A *sufficient* explanation contains content that the user requires to carry out their tasks. A subtlety in generating explanations that appeal to the user would be to tailor the explanation length to the user's needs and preferences, i.e., to avoid lengthy explanations with content that might not be useful to the user or that they already understand. Further, we acknowledge that the resourcefulness and sufficiency aspects of explanations might be hard to measure in real-time. However, we suggest that explainable knowledge-enabled systems should be designed after an analysis of user requirements and utilize techniques to employ dynamic and static evaluation strategies to help realize these goals. More specifically, dynamic strategies could involve interactive mechanisms, such as the delivery of persuasive messages used by Maimone et al. [48], and static evaluation strategies could include user surveys conducted to evaluate the effectiveness of the systems, such as the one by Glass et al. [25].

- **Adapt to users' context:** Besides being user-centric, explanations need to be tailored to the user's *current scenario and context*. Explainable AI systems not only need to leverage information about the user (as may have been captured in a user profile [65,69]), but they also need to identify the user's intent and adapt the *explanation form* to connect to the user's mental model and align with the user's intent. For example, an explanation may include a contrastive hypothesis that relates to the user's intent or statistical evidence to provide more support to enhance a user's belief. In a later chapter, "Directions for Explainable Knowledge-enabled

Systems," in this book, we present different explanation types and their various focii that would allow AI systems to generate diverse explanations.

Overall, explanations should serve beyond their original aim to teach [70], and provide *trustworthy, transparent, unambiguous accounts* of automated tasks to end-users.

2.1.2. Explainable Knowledge-Enabled Systems

While many have attempted to define explanations (e.g., [17,71]), additional efforts have attempted to improve the generation of explanations (e.g., [25,39,54]) and tackle various aspects of explainability (e.g., [61,57]). To begin to address the need of building explainable, knowledge-enabled AI systems, we present a list of desirable properties from the synthesis of our literature review of past explanation work. Our review primarily spans knowledge representation in expert systems [71], provenance and reasoning efforts in the Semantic Web [26], user task-processing workflows in cognitive assistants [53,54], and efforts to reduce unintelligibility in the ML domain [3,23,27]. Additionally, we analyzed explanation requirements from current literature, answering an increased need for *user-comprehensibility* [43], *accountability* [17] and *user-focus* [57]. In our literature review in Section 3 we will highlight approaches that exhibit these properties.

- **Modularity**: A modular design, such as, the one proposed by Swartout and Moore [70], is desirable, as it would allow systems to adapt models and functioning to users' requirements and scenarios. This property would also allow for the AI system to include explanation facilities that tap into various modules to expose information requested by and conducive to the user's needs.

- **Interpretability**: Borrowing from Mittlestadt et al. [57] and Hasan and Gandon [31], we believe that the interpretability of explainable knowledge-enabled systems enables them to be transparent, lending to the ability to provide trace-based accounts of their working. Additionally, we utilize Gilpin et al's definition of interpretability as a "science of comprehending what a model did." However, if the models used in the system are not interpretable, we propose that they should consider including proxy methods to be interpretable, for example, utilizing linear proxy models proposed by Gilpin et al. [23] that serve as a simplified proxy of the full model.

- **Support provenance:** Paraphrasing from the explanation requirements suggested by Hasan and Gandon [31], we agree that explainable knowledge-enabled systems should store the provenance of the information that their models rely on beyond just metadata. We believe that the inclusion of provenance aids AI systems in generating *resourceful and sufficient* explanations for users, providing them with resources for further exploration.

- **Adapt to user's needs:** We propose that AI systems need to be *adaptive* and *interactive*, adapting their functioning and explanation generation capabilities to suit the user's requests and contexts. To this end, and to provide tailored explanations, Ribera and Lapedriza [64] have identified user categories (domain experts, AI researchers, and lay users) and presented their contrasting demands from an AI system. Further, the ability to be adaptive would be enhanced by a modular design, as suggested earlier, and would aid the system in generating explanations in various forms to suit the user's understanding and their needs.

- **Include explanation facilities:** Inspired by McGuinness et al.'s cognitive assistants explanation frameworks [53,54], we propose that the design of the explanation facilities should be addressed early and in detail in the design phase, to ensure that the AI system is capable of supporting the requirements of the explanation facilities within its design. Explanation facilities could constitute a wide-range of user-facing interfaces, such as, dialogue systems, visualizations, and feedback systems that the user interacts with and provides feedback to the AI system about the explanations generated or a need for further clarifications. Hence, since explanation facilities would require additional information, such as, provenance, and would need the system to incorporate feedback and adapt to context, we recommend that their design be coupled with the AI system design.
- **Include/Access a knowledge store**: We recommend that explainable knowledge-enabled systems store the *domain knowledge* they rely on, the *user's mental model* they appeal to, and the *explanation components* they are generating. Additionally, we relax the inclusion of knowledge in that an AI system might provide access to a knowledge store - as the system may host it, or it may use some other system's hosting and contribute to and access that store. By knowledge store, we refer to data storage mechanisms (KGs or semantic representations are preferred) that can store knowledge of various forms spanning categories such as background knowledge, domain knowledge, etc.
- **Support compliance and obligation checks:** In addition to hosting/accessing knowledge stores, we recommend that explainable knowledge-enabled systems store an encoding set of expert knowledge in their field of application. These encodings should be sufficient to determine if the system complies with the standards and practices in that field. Additionally, we also recommend that explainable knowledge-enabled systems attempt to adhere to standards for the proposed explainable AI models, such as [3,23]. Furthermore, we suggest that compliance and obligation checks be evaluated on the system post-construction.

2.2. Definitions

Having identified desirable properties for explanations and explainable knowledge-enabled systems, will now provide a set of definitions leveraging our review of the explanation literature and our analysis of the current AI landscape. Our goal is to reflect the needs of explainable AI in current times and provide a summary of the desirable properties to achieve better explainability.

2.2.1. Explanation

We define an explanation in the computational world as, "an account of the system, its workings, the *implicit and explicit* knowledge used in its reasoning processes and the specific decision, that is *sensitive* to the end-user's *understanding, context, and current needs.*"

2.2.2. Explainable Knowledge-Enabled Systems

We define "explainable knowledge-enabled systems" to be, "AI systems that include a representation of the domain knowledge in the field of application, have mechanisms to incorporate the *users' context*, are *interpretable*, and host *explanation facilities* that generate *user-comprehensible, context-aware, and provenance-enabled* explanations of the mechanistic functioning of the AI system and the knowledge used."

3. Approaches

We present past approaches that have addressed various aspects of explainability related to trust, transparency, provenance and interpretability. To the extent possible, we group publications by technical domain: knowledge-based systems, Semantic Web applications, cognitive assistants, and ML systems, in an attempt to show the progression of methods within those domains. In Section 3.1, we consider work from the 1970s-1990s that sought to utilize the trace explainability strengths of rule-based systems to explain the process used to arrive at decisions. In Section 3.2, we review provenance and explanation modeling efforts and posit them as contributors to the development of trustworthy and explainable semantic applications. In Section 3.3, we focus on efforts to explain task-based workflows in personal assistants and intelligent tutoring settings. We end with a review of papers that improve the interpretability and trust aspects of ML methods in Section 3.4. While each of these vast domains has large volumes of published literature, we restrict ourselves to seminal work on explainability in the domain or publications that have introduced novel techniques to tackle different aspects of explainability. As a conclusion of each domain subsection, we provide a brief summary of the methods utilized to address explainability and describe any lessons applicable for the development of future explainable AI methods.

Table 1 contains an evaluation of the foundational AI systems, reviewed against the criteria we defined for explainable knowledge-enabled systems (Section 2.1). The chronological order allows us to view trends in explainability over the years and also helps expose shifts in the areas of focus and strengths of the class of approaches. We observe that explanations were well-explored as a topic of interest in the AI community from the early 1990s - mid-2000s. We note that, even within the expert systems era, the AI architecture evolved from simply generating trace-based accounts of decisions to including modular explanation facilities ([11,13,70]) that sometimes could produce provenance-enabled ([13]), adaptive and user-customizable ([60]) explanations. Additionally, observe that, among other classes of approaches in our review, explanations have been best established in cognitive assistants, which also have the most direct impact on human decision-making capabilities. However, we notice that, with more recent systems in the Semantic Web and ML domains, there has been a shift in explainability from building explanation facilities to minimally ensuring that AI models are interpretable [63] and support provenance [50] for further tracing. Further, most AI systems in our review ([11,13,50,53,54,68,70,72]) satisfy the 'Compliance Checks' criteria by leveraging logical rule-based or other deductive reasoners to check or enforce compliance. Also, systems such as the Disciple-LTA and Common Ground Learning and Explanation (COGLE) deployed in critical settings of military and aviation, respectively, have features to allow both expert and lay users to provide feedback about the system's explanations and outputs. Hence, indicating that system supported features are partially driven by the domain of application. Finally, while our evaluation was conducted on a carefully selected set of approaches, our findings on explainability trends are in-line with a larger,

Table 1. Foundational explanation approaches and desired features of explainable knowledge-enabled systems

Year	System	Application	Knowledge Store	Interpretable	Explanation Facilities	Modular	Adaptive	Support Provenance	Compliance Checks
1977	MYCIN [68]	Healthcare	✓	✓					✓
1982	NEOMYCIN [13]	Healthcare	✓	✓	✓	✓		✓	✓
1989	CLASSIC [11]	General Purpose	✓	✓	✓	✓	✓		✓
1991	Explainable Expert System (EES) [70]	Program Advisor	✓	✓	✓	✓			✓
2004	Inference Web Framework [53]	General Purpose	✓	✓	✓	✓	✓	✓	✓
2005	Disciple-LTA [72]	Military	✓	✓	✓	✓	✓	✓	✓
2007	Integrated Cognitive Explanation Environment (ICEE) [54]	Office Assistant	✓	✓	✓	✓	✓	✓	✓
2009	Automated Policy Reasoning [39]	Judicial	✓	✓	✓		✓	✓	✓
2016	Local Interpretable Model-agnostic Explanations (LIME) [63]	General Purpose		✓	✓	✓			
2017	ReDrugs [49]	Medicine	✓	✓				✓	✓
2017 (ongoing)	Common Ground Learning and Explanation (COGLE) [28]	Unmanned Aircrafts	✓		✓	✓	✓		✓

systematic review conducted by Nunes and Jannach [59], who noted that explainability was best explored in the expert systems and cognitive assistants domains.

3.1. Knowledge-based systems

The 80s decade saw the rise of knowledge-based and expert systems, that were designed to assist humans where human resources were limited [16]. Expert systems and knowledge-based systems both contained an encoding of knowledge. More specifically, in the case of expert systems, the knowledge encoded was that of expert's knowledge, typically in the form of rules. In our review, we will not make distinctions between these two classes of systems and will focus on identifying the explainability components of these systems. From an implementation perspective, both of these systems required the engineering and encoding of multiple rules to support inference. This reliance on rules made these systems inherently explainable, as one could trace back the rules to identify the factors that lead to a conclusion. Subsequently, researchers have introduced different types of explanations [13,68], and approaches to improve explanation generation [11], and to introduce more granular content into explanations generated by these systems [70].

3.1.1. Early Expert Systems: MYCIN and NEOMYCIN

The MYCIN [67,68] paper was one of the first to introduce computer-based explanations, and, is regarded as a foundational and seminal work. The goal of the MYCIN system was to identify highly probable carriers of infectious diseases, and suggest treatments for the diseases. The system provided explanations by exposing the inference trace that lead to a decision. The system was able to trace back and expose the reasoning, that served as justifications of decisions. In particular, MYCIN provided *Why* and *How* explanations [16]. The *Why* explanations included facts and task-based information to address a user's queries. The *How* explanations explained the manner and trace in which the system generated the conclusion.

To enhance the *Why* and *How* explanations, a descendant of MYCIN - NEOMYCIN [13] produced strategic explanations comprised of meta-knowledge and the problem-solving strategies to adapt the MYCIN system to a teaching setting. NEOMYCIN built on MYCIN's inability to explain beyond the expert knowledge known to the system and added a component that leveraged explicit encodings of problem-solving strategies used to generate the medical knowledge for use in its explanations. To this end, the NEOMYCIN system used a meta-strategy to decide what portion of the rules to invoke from data sources, including an etiological taxonomy, disease knowledge, and causal associations. The metastrategy contained rules that a human would use to undertake tasks such as building hypothesis, pursuing them, identifying problems, etc. In essence, the NEOMYCIN system attempted to mimic human decision-solving, where one would eliminate a hypothesis based on the search space, and not by merely navigating the knowledge ("bridge concepts" [13]) that the system already holds. Further, NEOMYCIN introduced the idea of separating knowledge to make the system more accessible, which was further adopted by Moore and Swartout in their Explainable Expert System [70] effort, discussed later in this section. While the strategic explanations generated by NEOMYCIN are desirable, they might be onerous for user consumption due to a surplus of details.

3.1.2. Explainable Description Logics: CLASSIC

McGuinness and Borgida took an approach to explanation where each of the inferences that the underlying logical reasoning system could execute had a declarative explanation description and those individual explanation components could be used to build simple, complex, abstracted, or otherwise customized explanations [52]. Additionally, every expert rule that a knowledge-based system builder encoded in the system included a structured component that could be used to explain when that rule was used. These explanation "breadcrumbs" could then be used to assemble explanations when a user's actions triggered the execution of a rule.

The authors implemented their approach in the CLASSIC knowledge representation system, a description-logic-based language that provided a framework "to define structured concepts and make assertions about individuals in a knowledge base" [60]. The complete set of foundational inference rules that could be explained for the underlying description logic reasoner was also available for reuse in other systems [51]. This style of encoding axioms for every inference that a system could execute was also leveraged in the axiomatic semantics for other predecessors to today's description logic-based recommended language for encoding ontologies on the web: OWL [55]. The axioms for RDF, RDFS, and DAML+OIL were described in W3C Note[3] and then were used in a number of different reasoners to provide trace-based explanation capabilities.

---

[3]DAML+OIL axioms note link: `https://www.w3.org/TR/daml+oil-axioms`

3.1.3. Explainable Expert System

Moore and Swartout coined the term 'Explainable Expert Systems' (EES) in their widely-cited work [70]. The EES framework that aimed to provide explanations and was tested in a Program Enhancement Advisor setting. The explanations generated by the EES system borrowed from and had components of various knowledge sources including domain, problem-solving and system terminology. Further, the design of their EES system supported the generation of the various components of the explanations and were made of knowledge bases, a program writer, an explanation generator, an interpreter, and an execution trace. The EES system used a planning algorithm, wherein goals are reformulated if no viable match is found in the domain knowledge. The reformulation of goals was achieved by the representation of the domain knowledge into a concept hierarchy, via a language, such as, KL-ONE [12]. The EES framework was interactive in nature, and goals were reformulated based on user dialogue with the system. Additionally, users' queries were used as a cue to interleave domain and problem-solving knowledge traces into their explanations.

3.1.4. Summary

The explainable knowledge-based systems that we discussed introduced several types of explanations, including *Why, How, and Strategic* explanations (described earlier in Section 1.1). However, their reliance on encoding a large rule base makes them difficult to scale and extremely human-intensive to maintain. Today, we see the semi-automatic generation of rules and knowledge-base population via natural language processing and ontology-enabled extraction techniques. Many learnings from knowledge-based systems have been reused and expanded in the Semantic Web, as will be illustrated in Section 3.2.

3.2. Semantic Web

The creation of the World Wide Web (WWW) [8] made it possible to create content online and make existing content available online in digital formats. In their seminal paper, Berners-Lee, Hendler, and Lassila [9] state that the Semantic Web was intended to unify content being published online through tagging content with unique identifiers, or Uniform Resource Identifiers (URIs), representing the content utilizing well formed definitions from taxonomies and ontologies, and borrowing from the knowledge representation world to utilize structuring mechanisms for data. While these properties are desirable and necessary to enable data sharing and achieve a semantic understanding of digital content, they are not sufficient to make the content explainable to a broad range of users. However, the Semantic Web community has tackled the provenance aspect and trace-based aspects of explainability and developed several provisions to both include provenance in the semantic representation [26,42] and to supporting reasoning mechanisms, [34] to generate traces. As a direct consequence of the Semantic Web, the textual content is more accessible in knowledge graphs (KGs) via semantic representations [20]. Additionally, KG provisions have made it possible to provide justifications and provenance to suggestions. In this section, we will review some provenance encoding efforts and explainable semantic applications.

3.2.1. Provenance modeling efforts

There have been two somewhat recent foundational provenance efforts that paved the way for provenance-aware applications, namely the World Wide Web Consortium's work on a recommended standard for provenance on the web (PROV) with its associated encoding as an ontology PROV-O [42] and nanopublications [26]. Nanopublications provide a structure to associate triple statements with their provenance. In general, provenance is essential as it encodes information that can be used to explore where information came from and this information can be used to build trust in applications when they use this information to expose the evidence behind their recommendations.

3.2.2. Nanopublications

Nanopublications were conceived to help disambiguate and represent the context for scientific statements that were extracted from textual corpora and made available as triples. The authors identified that contextual information present in a document was imperative to understand a statement in relation to the full document. Hence, they designed nanopublications that provided a mechanism to associate metadata or annotations with statements. The schema of nanopublications has evolved over the years. In its current state,[4] nanopublications are composed of three named graph components, Assertions, Publication Information, and Provenance. The Publication Information graph stores metadata information about the creation of the content, or how it came to be, such as, the date of creation, author, etc. The Provenance graph contains metadata, such as, citation information. The assertion graph contains one or more subject-predicate-object statements with domain content.

Kuhn et al. [41] have proposed an Atomic, Independent, Declarative, and Absolute (AIDA) framework to encode atomic and indisputable assertion statements. They describe a metananopublication world in which nanopublications can be created from other nanopublications via different channels, for example, from authors creating content from scientific results, and from data mining algorithms generating nanopublications from existing unstructured data sources. Essentially through the metananopublications concept, the authors highlight that provenance can be interleaved and chained, to reflect the real world where multiple entities depend on each other at various levels of granularities.

3.2.3. The Provenance Ontology (PROV-O)

The PROV-O ontology [42] provides a formal mechanism to support comprehensive modeling of the provenance of digital objects. In their ontology, they support three primary forms of provenance contributors, agent-centered, object-centered, and process-centered forms. In PROV-O [5], provenance is modeled via three simple class types, i.e., 'entities'[6] which are generated by activities, and 'entities' and 'activities' that are 'associated with' and 'attributed to' agents, respectively. In the W3C note, the editors showcase the adequacy of the PROV-O ontology in modeling a use case where a blogger is exploring the provenance chain of a newspaper article while finding out who compiled the chart included in the article. The use case also illustrates that provenance needs to

---

[4]Nanopublication Guidelines: `http://nanopub.org/guidelines/working_draft/`
[5]PROV-O ontology W3C note: `https://www.w3.org/TR/prov-o/`
[6]Classes and properties are referred to by their label, and are enclosed within single quotes

be modeled comprehensively to ensure that users have a complete understanding of the information they are viewing.

There have been ontology alignment efforts on the PROV-O ontology to enhance usability and increase interoperability. These efforts include alignment of PROV-O with standard ontologies, such as, the TIME ontology, Semantic Sensor Network Ontology (SSN), and the Basic Formal Ontology (BFO). The PROV-O ontology has also served as a foundational ontology for several other provenance ontologies (e.g., Provenance for Clinical and Healthcare Research (ProvCare [73]) and Guideline Provenance Ontology (G-Prov [1])) that support provenance modeling in specific use cases with different levels of granularity.

3.2.4. Provenance and Related Semantic Knowledge Graphs

The Semantic Web community also allows for different alternatives of representing that information based on granularity and content needs such as named graphs, [7] reification, [8] etc., and there exist cross-domain open source KGs that host somewhat comparably rich provenance (e.g., Wikidata, [9] WebIsALOD [33]). Additionally, while we believe that provenance modeling is crucial to provide high-quality, trustworthy information to consumers, we acknowledge that it is not sufficient to capture user context or to personalize results. Recently, there has been an emergence of KGs that encode contextual and personal information [29,48], lending to the personalizing of semantic applications that are enabled by these KGs. Gyrard et al. [29] described the components of a personalized healthcare knowledge graph (PHKG) that are needed to monitor user health to help users combat chronic diseases, such as, asthma and obesity. In a similar effort, Maimone et al. developed Perkapp [48], a persuasive system that monitors people's lifestyles and persuades them to make healthier choices and stay on track. Their persuasive, knowledge-based system architecture contains a set of expert-generated rules and outputs persuasive context-aware messages to users based on their adherence to the rules.

3.2.5. Reasoning Efforts

We now present a selective overview of the reasoning efforts. We briefly introduced RDFS reasoning efforts in Section 3.1. RDFS reasoning results in justifications or trace-based accounts of *Why* a conclusion was made by the system, based on which rule fired. However, these justifications can be overwhelming for human consumption. To address this, Horridge et al. [37] proposed laconic and precise justifications that do not 1. conceal detail, 2. expose axioms that are relevant to the justification, and 3. are atomic, in that multiple fine-grained cores can be highlighted. Besides the laconic justification effort, there have been other efforts to improve explainability of justifications and we discuss one such effort, the AIR (Accountability in RDF or AMORD[10] [40] in RDF) language.

3.2.6. Explanations for Automated Policy Reasoning

AIR language that had a broader focus on modeling explanations serving to explain inference traces from policy reasoning. AIR is a Semantic Web-based rule language fo-

---

[7]Named Graphs: `https://www.w3.org/2009/07/NamedGraph.html`

[8]Reification: `https://www.w3.org/TR/rdf-primer/#reification`

[9]Wikidata: `https://www.wikidata.org/wiki/Wikidata:Main_Page`

[10]AMORD (A Miracle Of Rare Device) is an explanation system developed for MIT scheme in the 1970's

cused on generating and tracking explanation for inferences and actions [39]. The Massachusetts Institute of Technology (MIT) Decentralized Information Group developed the AIR language, as an extension to N3Logic [7] to support accountable privacy protection in Web-based information systems conforming to Linked Data principles. Accountability and privacy protection are enabled through auditable trace-based explanations. AIR supports *Linked Rules*, which can be combined and reused like Linked Data. Additionally, AIR explanations can be used for further reasoning.

AIR provides two independent ontologies. One ontology allows the specification of AIR rules,[11] and the other one allows describing justifications.[12] The reasoning steps of the AIR reasoner are considered as events and modeled as subclasses of `air:Event`. `air:Rule` represents rules, and it is defined as a subclass of `air:Operation`. The ontology also provides properties to enable representing variable mappings in the performed operations. AIR provides a means to write explicit explanations using the assertion property associated with rules. This property is composed of two components, `air:Statement`, which is the set of triples being asserted, and `air:Justification`, which is the explicit justification that needs to be associated with the statement.

Example policy reasoning with explanations using AIR:

Parts of the *Massachusetts Disability Discrimination Law* were translated into a computer interpretable policy using AIR. A user's phone records requesting some service and subsequently getting denied based on his disability recorded in the phone logs were captured in RDF. Once the AIR reasoner is invoked with the policy file, and the phone log in RDF, a user can visualize the annotated transaction log that contains the reasoning output. Figure 1 contains a partial proof tree with natural language assertions.

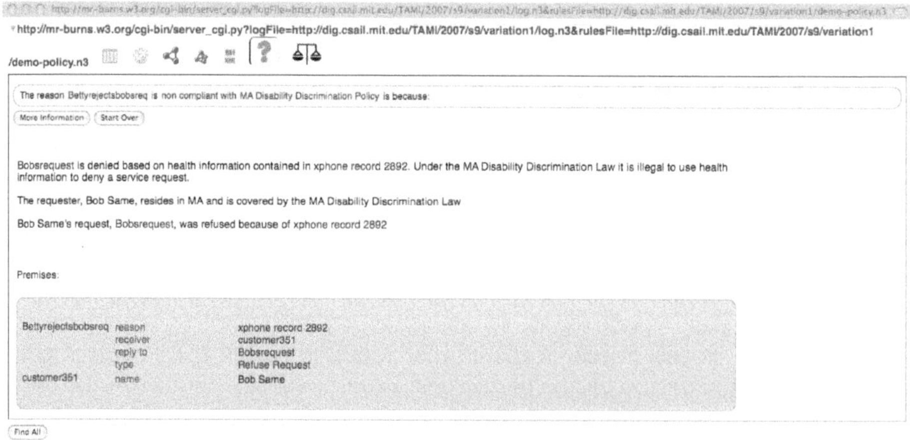

Figure 1. AIR Justification or Explanations View: Once a user clicks the "Why?" button, they will see a description appear in the "Because" box, and the premises that support the justification appear in the "Premises" box. When the user clicks the "More Information" button, the descriptions corresponding to outer rules in the proof tree will be appended to the "Because" box, and the "Premises" box is overwritten with the corresponding set of premises in the proof tree. When all the descriptions in the proof tree have been traversed, the message "No more information is available from the reasoner" will be displayed in the "Premises" box. At any given time, this proof exploration can be restarted by clicking the "Start Over" button. [Image taken from website [13]]

---

[11] AIR rules ontology: `http://dig.csail.mit.edu/TAMI/2007/amord/air`
[12] AIR justifications ontology: `http://dig.csail.mit.edu/2009/AIR/airjustification.n3`

3.2.7. Semantic applications

Aside from the various representation mechanisms described earlier that support prove-nance encoding and personalized content, there have been many semantic applications (e.g., [49,66]) enabled by these representations that are explainable. We briefly describe two of these efforts.

In our automatic breast cancer characterization effort [66], we developed a visual interface to assist physicians in their diagnosis process by providing justifications of the treatment rules that resulted in a stage change of a patient between changing guideline editions. We considered the 7th and 8th edition of the American Joint Committee on Cancer (AJCC) cancer staging guidelines [24]. Our system reasoned using a knowledge base of encoded cancer staging rules, and inferred the stage of the patient based on their metastasis parameters and biomarkers. Our system could automatically determine the staging, explain how the stage was derived, and explain any restaging that happened. In another effort, McCusker et al. developed a framework [49] that encoded semantic connections between drugs, proteins, and diseases and allowed users to look for potential repurposing of drugs. A novel aspect of this system was that the interface allowed the user to explore why a drug may be used to target a particular disease, thus having a potential causal explanation as opposed to many other drug repurposing efforts that focused only on correlations. The system also included weights on all of the links in the graph so that users could get a sense of how strongly the evidence supports a relationship.

The semantic applications we reviewed primarily utilize scientific evidence to present factual content, discover new content, and automate human-intensive tasks. In Section 3.3, we review explanation modeling frameworks, such as, the Inference Web [53], which also have semantic representations but are used in more typical cognitive assistant settings.

3.2.8. Summary

The Semantic Web efforts we described address various components of explainability. Although, even these interpretable systems, powered by KGs and ontologies, do not en-tirely address all aspects of explainability that we detail in Section 2. However, we be-lieve that semantic representations for explainability can evolve from the existing se-mantic representations for provenance, accountability and context. Hence, we believe that the strengths of the Semantic Web, coupled with ML methods, will be a significant contributor to hybrid explainable AI systems.

3.3. Cognitive Assistants

Cognitive Assistants are systems that are used to "augment human intelligence" [21] and aid humans in decision-making and problem-solving. These assistants have grown from their former role of professional assistants, educating users in a particular domain, to be-ing widely accessible as personal assistants, aiding users in their everyday tasks. These assistants function in a tight coupling with the user and, hence, their design, knowledge bases, and interactions are driven by users' cognitive capabilities and needs. Further, these assistants play various roles from fostering positive behavior change, to training people with the necessary problem-solving skills in a domain, to providing tailored in-

---

[13] Image available at: http://dig.csail.mit.edu/TAMI/2008/JustificationUI/howto.html

formation based on an understanding of user context [19]. As the proliferation of general purpose, conversational cognitive assistants grows, it will become increasingly important that they include a representation of the user's goals, and "theory-of-mind" elements that support effective communication and collaboration [22].

3.3.1. DARPA PAL program

An ambitious and multi-university program, the Defense Advanced Research Projects Agency (DARPA) program, Personal Assistant that Learns (PAL),[14] gave rise to the Cognitive Assistant that Learns and Organizes (CALO) system. CALO was a large effort including over 20 collaboration organizations aimed at building a cognitive agent that can assist in a wide range of day-to-day office-related tasks, including sending out emails, memos, maintaining a to-do list [14], etc. Henceforth, several projects leveraged the CALO work, the most famous is Apple's personal assistant Siri. In our review, we will cover some of the seminal explainable cognitive assistants [53,54] and user studies [25] that resulted from or were refined within the CALO project, that are explainable in their own right.

Inference Web was one of the early modular explanation frameworks, and it built upon the strengths from the Semantic Web [32], Description Logics [4], and expert systems communities, to generate explanations for distributed, web-based systems that were interacting with users. The framework provided explanations that contained the provenance of the information (both implicit and explicit), and the proof for inference traces to novice users and agents alike. Additionally, the framework could abstract explanations to suit users' understanding and to avoid lengthy proofs that would overwhelm the users (similar to the breadcrumbs features provided by the CLASSIC system (Section 3.1.2)). Besides the ability to abstract explanations, the framework was also capable of providing explanations in different formats and even had a built-in explanation dialogue that would display questions and answers. Users could then interact with the answers and pose follow-up questions. The framework achieved its explanation capabilities via a modular architecture consisting of an IWBase, a data repository of the metainformation about the information used by the framework; an IWAbstractor, abstractor component that converted lengthy Proof Markup Language (PML) [15] proofs to PML explanations; an IWExplainer, an explanation dialogue component that would generate explanations for users; and an IWBrowser, a browser for displaying the explanations. While the Inference Web framework did not include a context-specific component, it provided some context modeling options and was capable of providing a wide range of customized explanation capabilities that included direct support for encoding trust and user models.

McGuinness et al. [54] expanded on their earlier Inference Web [53] framework, and developed an Integrated Cognitive Explanation Environment (ICEE) that generated explanations for task reasoning. ICEE served as an explanation component on the CALO system, in which multiple reasoning techniques, including task processing, numerous learning components, along with statistical and deductive methods, all worked together. Since CALO served as a cognitive assistant in the workplace, the tasks involved processing workplace automation activities, such as requesting quotes from different sources (e.g., *GetQuotes* was one of the sub-tasks [54]). Additionally, the reasoning techniques used in CALO used multiple knowledge sources to generate conclusions that needed to

---

[14]PAL: https://www.darpa.mil/about-us/timeline/personalized-assistant-that-learns

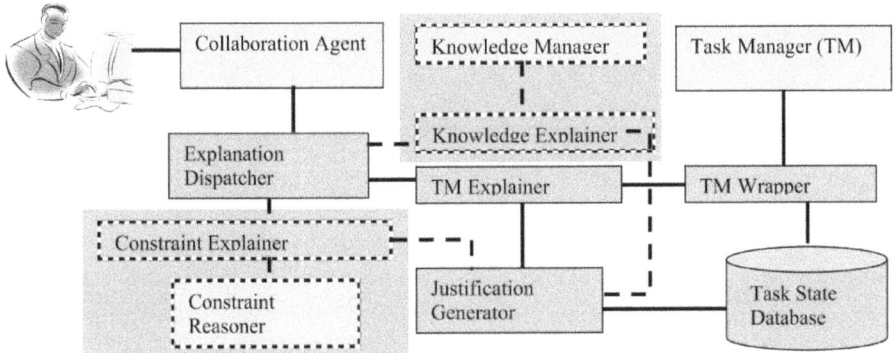

Figure 2. An activity flow diagram of the Integrated Cognitive Explanation Environment (ICEE) that was utilized to explain task-processing systems in the CALO project taken from McGuinness et al. [54].

be explained. The ICEE explanation architecture (shown in Figure 2) consisted of several components critical to generating explanations: an *explanation dispatcher* that interpreted a user's explanation request and invoked different reasoning components based on the type of explanation request, a *task manager explainer* that further invoked task manager wrappers to gather task execution information, a *task state database* that maintained the execution traces and states of the tasks, and a *justification generator* that created explanations from the task execution processing information.

The authors conducted a user study aimed at understanding the types of questions that users wanted answered. These explanation request types included questions about the motivation of a task, status, execution history, forward-looking execution plans, task ordering, or explicit questions about time [54]. The classifications of these explanation requests into different request types helped invoke appropriate explanation strategies. Additionally, the system hosted introspective predicates were used to identify the types of information to be included in explanations based on the request's intent. Broadly, the introspective predicates were grouped into *basic procedure information*, metadata about task definitions; *execution information*, details about the task execution; and, *projection information*, information about future task processing. The ICEE framework provides an example of many of the components needed in explainable hybrid AI systems and demonstrated how they can be used to provide user-customized explanations.

Another noteworthy effort from CALO was Glass, et al. [25]'s user study that assessed the trust and understandability aspects of adaptive systems. They used the CALO system as an adaptive system use case in their study. Their findings grouped users' concerns into eight themes: 1). *High-level usability of complex prototypes*, 2). *being ignored*, 3). *context-sensitive questions*, 4). *granularity of feedback*, 5). *transparency*, 6). *provenance*, 7). *managing expectations*, and 8). *autonomy and verification*. While there were some system-related concerns that could be addressed via system improvements (high-level usability, verification), there were also other concerns, such as, provenance, the granularity of feedback, the transparency targeting the users' perception of trust in the agent. They found that the trust level of most users in the system increased significantly with the inclusion of provenance and context-sensitive aspects. Therefore, this study concluded that users who work with cognitive agents would like an interactive dialogue and personalized experience and would prefer provenance information to understand the working of these complex systems, to some degree. The themes identified in this paper remain desired features for our complex, hybrid systems of today that use both statistical ML and reasoning techniques.

3.3.2. Intelligent tutors

Intelligent tutoring is a sub-domain of cognitive assistants, where adaptive task-oriented systems are utilized for training humans in a particular domain. Hence, intelligent tutors need to appeal to the human cognition and understand and evolve their learning capabilities and grasp of the domain. In a seminal work, VanLeHan [75] noted that there are two loops to human tutoring, an inner and outer loop. He noted that the inner loop worked in tandem with the human, helping them at each step, assessing their competence, and updating the student model, while the outer loop identified a new task to execute based on the student's assessment. Enhancements have been proposed to VanLeHan's inner and outer loop proposition, one of which is a behavior graph [2] that kept track of the possible problem-solving strategies that students can adopt. The edges in a behavior graph represented the different ways in which students could solve problems, and the nodes represented the acceptable states. In general, intelligent tutors host an inherent, domain-specific knowledge component that is used to undertake tasks.

A use case on explainable, intelligent tutors was explored in a military setting by a Disciple-LTA [72] system. They used an iterative problem-solving approach in intelligence tasks to assist analysts. These tasks were broken down into executable steps to which evidence could be associated to find solutions (also termed as "task-reduction"). The solutions were then combined at the task level, or "solution-composition," to produce conclusions. A sample conclusion from this system was "There is strong evidence that Location-A is a training base for terrorist operations." [72] The Disciple-LTA architecture consisted of different reasoning agents: learners, tutors, and problem-solvers, all of which read from and wrote into the knowledge base of an ontology and its rules.

3.3.3. Summary

The cognitive assistant literature is vast and continues to grow with the emergence of personal assistants, such as, Apple's Siri, Amazon's Alexa, etc. In our review, we have covered explanation facilities in DARPA's CALO project [25,53,54], and have also briefly discussed Intelligent Tutors [2,72,75]. While the focus of explanations in the CALO cognitive assistant was on explaining task-based workflows, the underlying system contained a set of hybrid deductive reasoners coupled with numerous learning components, and thus is representative of today's hybrid learning systems. User requirements were utilized to design explanation strategies and determine the execution of the next task, dictated by user feedback. Cognitive assistants have begun to focus on the end-user, and are supporting facilities to account for user perspective, to some extent, unlike expert systems (Section 3.1) that focused primarily on generating explanations of inference traces.

3.4. Explainability in Machine Learning (ML)

ML algorithms have been rapidly advancing, proliferating in various domains, even high-precision domains, such as, healthcare and finance. However, these algorithms, are typically more opaque than previous expert systems (Section 3.1), semantic applications

(Section 3.2), and cognitive assistants (Section 3.3). Hence, the ML domain faces large challenges in addressing the trustworthiness, transparency, and intelligibility[15] of their models. Additionally, even within the ML domain, there has been a shift from the dependence on simpler linear algorithms that were less complex, to non-linear, "black-box" models, such as, deep learning [44]. While ML algorithms are often achieving high accuracy, they are typically unable to explain why they arrived at a classification or score (view the tradeoff in Figure 3). However, there have been techniques to circumvent these issues, such as, providing confidence scores for the results of models to induce trust (post-hoc interpretations [3,57]), attaching semantic information to results [5], presenting contrastive or counterfactual explanations to provide intuition for the model's functioning [74,76], etc. Formally, the interpretability techniques for ML models can be grouped into two categories [57], one class aimed at *post-hoc interpretations* that contain explanations about the results to provide perspective on the model's functioning, and the other aimed at improving *transparency* to offer an intuition for the model's functioning. We want to clarify that although ML models might not be considered traditional knowledge-enabled system candidates, we have included them in our review due to the emergence of hybrid systems composed of ML models and semantic methods. We believe that a review of explainability approaches in the ML domain will be fruitful for introducing explanation components into these hybrid systems.

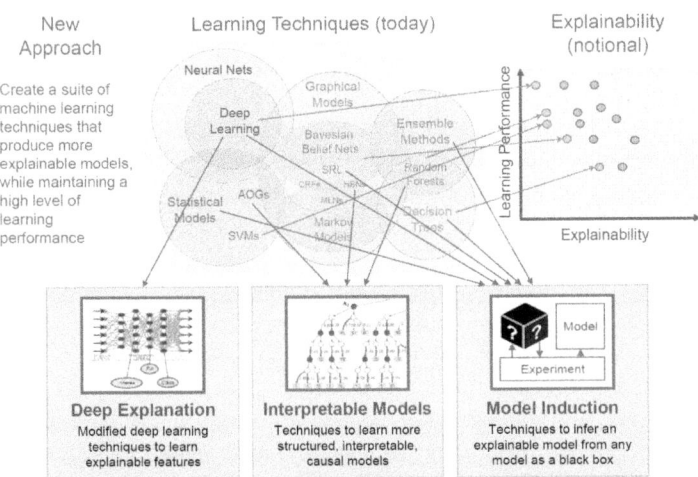

Figure 3. A high-level overview of the ML models' classes and the explanation techniques being developed as part of DARPA's eXplainable AI program. It is interesting to note the accuracy-explainability tradeoff depicted in the graph on the right, which shows that within the ML domain, simpler models which are oftentimes less accurate are often more explainable [Image taken from Gunning [27]].

---

[15]Our definition of intelligibility is very similar to the description proposed by Lipton [46] and Lou et al. [47], in that intelligible models are interpretable wherein the contribution of model features to a decision can be deciphered.

3.4.1. DARPA XAI Program

DARPA's eXplainable AI (XAI) program[16] focuses on building explainable models that achieve high accuracy and on methods to enable human users to trust and understand these models. We will discuss selected XAI efforts mentioned in the DARPA XAI reports [27,28] that have a knowledge explainability component to them.

Bau et. al. [5], have developed a *network dissection* technique to align the intermediate layer results of convolutional neural networks (CNN) with semantic concepts. They make two contributions, a *network dissection* technique to identify what the network is learning at each step by comparing it to semantic concepts, and the construction of *disentangled representation* to align encodings between the network's output and a semantic concept. The disentangled representations were designed to provide a notion of the "human perception of what it means for a concept to be mixed up" [5]. Further, the authors also assembled a new dataset, the Broadly and Densely Labeled Dataset (Broden) [78] of objects, that contained low-level compositions of objects used as semantic concepts. This work addresses the deep explanation component of Figure 3, wherein feature modifications are being made to make deep learning algorithms interpretable. Similarly, as part of the same program, a team of Charles River Analytica (CRA) researchers developed a technique to learn the causal nature of CNN activations [30]. In this work, Harradon et al. [30] construct a causal graph in-line with Judea Pearl's do-calculus [62] method. They ground the network activations in a $P(O,P,C)$ graph, where C represents concepts of network representations that humans can identify, P is the input, and O is the output. However, unlike the network dissection paper [5], the causal graph is learned via an unsupervised autoencoder method. Hence, it might be challenging to trust the causal graphs that are learned.

Since the XAI program by DARPA is an ongoing initiative, some of the work mentioned in the slideware[17] remains unpublished. However, we briefly summarize some of these unpublished methods that we believe are relevant to our explainability review. In the Common Ground Learning and Explanation (COGLE) project,[18] being led by PARC, a system is being built to explain to humans the workings of an autonomous Unmanned Aircraft System (UAS) testbed. The COGLE system explains the workings of the UAS reinforcement learning decision-making algorithm to users, conveys an understanding of the system's future behavior, and uses a common ground vocabulary to present these explanations. The common ground vocabulary is generated by including both human understandable and machine-understandable terminology, hence, hoping to ensure a dialogue between ML algorithms and humans. The common ground idea corroborates a requirement put forth by Doshi-Velez et al., [18] that "to build AI systems that can provide explanation in terms of human-interpretable terms, we must both list those terms and allow the AI system access to examples to learn them." In another effort, researchers at Rutgers have proposed a technique to choose optimal examples to explain a model's decision via Bayesian Teaching [77]. The explanation by the Bayesian Teaching method is an explanation by examples technique, wherein model-agnostic probabilistic methods

---

[16]DARPA XAI program website: `https://www.darpa.mil/program/explainable-artificial-intelligence`

[17]DARPA explainable AI slideware: `https://www.darpa.mil/attachments/explainableAIProgramUpdate.pdf`

[18]COGLE: `https://www.parc.com/blog/explainable-ai-an-overview-of-parcs-cogle-project-with-darpa/`

are used to identify the most probable data points that lead to a conclusion. The hypothesis that Yang et al. [77] present is that the data is most representative of the algorithm's conclusions, and humans tend to understand more intuitively through examples.

In summary, the DARPA XAI program (of which the report is a by-product [27]) is largely focused on improving explainability of deep learning models through local interpretation methods, or "knowing the reasons for specific decisions" [17] and post-hoc interpretations. These focus points, to some extent, address the trustworthiness and intelligibility aspects of the explainability of ML models.

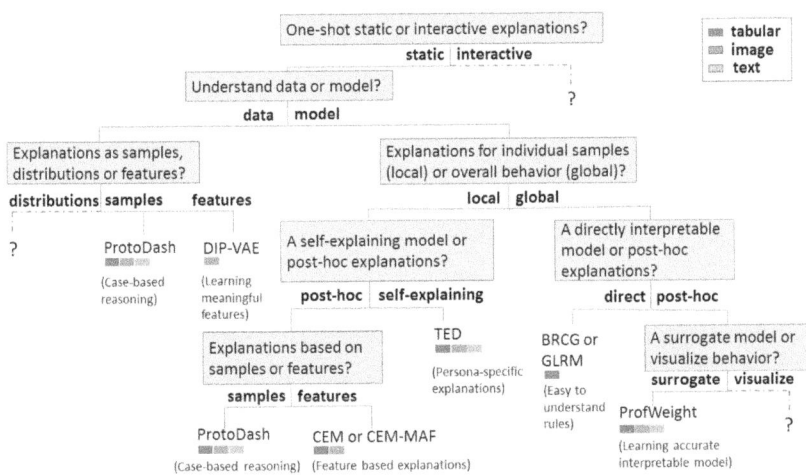

Figure 4. A decision-tree like visual overview of the taxonomy of explanations which encodes different factors ML models need to consider while designing explainable models. [Image taken from Arya et al. [3]]

3.4.2. Taxonomies in explainable ML

Besides the DARPA XAI program, there have been other recent efforts in the ML domain to support the explainability of ML models. A team of researchers from IBM Research have built the AI Fairness 360 [6] and AI Explainability 360 [3] toolkits to identify bias in datasets and ML algorithms, and to describe the explainability of ML models, respectively. In their AI fairness 360 toolkit, Bellamy et al. [6] define metrics to identify bias in three stages of the dataset, the algorithm, and the predictions of the algorithm, in their goal to improve fairness in the entire ML workflow. While, in Section 1, we noted that we do not account for fairness in explainability, we acknowledge that the exposition of the fairness of the algorithm and data could increase trust in the model. Furthermore, in the AI explainability 360 effort, Arya et al. [3] designed a taxonomy resource to provide a structure of the explanation space to benefit algorithm designers who are looking to include necessary components in explanations. More specifically, their taxonomy (Figure 4) helps in identifying methods to introduce local (explanations of portions of the model that lead to a conclusion), global (an explanation of the entire model), and post-hoc interpretations (explaining the results) of models via careful inclusion of features and mechanisms during the design of ML models. However, their taxonomy focused more on model interpretability and features of the model, rather than on intended use of the model by users.

Researchers at MIT conducted a literature review of published explainable AI papers and cataloged the explanation methods used by ML algorithms into a taxonomy [23]. Their taxonomy grouped papers into three categories, methods that emulate the processing of the data, explanations of representations (such as, the network dissection technique [5]), and explanation-producing networks. Their hope was for future methods to use the taxonomy as a reference to build explainable models. Additionally, they note that certain ML methods, such as, decision trees are more interpretable than black-box models and hence are being utilized as proxies [79] to explain the conclusions of these black-box models. Similarly, Gilpin et al. [23] proposed the Local Interpretable Model-agnostic Explanations (LIME) framework [63], that can be utilized to generate linear models on perturbations of the black-box model input to get a sense of the functioning of the black-box models.

3.4.3. Summary

From a review of the ML domain, we can infer that the explainability techniques being developed are mainly tackling challenges of model interpretability and generating post-hoc interpretations of the model's conclusions or input data. While these two broad categories might seem insufficient, the breadth of innovative approaches [3,5,76,77] being developed are promising and can help in building interpretable, and hybrid models, aided by explainable models (e.g., KGs, causal methods). In summary, what makes the models that we describe in this section candidates for explainable knowledge-enabled systems is that they utilize knowledge to provide an intuition for the functioning of unintelligible models [5], or to build a vocabulary (COGLE: [19]) to explain conclusions/inputs/workings of the algorithms. Additionally, prior knowledge of the requirements of explanations are being encoded as taxonomies [3,23] to serve as checks for future explainable models, and knowledge of existing linear models [63,79] are being leveraged to enhance the explanation capabilities of ML models. Orthogonally, the interpretability research in the ML domain is helping researchers understand that humans prefer richer, social, contrasting, and selective explanations [57].

4. Conclusion

We presented foundational approaches to explainable, knowledge-enabled systems, and identified themes for explainability within these approaches. We presented our definition of "explainable knowledge-enabled systems" to cover a broad range of past and present AI systems including expert systems, Semantic Web, cognitive assistants, and ML domains. Additionally, we believe that, with the increasing focus on explainable AI, we are at the cusp of a new era of AI where explainability plays a pivotal role in the adoption of AI systems. We provided synthesized, refined definitions of knowledge-enabled systems from a user perspective and included properties that are desirable for when a system needs to generate *provenance-aware, personalized, and context-aware* explanations.

---

[19]COGLE: `https://www.parc.com/blog/explainable-ai-an-overview-of-parcs-cogle-project-with-darpa/`

We reminded our readers that different AI domains and varying methodologies are differently suited for various aspects of explanations. The next-generation hybrid AI systems would benefit from these identified strengths, utilizing a potentially, carefully chosen combination of these techniques to provide more complete, satisfying explanations. For instance, we identified that trace-based explanation facilities are well-explored in expert systems, provenance encoding in the Semantic Web domain is capable of representing different granularities of evidence, the modular, task-based explanation facilities of cognitive assistants can generate atomic explanation components, and that interpretability efforts in the ML domain are giving rise to taxonomical checks for explainable AI models that can be adapted to other AI fields. However, we noted that these AI systems do not fully account for aspects such as user context and causality and are only capable of generating explanations belonging to a restricted set of explanation types. To address these issues, we present directions for research and describe different explanation types in a later chapter, "Directions for Explainable Knowledge-enabled Systems," that might play a key role in furthering explainable AI.

In conclusion, we believe that with the increased adoption of AI systems, there is an increased need for systems to be interpretable, adaptive, interactive, and, most importantly, able to generate explanations that not only provide an overview of the AI system, but serve as a means to educate users and help in their future explorations. To address these lofty goals of explainability, we believe that we need to learn from strengths of past foundational approaches and adapt/expand on them in the user-centric needs of the current AI landscape to build hybrid AI systems that are interpretable, knowledge-enabled, adaptive, and context and provenance-aware.

5. Acknowledgments

This work is partially supported by IBM Research AI through the AI Horizons Network. We thank our colleagues from IBM Research, Amar Das, Morgan Foreman and Ching-Hua Chen, and from RPI, James P. McCusker, and Rebecca Cowan, who greatly assisted the research and document preparation.

References

[1] Nkcheniyere N. Agu, Neha Keshan, Shruthi Chari, Oshani Seneviratne, James P. McCusker, Amar Das, and Deborah L. McGuinness. G-prov: Provenance management for clinical practice guidelines. In *Proc. of the Semantic Web solutions for large-scale biomedical data analytics Workshop*, page to appear. CEUR, 2019.

[2] Vincent Aleven, Bruce M Mclaren, Jonathan Sewall, and Kenneth R Koedinger. A new paradigm for intelligent tutoring systems: Example-tracing tutors. *Int. J. of Artificial Intelligence in Education*, 19(2):105–154, 2009.

[3] Vijay Arya, Rachel KE Bellamy, Pin-Yu Chen, Amit Dhurandhar, Michael Hind, Samuel C Hoffman, Stephanie Houde, Q Vera Liao, Ronny Luss, Aleksandra Mojsilović, et al. One explanation does not fit all: A toolkit and taxonomy of ai explainability techniques. *arXiv preprint arXiv:1909.03012*, 2019.

[4] Franz Baader, Ian Horrocks, and Ulrike Sattler. Description logics. In *Handbook on ontologies*, pages 3–28. Springer, 2004.

[5] David Bau, Bolei Zhou, Aditya Khosla, Aude Oliva, and Antonio Torralba. Network dissection: Quantifying interpretability of deep visual representations. In *Proc. of the IEEE Conf. on Computer Vision and Pattern Recognition*, pages 6541–6549, 2017.

[6]   Rachel KE Bellamy, Kuntal Dey, Michael Hind, Samuel C Hoffman, Stephanie Houde, Kalapriya Kannan, Pranay Lohia, Jacquelyn Martino, Sameep Mehta, Aleksandra Mojsilovic, et al. Ai fairness 360: An extensible toolkit for detecting, understanding, and mitigating unwanted algorithmic bias. *arXiv preprint arXiv:1810.01943*, 2018.

[7]   Tim Berners-Lee, Dan Connolly, Lalana Kagal, Yosi Scharf, and Jim Hendler. N3logic: A logical framework for the world wide web. *Theory and Practice of Logic Programming*, 8(3):249–269, 2008.

[8]   Tim Berners-Lee, Dimitri Dimitroyannis, A John Mallinckrodt, and Susan McKay. World wide web. *Computers in Physics*, 8(3):298–299, 1994.

[9]   Tim Berners-Lee, James Hendler, Ora Lassila, et al. The semantic web. *Scientific american*, 284(5):28–37, 2001.

[10]   Or Biran and Courtenay Cotton. Explanation and justification in machine learning: A survey. In *IJCAI-17 workshop on explainable AI (XAI)*, volume 8, page 1, 2017.

[11]   Alexander Borgida, Ronald J Brachman, Deborah L McGuinness, and Lori Alperin Resnick. Classic: A structural data model for objects. In *ACM Sigmod record*, volume 18, pages 58–67. ACM, 1989.

[12]   Ronald J Brachman and James G Schmolze. An overview of the kl-one knowledge representation system. In *Readings in artificial intelligence and databases*, pages 207–230. Elsevier, 1989.

[13]   William J Clancey and Reed Letsinger. *NEOMYCIN: Reconfiguring a rule-based expert system for application to teaching*. Dept. of Computer Sci., Stanford University Stanford, 1982.

[14]   Kenneth Conley and James Carpenter. Towel: Towards an intelligent to-do list. In *AAAI Spring Symp.: Interaction Challenges for Intelligent Assistants*, 2007.

[15]   Paulo Pinheiro Da Silva, Deborah L McGuinness, and Richard Fikes. A proof markup language for semantic web services. *Information Systems*, 31(4-5):381–395, 2006.

[16]   Jasbir S Dhaliwal and Izak Benbasat. The use and effects of knowledge-based system explanations: theoretical foundations and a framework for empirical evaluation. *Information systems research*, 7(3):342–362, 1996.

[17]   Finale Doshi-Velez and Been Kim. Towards a rigorous science of interpretable machine learning. *arXiv preprint arXiv:1702.08608*, 2017.

[18]   Finale Doshi-Velez, Mason Kortz, Ryan Budish, Chris Bavitz, Sam Gershman, David O'Brien, Stuart Schieber, James Waldo, David Weinberger, and Alexandra Wood. Accountability of AI under the law: The role of explanation. *arXiv preprint arXiv:1711.01134*, 2017.

[19]   Maria R Ebling. Can cognitive assistants disappear? *IEEE Pervasive Computing*, 15(3):4–6, 2016.

[20]   Lisa Ehrlinger and Wolfram Wöß. Towards a definition of knowledge graphs. *SEMANTiCS (Posters, Demos, SuCCESS)*, 48, 2016.

[21]   Douglas C Engelbart. Toward augmenting the human intellect and boosting our collective iq. *Communications of the ACM*, 38(8):30–33, 1995.

[22]   Robert G Farrell, Jonathan Lenchner, Jeffrey O Kephjart, Alan M Webb, Michael J Muller, Thomas D Erikson, David O Melville, Rachel KE Bellamy, Daniel M Gruen, Jonathan H Connell, et al. Symbiotic cognitive computing. *AI Magazine*, 37(3):81–93, 2016.

[23]   Leilani H Gilpin, David Bau, Ben Z Yuan, Ayesha Bajwa, Michael Specter, and Lalana Kagal. Explaining explanations: An approach to evaluating interpretability of machine learning. *arXiv preprint arXiv:1806.00069*, 2018.

[24]   Armando E Giuliano, James L Connolly, Stephen B Edge, Elizabeth A Mittendorf, Hope S Rugo, Lawrence J Solin, Donald L Weaver, David J Winchester, and Gabriel N Hortobagyi. Breast cancer—major changes in the American Joint Committee on Cancer eighth edition cancer staging manual. *CA: A Cancer J. for Clinicians*, 67(4):290–303, 2017.

[25]   Alyssa Glass, Deborah L McGuinness, and Michael Wolverton. Toward establishing trust in adaptive agents. In *Proc. of the 13th Int. Conf. on Intelligent user interfaces*, pages 227–236. ACM, 2008.

[26]   Paul Groth, Andrew Gibson, and Jan Velterop. The anatomy of a nanopublication. *Information Services & Use*, 30(1-2):51–56, 2010.

[27]   David Gunning. Explainable artificial intelligence (xai). *Defense Advanced Research Projects Agency (DARPA), nd Web*, 2, 2017.

[28]   David Gunning and David W Aha. Darpa's explainable artificial intelligence program. *AI Magazine*, 40(2):44–58, 2019.

[29]   Amelie Gyrard, Manas Gaur, Saeedeh Shekarpour, Krishnaprasad Thirunarayan, and Amit Sheth. Personalized health knowledge graph. In *Int. Semantic Web Conf. (ISWC) 2018 Contextualized Knowledge Graph Workshop*, 2018.

[30] Michael Harradon, Jeff Druce, and Brian Ruttenberg. Causal learning and explanation of deep neural networks via autoencoded activations. *arXiv preprint arXiv:1802.00541*, 2018.

[31] Rakebul Hasan and Fabien Gandon. Explanation in the semantic web: a survey of the state of the art, 2012.

[32] James Hendler and Eric Miller. Integrating applications on the semantic web. *J. of the Institute of Electrical Engineers of Japan*, Vol 122(10):676–680, 2002.

[33] Sven Hertling and Heiko Paulheim. Webisalod: providing hypernymy relations extracted from the web as linked open data. In *Int. Semantic Web Conf.*, pages 111–119. Springer, 2017.

[34] Aidan Hogan, Andreas Harth, and Axel Polleres. Scalable authoritative owl reasoning for the web. *Int. J. on Semantic Web and Information Systems (IJSWIS)*, 5(2), 2009.

[35] James Hollan, Edwin Hutchins, and David Kirsh. Distributed cognition: toward a new foundation for human-computer interaction research. *ACM Transactions on Computer-Human Interaction (TOCHI)*, 7(2):174–196, 2000.

[36] Andreas Holzinger, Chris Biemann, Constantinos S Pattichis, and Douglas B Kell. What do we need to build explainable ai systems for the medical domain? *arXiv preprint arXiv:1712.09923*, 2017.

[37] Matthew Horridge, Bijan Parsia, and Ulrike Sattler. Laconic and precise justifications in owl. In *Int. semantic web Conf.*, pages 323–338. Springer, 2008.

[38] Edwin Hutchins. The technology of team navigation, intellectual teamwork: social and technological foundations of cooperative work, 1, 1990.

[39] Lalana Kagal. Accountability In RDF (AIR) Web Rule Language, 2009.

[40] Johan de Kleer, Jon Doyle, Guy L Steele Jr, and Gerald Jay Sussman. AMORD explicit control of reasoning. *ACM SIGPLAN Notices*, 12(8):116–125, 1977.

[41] Tobias Kuhn, Paolo Emilio Barbano, Mate Levente Nagy, and Michael Krauthammer. Broadening the scope of nanopublications. In *Extended Semantic Web Conf.* Springer, 2013.

[42] Timothy Lebo, Satya Sahoo, Deborah McGuinness, Khalid Belhajjame, James Cheney, David Corsar, Daniel Garijo, Stian Soiland-Reyes, Stephan Zednik, and Jun Zhao. Prov-o: The prov ontology. *W3C recommendation*, 2013.

[43] Freddy Lecue. On the role of knowledge graphs in explainable ai. *Semantic Web J. (Forthcoming)*, 2019.

[44] Yann LeCun, Yoshua Bengio, and Geoffrey Hinton. Deep learning. *Nature*, 521(7553):436–444, 2015.

[45] Brian Y Lim, Anind K Dey, and Daniel Avrahami. Why and why not explanations improve the intelligibility of context-aware intelligent systems. In *Proc. of the SIGCHI Conf. on Human Factors in Computing Systems*, pages 2119–2128. ACM, 2009.

[46] Zachary C Lipton. The mythos of model interpretability. *Queue*, 16(3):31–57, 2018.

[47] Yin Lou, Rich Caruana, and Johannes Gehrke. Intelligible models for classification and regression. In *Proc. of the 18th ACM SIGKDD Int. Conf. on Knowledge discovery and data mining*, pages 150–158. ACM, 2012.

[48] Rosa Maimone, Marco Guerini, Mauro Dragoni, Tania Bailoni, and Claudio Eccher. Perkapp: A general purpose persuasion architecture for healthy lifestyles. *J. of biomedical informatics*, 82:70–87, 2018.

[49] James P McCusker, Michel Dumontier, Rui Yan, Sylvia He, Jonathan S Dordick, and Deborah L McGuinness. Finding melanoma drugs through a probabilistic knowledge graph. *PeerJ Computer Sci.*, 3:e106, 2017.

[50] James P McCusker, Sabbir M Rashid, Zhicheng Liang, Yue Liu, Katherine Chastain, Paulo Pinheiro, Jeanette A Stingone, and Deborah L McGuinness. Broad, interdisciplinary science in tela: An exposure and child health ontology. In *Proc. of the 2017 ACM on Web Sci. Conf.*, pages 349–357. ACM, 2017.

[51] Deborah L McGuinness. *Explaining reasoning in description logics*. PhD thesis, Rutgers University, 1996.

[52] Deborah L McGuinness and Alexander Borgida. Explaining subsumption in description logics. In *IJCAI (1)*, pages 816–821, 1995.

[53] Deborah L McGuinness and Paulo Pinheiro Da Silva. Explaining answers from the semantic web: The inference web approach. *Web Semantics: Sci., Services and Agents on the World Wide Web*, 1(4):397–413, 2004.

[54] Deborah L McGuinness, Alyssa Glass, Michael Wolverton, and Paulo Pinheiro Da Silva. Explaining task processing in cognitive assistants that learn. In *AAAI Spring Symp.: Interaction Challenges for Intelligent Assistants*, pages 80–87, 2007.

[55] Deborah L McGuinness, Frank Van Harmelen, et al. Owl web ontology language overview. *W3C recommendation*, 10(10):2004, 2004.

[56]   Tim Miller. Explanation in artificial intelligence: Insights from the social sciences. *Artificial Intelligence*, 267:1–38, 2019.

[57]   Brent Mittelstadt, Chris Russell, and Sandra Wachter. Explaining explanations in ai. In *Proc. of the Conf. on fairness, accountability, and transparency*, pages 279–288. ACM, 2019.

[58]   Donald A Norman. *The psychology of everyday things*. Basic books, 1988.

[59]   Ingrid Nunes and Dietmar Jannach. A systematic review and taxonomy of explanations in decision support and recommender systems. *User Modeling and User-Adapted Interaction*, 27(3-5):393–444, 2017.

[60]   Peter F Patel-Schneider, Deborah L McGuinness, Ronald J Brachman, and Lori Alperin Resnick. The classic knowledge representation system: Guiding principles and implementation rationale. *ACM SIGART Bulletin*, 2(3):108–113, 1991.

[61]   Judea Pearl. *Causality*. Cambridge university press, 2009.

[62]   Judea Pearl. Theoretical impediments to machine learning, 2017.

[63]   Marco Tulio Ribeiro, Sameer Singh, and Carlos Guestrin. Why should i trust you?: Explaining the predictions of any classifier. In *Proc. of the 22nd ACM SIGKDD Int. Conf. on knowledge discovery and data mining*, pages 1135–1144. ACM, 2016.

[64]   Mireia Ribera and Àgata Lapedriza. Can we do better explanations? a proposal of user-centered explainable ai. In *IUI Workshops*, 2019.

[65]   Elaine Rich. Stereotypes and user modeling. In *User models in dialog systems*, pages 35–51. Springer, 1989.

[66]   Oshani Seneviratne, Sabbir M Rashid, Shruthi Chari, James P McCusker, Kristin P Bennett, James A Hendler, and Deborah L McGuinness. Knowledge integration for disease characterization: A breast cancer example. In *Int. Semantic Web Conf.*, pages 223–238, San Francisco, USA, 2018. Springer.

[67]   Edward Shortliffe. *Computer-based medical consultations: MYCIN*. Elsevier, 2012.

[68]   Edward Hance Shortliffe. Mycin: a rule-based computer program for advising physicians regarding antimicrobial therapy selection. Technical report, Dept. of Computer Sci., Stanford University Stanford, 1974.

[69]   Kazunari Sugiyama, Kenji Hatano, and Masatoshi Yoshikawa. Adaptive web search based on user profile constructed without any effort from users. In *Proc. of the 13th Int. Conf. on World Wide Web*, pages 675–684. ACM, 2004.

[70]   William Swartout, Cecile Paris, and Johanna Moore. Explanations in knowledge systems: Design for explainable expert systems. *IEEE Expert*, 6(3):58–64, 1991.

[71]   William R Swartout and Johanna D Moore. Explanation in second generation expert systems. In *Second generation expert systems*, pages 543–585. Springer, 1993.

[72]   Gheorghe Tecuci, Mihai Boicu, Cindy Ayers, and David Cammons. Personal cognitive assistants for military intelligence analysis: Mixed-initiative learning, tutoring, and problem solving. In *First Int. Conf. on Intelligence Analysis*, pages 2–6. Citeseer, 2005.

[73]   Joshua Valdez, Matthew Kim, Michael Rueschman, Vimig Socrates, Susan Redline, and Satya S Sahoo. Provcare semantic provenance knowledgebase: evaluating scientific reproducibility of research studies. In *AMIA Annual Symp. Proc.*, volume 2017, page 1705. American Medical Informatics Association, 2017.

[74]   Jasper van der Waa, Marcel Robeer, Jurriaan van Diggelen, Matthieu Brinkhuis, and Mark Neerincx. Contrastive explanations with local foil trees. *arXiv preprint arXiv:1806.07470*, 2018.

[75]   Kurt Vanlehn. The behavior of tutoring systems. *Int. J.of artificial intelligence in education*, 16(3):227–265, 2006.

[76]   Sandra Wachter, Brent Mittelstadt, and Chris Russell. Counterfactual explanations without opening the black box: Automated decisions and the gdpr. *Harv. JL & Tech.*, 31:841, 2017.

[77]   Scott Cheng-Hsin Yang and Patrick Shafto. Explainable artificial intelligence via bayesian teaching. In *NIPS 2017 workshop on Teaching Machines, Robots, and Humans*, 2017.

[78]   Bolei Zhou, David Bau, Aude Oliva, and Antonio Torralba. Interpreting deep visual representations via network dissection. *IEEE transactions on pattern analysis and machine intelligence*, 2018.

[79]   Jan Ruben Zilke, Eneldo Loza Mencía, and Frederik Janssen. Deepred–rule extraction from deep neural networks. In *Int. Conf. on Discovery Sci.*, pages 457–473. Springer, 2016.

Knowledge Graphs for eXplainable Artificial Intelligence: Foundations, Applications and Challenges 49
I. Tiddi et al. (Eds.)
IOS Press, 2020
doi:10.3233/SSW200011

Knowledge Graph Embeddings and Explainable AI

Federico BIANCHI [a], Gaetano ROSSIELLO [b], Luca COSTABELLO [c],
Matteo PALMONARI [d], and Pasquale MINERVINI [e]

[a] *Bocconi University*
[b] *IBM Research AI*
[c] *Accenture Labs*
[d] *University of Milan-Bicocca*
[e] *University College London*

Abstract. Knowledge graph embeddings are now a widely adopted approach to knowledge representation in which entities and relationships are embedded in vector spaces. In this chapter, we introduce the reader to the concept of knowledge graph embeddings by explaining what they are, how they can be generated and how they can be evaluated. We summarize the state-of-the-art in this field by describing the approaches that have been introduced to represent knowledge in the vector space. In relation to knowledge representation, we consider the problem of explainability, and discuss models and methods for explaining predictions obtained via knowledge graph embeddings.

Keywords. Knowledge Graphs, Knowledge Graph Embeddings, Knowledge Representation, eXplainable AI

1. Introduction

A knowledge graph [39] (KG) is an abstraction used in knowledge representation to encode knowledge in one or more domains by representing entities like New York City and United States (i.e., nodes) and binary relationships that connect these entities; for example, New York City and United States are connected by the relationship country, i.e., New York City has United States as a country. Most of KGs also contains relationships that connect entities with *literals*, i.e., values from known data structures such as strings, numbers, dates, and so on; for example a relationship settled that connects New York City and the integer 1624 describe a property of the entity New York City. More in general, we can view a KG under a dual perspective: as a *directed labeled multi-graph*, where nodes represent entities or literals and labeled edges represent specific relationships between entities or between an entity and a literal, and as a set of *statements*, also referred to as *facts*, having the form of subject-predicate-object triples, e.g., (New York City, country, United States) and (New York City, settled, 1624). In the following, we will use the notation (h, r, t) (head, relation, tail) to identify a statement in KG, as frequent in the literature about KG embeddings.

The entities described in KGs are commonly organized using a set of *types*, e.g., City and Country, also referred to as concepts, classes or data types (when referred

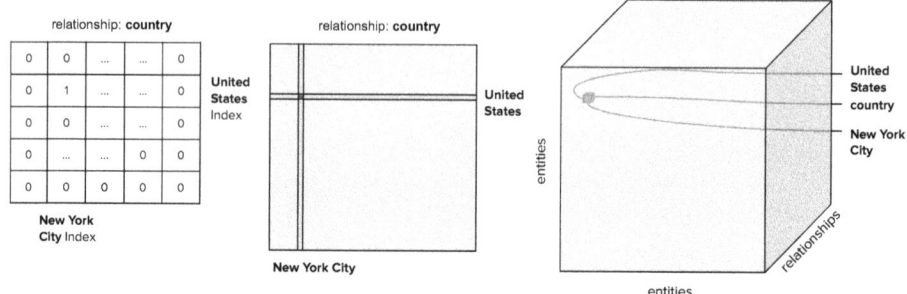

Figure 1. Binary adjacency representation of a KG.

to literals). For example, the statement (New York City, type, City) states that the entity New York City has type City. Indeed, this types are often defined in what is generally referred to as the *ontology* [21]. An ontology is a formal specification of the meaning of types and relationships expressed as a set of logical constraints and rules, which support automated reasoning. For example, DBpedia [3], a knowledge graph built upon information extracted from Wikipedia, describes more than 4 million entities and has 3 billion statements[1].

While KGs can be described using a graph, a nice and simple way to visualize a knowledge graph is considering it as a 3-order adjacency tensor (i.e., a 3-dimensional tensor describing the structure of the KG). Formally a 3-dimensional adjacency tensor is defined as $T \in \mathbb{R}^{N \times R \times N}$, where N is the number of entities and R is the number of relationships. Each dimension of the tensor corresponds to (head, relation, tail) respectively.

More formally, assume we have a KG $\mathcal{G} = \{(e_i, r_j, e_k)\} \subseteq \mathcal{E} \times \mathcal{R} \times \mathcal{E}$, where $\mathcal{E}$ and $\mathcal{R}$ denote the sets of entities and relations in the KG, respectively, with $|\mathcal{E}| = N$ and $|\mathcal{E}| = R$. The adjacency tensor $T \in \mathbb{R}^{N \times R \times N}$ is defined as follows:

$$T_{i,j,k} = \begin{cases} 1 & \text{if } (e_i, r_j, e_k) \in \mathcal{G}, \\ 0 & \text{otherwise.} \end{cases}$$

To visualize this, imagine a simple adjacency matrix that represents a single relation, such as the country relation: the two dimensions of the matrix correspond to the head entity and the tail entity. Each entity corresponds to an unique index: given a triple (New York City, country, United States), we have a 1 in the cell of the matrix corresponding to the intersection between the i-th row and the j-th column, where $i, j \in \mathbb{N}$ are the indices associated with New York City and United States, respectively. On the other hand, any cell in the adjacency matrix corresponding to triples not in the KG contains a 0. If we consider more than one relationship and we stack them together, we obtain a 3-dimensional tensor, generally referred to as the binary tensor representation of a KG. See Figure 1 for a simple visualization of this concept.

---

[1]https://wiki.dbpedia.org/about/facts-figures

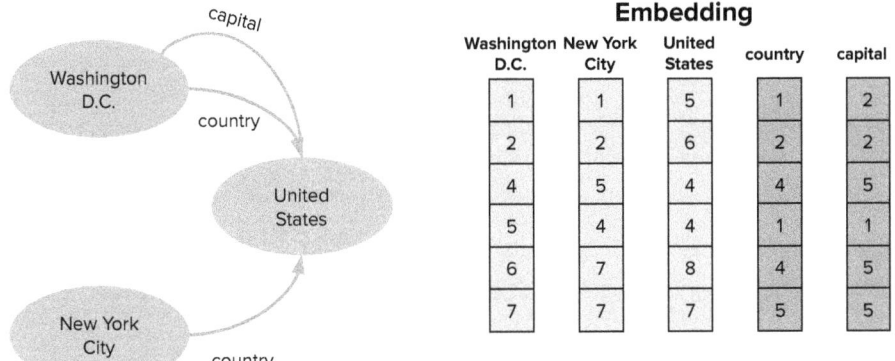

Figure 2. Starting from a knowledge graph, embedding methods generate representations of the elements of the knowledge graph that are embedded in a vector space. For example, these representations could be vectors. Vectors encode latent properties of the graph and for example similar entities tend to be described with similar vectors.

The term "knowledge graph embeddings" refers to the generation of vector representations of the elements that form a knowledge graph[2]. Essentially, what most methods do is to create a vector for each entity and each relation; these embeddings are generated in such a way to capture latent properties of the semantics in the knowledge graph: *similar* entities and *similar* relationships will be represented with *similar* vectors. Figure 2 provides an intuitive example of what a knowledge graph embedding method does. The tensor representation introduced above is frequently used in many KG embedding methods that learn embeddings by using dimensionality reduction techniques over the tensor.

The elements are generally represented in a vector space with low dimensionality (with values ranging from 100 dimensions to 1000 dimensions) and one key aspect is given by the notion of similarity: in a vector space similarity can be interpreted with the use of vector similarity measures (e.g., cosine similarity, in which two vectors are more similar if the angle between them is small).

An important task is to find ways to extend KGs adding new relationships between entities. This task is generally referred to as link prediction or knowledge graph completion. Adding new facts can be done with the use of logical inference. For example, from a triple (Washington D.C., capital, United States) we can infer (Washington D.C., country, United States). Inferring this last fact comes from background knowledge encoded in an axiom that specify that if a city is a capital of a country, it is also part of that country (e.g., as encoded by a first order logic rule such as $\forall X, Y : \text{capital}(X,Y) \Rightarrow \text{country}(X,Y)$). Unfortunately, many knowledge graphs have many observed facts and fewer axioms or rules [87].

KG embeddings can be used for link prediction, since they show interesting predictive abilities and are not directly constrained by logical rules. This property comes at the

---

[2]Note that knowledge graph embeddings are different from Graph Neural Networks (GNNs). KG embedding models are in general shallow and linear models and should be distinguished from GNNs [78], which are neural networks that take relational structures as inputs.

cost of not being directly interpretable (i.e., the vector representations now encode the latent meaning of the entity/relationship). The explainability of this prediction is often difficult because the result comes from the combination of latent factors that are embedded in a vector space and an evaluation of the inductive abilities of these methods is still an open problem [87].

Knowledge graph embeddings projected in the vector space tend to show interesting latent properties [61]; for example, *similar* entities tend to be close in the vector space. The value of similarity in the latent space is a function that depends on the way knowledge graph embeddings are generated. Similarity is also important under the point of view of explaining the meaning. For instance, we might not know the meaning of the entity New York City, but it can be inferred from its topic by looking at closest entities in the geometric space (i.e. Washington D.C. and United States).

The components of the vectors representing the entities and relations are not explainable themselves, and it can be hard to assign a natural language label that describes the meaning of that component. However, we can observe how different entities and relationships are related within the graph by analyzing its structure – which was also used to generate the vector-based representations. In addition, the training is driven by a similarity principle, which can be easily understood. For example, similar entities have similar embedding representations, and the same is true for similar relationships. Thus, while it is not possible to explain the exact difference between two vectors of two entities, we can refer to this similarity when using the vectors in more complex neural networks that use these vectors and the additional information to enrich the network capabilities.

Knowledge graph embeddings have been used in different contexts including recommendation [40,91,106], visual relationship detection [4] and knowledge base completion [11]. Moreover, knowledge graph embeddings can be used to integrate semantic knowledge inside deep neural networks, thus enriching the explainability of pure black-box neural networks [48,38], but they also come with some limitations.

In this chapter, we describe how to build embedding representations for knowledge graphs and how to evaluate them. We discuss related work of the field by mentioning the approaches that improved the state-of-the-art results. Then, we focus on knowledge graph embeddings to support explainability, i.e. how knowledge graph embeddings can be adopted to provide explanations by describing the relevant state-of-the-art approaches. Similarity comes has a key factor also in the context of explainability, in recommender systems for example, similarity is a key notion to express suggestions to users.

1.1. Overview of this Chapter

This chapter provides an overview of the field in which we describe how KG embeddings are generated and which are the most influential approaches in the filed up to date. Moreover, the chapter should also describe which are the possible usages for KG embeddings in the context of explainability. In the recent literature, many approaches for knowledge graph embeddings have been proposed; we summarize the most relevant models by focusing on the key ideas and their impact on the community.

In Section 2 we give a more detailed overview related to how a knowledge graph embedding method can be defined and trained. We will describe TransE [11], one of the most popular models, and then we will briefly explain how information that does not come from the knowledge graph can be used to extend the capabilities of the embedding models. This will be a general introduction that should help the reader understand how the methods introduced in the other sections work.

In Section 3, we describe the approaches we have selected. We summarize what researchers have experimented within the field, giving to the reader the possibility of exploring different possible ways of generating knowledge graph embeddings. Note that it is difficult to describe which is the best model for a specific task because evaluation results are greatly influenced by hyper-parameters (see Section 3.5). Nevertheless, we think that most of the approaches have laid the basis for further development in the field and are thus worth describing. We then describe how knowledge graph embeddings are evaluated, showing that the main task is link prediction and that the datasets used have changed over the years. Link prediction is a task that requires high explainability, something that in the context of knowledge graph embeddings is often missing. In general, ComplEx [88] is often considered as one of the best performing models [4] and gives stable results in inductive reasoning tasks [87].

Then, in Section 4, we focus on explainability. Explainability is a difficult term to define [53]. Knowledge graph embeddings are not explainable by default, because they are sub-symbolic representations of entities in which latent factors are encoded. Knowledge graph embeddings can be used for link prediction, but the prediction is the result of the combination of latent factors that are not directly interpretable. However, there is recent literature that explores the usage of embeddings in the context of explainable and logical inferences.

We conclude this chapter in Section 5, where we summarize our main conclusions and we describe possible future directions for the field.

Additional Resources   Several works that provide an overview of knowledge graph embeddings have been proposed in the literature. We point the reader to [28] that contains a nicely written survey of approaches that are meant to support the embedding of knowledge graph literals and to [92] for another overview on knowledge graph embeddings. As knowledge graph embeddings provide sub-symbolic representations of knowledge there is a recent increasing interest in finding ways to interpret how these representations interact [1]. Inductive capabilities of knowledge graph embeddings methods have been recently evaluated [87].

2. Knowledge Graph Embeddings

A Short Primer   In this first part, we are going to define the general elements that characterize a knowledge graph embedding method. To better illustrate how knowledge graph embeddings are created we focus our explanation on one of the seminal approaches of the field, TransE [11]. We will introduce how TransE embeddings can be generated and how a method like TransE can be extended to consider information that is not included in the set of triples. While we will describe TransE-specific concepts, most of what it is explained in this section is still valid for other methods in the state of the art.

Nowadays, a plethora of approaches to generate embedded representations of KGs exists [11,67,96,52,88]. In 2011, RESCAL [67] was the first influential model to create embedded representations of entities and relationships from a KG by relying on a tensor factorization approach upon the 3-dimensional tensor generated by considering subject entity, predicate entity and object entity as the 3 dimensions of the tensor. There are mainly three elements that are used to distinguish a method to generate KGs embedding: (i) the choice of the representations of entities and relationships, in general vector representations of real numbers are used [11,96], but there are methods that use matrices to represent relationships [67] and complex vectors to represent entities and relationships [88]; (ii) the so-called *scoring function*, which we will refer to as ϕ. This function is used to aggregate the information combing from a triple, and is generally referred to as the function that estimates the *likelihood* of the triple; lastly (iii) the loss function, which defines the objective being minimized during the training of the knowledge graph embedding model.

Changes in these three elements is what generally makes one model better than the other (although, see Section 3.5, where we explain the impact of different hyperparameters on the comparison). Scoring functions can be extended with many different information like, information coming from images [98] or numerical and relational features [26], in which the entity vector of a scoring function might be represented with the aggregation of image representations of that entity or textual content, an entity can be represented by aggregating the information contained inside its textual description. At the same time, loss functions can be extended considering different parameters, e.g., it is possible to extend a loss function by adding regularization. The interaction between the entity vectors and the relationship vectors is modulated by the score function. The score function computes a confidence value of the likelihood of a triple.

The learning process requires both positive and negative data in input and KGs contain only positive information. In KG embeddings the generation of negative is generally achieved generating *corrupted triples* i.e., triples that are false. For example, if in a knowledge graph we have the triple (New York City, country, United States), a simple corrupted triple is (United States, country, New York City). Note that despite these training procedures might have several limitations, different methods have been proposed to optimize the selection of good negative samples. One of the most advanced techniques is KBGAN [13] that proposes an adversarial method to generate effective negative training examples that can improve the representations of the knowledge graph embedding.

Making Knowledge Graph Embeddings   TransE [11] uses k-dimensional vectors to represent both entities and relationships; the score function that the authors propose as the following form $d(\mathbf{h}+\mathbf{r},\mathbf{t})$, where the d function can be the L1 or the L2 norm. The driving idea of this score function is that the sum of the subject vector with the predicate vector should generate the vector representation of the object as output (i.e. $\mathbf{h}+\mathbf{r} \approx \mathbf{t}$), in general the scoring function can be also defined as $d(\mathbf{h}+\mathbf{r},\mathbf{t}) = \|\mathbf{h}+\mathbf{r}-\mathbf{t}\|$. The loss function defined to learn the representations is instead:

$$\mathscr{L} = \sum_{h,r,t\in S} \sum_{h',r,t'\in S'_{h,r,t}} [\gamma+d(\mathbf{h}+\mathbf{r},\mathbf{t}) - d(\mathbf{h}'+\mathbf{r},\mathbf{t}')]_+,$$

where $[x]_+$ is the positive part of x and γ is a margin hyper-parameter. And $S'_{h,r,t}$ is the set of corrupted triples. $d(\mathbf{h}+\mathbf{r},\mathbf{t})$ is the score of the true triple while $d(\mathbf{h}'+\mathbf{r},\mathbf{t}')$ is the score of the true triple. This loss function favors low values of $d(\mathbf{h}+\mathbf{r},\mathbf{t})$ with respect to the corrupted triples, in such a way that the function can be effectively minimized. It is possible to optimize the representation through the use of gradient-based techniques that are now common in machine learning. Figure 3 shows how TransE combine entities and

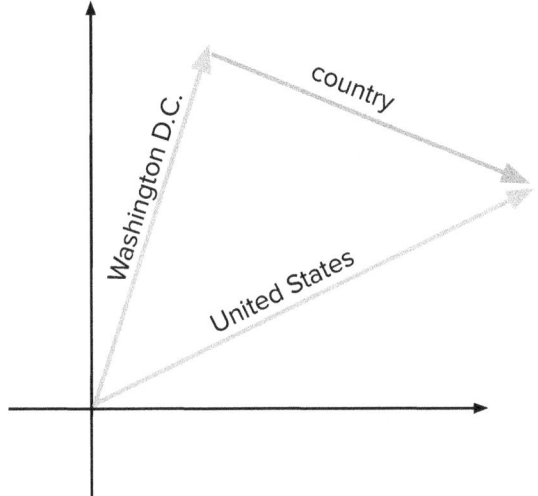

Figure 3. Example of how TransE represents and models the interactions between entities and relationships in vector space.

relationships in the scoring function. Through the training process, TransE learns vector representations of entities and relationships.

Augmenting Knowledge Graph Embeddings   Knowledge graph embeddings can be generated by considering information that is not included in the graph itself. Different methods have been introduced to extend knowledge graph embeddings by adding novel information outside from the one provided by knowledge graph triples and we will give a more detailed overview in the next section, here we describe a method that extends TransE using textual information; adding elements to the score function allows us to include novel information inside our representations.

Description-Embodied Knowledge Representation Learning (DKRL) [100] jointly learns a structure-based representation h_s (as TransE) and a description-based representation t_d that can be used in an integrated scoring function, thus combining the relative information coming from both text and facts. To extend with additional information a model like TransE, the scoring function can be extended to optimize also other representations. For example, DKRL uses the following scoring function:

$$\|\mathbf{h}_s + \mathbf{r} - \mathbf{t}_s\| + \|\mathbf{h}_d + \mathbf{r} - \mathbf{t}_d\| + \|\mathbf{h}_s + \mathbf{r} - \mathbf{t}_d\| + \|\mathbf{h}_d + \mathbf{r} - \mathbf{t}_s\|.$$

Optimizing this joint score function allows us to combine the information coming from both text and triples. In detail, DKRL uses convolutional neural networks to generate description based representations for the entities. Different information can be used to extend the embedding such as images, logical rules, and textual information. In general, the process to introduce new information relies on the extension of the scoring function. Often adding more information allows us to extend the capabilities of the model. For example, the use of text-based representations allows us to generate vector representations of entities for which we have a description but that are not present in the KG.

Method	Scoring Function	Representation
RESCAL [67], 2011	$\mathbf{h}^\top \mathbf{W}_r \mathbf{t}$	$\mathbf{h}, \mathbf{t} \in \mathbb{R}^d, \mathbf{W}_r \in \mathbb{R}^{d \times d}$
TransE [11], 2013	$-\|\mathbf{h} + \mathbf{r} - \mathbf{t}\|$	$\mathbf{h}, \mathbf{t}, \mathbf{r} \in \mathbb{R}^d$
DistMult [103], 2014	$\langle \mathbf{h}, \mathbf{r}, \mathbf{t} \rangle$	$\mathbf{h}, \mathbf{t}, \mathbf{r} \in \mathbb{R}^d$
HolE [66], 2016	$\langle \mathbf{r}, \mathbf{h} \otimes \mathbf{t} \rangle$	$\mathbf{h}, \mathbf{t}, \mathbf{r} \in \mathbb{R}^d$
ComplEx [88], 2016	$\mathrm{Re}(\langle \mathbf{h}, \mathbf{r}, \bar{\mathbf{t}} \rangle)$	$\mathbf{h}, \mathbf{t}, \mathbf{r} \in \mathbb{C}^d$
RotatE [82], 2019	$-\|\mathbf{h} \circ \mathbf{r} - \mathbf{t}\|^2$	$\mathbf{h}, \mathbf{t}, \mathbf{r} \in \mathbb{C}^d, |r_i| = 1$

Table 1. A short list with knowledge graph embedding approaches with the respective scoring functions and the representation space used for entities and relationships. Lowercase elements are vectors, while uppercase elements are matrices, $\otimes$ is the circular correlation. $\bar{\mathbf{t}}$ defines the complex conjugate of an $\mathbf{t}$ and Re denotes the real part of a complex vector. We sampled these approaches by considering the novelty they introduced at the time they were presented. Score functions are based on those published in [82,6].

3. State-of-the-art Knowledge Graph Embeddings

In this section, we review some of the algorithms that have been introduced in the state of the art. Our main objective is to give the reader an overview of the research that has been done until now and which are the key points in the knowledge graph embedding field.

3.1. Structure-based Embeddings

Approaches that focus on the use of knowledge graph facts have also been called *fact alone* methods by other authors [92]. Table 1 shows the different scoring function that can be used to define different knowledge graph embeddings methods. The two main categories of approaches are the *translational models* and the *bilinear models*. Transnational models are often based on learning the translations from the head entity to the tail entity (e.g., TransE) while bilinear models often tend to use a multiplicative approach and to represent the relationships as matrices in the vector space. In general, bilinear models obtain good results in the link prediction tasks [44]. Main models of this category are RESCAL [67], DistMult [103], ComplEx [88].

Translational Models We have described how TransE behaves in the previous section. Note that TransE does not efficiently learn the representations for 1-to-N relationships in a knowledge graph. This comes from how the scoring function is defined: suppose the existence of the triples (New York City, locatedIn, State of New York), (New York City, locatedIn, United States. Eventually, a scoring function consistent with $\mathbf{s} + \mathbf{p} \approx \mathbf{o}$, would make the entities State of New York and United States similar, since the elements $\mathbf{s}$ and $\mathbf{p}$ of the formula are fixed. Novel models in the translational group have been introduced to reduce the effect of this problem; we can cite in this category TransH [96] and TransR [52]. In general, translational models have the advantages of having a concise definition and getting good performances. In this same category, recent and relevant approaches are RotatE [82] and HAKE [107].

Bilinear Models RESCAL [67] is based on the factorization of the tensor (see Figure 2 and has a high expressive power due to the use of a full rank matrix for each relationship in the score function $\mathbf{h}^\top \mathbf{W}_r \mathbf{t}$, where the interaction between the elements comes under the form of vector-matrix products. At the same time, the full rank matrix is prone to overfitting [107] and thus researchers that studied bilinear models have added some constraints on those representations. Indeed, DistMult [103] interprets the matrix $\mathbf{W}_r$ as a diagonal matrix, not making difference between head entity and tail entity and thus forcing the modeling of symmetric relationships [44,87]: $\phi(h,r,t) = \phi(t,r,h)$, $\forall h,t$, that force symmetry even for anti-symmetric relationships (e.g., `country`, `hypernym`).

At the same time DistMult was extended by ComplEx that models the vectors in a complex vector space to better account for anti-symmetric relationships. HolE [66] uses circular correlation, a non commutative operation between vectors, that allows us to effectively surpass the $\phi(h,r,t) = \phi(t,r,h)$ problem that DistMult had. Note that it has been proved that HolE and ComplEx are isomorphic [36]. ANALOGY [54] is a model that extends the scoring function by considering analogical relationships that exist between entities given the relationships. In their paper [54], the authors have shown that DistMult, ComplEx and HolE are special cases of ANALOGY.

Neural Models   Another group with a lower number of proposed approaches consists of neural networks-based models; the Neural Tensor Network [81] is an approach for knowledge graph embeddings that uses a score function that contains a tensor multiplication, that depends on the relationship, to relate entity embeddings, this type of operation provides some interesting reasoning capabilities and was also used in later approaches as a support for reasoning using neural networks in a neural-symbolic model [80]. Instead, ConvE [18] introduces the use of convolutional layers, thus being closer to deep learning approaches. While effective, this method suffers from limited explainability and more variation given by the number of hyperparameters that increases with the number of layers [82].

Recent Approaches   We hereby summarize some recent approaches that have been introduced in the literature and that are relevant with respect to the results they obtained and the ideas that stand behind them.

- Hierarchy-Aware Knowledge Graph Embedding (HAKE) [107] is one of the few models that also consider the fact that elements in the knowledge graph belong to different levels of the hierarchy (e.g., the authors use the triple *arbor/cassia/palm, hypernym, tree* as an example of elements at different levels of the hierarchy). Using polar coordinates they are able to distribute the hierarchical knowledge inside the representations.
- RotatE [82] was introduced to provide a method to effectively represent symmetric properties in knowledge graph embeddings. The authors of this paper propose to use rotation in a complex space to support symmetry and other properties. In Figure 4 we show how rotation can effectively support the definition of relationships that are symmetric; the rotation allows you to interpret symmetry as a geometric property. Authors prove that their model, implemented inside a complex vector space, can capture properties like symmetry, inversion, and composition.
- TuckER [6] is a recent approach that also uses tensor factorization for knowledge graph embeddings obtaining good results over the link prediction task.
- Another recent approach tries to apply graph convolutional neural networks to generate knowledge graph embeddings, and this might influence a new way of dealing with knowledge graph structures [79].
- Contextualized Knowledge Graph Embeddings [31] (COKE) is a method that has been inspired by recent results of contextual representation of words [68]: using

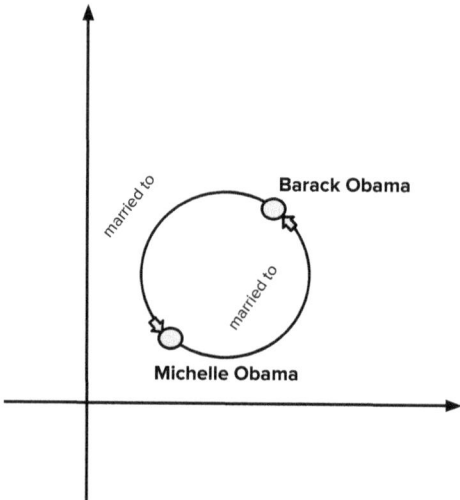

Figure 4. Example of how the use of rotation can support the definition of properties that are symmetric in the vector space. Image is adapted from [82].

transformers [89], the authors propose to capture the different meanings an entity can assume in different parts of the knowledge graph. For example, the entity Barack Obama is connected to entities related to politics, but also to the entity that represents members of his family, showing two different *contextual meanings* of the same entity. The main difference between COKE and other models is that it models the representations based on the context and thus, differently from other methods, it provides representations that are not static.

- SimplE [44] extends canonical Polyadic tensor decomposition (CP) [37] to provide good embeddings for link prediction. CP poorly performs on link prediction because it learns two independent embeddings for each entity. SimplE makes use of inverse relationships to jointly learn the two embeddings of each entity.
- Quantum embeddings [27] are a novel method to embed entities and relationships in a vector space and the representations are generated following ideas that come from quantum logic axioms [10]. These embeddings preserve the logical structure and can be used to do both reasoning and link prediction.

3.2. Enhanced Knowledge Graph Embeddings

While most of the previous approaches rely mainly on the use of the triples present in the knowledge graph to generate the vector representations; additional information (or different information) can be used inside the embeddings to generate vectors that account for a better representation. As noted by [92] attributes (like gender) need to be model in an efficient way: the attribute *male* is connected to multiple entities and thus model like TransE might not be adequate to treat this issue; in the literature, there are in fact models that have been proposed to account for better handling of these attributes [51].

Path-based Embeddings   While the most common approaches use a score function that is based on triples, more recent approaches try to consider also the information that comes from a path on the graph [50,33]. There are approaches that focus on the use of Recurrent Neural Networks (RNNs) to tackle the task of multi-hop predictions [104,16].

Distributional Embeddings   An alternative approach to generate embeddings comes from the computational linguistics field and it is represented by those models that view language under a distributional perspective in which the meaning of words in a language can be extracted from the usage of those words in the language. Word2vec [59] is a model that embeds words in the vector space by eventually putting words that appear in similar contexts in close positions of the vector space. In the same way, on Wikipedia using user-made links [7] or using entity linking [9] it is possible to generate embeddings of the entities of a knowledge graph using the word2vec algorithm [59]. For example, Wiki2vec[3] uses word2vec over Wikipedia text and generates the representations for both entities (by looking at links co-occurrence) and words. TEE [9] proposes to use entity linking to first disambiguate text and generate sequences of entities and then use the knowledge graph to replace the sequences of entities with sequences of most specific types; using word2vec one can generate entity and type embeddings based on the distribution in text. Methods that are based on entity linking suffer from low coverage, caused by the entity linking quality. In general, these models do not provide a direct way to embed relationships. Another prominent model in this category is RDF2Vec [72]: it uses an approach that combines techniques from the word embeddings community with knowledge graphs. It generates embeddings of entities and relationships by first creating a virtual document that contains lexicalized walks over the graph and then use word embeddings algorithm on the virtual document to create the representations.

Text-Enhanced Embeddings   There instead exists a variety of models that makes use of textual information [97,23,95,100,99,41,2] to enhance the performance of knowledge graph embeddings techniques. These pre-trained representations can be used to initialize knowledge graph embeddings and to generate representations that can, in some cases, outperform other baselines [103]. As stated in the previous section, the use of textual information can be useful to generate the representations of the entities even when they are not present in the knowledge base. For example, Text-enhanced Knowledge Embedding [97] (TEKE) focuses on Wikipedia inner links and replaces them with Freebase entities and then constructs a co-occurrence network of entities and words in the text; eventually, this information is used to enrich the contextual representation of the elements of the knowledge graph. Jointly [95] is an embedding method in which textual knowledge is used to enrich the representation of entities and relationships. In this work, both entities and words are aligned into a common vector space; vectors associated with words and entities that represent a common concept are then forced to be closer in the vector space by combining different loss functions. Description-Embodied Knowledge Representation Learning (DKRL) [100] includes the description of the entities in the representation. DKRL uses a convolutional layer to encode the description of the entity into a vector representation and use this representation in the loss function. Words vectors coming from the entity description can be initialized with the use of word2vec embeddings. The model learns two representations for each entity, one that is structure-based (i.e., like TransE)

---

[3]https://github.com/idio/wiki2vec

and one that is based on the descriptions. One key advantage of DKRL [100] is that it offers the possibility of doing zero-shot learning of entities by using the description of the entities themselves.

Image Enhanced Embeddings   Image-embodied Knowledge Representation Learning [101] (IKRL) provides a method to integrate images inside the scoring function of the knowledge graph embedding model. Essentially, IKRL uses multiple images for each entity and use the AlexNet convolutional neural network [46] to generate representations for the images; these representations are then selected and combined with the use of attention to be finally projected in the entity space, generating an image specific representation for images. Recently, approaches to exploit *multi-modal learning* on knowledge graph embeddings that combine image features and other information have also been introduced in the state-of-the-art [98,55].

Logic Enhanced Embeddings   There are approaches that account for the combination of logic and facts [93,29,30,74] for knowledge representation. KALE is a model that combines facts and rules using fuzzy logic [29]. There are other approaches that try to embed knowledge graphs by keeping the logical structure consistent, we mentioned embedding with quantum axioms in Section 3.1, but there are other methods that starts with the objective of doing logical reasoning over embedded representations [80,73] (we will present more details of these approaches in the Section 4, where we discuss explainability).

Researchers have shown that it is possible to combine facts and first-order formulae using a joint optimization process. In [75], the authors propose a general approach for incorporating first-order logic formulae in embedding representations. During training, their approach samples sets of entities, and jointly minimizes the negative likelihood of the data and a loss function measuring to which extent the model violates the given rules with respect to the sampled entities. A shortcoming of this approach is that it relies on a sampling procedure, and it provides no guarantees the model will still produce predictions that are consistent with the logic rules for entities that were not observed during training. To overcome this shortcoming, in [61] authors incorporate equivalency and inversion axioms between relations by only regularizing the relation representations during the training process, where the shape of the regularizers are derived from the axiom and the model formulations. A similar idea is followed by [17] for incorporating simple implications between two relations. In [63], authors propose using adversarial training for incorporating general first-order logic rules in entity and relation representations: during training, an adversary searches for entities where the model violates the given constraints, and the model is regularized in order to correct such violations. Entities can be searched either in entity or in entity embedding space; in the latter case, the problem of finding the entity embeddings where the model maximally violates the logic rules can be efficiently solved via gradient-based optimization.

Schema-Aware Embeddings   Few models in the state of the art focus on the differences between instances (i.e., entities) of a knowledge graph and concepts (like, Country, City and Place) [56]. Schema-rules can be useful to define constraints over score predictions. For example, they have been used to learn predicate specific parameters to decrease, in an adaptive way, the score of relationships that might be conflicting with schema rules [62].

TransC [56] proposes an interesting representation for concepts, in which each concept is represented as a sphere and each entity is a vector. An instance-of relationship can be easily verified by checking if the entity is contained inside the sphere. In one of the previous sections, we mentioned HAKE (Hierarchy-Aware Knowledge Embeddings) [107] as a recent method that considers the hierarchical topology in the embedding. This aspect is also important in the context of analysis over explainability: modeling ontologies is a needed step to learn how to model logical reasoning and provide justifiable inferences, however, not all methods are capable of modeling rules [32].

There are also approaches that considers the fact that the ontology can be used to provide better representations, for example Type-embodied Knowledge Representation Learning (TKRL) [102]. Given a triple h, r, t, the subject **h** and the object **t** are projected to the type spaces of this relation as $\mathbf{h}_r$ and $\mathbf{t}_r$, the projection matrices become type-specific. TKRL optimizes the following scoring function: $||\mathbf{h}_r + \mathbf{r} - \mathbf{t}_r||$. In this group we also include TRESCAL [14] an extension of RESCAL [67] that considers types in the tensor decomposition. On the other hand, there do exist approaches that generate the representations of ontology concept by taking in consideration the co-occurrence of types in text [9].

Hyperbolic Embeddings   Many approaches in the state-of-the-art rely on the use of representations in the Euclidean space. However, when dealing with the representations of tree-like structures (e.g., some ontologies can be interpreted as trees) Euclidean spaces have to rely on many dimensions and are not suited to represent trees. Euclidean geometries rely on Euclid's axiom of the parallel lines, but there do exist other geometries that do not consider it. Hyperbolic geometries allow us to use hyperbolic planes where trees can be effectively encoded. These approaches have been now widely used to represent tree-like structure [65,83,77] and received recognition in natural language processing [47,85,90]. In general, these approaches have been applied to ontological trees (e.g., the WordNet hierarchy) and cannot account for knowledge graph structures that are more complex. Recently, embedding in the hyperbolic plane has shown to be effective also for knowledge graphs [5,45] since they can provide better ways to model topological structures [45].

Temporal Knowledge Graph Embeddings   There are also approaches that are meant to account for temporality in knowledge graph embeddings by considering temporal link prediction (i.e., consider that some predicates, like *president of*, have values that change over time) and to study the evolution of knowledge graphs over time [42,22,25]. For example, recurrent neural networks can be used to learn time-aware relation representations [25].

3.3. Evaluation and Replication

Evaluation in knowledge graph embeddings is often based on link prediction. In general, the link prediction task can be defined as the task of finding an entity that can be used to complete the triple $(h, r, ?)$; for example, (New York City, country, ?), where ? is United States. To compute the answer for the incomplete triple generally the score function is used to estimate the *likelihood* of the entities. The procedure is the following: for each triple to test, we remove the head and we compute the value of the score function for each of the entities that we have in the dataset and we rank them from higher to

Dataset	# Entities	# Relations	Train	Validation	Test
FB15k	14,951	1,345	483,142	50,000	59,071
FB15k-237	14,505	237	272,115	17,535	20,466
WN18	40,943	18	141,442	5,000	5,000
WN18RR	40,943	11	86,835	2,824	2,924
YAGO3-10	123,182	37	1,079,040	5,000	5,000

Table 2. Number of entities, relationships and training, validation, test triples for the main dataset used in the state-of-the-art.

lowest. Then we collect the rank of the correct entity. The same is done by replacing the tail of the triple. At the end, the average rank is computed, this measure is called Mean Reciprocal Rank (MRR). Another measure that is often used in the link prediction setting is the HITS@K (with K commonly in $1, 3, 10$).

[11] uses a *filtering* setting that has become a standard of the evaluation. The evaluation of the MRR is influenced by the fact that some *correct* triples share entity and relationship (e.g., (United States, countryOf, ?) is true for multiple triples) and they can be ranked one over the other in the ranking list, thus biasing the results. What it is typically done when computing the MRR for a triple in this setting is to filter out the other triples that are true and that are present in the training/validation/test set.

FB15k [11] is a subset of Freebase while WN18 [11] is a Word-Net subset. FB15k and WN18 were both introduced in [11] and originally come with a training, validation and test split.

The quality of these two datasets has been argued in more recent work [86,18]. FB15k originally contained triples in the test set that are the inverse of those present in the training set, for example /award/award_nominee and /award_nominee/award. While those links are not false, they could bias the results by making the task easier for learning models (i.e., models can just learn that one relationship is the inverse of the other [86], and models that force symmetry, like DistMult, could perform better just because of the dataset used). The same problem was found in WN18 [18]. This brought researchers to introduce two novel datasets, a subset of the original ones, that do not contain easy-to-solve cases. FB15k-237 has been introduced by [86] and WN18RR was introduced by [18] and they are a subset of FB15K and WN18 respectively. Take into account that the DistMult model favored the symmetry between the relationships.

YAGO3-10 [57,18] has recently become quite popular, it contains a subset of the YAGO knowledge graph that consists of entities that have more than 10 relationships each. As noted by [18] the triples in this dataset account for descriptive attributes of people (e.g., as citizenship, gender, and profession). Another really important dataset is Countries [12], which is often used to evaluate how well knowledge graph embeddings learn long term logical dependencies. Note that while in general, the datasets used are the ones we described, some papers introduce new datasets when needed. For example, a subset of the YAGO dataset (namely YAGO39K) has been used to evaluate TransC a work that extended embeddings with the use of concepts [56].

In Table 2 we show numerical data related to these datasets. It is important to notice that these datasets are small with respect to the size of knowledge graphs (e.g., DBpedia has more than 4 million entities).

Link prediction is not the only task on which knowledge graph embedding are evaluated, often the evaluation takes into account the task of triple classification, that is the task of verifying if a triple is true or false (i.e., it is a binary classification task over input triples).

3.4. Open-source Projects on Knowledge Graph Embeddings

Many approaches in the literature share code to reproduce the results in the paper, but often code is written in different languages and does not allow efficient comparison between methods and extensions of the methods. However, there are now some libraries that can be used to replicate the results of different knowledge graph embeddings methods. We cite three and currently active repositories that are popularly used. OpenKE[4] [35], the main repository contains Pytorch code, but the authors made the code available also in Tensorflow. Ampligraph[5] [15], a Tensorflow library that introduces high-level APIs to generate embeddings. Finally, PyTorch BigGraph is another interesting library for knowledge graph embeddings that has been recently introduced by Facebook that can scale to billions of entities[6] [49].

3.5. Limitations of Knowledge Graph Embeddings

Different methods have been introduced in literature and all come with different training methods (e.g., different optimizers, different loss functions, different strategies for sampling negatives). Making the comparison between different methods often difficult and in general not directly possible.

The first hints of these limitations have been outlined in 2017, where a work has shown that most of the approaches introduced until then could be outperformed by the use of a simple well-tuned DistMult model [43]; the other two competitive models were ComplEx [88] and HolE [66]. As stated by the authors, there is the need to focus on different measures for the evaluation of knowledge graph embeddings[7] and for the intensive study of how hyperparameters are selected. Results are sometime more influenced by training epochs than from actual model complexity.

Recent work [84] shows that KGE models for link prediction are uncalibrated. This is problematic especially for triple classification tasks where users must define relation-specific thresholds, which can be difficult when working with a large number of relation types. Moreover, calibrated probabilities are crucial to provide trustworthy and interpretable decisions (e.g. drug-target discovery scenarios). The authors propose a heuristics that adopts Platt scaling or isotonic regression to calibrate KGE models even without ground truth negatives.

A very recent paper [76] has provided new evidence over the limitations of the evaluation of knowledge graph embedding approaches. Authors found that the results of the approaches vary significantly across studies and that they are very much dependent on experimental settings including hyperparameters and loss functions. The main result of this paper is that the conclusions drawn in different papers probably need to be revised in light of the results. Note that the paper address only structure-based embeddings (to which they refer to as pure knowledge graph embeddings), but since many of the en-

---

[4]https://github.com/thunlp/OpenKE
[5]https://github.com/Accenture/AmpliGraph
[6]https://github.com/facebookresearch/PyTorch-BigGraph
[7]Note that the work considered experiment over FB15k and WN18.

hanced models are based on knowledge graph embeddings, the conclusions drawn from them should also be revised. This paper suggests the lack of a predefined ground of comparison for the embeddings that was already hinted by the need of updating the evaluation datasets (see Section 3.3, where we explained the limitations of some of the state-of-the-art datasets). The same authors propose LibKGE[8] an open-source library for reproducible research on knowledge graph embeddings that might become useful in providing more robust results to the community.

4. Knowledge Graph Embeddings and Explainability

While explainability is a widely used term and its general meaning is intuitive, there is no agreed definition about what explainability in machine learning is [53]. Explainability in the context of knowledge graph has recently been outlined by [48,38]. In relation to knowledge graph embeddings, explainability has a difficult interpretation: while knowledge graphs are open and in general explainable in terms of direct relationships with other entities, knowledge graph embeddings are often referred to as sub-symbolic, since they represent elements in the vector space, thus losing the original interpretability that comes from logic. The difficulty of mapping vector space representations with logic has been outlined in different work [32,44] and that in general, some rules are impossible to learn with knowledge graph embeddings (i.e., as described by [32] DistMult can only model a restricted class of subsumption hierarchies). Moreover, explainability passes from the definition of methods that support logical reasoning, since logic offers a paradigm that supports reasoning and its inferences are justifiable and verifiable using logical axioms.

The problem in parts originates from the fact that there is no agreed view upon how to measure how explainable a system is; the quest of explainable artificial intelligence remains *how to build intelligent systems able to expose explanation in a human-comprehensible way* [48].

Explainability in knowledge graph embeddings is also important because these latent representations are affected by bias, and social biases have to be taken into consideration when using embeddings for prediction. In fact, as word embedding show stereotypical biases in the representation, evidence of bias in knowledge graph embeddings has been found [24]: males are more likely to be bakers while females are more likely to be home-keepers; this fact could greatly bias the link prediction of novel relationships, think for example of a link prediction system that predicts the most suitable person for a job. Explainability is important in the context of KG embedding because we need to be able to explain these inferences. Same requirement is needed by methods that study drugs effects [58].

What is generally missing is a methodology to effectively explain the predictions of knowledge graph embeddings. From their introduction in the state-of-the-art until now, embedding methods have been mainly evaluated and compared by considering only the accuracy on link prediction tasks. As already outlined in literature [69], studies should also be conducted to evaluate the interpretability and the reason why link prediction is feasible in knowledge graphs. For example, Completion Robustness and Interpretability

---

[8]https://github.com/uma-pi1/kge

via Adversarial Graph Edits (CRIAGE) [69] explore the robustness of the approaches by seeing how adding and removing facts affects the general performance of the models. CRIAGE can estimate the effect of those modifications and how they influence the predictions; moreover, it can be used to evaluate the sensitivity of the models towards the addition of fake facts. CRIAGE [69] can be indeed used to understand and explain knowledge graph embeddings prediction and explore the limitations and the advantages of different models. In this context, it is worth to cite the closely related, but introduced for graph neural networks, GNNExplainer [105]. GNNExplainer is the first work that provides an approach to make sense of the predictions of a graph network: it can be used to identify the most important parts and features of the graph neural network that influence the prediction of a particular instance (e.g., new link, new node label). While this model has been applied to graph neural network it might be possible to adapt it to knowledge graph embeddings.

[48] provides an overview of the challenges, the approaches and the limitations of Explainable Artificial Intelligence in different fields, such as machine learning, planning, natural language processing, computer vision, etc. In particular, the author focuses on how knowledge graphs could be used to support explanations in order to overtake the limitations in each field.

An advantage of knowledge graph generated representations, with respect to standard representations generated by deep learning algorithms, is that they come with a previous meaning: each entity vector has a connection with the knowledge graph from which it originates; even if the representation is sub-symbolic. Differently from words [59], knowledge graph embedding representations do not suffer from inheriting ambiguity and are can be thus be used more effectively to model reasoning and explainable systems. Moreover, knowledge graph embeddings are not ambiguous in contrast to "pure words" in sentences that are ambiguous; this last fact can also help in context of explainability, since it's favorable to provide explanations on something that is not ambiguous and that is linked to a knowledge base.

A key combination can come from the usage of knowledge graph embeddings with logical rules, that can provide justification and explainability over inferences. As stated by [48], knowledge graphs could provide a semantic layer to support tasks like question answering that are generally tackled with brute force approaches on text. Knowledge graphs can provide generalization capabilities using logic as the source of the generalization: the KG representations can, in fact, be used as sources of inputs to deep learning algorithms and can be used to bridge two worlds that are apart. Knowledge graph representations are linked to knowledge graphs and are thus connected to a source that has explicit connections.

In fact, there has been a recent spike in the interest for knowledge graph embedding used inside recommender systems to enhance the performance and the explainability of recommendation [40,91,106]. Deep Knowledge-Aware Network [91] is a deep network that is used to include external knowledge, trough the use of entity embeddings, inside a news recommendation system; the idea behind this model is to use the information in the knowledge graph to recommend to user news that have a high probability of being clicked. Instead of focusing on word-occurrence based method, like topic models, the proposed model search for more latent factors to use in the recommendation trough the use of embeddings. Instead, other researchers have combined embeddings with recurrent neural networks to account for the recommendation of items based on sequences of user interactions [40].

Many methods for recommendation have limitations regarding the explainability when a multi-hop reasoning is required. In attempt to address this shortcoming, a Knowledge-aware Path Recurrent Network (KPRN) is proposed in [94]. KPRN models the sequential dependencies that connect users and items by also considering the entities and the relationships in between. The running example in the paper is as follows if (Alice, Interact, Shape of You) & (Shape of You, SungBy, Ed Sheeran) & (Ed Sheeran, IsSingerOf, I SeeFire) then (Alice, Interact, I See Fire). LSTMs are used to model the sequences of entities and relationships and to predict a recommendation. The embedding of entities and relationships is similar to the path-based embeddings introduced in Section 3.2.

At the same time, the field of conversational agents has also taken into consideration the use of knowledge graph embeddings for explainable conversations [64]. OpenDialKG [64] is a corpus in which there is a parallel alignment between the knowledge graph and the dialogues. The authors of the paper propose also an attention-based model that can learn knowledge paths from entities mentioned in the dialog contexts and predicts novel entities that are relevant to the contexts of the dialog: paths provide explanations for entity used in reply to a dialog. Initialization of the model is done through the use of knowledge graph embeddings.

These last models are close to what has been outlined at the start of this section [48,38]: knowledge graphs can provide a semantic and explainable layer (i.e., for conversational agents and for recommendation) that can be useful not only to simply solve tasks but also to provide an effective way to interpret the black-box answers given by neural models.

4.1. Knowledge Graph Embeddings and Logical Reasoning

Logic is the main explanation paradigm for KGs and one important aspect we want KG embeddings to cover is how to account for axiomatic knowledge inside embeddings. Through a standard KG embedding model it is possible to perform several downstream tasks, such as triple validation or subject, object and relationship prediction. Knowledge graph embeddings model relational structure under the form of elements in a low dimensional vector space. While originally methods have been introduced to solve link prediction tasks, more recently many researchers have studied and explored the logical properties of knowledge graph embedding methods. The question that they try to answer is related to how can we effectively model logical knowledge inside a vector space.

In fact, a recent trend in literature is to propose embedding models that can effectively model some specific logical axioms inside the vector space. This attempt is related to the observation that pure translational approaches like TransE [11] are not capable of modeling symmetry in the relationships due to the choice of the score function.

ComplEx [88] was proposed as an extension of the DistMult approach in the complex space in which it is easier to model properties of relationships like anti-symmetry (remember that DistMult force symmetry between the relationships). Instead, as introduced above, RotatE [82] use rotations in a complex plane to capture properties like symmetry, antisymmetry, inversion, and composition. In fact, RotatE models each relationship as a rotation from the subject vector to the object vector in a complex hyperplane.

Still, a drawback of the approaches that are based on complex Euclidean geometry is that they require a large number of parameters to train.

A promising direction is how to perform complex logical queries using KGE models. For instance, a query "Predict communities C? in which user u is likely to upvote a post" might be expressed as $C?.\exists P : upvote(u, P) \land belong(P, C?)$. In [34] the authors propose a method to map and execute conjunctive queries in a vector space represented by KG embeddings, and further extended by [70] to support disjunctions. Recent work such as QUERY2BOX [71] goes as far as proposing a hybrid query processing framework. The authors propose a KGE-based query engine that addresses both conjunctive and disjunctive queries by modeling queries as bounding boxes in the embedding space. Besides its intrinsic interpretability - grounded in first-order logical queries it supports - this multi-hop reasoning framework shows how the interplay of KG embeddings and logical queries overcome missing information in the graph when delivering an answer.

There are approaches that try to combine sub-symbolic representations with reasoning systems: Logic Tensor Networks [80], for example, allows us to define a differential fuzzy logic language over data. Essentially, Logic Tensor Networks (LTN) create the representations for logical constants, functions, and predicates by embedding those in a vector space. While Logic Tensor Networks were not used directly to create knowledge graph embeddings, they have been used with good results on semantic image interpretation tasks [19,20]. Integrating embedding approaches with logical reasoning can account for more complex inferences: combining similarity with logical inferences can bring to interesting results in the field; for example, it is possible to use embedding similarity to extend reasoning on unknown entities. For example, [8] shows that combining entity embeddings with logical systems like LTNs can be useful to make inferences that are impossible for rule-based systems.

On a similar note, the Neural Theorem Prover (NTP) [73] is an extension of the Prolog programming language that uses embeddings in place of the strict unification provided by Prolog. For such a reason, they are also able to provide an explanation in the form of proof paths, for any given prediction.

While both LTN and NTP are not directly knowledge graph embedding methods they use or generate embeddings as part of their training procedure (e.g., LTN embeds elements in the vector space to support logical reasoning). The NTPs provide strong reasoning capabilities with the power of the neural network models but are not scalable to large knowledge bases. Indeed, recently NTPs were extended by the Greedy NTPs (GNTPs) [60] a model that greatly reduces the computational needs of NTPs, making it possible to use it on large knowledge bases by considering to prune reasoning paths that are not likely when doing inference. We mention again in this section the embeddings inspired by quantum physics have been proposed [27] that provide methodologies to reason over embedding by preserving the logical structure.

5. Summary and Future Directions

In this chapter, we have summarized the current state-of-the-art of knowledge graph embeddings by describing many different methods and their main properties. We have also outlined the limitations of these methods, that provide dense representations that while not directly interpretable, but are still connected to a knowledge graph and have thus relationships with other elements. In the context of explainability, we saw that some models are tightly related to logic and try to reconstruct it from the embeddings or to use the embedded representation to perform logical reasoning. However, the actual explainability of these methods is still low and approaches that try to account for it are recent.

The evolution of the methods in the literature has passed trough different dataset and the evaluation is still subject to a lot of variation due to hyperparameters choice and training procedures. Older approaches perform well when trained with new methodologies. There is the need to define a common ground for evaluation that also takes into account the many differences that each model proposes.

References

[1]   Carl Allen, Ivana Balazevic, and Timothy M Hospedales. On understanding knowledge graph representation. *arXiv preprint arXiv:1909.11611*, 2019.

[2]   Bo An, Bo Chen, Xianpei Han, and Le Sun. Accurate text-enhanced knowledge graph representation learning. In *Proceedings of the 2018 Conference of the North American Chapter of the Association for Computational Linguistics: Human Language Technologies, Volume 1 (Long Papers)*, pages 745–755, 2018.

[3]   Sören Auer, Christian Bizer, Georgi Kobilarov, Jens Lehmann, Richard Cyganiak, and Zachary Ives. Dbpedia: A nucleus for a web of open data. In *The semantic web*, pages 722–735. Springer, 2007.

[4]   Stephan Baier, Yunpu Ma, and Volker Tresp. Improving visual relationship detection using semantic modeling of scene descriptions. In *ISWC*, pages 53–68. Springer, 2017.

[5]   Ivana Balažević, Carl Allen, and Timothy Hospedales. Multi-relational poincar\'e graph embeddings. In *NIPS*, 2019.

[6]   Ivana Balazevic, Carl Allen, and Timothy Hospedales. TuckER: Tensor factorization for knowledge graph completion. In *EMNLP-IJCNLP*, pages 5188–5197, Hong Kong, China, November 2019. Association for Computational Linguistics.

[7]   Pierpaolo Basile, Annalina Caputo, Gaetano Rossiello, and Giovanni Semeraro. Learning to rank entity relatedness through embedding-based features. In *NLDB*, pages 471–477. Springer, 2016.

[8]   Federico Bianchi, Matteo Palmonari, Pascal Hitzler, and Luciano Serafini. Complementing logical reasoning with sub-symbolic commonsense. In *International Joint Conference on Rules and Reasoning*, pages 161–170. Springer, 2019.

[9]   Federico Bianchi, Matteo Palmonari, and Debora Nozza. Towards encoding time in text-based entity embeddings. In *ISWC*, 2018.

[10] Garrett Birkhoff and John Von Neumann. The logic of quantum mechanics. *Annals of mathematics*, pages 823–843, 1936.

[11] Antoine Bordes, Nicolas Usunier, Alberto Garcia-Duran, Jason Weston, and Oksana Yakhnenko. Translating embeddings for modeling multi-relational data. In *NIPS*, pages 2787–2795, 2013.

[12] Guillaume Bouchard, Sameer Singh, and Theo Trouillon. On approximate reasoning capabilities of low-rank vector spaces. In *2015 AAAI Spring Symposium Series*, 2015.

[13] Liwei Cai and William Yang Wang. Kbgan: Adversarial learning for knowledge graph embeddings. In *NAACL-HLT*, pages 1470–1480, 2018.

[14] Kai-Wei Chang, Wen-tau Yih, Bishan Yang, and Christopher Meek. Typed tensor decomposition of knowledge bases for relation extraction. In *EMNLP*, pages 1568–1579, 2014.

[15] Luca Costabello, Sumit Pai, Chan Le Van, Rory McGrath, Nicholas McCarthy, and Pedro Tabacof. AmpliGraph: a Library for Representation Learning on Knowledge Graphs, March 2019. doi = 10.5281/zenodo.2595043.

[16] Rajarshi Das, Arvind Neelakantan, David Belanger, and Andrew McCallum. Chains of reasoning over entities, relations, and text using recurrent neural networks. In *EACL*, pages 132–141, 2017.

[17] Thomas Demeester, Tim Rocktäschel, and Sebastian Riedel. Lifted rule injection for relation embeddings. In *EMNLP*, pages 1389–1399. The Association for Computational Linguistics, 2016.

[18] Tim Dettmers, Pasquale Minervini, Pontus Stenetorp, and Sebastian Riedel. Convolutional 2d knowledge graph embeddings. In *AAAI*, pages 1811–1818. AAAI Press, 2018.

[19] I Donadello, L Serafini, and AS d'Avila Garcez. Logic tensor networks for semantic image interpretation. In *IJCAI*, pages 1596–1602, 2017.

[20] Ivan Donadello and Luciano Serafini. Compensating supervision incompleteness with prior knowledge in semantic image interpretation. In *IJCNN*, pages 1–8. IEEE, 2019.

[21] Lisa Ehrlinger and Wolfram Wöß. Towards a definition of knowledge graphs. *SEMANTiCS (Posters, Demos, SuCCESS)*, 48, 2016.

[22] Cristóbal Esteban, Volker Tresp, Yinchong Yang, Stephan Baier, and Denis Krompaß. Predicting the co-evolution of event and knowledge graphs. In *2016 19th International Conference on Information Fusion (FUSION)*, pages 98–105. IEEE, 2016.

[23] Wei Fang, Jianwen Zhang, Dilin Wang, Zheng Chen, and Ming Li. Entity disambiguation by knowledge and text jointly embedding. In *CoNLL*, pages 260–269, 2016.

[24] Joseph Fisher. Measuring social bias in knowledge graph embeddings. *arXiv preprint arXiv:1912.02761*, 2019.

[25] Alberto García-Durán, Sebastijan Dumančić, and Mathias Niepert. Learning sequence encoders for temporal knowledge graph completion. *arXiv preprint arXiv:1809.03202*, 2018.

[26] Alberto Garcia-Duran and Mathias Niepert. Kblrn: End-to-end learning of knowledge base representations with latent, relational, and numerical features. *arXiv preprint arXiv:1709.04676*, 2017.

[27] Dinesh Garg, Shajith Ikbal Mohamed, Santosh K Srivastava, Harit Vishwakarma, Hima Karanam, and L Venkata Subramaniam. Quantum embedding of knowledge for reasoning. In *NIPS*, pages 5595–5605, 2019.

[28] Genet Asefa Gesese, Russa Biswas, Mehwish Alam, and Harald Sack. A survey on knowledge graph embeddings with literals: Which model links better literal-ly? *arXiv preprint arXiv:1910.12507*, 2019.

[29] Shu Guo, Quan Wang, Lihong Wang, Bin Wang, and Li Guo. Jointly embedding knowledge graphs and logical rules. In *Proceedings of the 2016 Conference on Empirical Methods in Natural Language Processing*, pages 192–202, 2016.

[30] Shu Guo, Quan Wang, Lihong Wang, Bin Wang, and Li Guo. Knowledge graph embedding with iterative guidance from soft rules. In *Thirty-Second AAAI Conference on Artificial Intelligence*, 2018.

[31] Swapnil Gupta, Sreyash Kenkre, and Partha Talukdar. Care: Open knowledge graph embeddings. In *EMNLP-IJCNLP*, pages 378–388, 2019.

[32] Víctor Gutiérrez-Basulto and Steven Schockaert. From knowledge graph embedding to ontology embedding? an analysis of the compatibility between vector space representations and rules. In *Sixteenth International Conference on Principles of Knowledge Representation and Reasoning*, 2018.

[33] Kelvin Guu, John Miller, and Percy Liang. Traversing knowledge graphs in vector space. In *EMNLP*, pages 318–327, 2015.

[34] William L. Hamilton, Payal Bajaj, Marinka Zitnik, Dan Jurafsky, and Jure Leskovec. Embedding logical queries on knowledge graphs. In *NeurIPS*, pages 2030–2041, 2018.

[35] Xu Han, Shulin Cao, Lv Xin, Yankai Lin, Zhiyuan Liu, Maosong Sun, and Juanzi Li. Openke: An open toolkit for knowledge embedding. In *EMNLP*, 2018.

[36] Katsuhiko Hayashi and Masashi Shimbo. On the equivalence of holographic and complex embeddings for link prediction. In *Proceedings of the 55th Annual Meeting of the Association for Computational Linguistics (Volume 2: Short Papers)*, pages 554–559, Vancouver, Canada, July 2017. Association for Computational Linguistics.

[37] Frank L. Hitchcock. The expression of a tensor or a polyadic as a sum of products. *Journal of Mathematics and Physics*, 6(1-4):164–189, 1927.

[38] Pascal Hitzler, Federico Bianchi, Monireh Ebrahimi, and Md Kamruzzaman Sarker. Neural-symbolic integration and the semantic web. *Semantic Web Journal*, pages 1–9, 2019.

[39] Aidan Hogan, Eva Blomqvist, Michael Cochez, Claudia d'Amato, Gerard de Melo, Claudio Gutierrez, José Emilio Labra Gayo, Sabrina Kirrane, Sebastian Neumaier, Axel Polleres, Roberto Navigli, Axel-Cyrille Ngonga Ngomo, Sabbir M. Rashid, Anisa Rula, Lukas Schmelzeisen, Juan Sequeda, Steffen Staab, and Antoine Zimmermann. Knowledge graphs, 2020.

[40] Jin Huang, Wayne Xin Zhao, Hong-Jian Dou, Ji-Rong Wen, and Edward Y. Chang. Improving sequential recommendation with knowledge-enhanced memory networks. In *SIGIR*, pages 505–514. ACM, 2018.

[41] Shoaib Jameel and Steven Schockaert. Entity embeddings with conceptual subspaces as a basis for plausible reasoning. In *ECAI*, 2016.

[42] Tingsong Jiang, Tianyu Liu, Tao Ge, Lei Sha, Sujian Li, Baobao Chang, and Zhifang Sui. Encod-

ing temporal information for time-aware link prediction. In *Proceedings of the 2016 Conference on Empirical Methods in Natural Language Processing*, pages 2350–2354, 2016.

[43] Rudolf Kadlec, Ondrej Bajgar, and Jan Kleindienst. Knowledge base completion: Baselines strike back. In *Proceedings of the 2nd Workshop on Representation Learning for NLP*, pages 69–74, 2017.

[44] Seyed Mehran Kazemi and David Poole. Simple embedding for link prediction in knowledge graphs. In *NIPS*, pages 4284–4295, 2018.

[45] Prodromos Kolyvakis, Alexandros Kalousis, and Dimitris Kiritsis. Hyperkg: Hyperbolic knowledge graph embeddings for knowledge base completion. *arXiv preprint arXiv:1908.04895*, 2019.

[46] Alex Krizhevsky, Ilya Sutskever, and Geoffrey E Hinton. Imagenet classification with deep convolutional neural networks. In *NIPS*, pages 1097–1105, 2012.

[47] Matt Le, Stephen Roller, Laetitia Papaxanthos, Douwe Kiela, and Maximilian Nickel. Inferring concept hierarchies from text corpora via hyperbolic embeddings. *arXiv preprint arXiv:1902.00913*, 2019.

[48] Freddy Lecue. On the role of knowledge graphs in explainable ai. *Semantic Web Journal*, 2019.

[49] Adam Lerer, Ledell Wu, Jiajun Shen, Timothee Lacroix, Luca Wehrstedt, Abhijit Bose, and Alex Peysakhovich. PyTorch-BigGraph: A Large-scale Graph Embedding System. In *SysML*, Palo Alto, CA, USA, 2019.

[50] Yankai Lin, Zhiyuan Liu, Huanbo Luan, Maosong Sun, Siwei Rao, and Song Liu. Modeling relation paths for representation learning of knowledge bases. In *EMNLP*, pages 705–714, 2015.

[51] Yankai Lin, Zhiyuan Liu, and Maosong Sun. Knowledge representation learning with entities, attributes and relations. In *Proceedings of the Twenty-Fifth International Joint Conference on Artificial Intelligence*, IJCAI'16, pages 2866–2872. AAAI Press, 2016.

[52] Yankai Lin, Zhiyuan Liu, Maosong Sun, Yang Liu, and Xuan Zhu. Learning entity and relation embeddings for knowledge graph completion. In *AAAI*, 2015.

[53] Zachary C. Lipton. The mythos of model interpretability. *Queue*, 16(3):30:31–30:57, June 2018.

[54] Hanxiao Liu, Yuexin Wu, and Yiming Yang. Analogical inference for multi-relational embeddings. In *Proceedings of the 34th International Conference on Machine Learning-Volume 70*, pages 2168–2178. JMLR. org, 2017.

[55] Ye Liu, Hui Li, Alberto Garcia-Duran, Mathias Niepert, Daniel Onoro-Rubio, and David S Rosenblum. Mmkg: Multi-modal knowledge graphs. In *European Semantic Web Conference*, pages 459–474. Springer, 2019.

[56] Xin Lv, Lei Hou, Juanzi Li, and Zhiyuan Liu. Differentiating concepts and instances for knowledge graph embedding. In *EMNLP*, pages 1971–1979, 2018.

[57] Farzaneh Mahdisoltani, Joanna Biega, and Fabian Suchanek. Yago3: A knowledge base from multilingual wikipedias. In *CIDR*, 2014.

[58] Brandon Malone, Alberto García-Durán, and Mathias Niepert. Knowledge graph completion to predict polypharmacy side effects. In *International Conference on Data Integration in the Life Sciences*, pages 144–149. Springer, 2018.

[59] Tomas Mikolov, Ilya Sutskever, Kai Chen, Greg S Corrado, and Jeff Dean. Distributed representations of words and phrases and their compositionality. In *NIPS*, pages 3111–3119, 2013.

[60] Pasquale Minervini, Matko Bošnjak, Tim Rocktäschel, Sebastian Riedel, and Edward Grefenstette. Differentiable reasoning on large knowledge bases and natural language. In *AAAI (to appear)*, 2020.

[61] Pasquale Minervini, Luca Costabello, Emir Muñoz, Vít Nováček, and Pierre-Yves Vandenbussche. Regularizing knowledge graph embeddings via equivalence and inversion axioms. In *ECML/PKDD (1)*, volume 10534 of *Lecture Notes in Computer Science*, pages 668–683. Springer, 2017.

[62] Pasquale Minervini, Claudia d'Amato, Nicola Fanizzi, and Floriana Esposito. Leveraging the schema in latent factor models for knowledge graph completion. In *SAC*, pages 327–332. ACM, 2016.

[63] Pasquale Minervini, Thomas Demeester, Tim Rocktäschel, and Sebastian Riedel. Adversarial sets for regularising neural link predictors. In *UAI*. AUAI Press, 2017.

[64] Seungwhan Moon, Pararth Shah, Anuj Kumar, and Rajen Subba. Opendialkg: Explainable conversational reasoning with attention-based walks over knowledge graphs. In *Proceedings of the 57th Annual Meeting of the Association for Computational Linguistics*, pages 845–854, 2019.

[65] Maximilian Nickel and Douwe Kiela. Poincaré embeddings for learning hierarchical representations. In *NIPS*, pages 6341–6350, 2017.

[66] Maximilian Nickel, Lorenzo Rosasco, and Tomaso Poggio. Holographic embeddings of knowledge graphs. In *AAAI*, 2016.

[67] Maximilian Nickel, Volker Tresp, and Hans-Peter Kriegel. A three-way model for collective learning

on multi-relational data. In *ICML*, volume 11, pages 809–816, 2011.

[68] Matthew E Peters, Mark Neumann, Mohit Iyyer, Matt Gardner, Christopher Clark, Kenton Lee, and Luke Zettlemoyer. Deep contextualized word representations. In *NAACL-HLT*, pages 2227–2237, 2018.

[69] Pouya Pezeshkpour, CA Irvine, Yifan Tian, and Sameer Singh. Investigating robustness and interpretability of link prediction via adversarial modifications. In *NAACL-HLT*, pages 3336–3347, 2019.

[70] Hongyu Ren, Weihua Hu, and Jure Leskovec. Query2box: Reasoning over knowledge graphs in vector space using box embeddings. *CoRR*, abs/2002.05969, 2020.

[71] Hongyu Ren*, Weihua Hu*, and Jure Leskovec. Query2box: Reasoning over knowledge graphs in vector space using box embeddings. In *ICLR*, 2020.

[72] Petar Ristoski, Jessica Rosati, Tommaso Di Noia, Renato De Leone, and Heiko Paulheim. Rdf2vec: Rdf graph embeddings and their applications. *Semantic Web*, pages 1–32, 2018.

[73] Tim Rocktäschel and Sebastian Riedel. End-to-end differentiable proving. In *NIPS*, pages 3788–3800, 2017.

[74] Tim Rocktäschel, Sameer Singh, and Sebastian Riedel. Injecting logical background knowledge into embeddings for relation extraction. In *HLT-NAACL*, pages 1119–1129. The Association for Computational Linguistics, 2015.

[75] Tim Rocktäschel, Sameer Singh, and Sebastian Riedel. Injecting logical background knowledge into embeddings for relation extraction. In *HLT-NAACL*, pages 1119–1129. The Association for Computational Linguistics, 2015.

[76] Daniel Ruffinelli, Samuel Broscheit, and Rainer Gemulla. You CAN teach an old dog new tricks! on training knowledge graph embeddings. In *International Conference on Learning Representations*, 2020.

[77] Frederic Sala, Christopher De Sa, Albert Gu, and Christopher Ré. Representation tradeoffs for hyperbolic embeddings. In Jennifer G. Dy and Andreas Krause, editors, *ICML*, volume 80 of *Proceedings of Machine Learning Research*, pages 4457–4466. PMLR, 2018.

[78] Franco Scarselli, Marco Gori, Ah Chung Tsoi, Markus Hagenbuchner, and Gabriele Monfardini. The graph neural network model. *IEEE Transactions on Neural Networks*, 20(1):61–80, 2008.

[79] Michael Schlichtkrull, Thomas N Kipf, Peter Bloem, Rianne Van Den Berg, Ivan Titov, and Max Welling. Modeling relational data with graph convolutional networks. In *ESWC*, pages 593–607. Springer, 2018.

[80] Luciano Serafini and Artur d'Avila Garcez. Logic tensor networks: Deep learning and logical reasoning from data and knowledge. *arXiv preprint arXiv:1606.04422*, 2016.

[81] Richard Socher, Danqi Chen, Christopher D Manning, and Andrew Ng. Reasoning with neural tensor networks for knowledge base completion. In *NIPS*, pages 926–934, 2013.

[82] Zhiqing Sun, Zhi-Hong Deng, Jian-Yun Nie, and Jian Tang. Rotate: Knowledge graph embedding by relational rotation in complex space. *arXiv preprint arXiv:1902.10197*, 2019.

[83] Ryota Suzuki, Ryusuke Takahama, and Shun Onoda. Hyperbolic disk embeddings for directed acyclic graphs. *arXiv preprint arXiv:1902.04335*, 2019.

[84] Pedro Tabacof and Luca Costabello. Probability Calibration for Knowledge Graph Embedding Models. In *ICLR*, 2020.

[85] Alexandru Tifrea, Gary Bécigneul, and Octavian-Eugen Ganea. Poincar\'e glove: Hyperbolic word embeddings. *arXiv preprint arXiv:1810.06546*, 2018.

[86] Kristina Toutanova and Danqi Chen. Observed versus latent features for knowledge base and text inference. In *Proceedings of the 3rd Workshop on Continuous Vector Space Models and their Compositionality*, pages 57–66, 2015.

[87] Théo Trouillon, Éric Gaussier, Christopher R Dance, and Guillaume Bouchard. On inductive abilities of latent factor models for relational learning. *Journal of Artificial Intelligence Research*, 64:21–53, 2019.

[88] Théo Trouillon, Johannes Welbl, Sebastian Riedel, Éric Gaussier, and Guillaume Bouchard. Complex embeddings for simple link prediction. In *ICML*, pages 2071–2080, 2016.

[89] Ashish Vaswani, Noam Shazeer, Niki Parmar, Jakob Uszkoreit, Llion Jones, Aidan N Gomez, Łukasz Kaiser, and Illia Polosukhin. Attention is all you need. In *NeurIPS*, pages 5998–6008, 2017.

[90] Manuel Vimercati, Federico Bianchi, Mauricio Soto, and Matteo Palmonari. Mapping lexical knowledge to distributed models for ontology concept invention. In *AI*IA 2019 – Advances in Artificial Intelligence*, pages 572–587, Cham, 2019. Springer International Publishing.

[91] Hongwei Wang, Fuzheng Zhang, Xing Xie, and Minyi Guo. DKN: deep knowledge-aware network for news recommendation. In *WWW*, pages 1835–1844. ACM, 2018.

[92] Quan Wang, Zhendong Mao, Bin Wang, and Li Guo. Knowledge graph embedding: A survey of approaches and applications. *IEEE Transactions on Knowledge and Data Engineering*, 29(12):2724–2743, 2017.

[93] William Yang Wang and William W Cohen. Learning first-order logic embeddings via matrix factorization. In *IJCAI*, pages 2132–2138, 2016.

[94] Xiang Wang, Dingxian Wang, Canran Xu, Xiangnan He, Yixin Cao, and Tat-Seng Chua. Explainable reasoning over knowledge graphs for recommendation. In *AAAI*, pages 5329–5336. AAAI Press, 2019.

[95] Zhen Wang, Jianwen Zhang, Jianlin Feng, and Zheng Chen. Knowledge graph and text jointly embedding. In *EMNLP*, volume 14, pages 1591–1601, 2014.

[96] Zhen Wang, Jianwen Zhang, Jianlin Feng, and Zheng Chen. Knowledge graph embedding by translating on hyperplanes. In *AAAI*, 2014.

[97] Zhigang Wang and Juan-Zi Li. Text-enhanced representation learning for knowledge graph. In *IJCAI*, pages 1293–1299, 2016.

[98] Zikang Wang, Linjing Li, Qiudan Li, and Daniel Zeng. Multimodal data enhanced representation learning for knowledge graphs. In *IJCNN*, pages 1–8. IEEE, 2019.

[99] Han Xiao, Minlie Huang, Lian Meng, and Xiaoyan Zhu. Ssp: semantic space projection for knowledge graph embedding with text descriptions. In *AAAI*, 2017.

[100] Ruobing Xie, Zhiyuan Liu, Jia Jia, Huanbo Luan, and Maosong Sun. Representation learning of knowledge graphs with entity descriptions. In *Thirtieth AAAI Conference on Artificial Intelligence*, 2016.

[101] Ruobing Xie, Zhiyuan Liu, Huanbo Luan, and Maosong Sun. Image-embodied knowledge representation learning. In *IJCAI*, pages 3140–3146, 2017.

[102] Ruobing Xie, Zhiyuan Liu, and Maosong Sun. Representation learning of knowledge graphs with hierarchical types. In *IJCAI*, pages 2965–2971, 2016.

[103] Bishan Yang, Wen-tau Yih, Xiaodong He, Jianfeng Gao, and Li Deng. Embedding entities and relations for learning and inference in knowledge bases. *arXiv preprint arXiv:1412.6575*, 2014.

[104] Wenpeng Yin, Yadollah Yaghoobzadeh, and Hinrich Schütze. Recurrent one-hop predictions for reasoning over knowledge graphs. In *Proceedings of the 27th International Conference on Computational Linguistics*, pages 2369–2378, 2018.

[105] Zhitao Ying, Dylan Bourgeois, Jiaxuan You, Marinka Zitnik, and Jure Leskovec. Gnnexplainer: Generating explanations for graph neural networks. In *NeurIPS*, pages 9240–9251, 2019.

[106] Fuzheng Zhang, Nicholas Jing Yuan, Defu Lian, Xing Xie, and Wei-Ying Ma. Collaborative knowledge base embedding for recommender systems. In *KDD*, pages 353–362. ACM, 2016.

[107] Zhanqiu Zhang, Jianyu Cai, Yongdong Zhang, and Jie Wang. Learning hierarchy-aware knowledge graph embeddings for link prediction. *arXiv preprint arXiv:1911.09419*, 2019.

Knowledge Graphs for eXplainable Artificial Intelligence: Foundations, Applications and Challenges   73
I. Tiddi et al. (Eds.)
IOS Press, 2020
doi:10.3233/SSW200012

Benchmarking the Lifecycle of Knowledge Graphs

Michael RÖDER [a,b], Mohamed Ahmed SHERIF [a], Muhammad SALEEM [a],
Felix CONRADS [a], and Axel-Cyrille NGONGA NGOMO [a,b]

[a] *DICE group, Department of Computer Science, Paderborn University, Germany*
[b] *Institute for Applied Informatics, Leipzig, Germany*

Abstract. The growing interest in making use of Knowledge Graphs for developing explainable artificial intelligence, there is an increasing need for a comparable and repeatable comparison of the performance of Knowledge Graph-based systems. History in computer science has shown that a main driver to scientific advances, and in fact a core element of the scientific method as a whole, is the provision of benchmarks to make progress measurable. Benchmarks have several purposes: (1) they highlight weak and strong points of systems, (2) they stimulate technical progress and (3) they make technology viable. Benchmarks are an essential part of the scientific method as they allow to track the advancements in an area over time and make competing systems comparable. This chapter gives an overview of benchmarks used to evaluate systems that process Knowledge Graphs.

Keywords. Benchmark, Knowledge Graphs, Linked Data

1. Introduction

As the chapters before already discussed, there is a growing interest in creating explainable artificial intelligence (AI) systems based on Knowledge Graphs (KGs). The effectiveness and efficiency of these systems heavily depends on the underlying KGs and the systems processing them. It is crucial for an AI system to work with valid data. To this end, the systems that generate and validate the KGs should achieve a high performance with respect to data quality. In a similar way, AI systems need to get access to the KGs. Taking into account that AI systems rely on a large amount of data, the efficiency and scalability of KG storages is of huge importance for explainable AI systems. Hence, there is an increasing need for a comparable and repeatable evaluation of the performance of systems that create, enhance, maintain and give access to KGs. History in computer science has shown that a main driver to scientific advances, and in fact a core element of the scientific method as a whole, is the provision of benchmarks to make progress measurable. Benchmarks have several purposes: (1) they highlight weak and strong points of systems, (2) they stimulate technical progress and (3) they make technology viable. Benchmarks are an essential part of the scientific method as they allow to track the advancements in an area over time and make competing systems comparable. The TPC benchmarks[1] demonstrate how benchmarks can influence an area of research. Even

---

[1] http://www.tpc.org/information/benchmarks.asp

though databases were already quite established in the early 90s, the benchmarking efforts resulted in algorithmic improvements (ignoring advances in hardware) of 15% per year, which translated to an order of magnitude improvement in an already very established area [32].

This chapter gives an overview of benchmarks used to evaluate systems that process KGs. For creating better comparability between different benchmarks, we determine that each benchmark comprises the following components:

- The definition of the functionality that will be benchmarked.
- A set of tasks T. Each task $t_j = (i_j, e_j)$ is a pair of input data (i_j) and expected output data (e_j).
- Background data B which is typically used to initialize the system.
- One ore more metrics, which for each task t_j receive the expected result e_j, as well as the result r_j provided by the benchmarked system.

The remainder of this chapter comprises two major parts. First, we will present the existing benchmark approaches for KG-processing systems. To structure the large list of benchmarks, we follow the steps of the Linked Data lifecycle [5, 50]. Second, we present existing benchmarking frameworks and briefly summarize their features before concluding the chapter.

2. Benchmarking the Linked Data (LD) steps

In [5, 50], the authors propose a lifecycle of LD and KGs comprising 8 steps. In this section, we will go through the single steps, briefly summarize the different actions they cover and how these actions can be benchmarked.

2.1. Extraction

A first step to enter the LD lifecycle is to extract information from unstructured or semi-structured representations and transform them into the RDF data model [50]. This field of information extraction is the subject of research since several decades. The Message Understanding Conference (MUC) introduced the first systematic comparison of information extraction approaches in 1993 [89]. Several other challenges followed, e.g., the Conference on Computational Natural Language Learning (CoNLL) [94], the Automatic Content Extraction (ACE) challenge [20], the Workshop on Knowledge Base Population (TAC-KBP) [43], the Senseval challenge [39], the Making Sense of Microposts workshop [10, 11, 67, 68], the Entity Recognition and Disambiguation (ERD) challenge [12] and the Open Knowledge Extraction challenge [60, 61, 86, 87].

2.1.1. Extraction Types

The extraction of knowledge from unstructured data comes with a wide range of different types. In [15], the authors propose a set of different extraction types that can be benchmarked. These definitions are further refined and extended in [71, 101]. A set of basic extraction functionalities for single entities can be distinguished as follows [71]:

Table 1. Summary of the Extraction types.

Type	Input i_j	Output e_j	Background data B
A2KB	d	$\{(\mu, u) \mid \mu \in M, u \in K \cup \mathrm{NIL}\}$	$K, \mathbb{T}$
C2KB	d	$U \subset K$	K
D2KB	(d, M)	$\{(\mu, u) \mid \mu \in M, u \in K \cup \mathrm{NIL}\}$	K
ERec	d	M	$\mathbb{T}$
ET	(d, M)	$\{(\mu, \mathbf{T}) \mid \mu \in M, \mathbf{T} \subset K\}$	K
RE	(d, M, U)	$\{(s, p, o) \mid s, o \in U, p \in \mathbb{P}\}$	$K, \mathbb{T}$
RT2KB	d	$\{(\mu, c) \mid c \in K\}$	$K, \mathbb{T}$

- *ERec*: For this type of extraction the input to the system is a plain text document d. The expected output are the mentions M of all entities within the text [71]. A set of entity types $\mathbb{T}$ is used as background data to define which types of entities should be marked in the texts.
- *D2KB*: The input for entity disambiguation (or entity linking) is a text d with already marked entity mentions $\mu \in M$. The goal is to map this set of *given* entities to entities from a given Knowledge Base (KB) K or to NIL. The latter represents the set of entities that are not present in K (also called emerging entities [35]). Although K is not part of the task (and the benchmark datasets do not contain it), it can be seen as background data of a benchmark.
- *Entity Typing (ET)*: The entity typing is similar to D2KB. Its goal is to map a set of *given* entity mentions to the type hierarchy of a KB.
- *C2KB*: The concept tagging (C2KB) aims to detect entities relevant for a given document. Formally, the function takes a plain text as input and returns a subset of the KB.

Based on these basic types, more complex types have been defined [71]:

- *A2KB*: This is a combination of the ERec and D2KB types and represents the classical named entity recognition and disambiguation. Thus, the input is a plain text document d and the system has to identify entities mentions μ and link them to K.
- *RT2KB*: This extraction type is the combination of entity recognition and typing, i.e., the goal is to identify entities in a given document set D and map them to the types of K.

For extracting more complex relations the *RE* experiment type is defined in [85, 86]. The input for the relation extraction is a text d with marked entity mentions $\mu \in M$ that have been linked to a knowledge base K. Let $u_j \in U$ be the URI of the j-th marking μ_j with $U \subset K \cup \mathrm{NIL}$. The goal is to identify the relation the entities have within the text and return it as triple. To narrow the amount of possible relations, a set of properties $\mathbb{P}$ is given as part of the background data. Table 1 summarizes the different extraction types.

2.1.2. Matchings

One of the major challenges when benchmarking a system is to define how the system's response can be matched to the expected answer.

Positional Matching. Some of the different extraction types described above aim to identify positions of entities within a given text. Two different strategies have been established to handle a comparison of the system's markings and expected markings [15, 71,101]. The *strong annotation matching* matches two markings if they have exactly the same positions. The *weak annotation matching* relaxes this condition. It matches two markings if they overlap with each other.

URI Matching. For the evaluation of the system performance with respect to several types of extraction, the matching of URIs is needed. Extraction systems can use different URIs from the creators of a benchmark, e.g., because the extraction system returns Wikipedia article URLs instead of DBpedia URIs. Since different URIs can point to the same real world entity, the matching of two URIs is not as trivial as the comparison of two strings. The authors of [71] propose a workflow for improving the fairness of URI matching:

1. *URI set retrieval.* Instead of representing a meaning as a single URI, it is represented as a set of URIs. This set can be expanded by crawling the Semantic Web graph using `owl:sameAs` links and redirects.
2. *URI set classification.* After expanding the URI sets, they are classified into these two classes. A URI set S is classified as $S \in C_{KB}$ if it contains at least one URI of K. Otherwise it is classified as $S \in C_{EE}$.
3. *URI set matching.* Two URI sets S_1, S_2 are matching if both are assigned to the C_{KB} class and the sets are overlapping or both sets are assigned to the C_{EE} class.

2.1.3. Key Performance Indicators

The performance of knowledge extraction systems is mainly measured using Precision, Recall and F1-measure. Since most benchmarking datasets comprise multiple tasks, Micro and Macro averages are used for summarizing the performance of the systems [15,71,101]. A special case is the comparison of entity types. Since the types can be arranged in a hierarchy, the hierarchical F-measure can be used for this kind of experiment [71]. For evaluating the systems' efficiency, the response time of the systems is a typical KPI [71, 101]. It should be noted that most benchmarking frameworks send the tasks sequentially to the extraction systems. In contrast to that, the authors of [87] introduced a stress test. During this test, tasks can be sent in parallel and the gaps between the tasks are reduced over time. For a comparison of the performance of the systems under pressure, a β metric is used, which combines the F-measure and the runtime of the system.

2.1.4. Datasets

Since the field of information extraction has been tackled for several years, a large number of datasets is available. Table 2 shows some example datasets. It is clear that the datasets vary a lot in their number of documents (i.e., the number of tasks), length of single documents and number of entities per document. All datasets listed in the table have been manually annotated. However, it is known that this type of datasets has two drawbacks. First, [38] showed that although the datasets are used as gold standards, they are not free of errors. Second, the size of the datasets is limited by the high costs of the manual annotation of documents. To this end, [58] proposed the automatic generation of annotated documents based on a given KB.

---

[2] http://www.yovisto.com/labs/ner-benchmarks/.

Table 2. Example benchmarks for knowledge extraction [71]. Collections of datasets, e.g., for a single challenge, have been grouped together.

Corpus	Task	Topic	|Documents|	Entities/Doc.	Words/Doc.
ACE2004 [65]	A2KB	news	57	5.37	373.9
AIDA/CoNLL [36]	A2KB	news	1393	25.07	189.7
AQUAINT [47]	A2KB	news	50	14.54	220.5
Derczynski IPM NEL [19]	A2KB	tweets	182	1.57	20.8
ERD2014 [12]	A2KB	queries	91	0.65	3.5
GERDAQ [16]	A2KB	queries	992	1.72	3.6
IITB [41]	A2KB	mixed	103	109.22	639.7
KORE 50^2	A2KB	mixed	50	2.88	12.8
Microposts2013 [11]	RT2KB	tweets	4265	1.11	18.8
Microposts2014 [10]	A2KB	tweets	3395	1.50	18.1
Microposts2015 [67]	A2KB	tweets	6025	1.36	16.5
Microposts2016 [68]	A2KB	tweets	9289	1.03	15.7
MSNBC [17]	A2KB	news	20	37.35	543.9
N^3 Reuters-128 [70]	A2KB	news	128	4.85	123.8
N^3 RSS-500 [70]	A2KB	RSS-feeds	500	1.00	31.0
OKE 2015 Task 1 [60]	A2KB, ET	mixed	199	5.11	25.5
OKE 2016 Task 1 [61]	A2KB, ET	mixed	254	5.52	26.6
Ritter [66]	RT2KB	news	2394	0.62	19.4
Senseval 2 [22]	ERec	mixed	242	9.86	21.3
Senseval 3 [45]	ERec	mixed	352	5.70	14.7
Spotlight Corpus^2	A2KB	news	58	5.69	28.6
UMBC [27]	RT2KB	tweets	12973	0.97	17.2
WSDM2012/Meij [9]	C2KB	tweets	502	1.87	14.4

2.2. Storage & Querying

After a critical mass of RDF data has been extracted, the data has to be stored, indexed and made available for querying in an efficient way [50]. Triplestores are data management systems for storing and querying RDF data. In this section, we discuss the different benchmarks used to assess the performance of triplestores. In particular, we highlight key features of triplestore benchmarks pertaining to the three main components of benchmarks, i.e., datasets, queries, and performance metrics. State-of-the-art triplestore benchmarks are analyzed and compared against these features. Most of the content in this section is adopted from [77].

2.2.1. Triplestore Benchmark Design Features

In general, triplestore benchmarks comprise three main components: (1) a set of RDF datasets, (2) a set of SPARQL queries, and (3) a set of performance metrics. With respect to the benchmark schema defined in Section 1, each task of a SPARQL benchmark comprises a single SPARQL query as input while the expected output data comprises the expected result of the query. The RDF dataset(s) are part of the Background data of a benchmark against which the queries are executed. In the following, we present key features of each of these components that are important to consider in the development of triplestore benchmarks.

Datasets.   Datasets used in triplestore benchmarks are either synthetic or selected from real-world RDF datasets [74]. The use of real-world RDF datasets is often regarded as useful to perform evaluation in close-to-real-world settings [48]. Synthetic datasets are useful to test the scalability of systems based on datasets of varying sizes. Synthetic dataset generators are utilized to produce datasets of varying sizes that can often be optimized to reflect the characteristics of real-world datasets [21]. Previous works [21,64] highlighted two key measures for selecting such datasets for triplestores benchmarking: (1) Dataset Structuredness and (2) Relationship Specialty. The formal definitions of these metrics can be found in [77]. However, observations from the literature (see e.g., [21,73]) suggest that other features such as varying number of triples, number of resources, number of properties, number of objects, number of classes, diversity in literal values, average properties and instances per class, average indegrees and outdegrees as well as their distribution across resources should also be considered.

The dataset structuredness and relationship specialty directly affect the result size, the number of intermediate results, and the selectivities of the triple patterns of a given SPARQL query. Therefore, they are important dataset design features to be considered during the generation of benchmarks [21,64,74].

SPARQL Queries.   The literature about SPARQL Queries [3,30,73,74,76] suggests that a SPARQL querying benchmark should vary the queries with respect to various features such as *query characteristics*: number of triple patterns, number of projection variables, result set sizes, query execution time, number of BGPs, number of join vertices, mean join vertex degree, mean triple pattern selectivities, BGP-restricted and join-restricted triple pattern selectivities, join vertex types, and highly used SPARQL clauses (e.g., LIMIT, OPTIONAL, ORDER BY, DISTINCT, UNION, FILTER, REGEX). All of these features have a direct impact on the runtime performance of triplestores. The formal definitions of many of the above mentioned features can be found in [77].

Performance Metrics.   Based on the previous triplestore benchmarks and performance evaluations [3,6,7,14,18,23,33,48,74,78,92,93,104] the performance metrics for such comparisons can be categorized as:

- *Query Processing Related*: The performance metrics in this category are related to the query processing capabilities of the triplestores. The query execution time is the central performance metric in this category. However, reporting the execution time for individual queries might not be feasible due to the large number of queries in the given benchmark. To this end, Query Mix per Hour (QMpH) and Queries per Second (QpS) are regarded as central performance measures to test the querying capabilities of the triplestores [7,48,74]. In addition, the query processing overhead in terms of the CPU and memory usage is important to measure during the query executions [78]. This also includes the number of intermediate results, the number of disk/memory swaps, etc.

- *Data Storage Related:* Triplestores need to load the given RDF data and mostly create indexes before they are ready for query executions. In this regard, the data loading time, the storage space acquired, and the index size are important performance metrics in this category [7,18,78,104].

- *Result Set Related:* Two systems can only be compared if they produce exactly the same results. Therefore, result set correctness and completeness are important metrics to be considered in the evaluation of triplestores [7,74,78,104].

- **Parallelism with/without Updates:** Some of the aforementioned triplestore performance evaluations [7, 14, 104] also measured the parallel query processing capabilities of the triplestores by simulating workloads from multiple querying agents with and without dataset updates.

2.2.2. Triplestore Benchmarks

Triplestore benchmarks can be broadly divided into two main categories, namely synthetic and real-data benchmarks.

Synthetic Triplestore Benchmarks. Synthetic benchmarks make use of the data (and/or query) generators to generate datasets and/or queries for benchmarking. Synthetic benchmarks are useful in testing the scalability of triplestores with varying dataset sizes and querying workloads. However, such benchmarks can fail to reflect the characteristics of real-world datasets or queries. The *Train Benchmark* (TrainBench) [92] uses a data generator that produces railway networks in increasing sizes and serializes them in different formats, including RDF. *The Waterloo SPARQL Diversity Test Suite* (WatDiv) [3] provides a synthetic data generator that produces RDF data with a tunable structuredness value and a query generator. The queries are generated from different query templates. *SP2Bench* [78] mirrors vital characteristics (such as power law distributions or Gaussian curves) of the data in the DBLP bibliographic database. *The Berlin SPARQL Benchmark* (BSBM) [7] uses query templates to generate any number of SPARQL queries for benchmarking, covering multiple use cases such as explore, update, and business intelligence. *Bowlogna* [18] models a real-world setting derived from the Bologna process and offers mostly analytic queries reflecting data-intensive user needs. The *LDBC Social Network Benchmark* (SNB) defines two workloads. First, the *Interactive* workload (SNB-INT) measures the evaluation of graph patterns in a localized scope (e.g., in the neighborhood of a person), with the graph being continuously updated [23]. Second, the *Business Intelligence* workload (SNB-BI) focuses on queries that mix complex graph pattern matching with aggregations, touching on a significant portion of the graph [93], without any updates. Note that these two workloads are regarded as two separate triplestore benchmarks based on the same dataset.

Triplestore Benchmarks Using Real Data. Real-data benchmarks make use of real-world datasets and queries from real user query logs for benchmarking. Real-data benchmarks are useful in testing triplestores more closely in real-world settings. However, such benchmarks may fail to test the scalability of triplestores with varying dataset sizes and querying workloads. *FEASIBLE* [74] is a cluster-based SPARQL benchmark generator, which is able to synthesize customizable benchmarks from the query logs of SPARQL endpoints. The *DBpedia SPARQL Benchmark* (DBPSB) [48] is another cluster-based approach that generates benchmark queries from DBpedia query logs, but employs different clustering techniques than FEASIBLE. The *FishMark* [6] dataset is obtained from FishBase[3] and provided in both RDF and SQL versions. The SPARQL queries were obtained from logs of the web-based FishBase application. *BioBench* [104] evaluates the performance of RDF triplestores with biological datasets and queries from five different real-world RDF datasets[4], i.e., Cell, Allie, PDBJ, DDBJ, and UniProt. Due to the size of the datasets, we were only able to analyze the combined data and queries of the first three.

---

[3]FishBase: http://fishbase.org/search.php
[4]BioBench: http://kiban.dbcls.jp/togordf/wiki/survey#data

Table 3 summarizes the statistics from selected datasets of the benchmarks.

Table 3. High-level statistics of the data and queries used on existing triplestore benchmarks. Both SNB-BI and SNB-INT use the same dataset and are therefore named as SNB for simplicity.

	Benchmark	Subjects	Predicates	Objects	Triples	Queries
Synthetic	Bowlogna [18]	2,151k	39	260k	12M	16
	TrainB. [92]	3,355k	16	3,357k	41M	11
	BSBM [7]	9,039k	40	14,966k	100M	20
	SP2Bench [78]	7,002k	5,718	19,347k	49M	14
	WatDiv [3]	5,212k	86	9,753k	108M	50
	SNB [23,93]	7,193k	40	17,544k	46M	21
Real	FishMark [6]	395k	878	1,148k	10M	22
	BioBench [104]	278,007k	299	232,041k	1,451M	39
	FEASIBLE [74]	18,425k	39,672	65,184k	232M	50
	DBPSB [48]	18,425k	39,672	65,184k	232M	25

2.3. Manual Revision & Authoring

Using SPARQL queries, the user can interact with the stored data directly, e.g., by correcting errors or adding additional information [50]. This is the third step of the Linked Data Lifecycle. However, since it mainly comprises user interaction, there are no automatic benchmarks for tools supporting this step. Hence, we will not look further into it.

2.4. Linking

For cleaned data originating from different sources, the generation of links between different information assets needs to be established [50]. The generation of such links between knowledge bases is one of the key steps of the Linked Data publication process.[5] A plethora of approaches has thus been devised to support this process [49].

The formal specification of Link Discovery adopted herein is akin to that proposed in [52]. Given two (not necessarily distinct) sets $\mathscr{S}$ resp. $\mathscr{T}$ of source resp. target resources as well as a relation R, the goal of LD is is to find the set $M = \{(s, \tau) \in \mathscr{S} \times \mathscr{T} : R(s, \tau)\}$ of pairs $(s, \tau) \in \mathscr{S} \times \mathscr{T}$ such that $R(s, \tau)$. In most cases, computing M is a non-trivial task. Hence, a large number of frameworks (e.g., SILK [37], LIMES [52] and KnoFuss [59]) aim to approximate M by computing the *mapping* $M' = \{(s, \tau) \in \mathscr{S} \times \mathscr{T} : \sigma(s, \tau) \geq \theta\}$, where σ is a similarity function and θ is a similarity threshold. For example, one can configure these frameworks to compare the dates of birth, family names and given names of persons across census records to determine whether they are duplicates. We call the equation which specifies M' a *link specification* (short LS; also called linkage rule in the literature, see e.g., [37]). Note that the Link Discovery problem can be expressed equivalently using distances instead of similarities in the following manner: Given two

---

[5]http://www.w3.org/DesignIssues/LinkedData.html

sets $\mathscr{S}$ and $\mathscr{T}$ of instances, a (complex) distance measure δ and a distance threshold $\theta \in [0, \infty[$, determine $M' = \{(s, \tau) \in \mathscr{S} \times \mathscr{T} : \delta(s, \tau) \leq \vartheta\}$.[6]

Under this so-called *declarative paradigm*, two entities s and τ are then considered to be linked via R if $\sigma(s, \tau) \geq \theta$. Naïve algorithms require $O(|\mathscr{S}||\mathscr{T}|) \in O(n^2)$ computations to output M'. Given the large size of existing knowledge bases, time-efficient approaches able to reduce this runtime are hence a central component of efficient link discovery, as link specifications need to be computed in acceptable times. This efficient computation is in turn the proxy necessary for machine learning techniques to be used to optimize the choice of appropriate σ and θ and thus ensure that M' approximates M well even when M is large [49]).

Benchmarks for the link discovery framework use tasks of the form $t_i = ((\mathscr{S}_i, \mathscr{T}_i, R_i), M_i)$. Depending on the given datasets $\mathscr{S}_i$ and $\mathscr{T}_i$, and the given relation R_i, a benchmark is able to make different demands on the Link discovery frameworks. To this end, such frameworks are designed to accommodate a large number of link discovery approaches within a single extensible architecture to address two main challenges measured by the benchmark:

1. *Time-efficiency*: The mere size of existing knowledge bases (e.g., 30+ billion triples in LinkedGeoData [88], 20+ billion triples in LinkedTCGA [75]) makes efficient solutions indispensable to the use of link discovery frameworks in real application scenarios. LIMES for example addresses this challenge by providing time-efficient approaches based on the characteristics of metric spaces [51, 54], orthodromic spaces [53] and filter-based paradigms [84].
2. *Accuracy*: The second key performance indicator is the accuracy provided by link discovery frameworks. Efficient solutions are of little help if the results they generate are inaccurate. Hence, LIMES also accommodates dedicated machine-learning solutions that allow the generation of links between knowledge bases with a high accuracy. These solutions abide by paradigms such as batch and active learning [55–57], unsupervised learning [57] and even positive-only learning [81].

The Ontology Evaluation Alignment Initiative (OAEI)[7] has performed yearly contests since 2005 to comparatively evaluate current tools for ontology and instance matching. The original focus has been on ontology matching, but since 2009 instance matching has also been a regular evaluation track. Table 4 (From [49]) gives an overview of the OAEI instance matching tasks in five contests from 2010 to 2014. Most tasks have only been used in one year while others like IIMB have been changed in different years. The majority of the linking tasks are based on synthetic datasets where values and the structural context of instances have been modified in a controlled way. Linking tasks cover different domains (life sciences, people, geography, etc.) and data sources (*DBpedia, Freebase, GeoNames, NYTimes,* etc.). Frequently, the benchmarks consist of several interlinking tasks to cover a certain spectrum of complexity. The number of instances are rather small in all tests with $9,958$ the maximum size of data source. The evaluation focus has been solely on the effectiveness (e.g., F-Measure) while runtime efficiency has not been measured. Almost all tasks focus on identifying equivalent instances (i.e., `owl:sameAs` links).

---

[6]Note that a distance function δ can always be transformed into a normed similarity function σ by setting $\sigma(x, y) = (1 + \delta(x, y))^{-1}$. Hence, the distance threshold ϑ can be transformed into a similarity threshold θ by means of the equation $\theta = (1 + \vartheta)^{-1}$.

[7]`http://www.ontologymatching.org`

We briefly characterize the different OAEI tasks as follows:

- *IIMB and Sandbox (SB)*. The IIMB benchmark has been part of the 2010, 2011 and 2012 contests and consists of 80 tasks using synthetically modified datasets derived from instances of 29 Freebase concepts. The number of instances varies from year to year but the instances have a very small size (e.g., at most 375 instances in 2012). The Sandbox (SB) benchmark from 2012 is very similar to IIMB but limited to 10 different tasks [2].
- *PR (Persons/Restaurant)*. This benchmark is based on real-person and restaurant-instance data that are artificially modified by adding duplicates and variations of property values. With 500–600 instances for the restaurant data and even less in the person data source, the dataset is relatively small. [24]
- *DI-NYT (Data Interlinking - NYT)*. This 2011 benchmark includes seven tasks to link about 10,000 instances from the NYT data source to DBpedia, Freebase and GeoNames instances. The perfect match result contains about 31,000 owl:sameAs links to be identified [25].
- *RDFT*. This 2013 benchmark is also of small size (430 instances) and uses several tests with differently modified DBpedia data. For the first time in the OAEI instance matching track, no reference mapping is provided for the actual evaluation task. Instead, training data with an appropriate reference mapping is given for each test case thereby supporting frameworks relying on supervised learning [31].
- *OAEI 2014*. Two benchmark tasks have to be performed in 2014. The first one (id-rec) requiring the identification of the same real-world book entities (owl:sameAs links). For this purpose, 1,330 book instances have to be matched with with 2,649 synthetically modified instances in the target dataset. Data transformations include changes like the substitution of book titles and labels with keywords as well as language transformations. In the second task (sim-rec) similarity of pairs of instances are determined, which do not reflect the same real-world entities. This addresses common preprocessing tasks, e.g., to reduce the search space for LD. In 2014, the evaluation platform SEALS [28], which has been used for ontology matching in previous years, is used for instance matching, too (see Section 3).

2.5. Enrichment

Linked Data Enrichment is an important topic for all applications that rely on a large number of knowledge bases and necessitate a unified view on this data, e.g., Question Answering frameworks, Linked Education and all forms of semantic mashups. In recent work, several challenges and requirements to Linked Data consumption and integration have been pointed out [46]. Several approaches and frameworks have been developed with the aim of addressing many of these challenges. For example, the R2R framework [8] addresses those by allowing mappings to be published across knowledge bases, mapping classes defining and property value transformation. While this framework supports a large number of transformations, it does not allow the automatic discovery of possible transformations. The Linked Data Integration Framework LDIF [79], whose goal is to support the integration of RDF data, builds upon R2R mappings and technologies such as SILK [37] and LDSpider[8]. The concept behind the framework is to enable users to

---

[8]http://code.google.com/p/ldspider/

Table 4. OAEI instance matching tasks over the years. "–" means not existing, "?" unclear from publication [49].

Year	Name	Input Format	Problem Type	Domains	LOD Sources	Link Type	Max. # Resources	Tasks
2010	DI	RDF	real	life sciences	diseasome drugbank dailymed sider	equality	5,000	4
	IIMB	OWL	artificial	cross-domain	Freebase	equality	1,416	80
	PR	RDF, OWL	artificial	people geography	–	equality	864	3
2011	DI-NYT	RDF	real	people geography organizations	NYTimes DBpedia Freebase Geonames	equality	9,958	7
	IIMB	OWL	artificial	cross-domain	Freebase	equality	1,500	80
2012	SB	OWL	artificial	cross-domain	Freebase	equality	375	10
	IIMB	OWL	artificial	cross-domain	Freebase	equality	375	80
2013	RDFT	RDF	artificial	people	DBpedia	equality	430	5
2014	id-rec	OWL	artificial	publications	?	equality	2,649	1
	sim-rec	OWL	artificial	publications	?	similarity	173	1

create periodic integration jobs via simple XML configurations. These configurations however have to be created manually. The same drawback holds for the Semantic Web Pipes[9], which follows the idea of Yahoo Pipes[10] to enable the integration of data in formats such as RDF and XML. By using Semantic Web Pipes, users can efficiently create semantic mashups by using a number of operators (such as getRDF, getXML, etc.) and connecting these manually within a simple interface. It begins by detecting URIs that stand for the same real-world entity and either merging them to one or linking them via `owl:sameAs`. Fluid Operations' Information Workbench[11] allows users to search through, manipulate and integrate for purposes such as business intelligence. The work presented in [13] describes a framework for semantic enrichment, ranking and integration of web videos. [1] presents semantic enrichment framework of *Twitter* posts. [34] tackles the linked data enrichment problem for sensor data via an approach that sees enrichment as a process driven by situations of interest.

To the best of our knowledge, DEER [80] is the first generic approach tailored towards learning enrichment pipelines of Linked Data given a set of atomic enrichment functions. DEER models RDF dataset enrichment workflows as ordered sequences of enrichment functions. These enrichment functions take as input exactly one RDF dataset and return

---

[9] http://pipes.deri.org/
[10] http://pipes.yahoo.com/pipes/
[11] http://www.fluidops.com/information-workbench/

an altered version of it by virtue of addition and deletion of triples, as any enrichment operation on a given dataset can be represented as a set of additions and deletions.

The benchmarking proposed by [80] aims to quantify how well the presented RDF data enrichment approach can automate the enrichment process. The authors thus assumed being given manually created training examples and having to reconstruct a possible enrichment pipeline to generate target concise bounded descriptions (CBDs[12]) resources from the source CBDs. Therefore, they used three publicly available datasets for generating the benchmark datasets:

1. From the biomedical domain, the authors chose *DrugBank*[13]. They chose this dataset because it is linked with many other datasets[14] from which the authors extracted enrichment data using their atomic enrichment functions. For evaluation, they deployed a manual enrichment pipeline M_{manual}, where they enriched the drug data found in *DrugBank* using abstracts dereferenced from *DBpedia*. Then, they conformed both *DrugBank* and *DBpedia* source authority URIs to one unified URI. For *DrugBank* they manually deployed two experimental pipelines:

   - $M_{DrugBank}^1 = (m_1, m_2)$, where m_1 is a dereferencing function that dereferences any dbpedia-owl:abstract from DBpedia and m_2 is an authority conformation function that conforms the *DBpedia* subject authority[15] to the target subject authority of *DrugBank*[16].
   - $M_{DrugBank}^2 = M_{DrugBank}^1 \mathbin{+\!\!+} m_3$, where m_3 is an authority conformation function that conforms *DrugBank*'s authority to the *Example* authority[17].

2. From the music domain, the authors chose the *Jamendo*[18] dataset. They selected this dataset as it contains a substantial amount of embedded information hidden in literal properties such as mo:biography. The goal of their enrichment process is to add a geospatial dimension to *Jamendo*, e.g., location of a recording or place of birth of a musician. To this end, the authors of [80] deployed a manual enrichment pipeline, in which they enriched *Jamendo*'s music data by adding additional geospatial data found by applying the NER of the NLP enrichment function against mo:biography. For *Jamendo* they manually deployed one experimental pipeline:

   - $M_{Jamendo}^1 = \{m_4\}$, where m_4 is an enrichment function that finds *locations* in mo:biography using natural language processing (NLP) techniques.

3. From the multi-domain knowledge base *DBpedia* [42] the authors selected the class AdministrativeRegion to be our third dataset. As DBpedia is a knowledge base with a complex ontology, they build a set of 5 pipelines of increasing complexity:

---

[12]https://www.w3.org/Submission/CBD/

[13]*DrugBank* is the Linked Data version of the DrugBank database, which is a repository of almost 5000 FDA-approved small molecule and biotech drugs, for RDF dump see http://wifo5-03.informatik.uni-mannheim.de/drugbank/drugbank_dump.nt.bz2

[14]See http://datahub.io/dataset/fu-berlin-drugbank for complete list of linked dataset with *DrugBank*.

[15]http://dbpedia.org

[16]http://wifo5-04.informatik.uni-mannheim.de/drugbank/resource/drugs

[17]http://example.org

[18]*Jamendo* contains a large collection of music-related information about artists and recordings, for RDF dump see http://moustaki.org/resources/jamendo-rdf.tar.gz

- $M_{DBpedia}^1 = \{m_5\}$, where m_5 is an authority conformation function that conforms the *DBpedia* subject authority to the *Example* target subject authority.
- $M_{DBpedia}^2 = m_6 + \!\!+ M_{DBpedia}^1$, where m_6 is a dereferencing function that dereference any dbpedia-owl:ideology and $+ \!\!+$ is the list append operator.
- $M_{DBpedia}^3 = M_{DBpedia}^2 + \!\!+ m_7$, where m_7 is a NLP function that finds *all* named entities in dbpedia-owl:abstract.
- $M_{DBpedia}^4 = M_{DBpedia}^3 + \!\!+ m_8$, where m_8 is a filter function that filters for abstracts.
- $M_{DBpedia}^5 = M_{DBpedia}^3 + \!\!+ m_9$, where m_9 is a predicate conformation function that conforms the source predicate dbpedia-owl:abstract to the target predicate of dcterms:abstract.

Altogether, The authors manually generated a set of 8 pipelines, which they then applied against their respective datasets. The resulting pairs of CBDs were used to generate the positive examples, which were simply randomly selected pairs of distinct CBDs. All generated pipelines are available at the project web site.[19]

2.6. Quality Analysis

Since Linked Data origins from different publishers, a variety of information quality exists and different strategies exists to assess them [50]. Since several previous steps are extracting and generating triples automatically, an important part of the quality analysis is the evaluation of single facts with respect to their veracity. These fact validation systems (also known as fact checking systems) take a triple (s, p, o) as input i_j and return a veracity score as output [90].

An extension to the fact validation task is the temporal fact validation. A temporal fact validation system takes a point in time as additional input. It validates whether the given fact was true at the given point in time. However, to the best of our knowledge, [29] is the only approach that tackles this task and FactBench is the only dataset available for benchmarking such a system.

2.6.1. Validation system types

Most of the fact validation systems use reference knowledge to validate a given triple. There are two major types of knowledge which can be used—structured and unstructured knowledge [90].

Approaches relying on structured knowledge use a reference knowledge base to search for patterns or paths supporting or refuting the given fact. Other approaches transfer the knowledge base into an embedding space and calculate the similarity between the entities positions in the space and the positions the entities should have if the fact is true [90]. For all these approaches, it is necessary that the single IRIs of the fact's subject, predicate and object are available in the knowledge base. Hence, the knowledge base the facts of a fact validation benchmark rely on is background knowledge a benchmarked fact validation system needs to have.

The second group of approaches is based on unstructured—in most cases textual—knowledge [29,90]. These approaches are generating search queries based on the give fact and search for documents providing evidences for the fact. To this end, it is necessary for

---

[19]https://github.com/GeoKnow/DEER/evaluations/pipeline_learner

such an approach to be aware of the subject's and object's label. Additionally, a pattern how to formulate a fact with respect to the given predicate might be necessary.

2.6.2. Datasets

Several datasets have been created during the last years. Table 5 gives an overview. *FactBench* [29] is a collection of 7 datasets.[20] The facts of the datasets have a time range attached which shows at which point in time the facts are true. The datasets share 1500 true facts selected from DBpedia and Freebase using 10 different properties.[21] However, the datasets differ in the way the 1500 false facts are derived from true facts.

- *Domain*: The subject is replaced by a random resource.
- *Range*: The object is replaced by a random resource.
- *Domain-Range*: Subject and object are replaced as described above.
- *Property*: The predicate of the triple is replaced with a randomly chosen property.
- *Random*: A triple is generated randomly.
- *Date*: The time range of a fact is changed. If the range is a single point in time, it is randomly chosen from a gaussian distribution which has its mean at the original point in time and a variance of 5 years. For time intervals, the start year and the duration are drawn from two Gaussian distributions.
- *Mix*: A mixture comprising one sixth of each of the sets above.

It has to be noted that all changes are done in a way that makes sure that the subject and object of the generated false triple follow the domain and range restrictions of the fact's predicate. In all cases, the generated fact must not be made present in the knowledge base.

In [82], the authors propose several datasets based on triples from the DBpedia. *CapitalOf #1* comprises *capitalOf* relations of the 5 largest US cities. If the correct city is not within the top 5 cities, an additional fact with the correct city is added. *CapitalOf #2* comprises the same 50 correct triples. Additionally, for each capital four triples with a wrong state are created. The *US Civil War* dataset comprises triples connecting military commanders to decisive battles of the US Civil war. The *Company CEO* dataset comprises 205 correct connections between CEOs and their company using the *keyPerson* property. 1025 incorrect triples are created by randomly selecting a CEO and a company from the correct facts. The *NYT Bestseller* comprises 465 incorrect random pairs of authors and books as well as 93 true triples of the New York Times bestseller lists between 2010 and 2015. The *US Vice-President* contains 47 correct and 227 incorrect pairs of vice-presidents and presidents of the United States. Additionally, the authors create two datasets based on SemMedDB. The *Disease* dataset contains triples marking an amino acid, peptide or protein as a cause of a disease or syndrome. It comprises 100 correct and 457 incorrect triples. The *Cell* dataset connects cell functions with the gene that causes them. It contains 99 correct and 435 incorrect statements.

In [83], the authors propose several datasets. *FLOTUS* comprises US presidents and their spouses. The *NBA-Team* contains triples assigning NBA players to teams. The *Oscars* dataset comprises triples related to movies. Additionally, the authors reuse triples from the Google Relation Extraction Corpora (*GREC*) containing triples about the *birthplace*,

---

[20]https://github.com/DeFacto/FactBench

[21]The dataset has 150 true and false facts for each of the following properties: *award, birthPlace, deathPlace, foundationPlace, leader, team, author, spouse, starring* and *subsidiary*.

Table 5. Summary of benchmark datasets for fact validations.

Dataset	Facts			Temporal
	True	False	Total	
Birthplace/Deathplace ([91])	206	206	412	no
CapitalOf #1 ([82])	50	209	259	no
CapitalOf #2 ([82])	50	200	250	no
Cell ([82])	99	435	534	no
Company CEO ([82])	205	1025	1230	no
Disease ([82])	100	457	557	no
FactBench Date ([29])	1 500	1 500	3 000	yes
FactBench Domain ([29])	1 500	1 500	3 000	yes
FactBench Domain-Range ([29])	1 500	1 500	3 000	yes
FactBench Mix ([29])	1 500	1 560	3 060	yes
FactBench Property ([29])	1 500	1 500	3 000	yes
FactBench Random ([29])	1 500	1 500	3 000	yes
FactBench Range ([29])	1 500	1 500	3 000	yes
FLOTUS ([83])	16	240	256	no
GREC-Birthplace ([83])	273	819	1 092	no
GREC-Deathplace ([83])	126	378	504	no
GREC-Education ([83])	466	1 395	1 861	no
GREC-Institution ([83])	1 546	4 638	6 184	no
NBA-Team ([83])	41	143	164	no
NYT Bestseller ([82])	93	465	558	no
Oscars ([83])	78	4 602	4 680	no
US Civil War ([82])	126	584	710	no
US Vice-President ([82])	47	227	274	no
WSDM-Nationality ([83])	50	150	200	no
WSDM-Profession ([83])	110	330	440	no

deathplace, *education* and *institution* of famous people. The ground truth for these triples is derived using crowd sourcing. The *profession* and *nationality* datasets are derived from the WSDM Cup 2017 Triple Scoring challenge. Since the challenge only provides true facts, false facts have been randomly drawn.

In [91], the authors claim that several approaches for fact validation do not take the predicate into account and that for most of the existing benchmarking datasets, checking the connection between the subject and object is already sufficient. For creating a more difficult dataset, the authors query a list of persons from DBpedia that have their birth- and death places in two different countries. They use these triples as true facts and swap birth- and deathplace to create wrong facts.

2.6.3. Key Performance Indicators

The performance of a fact validation system can be measured regarding its effectiveness and efficiency. To measure the effectiveness, the Area under ROC is a common choice [90]. Interpreting the validation as a binary classification task allows the usage of Precision, Recall and F1-measure. However, this comes with the search of a threshold for the minimal veracity value that can still be accepted as true [91]. The efficiency is typically measured with respect to the runtime of a fact validation system [90].

2.7. Evolution & Repair

If problems within a KG are detected, repairing and managing the evolution of the data is necessary [50]. Since repair tools mainly support a manual task, and are therefore hard to benchmark automatically, we will focus on the benchmarking of versioning systems. These systems work similarly to SPARQL stores described in Section 2.2. However, instead of answering a query based on a single RDF graph, they allow the querying of data from a single or over different versions of the graph [26].

With respect to the proposed benchmark schema, the benchmarks for versioning systems are very similar to the triple store benchmarks. A benchmark dataset comprises several versions of a knowledge base, a set of queries and a set of expected results for these queries. The knowledge base versions can be seen as background data that is provided at the beginning of the benchmarking. The input for a task is a single query and the expected output is the expected query result. The benchmarked versioning system has to answer the query based on the provided knowledge base versions.

2.7.1. Query Types

In the literature, different types of queries are defined, which a versioning system needs to be able to handle. The authors in [26] provide the following 6 queries:

- *Version materialization queries* retrieve the full version of a knowledge base for a given point in time.
- *Single-version structured queries* retrieve a subset of the data of a single version.
- *Cross-version structured queries* retrieve data across several versions.
- *Delta materialization queries* retrieve the differences between two or more versions.
- *Single-delta structured queries* retrieve data from a single delta of two versions.
- *Cross-delta structured queries* retrieve data across several deltas.

The authors in [62,63] create a more fine-grained structure providing 8 different types of queries.

2.7.2. Datasets

The BEAR benchmark dataset proposed in [26] comprises three parts—BEAR-A, BEAR-B, and BEAR-C. BEAR-A comprises 58 versions of a single real-world knowledge base taken from the Dynamic Linked Data Observatory.[22] The set of queries comprises triple pattern queries and is manually created by the authors to cover all basic functionalities a versioning system has to provide. Additionally, it is ensured that the queries give different results for all versions while they are ε-stable, i.e., the cardinalities of the results across the versions never exceed $(1 \pm \varepsilon)$ of the mean cardinality.

The BEAR-B dataset relies on the DBpedia Live endpoint. The authors of [26] took the changesets from August to October 2015 reflecting changes in the DBpedia triggered by edits in the Wikipedia. The dataset comprises data of the 100 most volatile

---

[22]http://swse.deri.org/dyldo/

resources and the changes to it. The data is provided in three granularities—the *instant* application of changes leads to 21,046 different versions. Additionally, the authors applied summarizations *hourly* and *daily*, leading to 1,299 and 89 versions, respectively. The queries for this dataset are taken from the LSQ dataset [72].

The BEAR-C dataset relies on 32 snapshots of the European Open Data portal.[23] Each snapshot comprises roughly 500m triples describing datasets of the open data portal. The authors create 10 queries that should be too complex to be solved by existing versioning systems "in a straightforward and optimized way" [26].

Evogen is a dataset generator proposed in [44]. It relies on the LUBM generator [33] and generates additional versions based on its configuration. Based on which delta the generator has used to create different versions, the 14 LUBM queries are adapted to the generated data.

The SPBv dataset generator proposed in [63] is an extension of the SPB generator [40], creating RDF based on the BBC core ontology. It mimics the evolution of journalistic articles in the world of online journalism. While new articles are published, already existing articles are changed over time and different versions of articles are created.

2.7.3. Key Performance Indicators

The main key performance indicator used for versioning systems is the query runtime. Analyzing these runtimes shows for which query type a certain versioning system has a good or bad performance. A second indicator is the space used by the versioning system to store the data [26, 63]. In addition to, [63] proposes the measurement of the time a system needs to store the initial version of the knowledge base and the time it needs to apply the changes to create newer versions.

2.8. Search, Browsing & Exploration

The user has to be enabled to access the LD in a fast and user friendly way [50]. This need has led to the development of keyword search tools and question answering systems for the Web of Data. As a result of the interest in these systems, a large number of evaluation campaigns have been undertaken [100]. For example, the TREC conference started a question answering track to provide domain-independent evaluations over unstructured corpora [102]. Another series of challenges is the BioASQ series [96], which seeks to evaluate QA systems on biomedical data. In contrast to previous series, systems must use RDF data in addition to textual data. For the NLQ shared task, a dataset has been released that is answerable purely by DBpedia and SPARQL. Another series of challenges is the Question Answering over Linked Data (QALD) campaign [97–99]. It includes different types of question answering benchmarks that are (1) purely based on RDF data, (2) based on RDF and textual data, (3) statistical data, (4) data from multiple KBs or (5) based in the music-domain.

Alongside the main question answering task (QA), the authors of [100] define 5 sub tasks that are used for deep analysis of the performance of question answering systems.

- *QA*: The classical question answering task uses a plain question q_i as input and expects a set of answers A_i as output. Since the answering of questions presumes certain knowledge, most question answering datasets define a knowledge base K

---
[23]http://data.europa.eu/euodp/en/data/

Table 6. Summary of the question answering tasks.

Task	Input i_j	Output e_j	Background data B
QA	q	$A \subset K$	K
C2KB	q	$U \subset K$	K
P2KB	q	$P \subset K$	K
RE2KB	q	$\{(s,p,o)\,\vert\,s,p,o \in K \cup V\}$	K
AT	q	$\alpha \in \mathbb{A}$	$\mathbb{A}$
AIT2KB	q	$\mathbf{T} \subset \mathbb{T}$	$\mathbb{T}$

as background knowledge for the task. It should be noted that A_i might contain URIs, labels or a literal (like a boolean value). Matching URIs and labels can be a particularly difficult task for a question answering benchmarking framework.

- *C2KB*: This sub-task aims to identify all relevant resources for the given question. It is explained in more detail in Section 2.1.
- *P2KB*: This sub-task is similar to C2KB but focusses on the identification of properties P that are relevant for the given question.
- *RE2KB*: This sub-task evaluates triples that the question answering system extracted from the given search query. The expected answer comprises triples that are needed to build the SPARQL query for answering the question. Note that these triples can contain resources, literals or variables. Two triples are the same if their three elements—subject, predicate and object—are the same. If the triples comprise variables, they must be at the same position while the label of the variable is ignored.
- *AT*: This sub task identifies the answer type α of the given question. The answer types $\mathbb{A}$ are defined by the benchmark dataset. In [99], the authors define 5 different answer types: `date`, `number`, `string`, `boolean` and `resource`, where a resource can be a single URI or a set of URIs.
- *AIT2KB*: This sub-task aims to measure whether the benchmarked question answering system is able to identify the correct type(s) of the expected resources. If the answer does not contain any resources, the set of types $\mathbf{T}$ is expected to be empty. Similar to the ERec task in Section 2.1, a set of entity types $\mathbb{T}$ is used as background data for this task.

The tasks and their formal descriptions are summarized in Table 6. The key performance indicators used for the different tasks are the Macro and Micro variants of Precision, Recall and F1-measure. The efficiency of the systems is evaluated by measuring the runtime a system needs to answer a query [100].

Table 7 lists datasets based on DBpedia and their features. It is clear that most of the datasets originate from the QALD challenge and contain a small number of questions. This mainly results from the high costs of the manual curation. At the same time, evolving knowledge bases cause a similar problem of outdated datasets, as described in Section 2.1.4. Questions that have been answered on previous versions of a knowledge base might not be answerable on new versions and vice versa. Additionally, the URIs of the resources listed as answers might be different in new versions. A step towards automating the creation of questions is the LC-QuAD dataset [95]. The tool for creating this dataset uses SPARQL templates to generate SPARQL queries and their corresponding questions. However, human annotators are still necessary to check the questions and manually repair faulty questions.

Table 7. Example datasets for benchmarking question answering systems and their features [95, 100].

Dataset	#Questions	Knowledge Base
LC-QuAD	5000	DBpedia 2016-04
NLQ shared task 1	39	DBpedia 2015-04
QALD1_Test_dbpedia	50	DBpedia 3.6
QALD1_Train_dbpedia	50	DBpedia 3.6
QALD1_Test_musicbrainz	50	MusicBrainz (dump 2011)
QALD1_Train_musicbrainz	50	MusicBrainz (dump 2011)
QALD2_Test_dbpedia	99	DBpedia 3.7
QALD2_Train_dbpedia	100	DBpedia 3.7
QALD3_Test_dbpedia	99	DBpedia 3.8
QALD3_Train_dbpedia	100	DBpedia 3.8
QALD3_Test_esdbpedia	50	DBpedia 3.8 es
QALD3_Train_esdbpedia	50	DBpedia 3.8 es
QALD4_Test_Hybrid	10	DBpedia 3.9 + long abstracts
QALD4_Train_Hybrid	25	DBpedia 3.9 + long abstracts
QALD4_Test_Multilingual	50	DBpedia 3.9
QALD4_Train_Multilingual	200	DBpedia 3.9
QALD5_Test_Hybrid	10	DBpedia 2014 + long abstracts
QALD5_Train_Hybrid	40	DBpedia 2014 + long abstracts
QALD5_Test_Multilingual	49	DBpedia 2014
QALD5_Train_Multilingual	300	DBpedia 2014
QALD6_Train_Hybrid	49	DBpedia 2015-10 + long abstracts
QALD6_Train_Multilingual	333	DBpedia 2015-10

3. Benchmarking platforms

During recent years, several benchmarking platforms have been developed for a single, a subset or all steps of the LD lifecycle. In this Section, we give a brief overview of some of these platforms.

The BAT-framework [15] is a one of the first benchmarking frameworks developed for the extraction step of the LD lifecycle. Its aim is to facilitate the benchmarking of named entity recognition, named entity disambiguation and concept tagging approaches.

GERBIL [71, 101] is an effort of the knowledge extraction community to enhance the evaluation of knowledge extraction systems. Based on the central idea of the BAT framework (to create a single evaluation framework that eases the comparison and enables the repeatability of experiments), GERBIL goes beyond these concepts in several ways. By offering the benchmarking of knowledge extraction systems via web service API calls, as well as the addition of user defined web service URLs and datasets, GERBIL enables users to add their own systems and datasets in an easy way. Additionally, the GERBIL community runs an instance of the framework that can be used for free.[24] The success

---

[24]http://w3id.org/gerbil

of the GERBIL framework led to its deployment in other areas. GERBIL QA transfers the concept of a benchmarking platform based on web services into the area of question answering [100].[25] GERBIL KBC is developed to support the evaluation of knowledge base curation systems—mainly fact validation systems.[26]

Iguana [14] is a SPARQL benchmark execution framework [27] that tackles the problem of a fair, comparable and realistic SPARQL benchmark execution. It consists of a *core* that executes the benchmark queries against the benchmarked triplestores and the *result processor* that calculates metric results. To tackle the problem of a realistic benchmark, Iguana implements a highly configurable stress test, which consists of several user pools that in themselves comprise several threads, representing simulated users. Each user pool consists of either SPARQL queries or SPARQL updates that are executed by its threads against the benchmarked triplestore.

The SEALS platform [103] is one of the major results of the Semantic Evaluation At Large Scale (SEALS) project.[28] It offers the benchmarking of LD systems in different areas like ontology reasoning and ontology matching. It enables the support of different benchmarks by offering a Web Service Business Process Execution Language (WSBPEL) [4] interface. This interface can be used to write scripts covering the entire lifecycle of a single evaluation. The platform aims to support evaluation campaigns and has been used in several campaigns during recent years [28].

HOBBIT [69] is the first holistic Big Linked Data benchmarking platform. The platform is available as open-source project and as an online platform.[29] Compared to the previously mentioned benchmarking platforms, the HOBBIT platform offers benchmarks for all steps of the LD lifecycle that can be benchmarked automatically. For example, it contains all benchmarks the previously described GERBIL platforms implement. Additionally, it ensures the comparability of benchmark results by executing the benchmarked systems in a controlled environment using the Docker container technology.[30] The same technology supports the benchmarking of distributed systems and the execution of distributed benchmarks. The latter is necessary to be able to generate a sufficient amount of data to evaluate the scalability of the benchmarked system.

4. Conclusion

In this chapter, we presented an overview of benchmarking approaches for the different steps of the Linked Data lifecycle. These benchmarks are important for the usage and further development of KG-based systems since they enable a comparable evaluation of the system's performance. Hence, for the development of explainable artificial intelligence based on KGs these benchmarks will play a key role to identify the best KG-based systems for interacting with the KG. In future works, these general benchmarks might be adapted towards special requirements explainable artificial intelligence approaches might raise with respect to their underlying KG-based systems.

---

[25]http://w3id.org/gerbil/qa
[26]http://w3id.org/gerbil/kbc
[27]https://github.com/dice-group/iguana
[28]http://www.seals-project.eu/
[29]https://github.com/hobbit-project/platform, https://master.project-hobbit.eu
[30]https://docker.com

References

[1] F. Abel, Q. Gao, G.-J. Houben, and K. Tao. Semantic enrichment of twitter posts for user profile construction on the social web. In *Proc. of ESWC*, pages 375–389. Springer, 2011.

[2] J. Aguirre, K. Eckert, J. Euzenat, A. Ferrara, W. R. van Hage, L. Hollink, C. Meilicke, A. Nikolov, D. Ritze, F. Scharffe, et al. Results of the Ontology Alignment Evaluation Initiative 2012. In *Proceedings of the 7th International Workshop on Ontology Matching*, pages 73–115, 2012.

[3] G. Aluç, O. Hartig, M. T. Özsu, and K. Daudjee. Diversified stress testing of RDF data management systems. In *ISWC*, pages 197–212. 2014.

[4] A. Alves, A. Arkin, S. Askary, C. Barreto, B. Bloch, F. Curbera, M. Ford, Y. Goland, A. Guízar, N. Kartha, et al. Web Services Business Process Execution Language Version 2.0. Oasis standard, W3C, April 2007.

[5] S. Auer and J. Lehmann. Creating knowledge out of interlinked data. *Semant. web*, 1(1,2):97–104, Apr. 2010.

[6] S. Bail, S. Alkiviadous, B. Parsia, D. Workman, M. van Harmelen, R. S. Gonçalves, and C. Garilao. FishMark: A linked data application benchmark. In *Proceedings of the Joint Workshop on Scalable and High-Performance Semantic Web Systems*, volume 943, pages 1–15. CEUR-WS.org, 2012.

[7] C. Bizer and A. Schultz. The Berlin SPARQL benchmark. *Int. J. Semantic Web Inf. Syst.*, 5(2):1–24, 2009.

[8] C. Bizer and A. Schultz. The r2r framework: Publishing and discovering mappings on the web. *COLD*, 665, 2010.

[9] R. Blanco, G. Ottaviano, and E. Meij. Fast and space-efficient entity linking in queries. In *Proceedings of the eighth ACM international conference on Web search and data mining*, 2015.

[10] A. E. Cano, G. Rizzo, A. Varga, M. Rowe, M. Stankovic, and A.-s. Dadzie. Making sense of microposts: (#microposts2014) named entity extraction & linking challenge. In *Proceedings of the 4th Workshop on Making Sense of Microposts*, volume 1141, pages 54–60, 2014. co-located with the 23rd International World Wide Web Conference (WWW 2014) Edited by Matthew Rowe, Milan Stankovic, Aba-Sah Dadzie.

[11] A. E. Cano Basave, A. Varga, M. Rowe, M. Stankovic, and A.-S. Dadzie. Making sense of microposts (#msm2013) concept extraction challenge. In A. E. Cano, M. Rowe, M. Stankovic, and A.-S. Dadzie, editors, *#MSM2013 : concept extraction challenge at Making Sense of Microposts 2013*, pages 1–15. CEUR-WS.org, BRA, 2013. Cano Basave, AE, Varga, A, Rowe, M, Stankovic, M & Dadzie, A-S: Making sense of microposts (#MSM2013) concept extraction challenge. Proc. of the workshop on 'Making Sense of Microposts' co-located with the 22nd international World Wide Web conference (WWW'13), Rio de Janeiro, Brazil, 13 May, ceur-ws.org/Vol-1019/msm2013-challenge-report.pdf.

[12] D. Carmel, M.-W. Chang, E. Gabrilovich, B.-J. P. Hsu, and K. Wang. Erd'14: Entity recognition and disambiguation challenge. In *37th international ACM SIGIR conference on Research & development in information retrieval*, 2014.

[13] S. Choudhury, J. G. Breslin, and A. Passant. *Enrichment and ranking of the youtube tag space and integration with the linked data cloud.* Springer, 2009.

[14] F. Conrads, J. Lehmann, M. Saleem, M. Morsey, and A.-C. N. Ngomo. Iguana: A generic framework for benchmarking the read-write performance of triple stores. In *Proceedings of the 16th International Semantic Web Conference (ISWC)*. Springer, 2017.

[15] M. Cornolti, P. Ferragina, and M. Ciaramita. A framework for benchmarking entity-annotation systems. In *22nd World Wide Web Conference*, 2013.

[16] M. Cornolti, P. Ferragina, M. Ciaramita, S. Rüd, and H. Schütze. A piggyback system for joint entity mention detection and linking in web queries. In *Proceedings of the 25th International Conference on World Wide Web*, pages 567–578, Republic and Canton of Geneva, Switzerland, 2016. International World Wide Web Conferences Steering Committee.

[17] S. Cucerzan. Large-scale named entity disambiguation based on Wikipedia data. In *Proceedings of the 2007 Joint Conference on Empirical Methods in Natural Language Processing and Computational Natural Language Learning (EMNLP-CoNLL)*, pages 708–716, Prague, Czech Republic, June 2007. Association for Computational Linguistics.

[18] G. Demartini, I. Enchev, M. Wylot, J. Gapany, and P. Cudré-Mauroux. BowlognaBench - benchmarking RDF analytics. In *Data-Driven Process Discovery and Analysis SIMPDA*, volume 116, pages 82–102. Springer, 2011.

[19]   L. Derczynski, D. Maynard, G. Rizzo, M. van Erp, G. Gorrell, R. Troncy, J. Petrak, and K. Bontcheva.
       Analysis of named entity recognition and linking for tweets. *Information Processing and Management*,
       51(2):32–49, 2015.

[20]   G. R. Doddington, A. Mitchell, M. A. Przybocki, L. A. Ramshaw, S. Strassel, and R. M. Weischedel.
       The automatic content extraction (ACE) program-tasks, data, and evaluation. In *LREC*, 2004.

[21]   S. Duan, A. Kementsietsidis, S. Kavitha, and O. Udrea. Apples and oranges: A comparison of RDF
       benchmarks and real RDF datasets. In *SIGMOD*, pages 145–156. ACM, 2011.

[22]   P. Edmonds and S. Cotton. Senseval-2: Overview. In *The Proceedings of the Second International
       Workshop on Evaluating Word Sense Disambiguation Systems*, pages 1–5, Stroudsburg, PA, USA, 2001.
       Association for Computational Linguistics.

[23]   O. Erling, A. Averbuch, J. Larriba-Pey, H. Chafi, A. Gubichev, A. Prat-Pérez, M. Pham, and P. A. Boncz.
       The LDBC Social Network Benchmark: Interactive workload. In *SIGMOD*, pages 619–630. ACM,
       2015.

[24]   J. Euzenat, A. Ferrara, C. Meilicke, J. Pane, F. Scharffe, P. Shvaiko, H. Stuckenschmidt, O. Sváb-
       Zamazal, V. Svátek, and C. T. dos Santos. Results of the Ontology Alignment Evaluation Initiative 2010.
       In *Proceedings of the 5th International Workshop on Ontology Matching (OM-2010)*, pages 85–117,
       2010.

[25]   J. Euzenat, A. Ferrara, W. R. van Hage, L. Hollink, C. Meilicke, A. Nikolov, D. Ritze, F. Scharffe,
       P. Shvaiko, H. Stuckenschmidt, et al. Results of the Ontology Alignment Evaluation Initiative 2011. In
       Proceedings of the 6th International Workshop on Ontology Matching, pages 85–113, 2011.

[26]   J. D. Fernández, J. Umbrich, A. Polleres, and M. Knuth. Evaluating query and storage strategies for
       RDF archives. *Semantic Web*, 10:247–291, 2019.

[27]   T. Finin, W. Murnane, A. Karandikar, N. Keller, J. Martineau, and M. Dredze. Annotating named entities
       in twitter data with crowdsourcing. In *Proceedings of the NAACL HLT 2010 Workshop on Creating
       Speech and Language Data with Amazon's Mechanical Turk*, pages 80–88, Stroudsburg, PA, USA, 2010.
       Association for Computational Linguistics.

[28]   R. García-Castro and S. N. Wrigley. SEALS Methodology for Evaluation Campaigns. Technical report,
       Seventh Framework Programme, 2011.

[29]   D. Gerber, D. Esteves, J. Lehmann, L. Bühmann, R. Usbeck, A.-C. N. Ngomo, and R. Speck. Defacto—
       temporal and multilingual deep fact validation. *Journal of Web Semantics*, 35:85–101, 2015. Machine
       Learning and Data Mining for the Semantic Web (MLDMSW).

[30]   O. Görlitz, M. Thimm, and S. Staab. SPLODGE: systematic generation of SPARQL benchmark queries
       for linked open data. In *ISWC*, volume 7649, pages 116–132. Springer, 2012.

[31]   B. C. Grau, Z. Dragisic, K. Eckert, J. Euzenat, A. Ferrara, R. Granada, V. Ivanova, E. Jiménez-Ruiz, A. O.
       Kempf, P. Lambrix, et al. Results of the Ontology Alignment Evaluation Initiative 2013. In *Proceedings
       of the 8th International Workshop on Ontology Matching co-located with the 12th International Semantic
       Web Conference*, pages 61–100, 2013.

[32]   J. Gray and C. Levine. Thousands of DebitCredit Transactions-Per-Second: Easy and Inexpensive.
       Technical report, Microsoft Research, 2005.

[33]   Y. Guo, Z. Pan, and J. Heflin. LUBM: a benchmark for OWL knowledge base systems. *J. Web Sem.*,
       3(2-3):158–182, 2005.

[34]   S. Hasan, E. Curry, M. Banduk, and S. O'Riain. Toward situation awareness for the semantic sensor
       web: Complex event processing with dynamic linked data enrichment. *Semantic Sensor Networks*,
       page 60, 2011.

[35]   J. Hoffart, Y. Altun, and G. Weikum. Discovering emerging entities with ambiguous names. In
       Proceedings of the 23rd International Conference on World Wide Web, pages 385–396, New York, NY,
       USA, 2014. ACM.

[36]   J. Hoffart, M. A. Yosef, I. Bordino, H. Fürstenau, M. Pinkal, M. Spaniol, B. Taneva, S. Thater, and
       G. Weikum. Robust disambiguation of named entities in text. In *Proceedings of the 2011 Conference on
       Empirical Methods in Natural Language Processing*, pages 782–792, Edinburgh, Scotland, UK., July
       2011. Association for Computational Linguistics.

[37]   R. Isele, A. Jentzsch, and C. Bizer. Efficient multidimensional blocking for link discovery without
       losing recall. In *Proceedings of the 14th International Workshop on the Web and Databases 2011*, 2011.

[38]   K. Jha, M. Röder, and A.-C. Ngonga Ngomo. All That Glitters is not Gold – Rule-Based Curation of
       Reference Datasets for Named Entity Recognition and Entity Linking. In *The Semantic Web. Latest
       Advances and New Domains: 14th International Conference, ESWC 2017, Proceedings*. Springer

International Publishing, 2017.

[39] A. Kilgarriff. Senseval: An exercise in evaluating word sense disambiguation programs. *1st LREC*, 1998.

[40] V. Kotsev, N. Minadakis, V. Papakonstantinou, O. Erling, I. Fundulaki, and A. Kiryakov. Benchmarking RDF Query Engines: The LDBC Semantic Publishing Benchmark. In *BLINK@ISWC*, 2016.

[41] S. Kulkarni, A. Singh, G. Ramakrishnan, and S. Chakrabarti. Collective annotation of wikipedia entities in web text. In *Proceedings of the 15th ACM SIGKDD International Conference on Knowledge Discovery and Data Mining*, pages 457–466, New York, NY, USA, 2009. Association for Computing Machinery.

[42] J. Lehmann, R. Isele, M. Jakob, A. Jentzsch, D. Kontokostas, P. N. Mendes, S. Hellmann, M. Morsey, P. van Kleef, S. Auer, et al. DBpedia - a large-scale, multilingual knowledge base extracted from wikipedia. *Semantic Web Journal*, 6(2):167–195, 2015.

[43] P. McNamee. Overview of the TAC 2009 knowledge base population track, 2009.

[44] M. Meimaris and G. Papastefanatos. The EvoGen Benchmark Suite for Evolving RDF Data. In *MEPDaW/LDQ@ ESWC*, pages 20–35, 2016.

[45] R. Mihalcea, T. Chklovski, and A. Kilgarriff. The Senseval-3 English Lexical Sample Task. In *Proceedings of Senseval-3: Third International Workshop on the Evaluation of Systems for the Semantic Analysis of Text*. Association for Computational Linguistics (ACL), 2004.

[46] I. Millard, H. Glaser, M. Salvadores, and N. Shadbolt. Consuming multiple linked data sources: Challenges and experiences. In *COLD Workshop*, 2010.

[47] D. Milne and I. H. Witten. Learning to link with wikipedia. In *Proceedings of the 17th ACM Conference on Information and Knowledge Management*, pages 509–518, New York, NY, USA, 2008. Association for Computing Machinery.

[48] M. Morsey, J. Lehmann, S. Auer, and A. N. Ngomo. DBpedia SPARQL benchmark - performance assessment with real queries on real data. In *ISWC*, volume 7031, pages 454–469. Springer, 2011.

[49] M. Nentwig, M. Hartung, A. N. Ngomo, and E. Rahm. A survey of current link discovery frameworks. *Semantic Web*, 8(3):419–436, 2017.

[50] A.-C. N. Ngomo, S. Auer, J. Lehmann, and A. Zaveri. *Introduction to Linked Data and Its Lifecycle on the Web*, pages 1–99. Springer International Publishing, Cham, 2014.

[51] A. N. Ngomo. Link discovery with guaranteed reduction ratio in affine spaces with minkowski measures. In *The Semantic Web - ISWC 2012 - 11th International Semantic Web Conference, Boston, MA, USA, November 11-15, 2012, Proceedings, Part I*, pages 378–393, 2012.

[52] A. N. Ngomo. On link discovery using a hybrid approach. *J. Data Semantics*, 1(4):203–217, 2012.

[53] A. N. Ngomo. ORCHID - reduction-ratio-optimal computation of geo-spatial distances for link discovery. In *The Semantic Web - ISWC 2013 - 12th International Semantic Web Conference, Sydney, NSW, Australia, October 21-25, 2013, Proceedings, Part I*, pages 395–410, 2013.

[54] A. N. Ngomo and S. Auer. LIMES - A time-efficient approach for large-scale link discovery on the web of data. In *IJCAI 2011, Proceedings of the 22nd International Joint Conference on Artificial Intelligence*, pages 2312–2317, 2011.

[55] A. N. Ngomo, J. Lehmann, S. Auer, and K. Höffner. RAVEN - active learning of link specifications. In *Proceedings of the 6th International Workshop on Ontology Matching*, pages 25–36, 2011.

[56] A. N. Ngomo and K. Lyko. EAGLE: efficient active learning of link specifications using genetic programming. In *The Semantic Web: Research and Applications - 9th Extended Semantic Web Conference, ESWC 2012, Heraklion, Crete, Greece, May 27-31, 2012. Proceedings*, pages 149–163, 2012.

[57] A. N. Ngomo and K. Lyko. Unsupervised learning of link specifications: deterministic vs. non-deterministic. In *Proceedings of the 8th International Workshop on Ontology Matching co-located with the 12th International Semantic Web Conference*, pages 25–36, 2013.

[58] A. N. Ngomo, M. Röder, D. Moussallem, R. Usbeck, and R. Speck. BENGAL: an automatic benchmark generator for entity recognition and linking. In E. Krahmer, A. Gatt, and M. Goudbeek, editors, *Proceedings of the 11th International Conference on Natural Language Generation*, pages 339–349. Association for Computational Linguistics, 2018.

[59] A. Nikolov, V. S. Uren, and E. Motta. Knofuss: a comprehensive architecture for knowledge fusion. In *Proceedings of the 4th International Conference on Knowledge Capture*, pages 185–186, 2007.

[60] A.-G. Nuzzolese, A. Gentile, V. Presutti, A. Gangemi, D. Garigliotti, and R. Navigli. Open knowledge extraction challenge. In *Semantic Web Evaluation Challenges*, volume 548, pages 3–15. Springer International Publishing, 2015.

[61]   A. G. Nuzzolese, A. L. Gentile, V. Presutti, A. Gangemi, R. Meusel, and H. Paulheim. The second open
        knowledge extraction challenge. In H. Sack, S. Dietze, A. Tordai, and C. Lange, editors, *Semantic Web
        Challenges*, pages 3–16, Cham, 2016. Springer International Publishing.
[62]   V. Papakonstantinou, G. Flouris, I. Fundulaki, K. Stefanidis, and G. Roussakis. Versioning for Linked
        Data: Archiving Systems and Benchmarks. In *BLINK@ISWC*, 2016.
[63]   V. Papakonstantinou, G. Flouris, I. Fundulaki, K. Stefanidis, and Y. Roussakis. Spbv: Benchmarking
        linked data archiving systems. In *BLINK/NLIWoD3@ISWC*, 2017.
[64]   S. Qiao and Z. M. Özsoyoglu. RBench: Application-specific RDF benchmarking. In *SIGMOD*, pages
        1825–1838. ACM, 2015.
[65]   L. Ratinov, D. Roth, D. Downey, and M. Anderson. Local and global algorithms for disambiguation to
        wikipedia. In *ACL*, 2011.
[66]   A. Ritter, S. Clark, Mausam, and O. Etzioni. Named entity recognition in tweets: An experimental study.
        In *EMNLP*, 2011.
[67]   G. Rizzo, A. Cano Basave, B. Pereira, and A. VARGA. Making sense of microposts (#microposts2015)
        named entity recognition & linking challenge. 05 2015.
[68]   G. Rizzo, M. van Erp, J. Plu, and R. Troncy. Making Sense of Microposts (#Microposts2016) Named
        Entity rEcognition and Linking (NEEL) Challenge. pages 50–59, 2016.
[69]   M. Röder, D. Kuchelev, and A.-C. N. Ngomo. Hobbit: A platform for benchmarking big linked data.
        Data Science, PrePress(PrePress):1–21, 2019.
[70]   M. Röder, R. Usbeck, S. Hellmann, D. Gerber, and A. Both. N3 - a collection of datasets for named
        entity recognition and disambiguation in the nlp interchange format. In *9th LREC*, 2014.
[71]   M. Röder, R. Usbeck, and A. N. Ngomo. GERBIL - benchmarking named entity recognition and linking
        consistently. *Semantic Web*, 9(5):605–625, 2018.
[72]   M. Saleem, M. I. Ali, A. Hogan, Q. Mehmood, and A. N. Ngomo. LSQ: the linked SPARQL queries
        dataset. In *ISWC*, volume 9367, pages 261–269. Springer, 2015.
[73]   M. Saleem, A. Hasnain, and A. N. Ngomo. LargeRDFBench: A billion triples benchmark for SPARQL
        endpoint federation. *J. Web Sem.*, 48:85–125, 2018.
[74]   M. Saleem, Q. Mehmood, and A.-C. Ngonga Ngomo. FEASIBLE: a Feature-based SPARQL Benchmark
        Generation Framework. In *International Semantic Web Conference (ISWC)*, 2015.
[75]   M. Saleem, S. S. Padmanabhuni, A. N. Ngomo, J. S. Almeida, S. Decker, and H. F. Deus. Linked cancer
        genome atlas database. In *I-SEMANTICS 2013 - 9th International Conference on Semantic Systems,
        ISEM '13, Graz, Austria, September 4-6, 2013*, pages 129–134, 2013.
[76]   M. Saleem, C. Stadler, Q. Mehmood, J. Lehmann, and A. N. Ngomo. SQCFramework: SPARQL query
        containment benchmark generation framework. In *K-CAP*, pages 28:1–28:8, 2017.
[77]   M. Saleem, G. Szárnyas, F. Conrads, S. A. C. Bukhari, Q. Mehmood, and A.-C. Ngonga Ngomo. How
        representative is a sparql benchmark? an analysis of rdf triplestore benchmarks? In *The World Wide
        Web Conference*, pages 1623–1633. ACM, 2019.
[78]   M. Schmidt, T. Hornung, M. Meier, C. Pinkel, and G. Lausen. SP2Bench: A SPARQL performance
        benchmark. In *Semantic Web Information Management - A Model-Based Perspective*, pages 371–393.
        2009.
[79]   A. Schultz, A. Matteini, R. Isele, C. Bizer, and C. Becker. LDIF - linked data integration framework. In
        COLD, 2011.
[80]   M. Sherif, A.-C. Ngonga Ngomo, and J. Lehmann. Automating RDF dataset transformation and
        enrichment. In *12th Extended Semantic Web Conference, Portorož, Slovenia, 31st May - 4th June 2015*.
        Springer, 2015.
[81]   M. Sherif, A.-C. Ngonga Ngomo, and J. Lehmann. WOMBAT - A Generalization Approach for
        Automatic Link Discovery. In *14th Extended Semantic Web Conference, Portorož, Slovenia, 28th May -
        1st June 2017*. Springer, 2017.
[82]   B. Shi and T. Weninger. Discriminative predicate path mining for fact checking in knowledge graphs.
        Knowledge-Based Systems, 104:123–133, 2016.
[83]   P. Shiralkar, A. Flammini, F. Menczer, and G. L. Ciampaglia. Finding streams in knowledge graphs to
        support fact checking. In *2017 IEEE International Conference on Data Mining (ICDM)*, pages 859–864.
        IEEE, 2017.
[84]   T. Soru and A. N. Ngomo. Rapid execution of weighted edit distances. In *Proceedings of the 8th
        International Workshop on Ontology Matching co-located with the 12th International Semantic Web
        Conference*, pages 1–12, 2013.

[85] R. Speck and A.-C. Ngomo Ngonga. On extracting relations using distributional semantics and a tree generalization. In *Knowledge Engineering and Knowledge Management*. Springer International Publishing, 2018.

[86] R. Speck, M. Röder, F. Conrads, H. Rebba, C. C. Romiyo, G. Salakki, R. Suryawanshi, D. Ahmed, N. Srivastava, M. Mahajan, et al. Open knowledge extraction challenge 2018. In D. Buscaldi, A. Gangemi, and D. Reforgiato Recupero, editors, *Semantic Web Challenges*, pages 39–51, Cham, 2018. Springer International Publishing.

[87] R. Speck, M. Röder, S. Oramas, L. Espinosa-Anke, and A.-C. Ngonga Ngomo. Open knowledge extraction challenge 2017. In M. Dragoni, M. Solanki, and E. Blomqvist, editors, *Semantic Web Challenges*, pages 35–48, Cham, 2017. Springer International Publishing.

[88] C. Stadler, J. Lehmann, K. Höffner, and S. Auer. Linkedgeodata: A core for a web of spatial open data. *Semantic Web*, 3(4):333–354, 2012.

[89] B. M. Sundheim. Tipster/MUC-5: Information extraction system evaluation. In *Proceedings of the 5th Conference on Message Understanding*, 1993.

[90] Z. H. Syed, M. Röder, and A.-C. N. Ngomo. Unsupervised discovery of corroborative paths for fact validation. In C. Ghidini, O. Hartig, M. Maleshkova, V. Svátek, I. Cruz, A. Hogan, J. Song, M. Lefrançois, and F. Gandon, editors, *The Semantic Web – ISWC 2019*, pages 630–646, Cham, 2019. Springer International Publishing.

[91] Z. H. Syed, M. Röder, and A.-C. Ngonga Ngomo. Factcheck: Validating rdf triples using textual evidence. In *Proceedings of the 27th ACM International Conference on Information and Knowledge Management*, pages 1599–1602, New York, NY, USA, 2018. Association for Computing Machinery.

[92] G. Szárnyas, B. Izsó, I. Ráth, and D. Varró. The Train Benchmark: Cross-technology performance evaluation of continuous model queries. *Softw. Syst. Model.*, 17(4):1365–1393, 2018.

[93] G. Szárnyas, A. Prat-Pérez, A. Averbuch, J. Marton, M. Paradies, M. Kaufmann, O. Erling, P. A. Boncz, V. Haprian, and J. B. Antal. An early look at the LDBC social network benchmark's business intelligence workload. In *Proceedings of the 1st ACM SIGMOD Joint International Workshop on Graph Data Management Experiences & Systems (GRADES) and Network Data Analytics (NDA)*, pages 9:1–9:11, 2018.

[94] E. F. Tjong Kim Sang and F. De Meulder. Introduction to the CoNLL-2003 Shared Task: Language-Independent Named Entity Recognition. In *Proceedings of CoNLL-2003*, 2003.

[95] P. Trivedi, G. Maheshwari, M. Dubey, and J. Lehmann. Lc-quad: A corpus for complex question answering over knowledge graphs. In C. d'Amato, M. Fernandez, V. Tamma, F. Lecue, P. Cudré-Mauroux, J. Sequeda, C. Lange, and J. Heflin, editors, *The Semantic Web – ISWC 2017*, pages 210–218, Cham, 2017. Springer International Publishing.

[96] G. Tsatsaronis, G. Balikas, P. Malakasiotis, I. Partalas, M. Zschunke, M. R. Alvers, D. Weissenborn, A. Krithara, S. Petridis, D. Polychronopoulos, et al. An overview of the BIOASQ large-scale biomedical semantic indexing and question answering competition. *BMC Bioinformatics*, 16:138, 2015.

[97] C. Unger, C. Forascu, V. Lopez, A. N. Ngomo, E. Cabrio, P. Cimiano, and S. Walter. Question answering over linked data (QALD-4). In *CLEF*, pages 1172–1180, 2014.

[98] C. Unger, C. Forascu, V. Lopez, A. N. Ngomo, E. Cabrio, P. Cimiano, and S. Walter. Question answering over linked data (QALD-5). In *CLEF*, 2015.

[99] C. Unger, A.-C. N. Ngomo, and E. Cabrio. *6th Open Challenge on Question Answering over Linked Data (QALD-6)*, pages 171–177. Springer International Publishing, Cham, 2016.

[100] R. Usbeck, M. Röder, M. Hoffmann, F. Conrads, J. Huthmann, A. Ngonga Ngomo, C. Demmler, and C. Unger. Benchmarking Question Answering Systems. *Semantic Web*, 10(2):293–304, 2019.

[101] R. Usbeck, M. Röder, A.-C. Ngonga Ngomo, C. Baron, A. Both, M. Brümmer, D. Ceccarelli, M. Cornolti, D. Cherix, B. Eickmann, et al. GERBIL – general entity annotation benchmark framework. In *24th WWW conference*, 2015.

[102] E. M. Voorhees et al. The trec-8 question answering track report. In *Trec*, volume 99, pages 77–82, 1999.

[103] S. N. Wrigley, R. García-Castro, and L. Nixon. Semantic evaluation at large scale (seals). In *Proceedings of the 21st International Conference on World Wide Web*, pages 299–302, New York, NY, USA, 2012. Association for Computing Machinery.

[104] H. Wu, T. Fujiwara, Y. Yamamoto, J. T. Bolleman, and A. Yamaguchi. BioBenchmark Toyama 2012: An evaluation of the performance of triple stores on biological data. *J. Biomedical Semantics*, 5:32, 2014.

Part 2

Applications

Knowledge Graphs for eXplainable Artificial Intelligence: Foundations, Applications and Challenges 101
I. Tiddi et al. (Eds.)
IOS Press, 2020
doi:10.3233/SSW200014

Knowledge-Aware Interpretable Recommender Systems

Vito Walter ANELLI [a], Vito BELLINI [a], Tommaso DI NOIA [a], and
Eugenio DI SCIASCIO [a]

[a] *Politecnico di Bari, Bari, Italy*

Abstract. Recommender systems are everywhere, from e-commerce to streaming platforms. They help users lost in the maze of available information, items and services to find their way. Among them, over the years, approaches based on machine learning techniques have shown particularly good performance for top-N recommendations engines. Unfortunately, they mostly behave as black-boxes and, even when they embed some form of description about the items to recommend, after the training phase they move such descriptions in a latent space thus loosing the actual explicit semantics of recommended items. As a consequence, the system designers struggle at providing satisfying explanations to the recommendation list provided to the end user. In this chapter, we describe two approaches to recommendation which make use of the semantics encoded in a knowledge graph to train interpretable models which keep the original semantics of the items description thus providing a powerful tool to automatically compute explainable results. The two methods relies on two completely different machine learning algorithms, namely, factorization machines and autoencoder neural networks. We also show how to measure the interpretability of the model through the introduction of two metrics: semantic accuracy and robustness.

Keywords. Recommender Systems, Knowledge Graphs, DBpedia, Interpretablity, Explanations, eXplainable AI

1. Introduction

Nowadays, it is well recognized that model-based approaches to recommendation can recommend items with a very high level of accuracy. Unfortunately, even when the model embeds content-based information, if we move to a latent space we miss references to the actual semantics of recommended items and, consequently, this makes non-trivial the interpretation of a recommendation process.

On the other side, transparency and interpretability of predictive models are gaining momentum since they have been identified as a key element in the next generation of recommendation algorithms. Interpretability may increase user awareness in the decision-making process and lead to fast (efficiency), conscious and right (effectiveness) decisions. When equipped with interpretability of recommendation results, a system ceases to be just a black-box [1,2,3] and users are more willing to extensively exploit the predictions [4,5]. Indeed, transparency increases their trust [6] (also exploiting specific semantic structures [7]), and satisfaction in using the system. Among interpretable models for Recommender Systems (RS), we may distinguish between those based on Content-based

(CB) approaches and those based on Collaborative filtering (CF) ones. CB algorithms provide recommendations by exploiting the available content and matching it with a user profile [8,9]. The use of content features makes easier to develop an interpretable model even though attention has to be paid since a CB approach *"lacks serendipity and requires extensive manual efforts to match the user interests to content profiles"* [10]. On the other hand, the interpretation of CF results will inevitably reflect the approach adopted by the algorithm. For instance, an item-based and a user-based recommendation could be interpreted, respectively, as *"other users who have experienced A have experienced B"* or *"similar users have experienced B"*. Unfortunately, things change when we adopt more powerful and accurate Deep Learning [11] or model-based algorithms and techniques for the computation of a recommendation list. Such approaches project items and users in a new vector space of latent features [12] thus making the final result not directly interpretable. In the last years, many approaches have been proposed that take advantage of side information in recommendation algorithms to enhance the performance of latent factor models. Side information can refer to items as well as users [13] and can be either structured [14,15] or semi-structured [16,17,18]. Interestingly, in [10] the authors argue about a new generation of knowledge-aware recommendation engines able to exploit information encoded in knowledge graphs (KG) to produce meaningful recommendations: *"For example, with knowledge graph about movies, actors, and directors, the system can explain to the user a movie is recommended because he has watched many movies starred by an actor"*.

In this chapter we show how to properly inject semantics-aware data coming from an RDF knowledge graph[1] in model-based recommendation algorithms in order to go beyond a black-box approach and transform them in interpretable models. In the next section we will focus on factorization machines [19] while in Section 3 we will analyze a deep learning model based on autoencoder neural networks [20]. During the evaluation of the two approaches in terms of precision and interpretability of the final model, we refer to different dimensions of an RDF dataset. In particular, we know that an RDF knowledge graph encodes different types of information:

- **Factual.** This refers to statements that describe attributes of an entity such as *Star Wars: Episode IV – A New Hope was directed by the George Lucas* or *Jumanji is located in British Columbia*;
- **Categorical.** It is mainly used to state something about the subject of an entity. In this direction, the categories of Wikipedia pages are an excellent example. Categories can be used to cluster entities and are often organized hierarchically thus making possible to define them in a more generic or specific way;
- **Ontological.** This is a more restrictive and formal way to classify entities via a hierarchical structure of classes. Differently from categories, sub-classes and super-classes are connected through IS-A (transitive) relations.

We will show how the selection of these three classes of knowledge —and their combinations— may affect the final performance of a knowledge-aware recommender system.

The chapter is structured as follows: in the next section we introduce and discuss a model based on knowledge-aware factorization machines for recommender systems

---

[1]We mainly refer to DBpedia.

while in Section 3 we describe a deep learning model based on autoencoders that embeds a knowledge-graph in its structure. Section 4 is devoted to a brief description of related literature. Conclusion and future work close the chapter.

2. Knowledge-aware Hybrid Factorization Machines for Top-N Recommendation

As shown in [21], factorization models have proven their strength in recommendation scenarios. Main advantages of factorization models are their effectiveness in dealing with very sparse settings and their prediction accuracy thanks to the subtle modeling of user-item interactions. Several factorization models have been proposed in the literature and, among them, factorization machines generalize most of the factorization models unifying this class of algorithms. Here we report the definition related to a second order features-interaction factorization model for a recommendation problem involving only implicit ratings. Nevertheless, the model can be easily extended to a more expressive representation by taking into account, e.g., demographic and social information [22], multi-criteria [23], and even relations between contexts [24]. We build for each user $u \in U$ and each item $i \in I$ a binary vector $\mathbf{x}^{\mathbf{ui}} \in \mathbb{R}^{1 \times n}$, with $n = |U| + |I|$, representing the interaction between u and i in the original user-item rating matrix. In this modeling, $\mathbf{x}^{\mathbf{ui}}$ contains only two 1 values corresponding to u and i while all the other values are set to 0 (see Fig. 1). $\mathbf{X} \in \mathbb{R}^{n \times m}$ is a matrix that contains as rows all the possible $\mathbf{x}^{\mathbf{ui}}$ we can build starting from the original user-item rating matrix as shown in Fig. 1.

x^1	1	0	0	0	...	1	0	0	0	0	...
x^2	1	0	0	0	...	0	1	0	0	0	...
x^3	1	0	0	0	...	0	0	1	0	0	...
x^4	0	1	0	0	...	0	0	1	0	0	...
x^5	0	1	0	0	...	0	0	0	1	0	...
x^6	0	0	1	0	...	1	0	0	0	0	...
x^7	0	0	1	0	...	0	0	1	0	0	...
	U_1	U_2	U_3	U_4	...	I_1	I_2	I_3	I_4	I_5	...
		User					Item				

Figure 1. A visual representation of $\mathbf{X}$ for sparse real valued vectors $\mathbf{x}^{\mathbf{ui}}$.

The FM score for each vector $\mathbf{x}$ is computed as follows:

$$\hat{y}(\mathbf{x}^{\mathbf{ui}}) = w_0 + \sum_{j=1}^{n} w_j \cdot x_j + \sum_{j=1}^{n} \sum_{p=j+1}^{n} x_j \cdot x_p \cdot \sum_{f=1}^{k} v_{(j,f)} \cdot v_{(p,f)} \qquad (1)$$

where the parameters the model learns are: w_0 representing the global bias; w_j giving the importance to every single x_j; the pair $v_{(j,f)}$ and $v_{(p,f)}$ in $\sum_{f=1}^{k} v_{(j,f)} \cdot v_{(p,f)}$ measuring the strength of the interaction between each pair of variables: x_j and x_p. The latent factors number is denoted as k and its value is usually chosen at design time when implementing the FM.

If we want to make a factorization machine interpretable, we need a way to give an explicit semantics to latent factors. In this respect, knowledge graphs may result very useful since they provide information about several and different domains [25]. In a knowledge graph, each triple represents the connection $\sigma \xrightarrow{\rho} \omega$ between two nodes, named *subject* (σ) and *object* (ω), through the *relation* (*predicate*) ρ. Following [26], we bind the set of features retrieved from a knowledge graph to the latent factors of a Factorization Machine model. Since we are tackling a top-N recommendation problem, we use a Bayesian Personalized Ranking (BPR) criterion [27] to train our model. In [28], authors originally proposed to encode a Linked Data knowledge graph within a vector space model with the aim of developing a CB recommender system. Given $I = \{i_1, i_2, \ldots, i_N\}$ as the set of items in a catalog and their associated triples $\langle i, \rho, \omega \rangle$ in a knowledge graph KG, we build the set of all possible features as $F = \{\langle \rho, \omega \rangle \mid \langle i, \rho, \omega \rangle \in \text{KG with } i \in I\}$. We can then represent each item as a vector of weights $\mathbf{i} = [v_{(i,1)}, \ldots, v_{(i,\langle \rho, \omega \rangle)}, \ldots, v_{(i,|F|)}]$, where $v_{(i,\langle \rho, \omega \rangle)}$ is calculated as the normalized TF-IDF value for $\langle \rho, \omega \rangle$ as follows:

$$v_{(i,\langle \rho, \omega \rangle)} = \underbrace{\frac{|\{\langle \rho, \omega \rangle \mid \langle i, \rho, \omega \rangle \in \text{KG}\}|}{\sqrt{\sum_{\langle \rho, \omega \rangle \in F} |\{\langle \rho, \omega \rangle \mid \langle i, \rho, \omega \rangle \in \text{KG}\}|^2}}}_{TF^{\text{KG}}} \cdot \log \underbrace{\frac{|I|}{|\{j \mid \langle j, \rho, \omega \rangle \in \text{KG and } j \in I\}|}}_{IDF^{\text{KG}}}$$

(2)

Since the numerator of TF^{KG} can only take values 0 or 1 and each feature under the root in the denominator has value 0 or 1, then $v_{(i,\langle \rho, \omega \rangle)}$ is zero if $\langle \rho, \omega \rangle \notin \text{KG}$.

$$v_{(i,\langle \rho, \omega \rangle)} = \frac{\log |I| - \log |\langle j, \rho, \omega \rangle \cap \text{KG} | j \in I|}{\sqrt{\sum_{\langle \rho, \omega \rangle \in F} |\{\langle \rho, \omega \rangle \mid \langle i, \rho, \omega \rangle \in \text{KG}\}|}}$$

(3)

Analogously, when we have a set U of users, we may represent them using the features that describe the items they enjoyed in the past. In the following, when no confusion arises, we use f to denote a feature $\langle \rho, \omega \rangle \in F$. Given a user u, if we denote with I^u the set of the items enjoyed by u, we may introduce the vector $\mathbf{u} = [v_{(u,1)}, \ldots, v_{(u,f)} \ldots, v_{(u,|F|)}]$, where $v_{(u,f)}$ is:

$$v_{(u,f)} = \frac{\sum_{i \in I^u} v_{(i,f)}}{|\{i \mid i \in I^u \text{ and } v_{(i,f)} \neq 0\}|}$$

Given the vectors $\mathbf{u}_j$, with $j \in [1 \ldots |U|]$, and $\mathbf{i}_p$, with $p \in [1 \ldots |I|]$, we build the matrix $\mathbf{V} \in \mathbb{R}^{n \times |F|}$ (see Fig. 2) where the first $|U|$ rows have a one-to-one mapping with $\mathbf{u}_j$ while the last ones correspond to $\mathbf{i}_p$. If we go back to Equation (1) we may see that, for each $\mathbf{x}$, the term $\sum_{j=1}^{n} \sum_{p=j+1}^{n} x_j \cdot x_{j'} \cdot \sum_{f=1}^{k} v_{(j,f)} \cdot v_{(p,f)}$ is not zero only once, i.e., when both x_j and x_p are equal to 1. In the matrix depicted in Fig. 1, this happens when there is an interaction between a user and an item. Moreover, the summation $\sum_{f=1}^{k} v_{(j,f)} \cdot v_{(p,f)}$ represents the dot product between two vectors: $\mathbf{v}_j$ and $\mathbf{v}_p$ with a size equal to k. Hence, $\mathbf{v}_j$ represents a latent representation of a user, $\mathbf{v}_p$ that of an item within the same latent space, and their interaction is evaluated through their dot product. In order to inject the knowledge coming from KG into a factorization machine, we set $k = |F|$ in Equation (1). In other words, we impose the number of latent factors equal to the number of features that describe all the items in the catalog. We want to stress here that our aim is not to

	_ dbc:Space_adventure_films	_ dbc:Films_set_in_the_future	_ dbc:American_science_fiction_films	_ dbc:1980s_science_fiction_action_films	_ dbc:Paramount_Pictures_films	_ dbc:Midlife_crisis_films	_ dbc:American_sequel_films	
v_1	0	0.88	0.81	0.7	0	0.60	0.53	...
v_2	1.3	1.12	0.91	0.84	0.65	0.59	0.58	...
v_3	0.5	0	0.71	0	0.28	0.35	0	...
v_4	0	0	0.31	0	0	0	0.6	...
v_5	0	0	0	0	0.18	0	0	...
v_6	0	0.12	0.22	0	0	0	0	...
v_7	1.23	1.03	0.89	0.85	0.56	0.3	0.61	...

Figure 2. Example of real valued feature vectors for different items v_j. For lack of space we omitted the predicate *dcterms:subject*

represent each feature through a latent vector, but to map each factor with an explicit feature in order to obtain latent vectors that are made of explicit semantic features. To this aim, we initialize the parameters $\mathbf{v}_j$ and $\mathbf{v}_p$ with their corresponding rows from $\mathbf{V}$ which in turn represent respectively $\mathbf{u}_j$ and $\mathbf{i}_p$. In this way, we try to identify each latent factor with a corresponding explicit feature. The rationale behind this idea is once the model has been trained, the resulting matrix $\hat{\mathbf{V}}$ still refers to the original features but it contains better values for $v_{(j,f)}$ and $v_{(p,f)}$ that take into account also the latent interactions between users, items and features. It is noteworthy that after the training phase $\mathbf{u}_j$ and $\mathbf{i}_p$ (corresponding to $v_{(j,f)}$ and $v_{(p,f)}$ in $\mathbf{V}$) contain non-zero values also for features that are not originally in the description of the user u or of the item i. At this point, if we extract the items vectors $\mathbf{v}_j$ from the matrix $\hat{\mathbf{V}}$, we may leverage optimal values of item vectors to implement an item-kNN recommendation approach. Similarities between each pair of items i and j are measured by evaluating the cosine similarity of their corresponding vectors in $\hat{\mathbf{V}}$:

$$cs(i,j) = \frac{\mathbf{v}_i \cdot \mathbf{v}_j}{\| \mathbf{v}_i \| \cdot \| \mathbf{v}_j \|}$$

Let N^i be the set of neighbors for the item i which contains the most similar items to i according to the selected similarity measure. We may choose i such that $i \notin I^u$ and a user u ad then predict the score assigned by u to i as:

$$score(u,i) = \frac{\sum\limits_{j \in N^i \cap I^u} cs(i,j)}{\sum\limits_{j \in N^i} cs(i,j)} \qquad (4)$$

From now on we will refer to this knowledge-aware factorization machine approach as kaHFM. Factorization machines can be easily trained to reduce the prediction error by using different optimization algorithms such as gradient descent methods, alternating least-squares (ALS) and MCMC. Since we formulated our problem as a *top-N* recommendation task, following [29], we trained kaHFM by using Bayesian Personalized Ranking Criterion (BPR) as a learning to rank approach. The BPR criterion is optimized using a stochastic gradient descent algorithm on a set D_S of triples (u, i, j), with $i \in I^u$ and $j \notin I^u$, selected through a random sampling from a uniform distribution. At the end of the training phase, we can use the optimal model parameters for the item recommendation step.

In Table 1 we show an example for categorical values obtained after the training (in the column kaHFM) together with the original TF-IDF ones computed for a movie from the Yahoo! Movies[2] dataset.

kaHFM	TF-IDF	Predicate	Object
1.3669	0.2584	dct:subject	dbc:Space_adventure_films
1.1252	0.2730	dct:subject	dbc:Films_set_in_the_future
0.9133	0.2355	dct:subject	dbc:American_science_fiction_action_films
0.8485	0.3190	dct:subject	dbc:1980s_science_fiction_films
0.6529	0.1549	dct:subject	dbc:Paramount_Pictures_films
0.5989	0.3468	dct:subject	dbc:Midlife_crisis_films
0.5940	0.1797	dct:subject	dbc:American_sequel_films
0.5862	0.2661	dct:subject	dbc:Film_scores_by_James_Horner
0.5634	0.2502	dct:subject	dbc:Films_shot_in_San_Francisco
0.5583	0.1999	dct:subject	dbc:1980s_action_thriller_films

Table 1. Top-10 features computed by kaHFM for the movie "Star Trek II - The Wrath of Khan".

2.1. Semantic Accuracy and Generative Robustness

kaHFM allows us to keep the meaning of the "latent" factors computed via a factorization machine, which turns out to be exploitable in order to interpret the recommended results. We propose an automated offline evaluation procedure to measure the *Semantic Accuracy* with the aim of verifying that kaHFM preserves the semantics of the features in **V** after the training phase. Furthermore, we define as *Robustness* the ability to assign a higher value to important features after one or more feature removal.

Semantic Accuracy.   The rationale behind Semantic Accuracy is to evaluate, given an item i, how well kaHFM is able to correctly predict its original features available in the computed top-K list $\mathbf{v}_i$. In other words, given the set of features of i represented by $F^i = \{f_1^i, \ldots, f_m^i, \ldots f_M^i\}$, with $F^i \subseteq F$, we check if the values in $\mathbf{v}_i$, corresponding to $f_{m,i} \in F^i$, are higher than those corresponding to $f \notin F^i$. Regarding the feature set M that initially describes i, we see how many features appear in the set $top(\mathbf{v}_i, M)$ representing the top-M features in $\mathbf{v}_i$. We then normalize this number by the size of F^i and average on all the items within the catalog I.

$$\text{Semantic Accuracy (SA@}M\text{)} = \frac{\sum_{i \in I} \frac{|top(\mathbf{v}_i, M) \cap F^i|}{|F^i|}}{|I|}$$

It not unusual to deal with scenarios for which we may have $|F| \gg M$. Therefore, we might also consider to measure the accuracy for different sizes of the top list. Since we

---
[2]http://research.yahoo.com/Academic_Relations

can describe items by using different number of features, the size of the top list might be a function of the original size of the features set that describes an item. In this direction, we measured SA@nM with $n \in \{1,2,3,4,5,\ldots\}$ and then we evaluated the number of features in F^i which are available in the top-$n \cdot M$ elements of $\mathbf{v}_i$.

$$SA@nM = \frac{\sum_{i \in I} \frac{|top(\mathbf{v}_i, n \cdot M) \cap F^i|}{|F^i|}}{|I|}$$

Robustness. Although SA@nM may result very useful to check whether kaHFM assigns weights according to the original description of item i, we still do not know if a high value in $\mathbf{v}_i$ really means that the corresponding feature is important to define i. In other words, are we sure that kaHFM provides a real mapping between latent factors and explicit features for i which in turn are the most important to describe the item? To provide a way of measuring "meaningfulness" for a given feature, we hypothesize that a particular feature $\langle \rho, \omega \rangle$ is useful for representing an item i, but the corresponding triple $\langle i, \rho, \omega \rangle$ is not described in the knowledge graph. In case kaHFM were effective in generating weights for unknown features, it should determine the importance of that feature and change its value to make it join the Top-K features in $\mathbf{v}_i$. Following this investigation, the rationale behind robustness is then to "forget" a triple involving i and check whether kaHFM is able to generate it back. We performed the following steps in order to implement this process:

- we train kaHFM to obtain optimal values v_i for all the features in F^i;
- we identify the feature $f_{MAX}^i \in F^i$ with the highest value in v_i;
- we retrain the model initializing $f_{MAX}^i = 0$ and we compute v_i'.

After the above steps, if $f_{MAX}^i \in top(v_i', M)$ then we can say that kaHFM shows a high robustness in identifying important features. In a catalog I, we want define the *Robustness for 1 removed feature @M* (1-Rob@M) as the number of items for which $f_{MAX}^i \in top(v_i', M)$ divided by the size of I.

$$1\text{-Rob@}M = \frac{\sum_{i \in I} |\{i \mid f_{MAX}^i \in top(v_i', M)\}|}{|I|}$$

Similarly to SA@nM, we may define 1-Rob@nM.

Experimental Evaluation. In this section, we provide details for all the three experiments we performed. Particularly, we want to test if:

- kaHFM's recommendations are accurate;
- kaHFM preserves the semantics of original features;
- kaHFM promotes significant features.

Datasets. We evaluated kaHFM's performance on two well-known datasets widely adopted in the recommender systems field on movie domain. Yahoo!Movies (Yahoo! Webscope dataset ydata-ymovies-user-movie-ratings-content-v1_0)[3] contains movies ratings on a [1..5] scale generated on Yahoo! Movies up to November 2003. It provides

---

[3]http://research.yahoo.com/Academic_Relations

content, demographic and mappings to `MovieLens` and `EachMovie` datasets. `Facebook Movies` dataset has been released for the Linked Open Data challenge co-located with ESWC 2015[4]. It contains implicit feedback only and it provides for each item a mapping to DBpedia. To map items in `Yahoo!Movies` and other datasets, we extracted all the updated items-features mappings and we made them publicly available[5]. Datasets statistics are shown in Table 2.

Dataset	#Users	#Items	#Transactions	#Features	Sparsity
Yahoo! Movies	4000	2,626	69,846	988,734	99.34%
Facebook Movies	32143	3,901	689,561	180,573	99.45%

Table 2. Datasets statistics.

Experimental Setting. In order to evaluate the proposed method with respect to other algorithms, we followed the "All Unrated Items" [30] protocol. We split the datasets using the Hold-Out 80-20, so we retained for every user the 80% of their ratings in the training set and moved the remaining 20% in the test set. Furthermore, a temporal split has been performed [31,32] whenever timestamps associated to every transaction is available.
Extraction. Thanks to the publicly available mappings, we have the DBpedia link for each of the items in datasets listed in Table 2. Exploiting this mapping, we fetched all the $\langle \rho, \omega \rangle$ pairs associated to items. Some features had been excluded, in particular we excluded features based on the following predicates: `owl:sameAs`, `dbo:thumbnail`, `foaf:depiction`, `prov:wasDerivedFrom`, `foaf:isPrimaryTopicOf`.
Selection. We used three different settings to perform experiments because we want to analyze the impact of the different kind of features. Features have been chosen depending on their presence in all the different domains and because of their factual, categorical or ontological meaning.
Filtering. In this step we remove irrelevant features that bring negligible value to the recommendation task, but, at the same time, pose scalability issues. We followed the approach presented in [26] for the pre-processing phase, and [33] with a unique threshold. Thresholds (corresponding to *tm* [26], and *p* [33] for missing values) and the considered features for each dataset are represented in Table 3.

Datasets	Threshold	Categorical Setting		Ontological Setting		Factual Setting	
		Total	Selected	Total	Selected	Total	Selected
`Yahoo!Movies`	99.62	26155	747	38699	1240	950035	3186
`Facebook Movies`	99.74	8843	1103	13828	1848	166745	5427

Table 3. Considered features in the different settings

2.2. Accuracy Evaluation

The objective of this evaluation is to verify whether the `Linked Data` injected in a controlled fashion can positively affect the training of Factorization Machines. To this aim, we do not compare kaHFM w.r.t. other state-of-art interpretable models but only with algorithms that are more related to our approach. We compared kaHFM[6] w.r.t. a canonical 2-

---

[4]`https://2015.eswc-conferences.org/program/semwebeval.html`
[5]`https://github.com/sisinflab/LinkedDatasets/`
[6]`https://github.com/sisinflab/HybridFactorizationMachines`

degree Factorization Machine where users and items are intended as features of the original formulation. We optimized the recommendation list ranking via BPR (BPR-FM). In order to keep the expressiveness of the model, the same number of hidden factors have been used (see the "Selected" column in Table 3). Furthermore, we used items similarity [34] in the last step of our approach (see Equation (4)), for this reason, we compared kaHFM against an *Attribute Based Item-kNN* (ABItem-kNN) algorithm. In ABItem-kNN each item is represented by a vector of weights which are calculated through a TF-IDF model. In this model, the attributes are computed via Equation (2). Nevertheless, we also compared kaHFM against a pure Item-kNN, which is an item-based implementation of the k-nearest neighbors algorithm. It finds the k-nearest item neighbors based on Pearson Correlation. Regarding BPR parameters, *learning rate, bias regularization, user regularization, positive item regularization*, and *negative item regularization* have been set respectively to 0.05, 0, 0.0025, 0.0025 and 0.00025. Following [29], we adopted a sampler "without replacement" in order to sample the triples as suggested by authors. We also compared kaHFM against the corresponding User-based nearest neighbor scheme, and Most-Popular, a simple baseline that shows high performance in specific scenarios [35]. Since our method relies on knowledge-graphs, we considered mandatory a comparison against a pure content-based baselines such as a Vector Space Model (*VSM*) [28]. As evaluation metrics for our approach, we measured accuracy through Precision@N (*Prec@N*) and Normalized Discounted Cumulative Gain (*nDCG@N*) [36]. The evaluation has been performed considering Top-10 [35] recommendations for all the datasets. When a rating score was available (Yahoo!Movies), a *Threshold-based relevant items* condition [37,38] was adopted with a relevance threshold of 4 over 5 stars in order to take into account only relevant items. In Fig. 3 results of our experiments regarding accuracy are showed. In all the tables we highlight in **bold** the best result while we underline the second one. Statistically significant results are denoted with a * mark considering Student's paired t-test with a 0.05 level. When Categorical and Ontological information are used, our method is the most accurate, as evidenced in Yahoo!Movies experiments. Very interestingly, even though Yahoo!Movies mapping is affected by a strong popularity bias, only the Factual setting leads our approach to be less effective then ABItem-kNN. In Facebook Movies we see a very consistent improvement of accuracy as it almost doubles up the ABItem-kNN algorithm values. We compared kaHFM against ABItem-kNN to verify whether the collaborative trained features might lead to better similarity values. We believe that this hypothesis is confirmed since in former experiments kaHFM beats ABItem-kNN in almost all settings. It turns out that collaborative trained features achieve better results in terms of accuracy. Moreover, we want to assess if the initialization of latent factors through a knowledge-graph based approach may improve the performance of Factorization Machines. kaHFM always beats BPR-FM, we suppose that this happens because the random initialization takes a while to converge towards an optimal solution. Finally, we want to check if collaborative trained features lead to better results in terms of accuracy w.r.t. a purely informativeness-based knowledge-graph-aware version of Vector Space Model. Our experiments confirm that kaHFM beats *VSM* in almost all cases. In order to strengthen the results we got, we computed recommendations with 0,1,5,10,15,30 iterations. In the interest of brevity, we report here[7] only the plots for Categorical setting (Fig. 3) It is worth to mention that for all the cases we considered,

---

[7]Results of the full experiments: https://github.com/sisinflab/papers-results/tree/master/kahfm-results/

	Facebook	Yahoo!	
Categorical Setting (CS)	P@10	P@10	nDCG@10
ABItem-kNN	0.0173*	0.0421*	0.1174*
BPR-FM	0.0158*	0.0189*	0.0344*
MostPopular	0.0118*	0.0154*	0.0271*
ItemKnn	0.0262*	0.0203*	0.0427*
UserKnn	0.0168*	0.0231*	0.0474*
VSM	0.0185*	0.0385*	0.1129*
kaHFM	**0.0296**	**0.0524**	**0.1399**
Ontological Setting (OS)	P@10	P@10	nDCG@10
ABItem-kNN	0.0172	0.0427*	0.1223*
BPR-FM	0.0155*	0.0199*	0.0356*
MostPopular	0.0118*	0.0154*	0.0271*
ItemKnn	0.0263*	0.0203*	0.0427*
UserKnn	0.0168*	0.0232*	0.0474*
VSM	0.0181*	0.0349*	0.1083*
kaHFM	**0.0273**	**0.0521**	**0.1380**
Factual Setting (FS)	P@10	P@10	nDCG@10
ABItem-kNN	0.0234	0.0619	**0.1764**
BPR-FM	0.0157	0.0177	0.0305
MostPopular	0.0123	0.0154	0.0271
ItemKnn	**0.0273**	0.0203	0.0427
UserKnn	0.0176	0.0232	0.0474
VSM	0.0219	**0.0627**	0.1725
kaHFM	0.0240	0.0564	0.1434

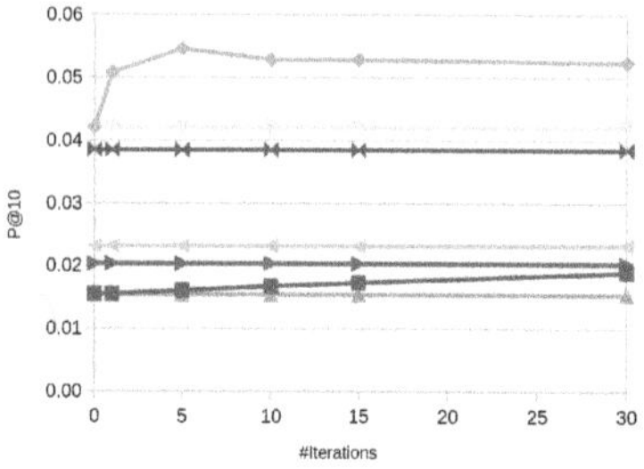

(a) Yahoo!Movies 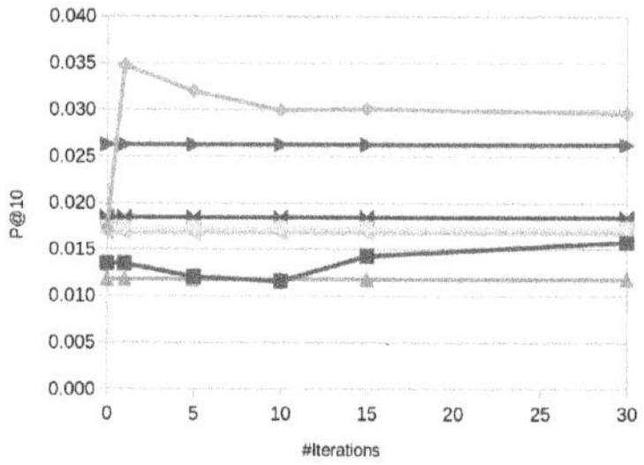   (b) Facebook Movies

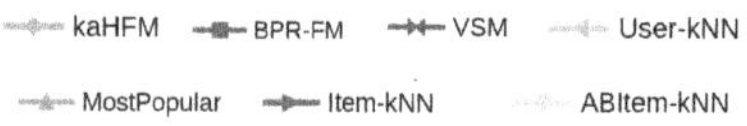

Figure 3. Accuracy results for Facebook Movies, and Yahoo!Movies. In figures: Precision@10 varying # iterations 0, 1, 5 , 10 , 15, 30

we show the best performance in one of these iterations. Nevertheless, in all the datasets we can notice a positive influence of the initialization of the feature vectors, with very similar performances to the ones depicted in [29].

2.3. Semantic Accuracy

Previous experiments showed that kaHFM is effective in terms of accuracy in recommendation scenarios. As a practical matter, we proved that:

- initializing latent factors with content-based weights leads to better performance with kaHFM;

- the obtained fine-tuned items vectors are better than the original ones in a *top-N* item recommendation scenario;
- results are dependent on the features we extract from the Knowledge Graph.

However, even though the proposed method outperforms the baselines, we still do not know if the original semantics of the features is preserved in the new space. In Section 2.1 we described `Semantics Accuracy` (*SA@nM*) as a metric to automatically assess if the importance calculated by `kaHFM` and associated to each feature reflects the actual meaning of that feature. Thus, we measured `SA@nM` with $n \in \{1,2,3,4,5\}$ and $M = 10$, and evaluated the number of ground features available in the top-nM elements of $\mathbf{v}_i$ for each dataset. Regarding the Categorical setting, results are showed in Table 4.

Semantics Accuracy	SA@M	SA@2M	SA@3M	SA@4M	SA@5M	F.A.
Yahoo!Movies	0.847	0.863	0.865	0.868	0.873	12.143
Facebook Movies	0.864	0.883	0.889	0.894	0.899	12.856

Table 4. Semantics Accuracy results for different values of M. F.A. denotes the Feature Average number per item.

2.4. Generative Robustness

From previous experiments, it follows that features calculated through `kaHFM` keep their original semantics if already present in the item description. In section 2.1, we described a procedure to measure the capability of `kaHFM` to compute meaningful features. Here, we calculate `1-Rob@nM` for the two adopted datasets. Results are showed in Table 5. In this case, we concentrate on the CS setting which provides the best results in

1-Robustness	1-Rob@M	1-Rob@2M	1-Rob@3M	1-Rob@4M	1-Rob@5M	F.A.
Yahoo!Movies	0.487	0.645	0.713	0.756	0.793	12.143
Facebook Movies	0.821	0.945	0.970	0.980	0.984	12.856

Table 5. 1-Robustness for different values of M. Column F.A. denotes the Feature Average number per item.

terms of accuracy. To achieve a better understanding of the results, we start focusing on `Yahoo!Movies` for which apparently `kaHFM` has bad performance. In Table 4 we show that `kaHFM` was able to guess 10 on 12 different features for `Yahoo!Movies`. In this experiment, we remove one of the ten features (thus, based on Table 4, `kaHFM` will guess an average of $10 - 1 = 9$ features). Since the number of features is 12 we have 3 remaining "slots". We want now assess if `kaHFM` is able to guess the removed feature in these "slots". Results of this experiment are showed in Table 5; as we can see, our method is able to put the removed feature in one of the three slots the 48.7% of the times starting from 747 overall features.

3. Knowledge-aware Autoencoder

In the last decade, Deep Learning (DL) has gained momentum as a disruptive technology. Several successes have largely proved it and, recently, researches have adopted DL for tackling the recommendation problem [39]. In this direction, DL recommendation techniques have shown to outperform state-of-the-art models regarding the accuracy of recommendations. Among the different DL techniques, Autoencoders are a Deep Neural Network (DNN) configuration often adopted for rating prediction task in a recommendation scenario. This configuration represents data in a low dimensional space preserving the important information for the recommendation process. Here, we describe SE-MAUTO. An Autoencoder configuration that mimics the semantics-aware topology of a Knowledge Graph (KG). SEMAUTO leverages the knowledge coming from a KG and combines it with the performance of an Autoencoder.

Autoencoders. Autoencoders are a special configuration of Artificial Neural Nets (ANNs). It is an unsupervised learning algorithm that aims to replicate the input into the output layer. It takes advantage of a latent representation of data to reproduce the fed input. More formally, we can say that Autoencoder training corresponds to learning an approximate identity function, producing $\hat{x}$ similar to x. A typical Autoencoder is graphically represented in Figure 4.

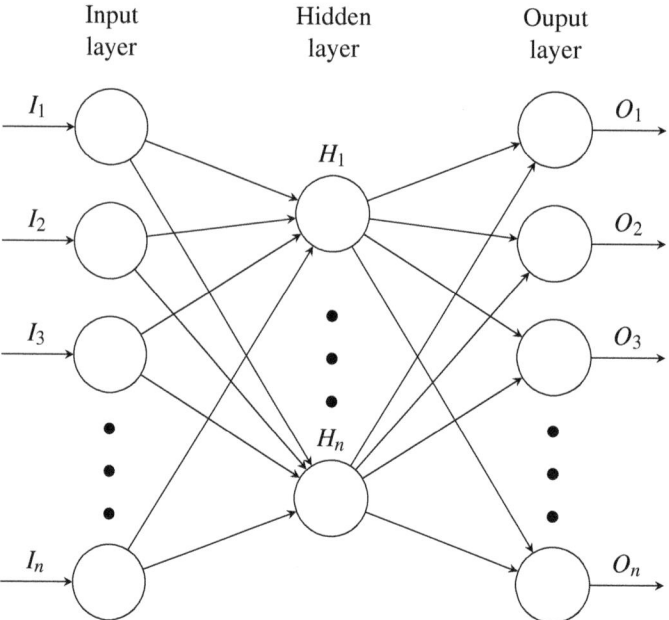

Figure 4. Architecture of an Autoencoder Neural Network.

Reproducing the input on the output layer, and hence learning an approximation of the identity function, is intuitive. However, the topology of the network we choose has many side-effects on the resulting function. As an example, if we limit the number of neurons in the hidden layer, the resulting function will seek correlations and combinations among input neurons to rebuild it. If we suppose to set 20 neurons in the hidden layer, while the input is composed of 100 neurons (i.e., 10×10 pixel image), the network can only use those 20 neurons to reconstruct the input. Thus, the network will learn a compressed representation of the input. A simple autoencoder designed to learn a low-dimensional representation is shown in Figure 4. Most Autoencoder configurations include only a single hidden layer. However, with the spread of DL, we are witnessing the proposal of many configurations that include several hidden layers. These Deep Autoencoders have more capacity and expressiveness, and hence they can perform a better approximation of the identity function [40].

Unfortunately, despite the excellent performance of Autoencoders, they behave like black boxes. Since they make use of latent representations, we cannot understand the reason why a compressed representation gives an output.

Semantics-Aware Autoencoder. The main intuition behind SEMAUTO is reflecting the KG connections between entities in a neural network. In detail, the same triples that describe items in the original KG activate the connections from layer i to layer i+1, as depicted in Figure 5.

In this pictorial representation, we have represented only categorical information into the autoencoder and we have omitted factual. These two sets of information in DBpedia have some peculiarities:

- the amount of categorical information is higher than the factual one. Regarding movies, the overall number of categories exceeds the number of entities reached by factual information;
- categorical information is more equally distributed over the items. In particular, categorical information can connect more items via the same category.

The idea is that a positive vote for *Cloud Atlas* could be a signal of preference toward the corresponding category *Post-apocalyptic films*.

We have leveraged the DBpedia categorical information to define the topology of the Neural Network. In particular, we have built a separate Autoencoder for each user on the platform, exploiting the items' descriptions available in DBpedia. This choice let us represent users with a different number of neurons, based on their interactions with the platform.

Let us define n as the number of items rated by user u. Let $C_i = \{c_{i1}, c_{i2}, \ldots, c_{im}\}$ be the set of m nodes (representing, e.g., categorical information) associated in the KG to the item i. Finally, let $F^u = \bigcup_{i=1}^{n} C_i$ be the set of features mapped into the hidden layer for the u, with $|F^u|$ being the overall number of units in the hidden layer.

It is worth to notice that the resulting network is not fully connected since it reflects the connections in the KG. Additionally, bias units are unnecessary, because they have no equivalent in the KG.

Moreover, the hidden layer units represent the categorical knowledge in KG. Once we start training the model, we take advantage of backpropagation algorithms to update the weights minimizing the prediction error for the user-item rating.

A possible interpretation for these weights is the importance given to them by the user for generating the rating score.

3.1. User profiles

At the end of the training phase, a new user-features latent representation is made available to the system.

Thanks to the categorical information encoded in the hidden layer, the method learns to predict user-item ratings employing the semantics of items.

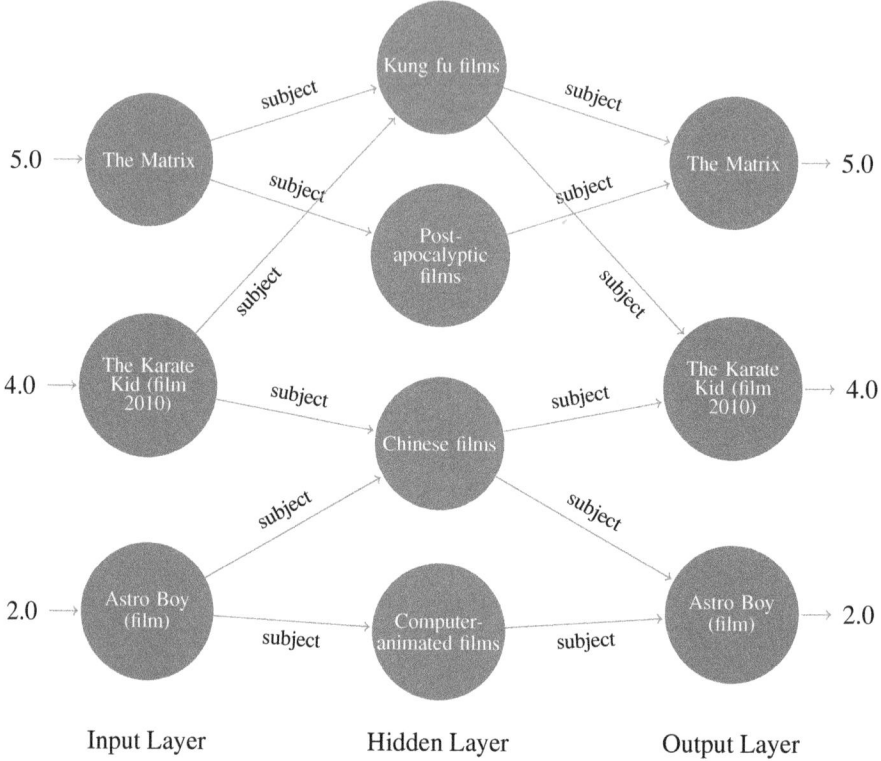

Figure 5. Architecture of a semantic autoencoder.

In the present work, we have adopted, as an activation function, the well known sigmoid $\sigma(x) = \frac{1}{1+e^{-x}}$ since we have normalized the input to be in the range $[0, 1]$. We have trained the autoencoders for 10,000 epochs using a learning rate of $r = 0.03$. The weights are initialized to random values as suggested by Xavier et al. in [41].

The resulting autoencoders contain much useful user information. In detail, we can build the user profile extracting the values of the weights. Since each node in the hidden layer corresponds to an explicit feature, we may assume that those values correspond to the user-feature importance in the user profile.

For a user u, the importance of a feature c is the summation of the weights $w_k^u(c)$ associated to the edges entering a node in the hidden layer. That unit represents the KG category c specialized on user u since we have trained the autoencoder with her ratings. More formally, we have:

$$\omega^u(c) = \sum_{k=1}^{|In(c)|} w_k^u(c)$$

where $In(c)$ is the set of the connections entering the unit that represents the feature c. We recall that, since the autoencoder is not fully connected, $|In(c)|$ is highly dependant on the connections between the items and the category c in KG.

Now we can leverage those weights to build a user profile. We model it as a weighted vector, in which each position is associated with a categorical feature.

Let F^u be the overall set of categories connected to the items rated by u and let $F = \bigcup_{u \in U} F^u$ be the overall set of features considering the entire population. For each user $u \in U$ and for each feature $c \in F$ we have the user profile defined as:

$$P(u) = \{ \langle c, \omega \rangle \mid \omega = \omega^u(c) \text{ if } c \in F^u \}$$

However, since users have rated a different number of items, we will witness different user profiles' dimensions. Also, as users rate only a small fraction of the catalog, the majority of the features for each user remains without a value. To compute those values we have taken advantage of unsupervised learning motivated by *word2vec* [42]. *word2vec* is designed to compute word embeddings exploiting the distribution of words in sentences of a corpus. It projects semantically similar words to close points in a new latent space. Even though two words never co-occur in the same sentence, we are still able to compute their similarity. More formally, let $[x_1, \ldots, x_n]$ be a word sequence in a window. *word2vec* will estimate the probability that a word is the element of the sequence $p(x' \mid [x_1, \ldots, x_n])$. In the current setting, instead of sequences of words, we are dealing with sequences of categories in the user profile. *word2vec* will, therefore, estimate the weight for the missing features $c' \notin F^u$ to be part of the sequence. To estimate the scores, we first need to generate the corpus with all the user profiles $P(u)$. Exploiting ω we can order the features within the profiles. Second, we need to associate a consistent value for the ordered elements $c \in F^u$ on all $u \in U$ (with different profiles' sizes). Formally, we transform the original set $P(u)$ to a sequence of categories $s(u)$. In detail, we map each $\langle c, \omega \rangle \in P(u)$ to $\langle c, norm(\omega) \rangle$ using *norm* as a mapping function:

$$norm : [0,1] \mapsto \{0.1, 0.2, 0.3, \ldots, 1\}$$

that linearly maps[8] a value in the interval $[0,1]$ to a real value in the set $\{0.1, 0.2, 0.3, \ldots, 1\}$. The new pairs form the set

$$P^{norm}(u) = \{ \langle c, norm(\omega) \rangle \mid \langle c, \omega \rangle \in P(u) \}$$

For each normalized user profile set $P^{norm}(u)$ we build the corresponding sequence

$$s(u) = [\ldots, \langle c_i, norm(\omega_i^u) \rangle, \ldots \langle c_j, norm(\omega_j^u) \rangle, \ldots]$$

with $\omega_i^u \geq \omega_j^u$.

The set $S = \{s(u) \mid u \in U\}$ is the corpus we can feed the *word2vec* algorithm with. Then, *word2vec* will be able to discover features patterns following to categories distribution over all users. We take advantage of user's sequence of features $s(u)$ to estimate the probability of $\langle c', norm(\omega') \rangle \in \bigcup_{v \in U} P^{norm}(v) - P^{norm}(u)$ to belong to the context. This probability is a measure of importance of the category for u. Consequently, we estimate $p(\langle c', norm(\omega') \rangle \mid s(u))$.

It is important to highlight that $c' \in F^u$ can appear in several pairs having c' as first category in $\bigcup_{v \in U} P^{norm}(v) - P^{norm}(u)$. As an example, the category dbc:Kung_fu_films may appear in $\langle$dbc : Kung_fu_films, $0.2\rangle$ and $\langle$dbc : Kung_fu_films, $0.5\rangle$, along with

---

[8]In this work we adopt a standard minmax normalization.

the related probabilities $p(\langle \text{dbc}:\text{Kung\_fu\_films}, 0.2 \rangle \mid s(u))$, $p(\langle \text{dbc}:\text{Kung\_fu\_films}, 0.5 \rangle \mid s(u))$. In these situations, we choose the category pair with the highest probability since we require to add the category $\text{dbc}:\text{Kung\_fu\_films}$ and the associated weight only once in the user profile. After this processing, we obtain a new user profile:

$$\hat{P}(u) = P(u) \cup \{\langle c, \omega \rangle \mid \underset{\omega \in \{0.1,\ldots,1\}}{\text{argmax}} \ p(\langle c, \omega \rangle \mid s(u)) \text{ and } \langle c, \omega \rangle \notin P^{norm}(u)\}$$

It is worth noticing that this new user profile $\hat{P}(u)$ acknowledges collaborative informa-tion, while the initial $P(u)$ makes use of only content knowledge. This is since $\hat{P}(u)$ is built using the set S that represents information coming from all the users.

3.2. Computing Recommendations

The choice of representing user profiles as weighted vectors is particularly useful to compute recommendations adopting a user-based k Nearest Neighbors (kNN) approach. As in Vector Space Model, the user profile represents the projection of the user in a new multi-dimensional space, where the similarity between the users u and v can be easily computed exploiting Cosine Vector Similarity. Then, the k most similar users (for user u) are used to estimate the rating r for the item i as a weighted average of the ratings on i among the neighbors:

$$r(u,i) = \frac{\sum_{j=1}^{k} sim(u,v_j) \cdot r(v_j,i)}{\sum_{j=1}^{k} sim(u,v_j)} \tag{5}$$

where $r(v_j,i)$ is the rating assigned to i by the user v_j. We are now able to provide top-N recommendations for each user ordering the ratings computed with Equation (5).

3.3. Experiments

We have tested SEMAUTO using three well-known datasets. In detail, the first part of this section is devoted to introducing these datasets. Later, we introduce the adopted evaluation protocol along with the evaluation metrics chosen. A detailed discussion of the experimental results closes the section. For the sake of reproducibility, we have made available a public implementation of the method[9].

Dataset.   We have evaluated the performance of the competing methods considering three well-known datasets belonging to three different domains. The statistics of the datasets are depicted in Table 6.

	#users	#items	#ratings	sparsity
MovieLens 20M	138,493	26,744	20,000,263	99.46%
Amazon Digital Music	478,235	266,414	836,006	99.99%
LibraryThing	7,279	37,232	626,000	99.77%

Table 6. Datasets

---

[9]https://github.com/sisinflab/SEMAUTO-2.0

For MovieLens 20M[10] we have considered a mapping containing 22,959 items, for Amazon Digital Music[11] we have mapped 4,077 items, and for LibraryThing[12] we have considered 9,926 items. For these experiments, only the items with a mapping to DBpedia were considered.

Evaluation protocol. As evaluation protocol, we have considered the "all unrated items" protocol [43]. In this protocol, all the items but those already rated by user u are considered candidate items. We have split the original data adopting a Hold-Out 80-20 strategy, in which the 80% of user ratings are retained as a training set. The remaining 20% is considered as the test set. Here, we show how we evaluated the performances of our methods in recommending items.

As evaluation metrics, we adopted some well-known accuracy and diversity metrics. As for accuracy, we have measured Precision, Recall, F-1 score, nDCG [44], while for diversity we have computed Aggregate Diversity, and Gini index as a measure of sales diversity [45].

Results Discussion. We have compared SEMAUTO against some well-known state-of-art recommendation algorithms: BPRMF, WRMF and a single-layer autoencoder for rating prediction. BPRMF [29] is a simple Matrix Factorization algorithm optimized adopting the Bayesian Personalized Ranking criterion. WRMF [46,47] is a Weighted Regularized Matrix Factorization method that makes use of regularized Least-Squares (LS), and uses a weighting matrix to differentiate the observed positive feedback from the others. BPRMF and WRMF can be enhanced to take advantage of side information, i.e., the description of items content. In detail, in this experimental evaluation, we have extracted the categorical information from the DBpedia KG and used it as side information. We have computed BPRMF and WRMF recommendation lists adopting the publicly available MyMediaLite[13] implementation. On the other side, the Autoencoder was implemented by scratch using Keras[14]. Also, we have performed the Wilcoxon Signed Rank test to assess the statistical significance of the results. The resulting *p-values* are constantly lower than 0.05.

Table 8 shows the results of the competing methods on the three aforementioned datasets. As you may notice, regarding SEMAUTO, we have considered different values for the size of the neighborhood k.

Concerning accuracy, it is worth noticing that SEMAUTO outperforms the considered baselines on MovieLens 20M and Amazon Digital Music. However, on the LibraryThing dataset, the results show a very similar behavior between the methods, with a slightly better performance shown by fully connected Autoencoder.

As for diversity, SEMAUTO behaves better than the competing algorithms. In detail, the results show that the recommendation lists are much more tailored to users, preserving the accuracy of recommendations. Finally, in the cases in which the accuracy results are very close to another method, our method provides differentiated lists and a much higher overall number of items.

---

[10]https://grouplens.org/datasets/movielens/20m/
[11]http://jmcauley.ucsd.edu/data/amazon/
[12]https://www.librarything.com
[13]http://mymedialite.net
[14]https://keras.io

	avg #features	std	avg #features/avg #items
Movielens 20M	1015.87	823.26	8.82
Amazon Digital Music	7.22	9.77	5.17
LibraryThing	206.88	196.64	1.96

Table 7. Summary of hidden units for mapped items only.

Table 7 shows that SEMAUTO performs better in domains with highly described items. This finding is clear if we observe the number of hidden units. This is likely due to the high expressiveness of the model, as suggested by the Universal Approximation Theorem. Consequently, SEMAUTO shows better performance on the MovieLens 20M dataset than the others. On the other side, on the LibraryThing dataset, SEMAUTO shows worse performance since we have not sufficient categories to make an expressive enough model.

4. Related Work

In the past few years, many interpretable recommendation models based on matrix factorization have been proposed. As is well known, matrix factorization approaches are not easy interpretable because the meaning of their latent factors is unknown. One of the first attempts to address this problem was proposed in [16] in which the authors propose Explicit Factor Model (EFM). In their work, a matrix factorization framework takes as input both products' features and users' opinions extracted with phrase-level sentiment analysis from users' reviews. Thereafter, few improvements to EFM have been proposed to deal with temporal dynamics [48] and to use tensor factorization [18]. Specifically, in the latter the aim is to predict both user preferences on features (extracted from textual reviews) and items; in their work, the authors adopted the Bayesian Personalized Ranking (BPR) criterion [29]. Advances in MF-based recommendation models which are interpretable have been proposed lately with Explainable Matrix Factorization (EMF) [49] in which models rely on neighbors to compute explanations. In the same way, an interpretable Restricted Boltzmann Machine model has been proposed in [50]. It learns a network model (with an additional visible layer) that takes into account a degree of explainability. Finally, an interesting work incorporates sentiments and ratings into a matrix factorization model, named Sentiment Utility Logistic Model (SULM) [17]. In another work, recommendations are computed by generating and ranking personalized explanations in the form of explanation chains [51]. Other methods exploits clustering techniques to provide an explanation, for instance in [52] the proposed method provides interpretable recommendations from positive examples based on the detection of co-clusters between users (clients) and items (products). In [53] authors propose a Multi Level Attraction Model (MLAM) in which they build two attraction models, for cast and story. The interpretability of the model is then provided in terms of attractiveness of Sentence level, Word level, and Cast member. Differently, in [54], authors train a matrix factorization model in order to compute a set of association rules that interprets the obtained recommendations. In [55], authors prove that given the conversion probabilities for all actions of customer features, the original historical data is transformable into a new space

	k	F1	Prec.	Recall	nDCG	Gini	aggrdiv
MOVIELENS 20M							
AUTOENCODER	–	0.21306	0.21764	0.20868	0.24950	0.01443	1587
BPRMF	–	0.14864	0.15315	0.14438	0.17106	**0.00375**	3263
BPRMF + SI	–	0.16838	0.17112	0.16572	0.19500	0.00635	3552
WRMF	–	0.19514	0.19806	0.19231	0.22768	0.00454	766
WRMF + SI	–	0.19494	0.19782	0.19214	0.22773	0.00450	759
SEMAUTO	5	0.18857	0.18551	0.19173	0.21941	0.01835	<u>**5214**</u>
	10	0.21268	0.21009	0.21533	0.24945	0.01305	3350
	20	0.22886	0.22684	0.23092	0.27147	0.01015	2417
	40	0.23675	0.23534	0.23818	0.28363	0.00827	1800
	50	0.23827	0.23686	0.23970	0.28605	0.00780	1653
	100	**0.23961**	**0.23832**	**0.24090**	**0.28924**	<u>0.00662</u>	1310
AMAZON DIGITAL MUSIC							
AUTOENCODER	–	0.00060	0.00035	0.00200	0.00102	0.33867	**3559**
BPRMF	–	0.01010	0.00565	0.04765	0.02073	**0.00346**	539
BPRMF + SI	–	0.00738	0.00413	0.03480	0.01624	0.06414	2374
WRMF	–	0.02189	0.01236	0.09567	0.05511	0.01061	103
WRMF + SI	–	0.02151	0.01216	0.09325	0.05220	0.01168	111
SEMAUTO	5	0.01514	0.00862	0.06233	0.04365	<u>0.03407</u>	3378
	10	0.01920	0.01091	0.07994	0.05421	0.05353	3449
	20	0.02233	0.01267	0.09385	0.06296	0.08562	3523
	40	0.02572	0.01460	0.10805	0.06980	0.14514	3549
	50	0.02618	0.01486	0.10974	0.07032	0.17192	<u>3549</u>
	100	**0.02835**	**0.01608**	**0.11964**	**0.07471**	0.24859	3448
LIBRARYTHING							
AUTOENCODER	–	**0.01562**	**0.01375**	**0.01808**	**0.01758**	0.07628	2328
BPRMF	–	0.01036	0.00954	0.01134	0.01001	0.06764	3140
BPRMF + SI	–	0.01065	0.00994	0.01148	0.01041	0.10753	**4946**
WRMF	–	0.01142	0.01071	0.01223	0.01247	**0.00864**	439
WRMF + SI	–	0.01116	0.01030	0.01217	0.01258	0.00868	442
SEMAUTO	5	0.00840	0.00764	0.00931	0.00930	0.13836	<u>4895</u>
	10	0.01034	0.00930	0.01163	0.01139	0.07888	3558
	20	0.01152	0.01029	0.01310	0.01248	0.04586	2245
	40	0.01195	0.01073	0.01347	0.01339	0.02800	1498
	50	0.01229	0.01110	0.01378	0.01374	0.02403	1312
	100	<u>0.01278</u>	<u>0.01136</u>	<u>0.01461</u>	<u>0.01503</u>	<u>0.01521</u>	873

Table 8. Experimental Results

so that the computation of a set of interpretable recommendation rules allows the model to provide an explanation. The core of our model is a general Factorization Machines (FM) model [56]. Nowadays FMs are the most widely used factorization models because they offer a number of advantages w.r.t. other latent factors models such as SVD++ [57], PITF [58], FPMC [59]. First and foremost, FMs are designed for a generic prediction task, on the contrary, others factorization models are usually deployed for specific tasks

[60]. In addition, it is a linear model and parameters can be estimated accurately even in presence of high sparsity data. At the same time, several improvements have been proposed for FMs, such as Neural Factorization Machines [61] that leverage neural networks to capture non linear structure of real-world data. Moreover, Attentional Factorization Machines use an attention network to learn the importance of feature interactions [62]. Finally, FMs have been specialized to better work as Context-Aware recommender systems [63].

5. Conclusion and Future Work

Recommender systems are, with no doubt, part of our daily life and as such they have the power to drive our decisions. Based on machine learning techniques, their are getting more and more complicated from an algorithmic point of view and they act as black-boxes while computing recommendation list. This calls for a new generation of machine learning algorithms that can be interpretable by a human user and, whenever possible, provide human-readable explanations. In this respect, knowledge graphs play a crucial role in the development of this new breed of tools thanks to the explicit semantics encoded in their well curated data. Indeed, they can be injected within a recommender system algorithm thus allowing them to provide a semantically-enriched interpretation of the results they compute. In this chapter we have presented two algorithms fed by DBpedia, kaHFM and SEMAUTO, based on machine learning techniques, namely factorization machines and autoencoder neural networks, which are able to compute interpretable recommendation lists. We have shown that, not only they train interpretable models but their performances are comparable with, and can also beat, state-of-the-art algorithms specifically designed to implement recommender systems. Moreover, experimental results have shown an interesting dependency of the performance of an algorithm from the kind of knowledge injected in the training process. Specifically, we have shown that results may change in the presence of categorical, factual or ontological knowledge extracted from a source knowledge graph. The concepts, ideas and motivation behind the development of kaHFM and SEMAUTO pave the way to the design of new interpretable algorithms for recommender systems able to automatically generate human-understandable explanations.

References

[1] R.R. Sinha and K. Swearingen, The role of transparency in recommender systems, in: *Extended abstracts of the 2002 Conference on Human Factors in Computing Systems, CHI 2002, Minneapolis, Minnesota, USA, April 20-25, 2002*, L.G. Terveen and D.R. Wixon, eds, ACM, 2002, pp. 830–831. doi:10.1145/506443.506619.

[2] N. Tintarev and J. Masthoff, Designing and Evaluating Explanations for Recommender Systems, in: *Recommender Systems Handbook*, F. Ricci, L. Rokach, B. Shapira and P.B. Kantor, eds, Springer, 2011, pp. 479–510. doi:10.1007/978-0-387-85820-3_15.

[3] M. Zanker, The influence of knowledgeable explanations on users' perception of a recommender system, in: *Sixth ACM Conference on Recommender Systems, RecSys '12, Dublin, Ireland, September 9-13, 2012*, P. Cunningham, N.J. Hurley, I. Guy and S.S. Anand, eds, ACM, 2012, pp. 269–272. doi:10.1145/2365952.2366011.

[4]   N. Tintarev and J. Masthoff, A Survey of Explanations in Recommender Systems, in: *Proceedings of the 23rd International Conference on Data Engineering Workshops, ICDE 2007, 15-20 April 2007, Istanbul, Turkey*, IEEE Computer Society, 2007, pp. 801–810. doi:10.1109/ICDEW.2007.4401070.

[5]   J.L. Herlocker, J.A. Konstan and J. Riedl, Explaining collaborative filtering recommendations, in: *CSCW 2000, Proceeding on the ACM 2000 Conference on Computer Supported Cooperative Work, Philadelphia, PA, USA, December 2-6, 2000*, W.A. Kellogg and S. Whittaker, eds, ACM, 2000, pp. 241–250. doi:10.1145/358916.358995.

[6]   R. Falcone, A. Sapienza and C. Castelfranchi, The Relevance of Categories for Trusting Information Sources, *ACM Trans. Internet Techn.* **15**(4) (2015), 13:1–13:21. doi:10.1145/2803175.

[7]   N. Drawel, H. Qu, J. Bentahar and E. Shakshuki, Specification and automatic verification of trust-based multi-agent systems, *Future Generation Computer Systems* (2018). doi:10.1016/j.future.2018.01.040.

[8]   M.J. Pazzani and D. Billsus, Content-Based Recommendation Systems, in: *The Adaptive Web, Methods and Strategies of Web Personalization*, P. Brusilovsky, A. Kobsa and W. Nejdl, eds, Lecture Notes in Computer Science, Vol. 4321, Springer, 2007, pp. 325–341. doi:10.1007/978-3-540-72079-9_10.

[9]   H.S.M. Cramer, V. Evers, S. Ramlal, M. van Someren, L. Rutledge, N. Stash, L. Aroyo and B.J. Wielinga, The effects of transparency on trust in and acceptance of a content-based art recommender, *User Model. User-Adapt. Interact.* **18**(5) (2008), 455–496. doi:10.1007/s11257-008-9051-3.

[10] Y. Zhang and X. Chen, Explainable Recommendation: A Survey and New Perspectives, *CoRR* **abs/1804.11192** (2018). http://arxiv.org/abs/1804.11192.

[11] S. Chakraborty, R. Tomsett, R. Raghavendra, D. Harborne, M. Alzantot, F. Cerutti, M.B. Srivastava, A.D. Preece, S. Julier, R.M. Rao, T.D. Kelley, D. Braines, M. Sensoy, C.J. Willis and P. Gurram, Interpretability of deep learning models: A survey of results, in: *2017 IEEE SmartWorld, Ubiquitous Intelligence & Computing, Advanced & Trusted Computed, Scalable Computing & Communications, Cloud & Big Data Computing, Internet of People and Smart City Innovation, SmartWorld/SCALCOM/UIC/ATC/CBDCom/IOP/SCI 2017, San Francisco, CA, USA, August 4-8, 2017*, IEEE, 2017, pp. 1–6. doi:10.1109/UIC-ATC.2017.8397411.

[12] Y. Koren, R.M. Bell and C. Volinsky, Matrix Factorization Techniques for Recommender Systems, *IEEE Computer* **42**(8) (2009), 30–37. doi:10.1109/MC.2009.263.

[13] X. Wang, X. He, F. Feng, L. Nie and T. Chua, TEM: Tree-enhanced Embedding Model for Explainable Recommendation, in: *Proceedings of the 2018 World Wide Web Conference on World Wide Web, WWW 2018, Lyon, France, April 23-27, 2018*, P. Champin, F.L. Gandon, M. Lalmas and P.G. Ipeirotis, eds, ACM, 2018, pp. 1543–1552. doi:10.1145/3178876.3186066.

[14] Z. Sun, J. Yang, J. Zhang, A. Bozzon, L. Huang and C. Xu, Recurrent knowledge graph embedding for effective recommendation, in: *Proceedings of the 12th ACM Conference on Recommender Systems, RecSys 2018, Vancouver, BC, Canada, October 2-7, 2018*, S. Pera, M.D. Ekstrand, X. Amatriain and J. O'Donovan, eds, ACM, 2018, pp. 297–305. doi:10.1145/3240323.3240361.

[15] V.W. Anelli and T.D. Noia, 2nd Workshop on Knowledge-aware and Conversational Recommender Systems - KaRS, in: *Proceedings of the 28th ACM International Conference on Information and Knowledge Management, CIKM 2019, Beijing, China, November 3-7, 2019*, W. Zhu, D. Tao, X. Cheng, P. Cui, E.A. Rundensteiner, D. Carmel, Q. He and J.X. Yu, eds, ACM, 2019, pp. 3001–3002. doi:10.1145/3357384.3358805.

[16] Y. Zhang, G. Lai, M. Zhang, Y. Zhang, Y. Liu and S. Ma, Explicit factor models for explainable recommendation based on phrase-level sentiment analysis, in: *The 37th Int. Conf. on Research and Development in Information Retrieval, SIGIR '14, Gold Coast , QLD, Australia*, S. Geva, A. Trotman, P. Bruza, C.L.A. Clarke and K. Järvelin, eds, ACM, 2014, pp. 83–92. ISBN ISBN 978-1-4503-2257-7. doi:10.1145/2600428.2609579.

[17] K. Bauman, B. Liu and A. Tuzhilin, Aspect Based Recommendations: Recommending Items with the Most Valuable Aspects Based on User Reviews, in: *Proceedings of the 23rd ACM SIGKDD International Conference on Knowledge Discovery and Data Mining, Halifax, NS, Canada, August 13 - 17, 2017*, ACM, 2017, pp. 717–725. doi:10.1145/3097983.3098170.

[18] X. Chen, Z. Qin, Y. Zhang and T. Xu, Learning to Rank Features for Recommendation over Multiple Categories, in: *Proceedings of the 39th International ACM SIGIR conference on Research and Development in Information Retrieval, SIGIR 2016, Pisa, Italy, July 17-21, 2016*, R. Perego, F. Sebastiani, J.A. Aslam, I. Ruthven and J. Zobel, eds, ACM, 2016, pp. 305–314. doi:10.1145/2911451.2911549.

[19] V.W. Anelli, T.D. Noia, E.D. Sciascio, A. Ragone and J. Trotta, How to Make Latent Factors Interpretable by Feeding Factorization Machines with Knowledge Graphs, in: *The Semantic Web - ISWC*

2019 - Proc. of 18th Int. Semantic Web Conf., Auckland, New Zealand, Part I, C. Ghidini, O. Hartig, M. Maleshkova, V. Svátek, I.F. Cruz, A. Hogan, J. Song, M. Lefrançois and F. Gandon, eds, Lecture Notes in Computer Science, Vol. 11778, Springer, 2019, pp. 38–56. doi:10.1007/978-3-030-30793-6_3.

[20]   V. Bellini, T.D. Noia, E.D. Sciascio and A. Schiavone, Semantics-Aware Autoencoder, *IEEE Access* **7** (2019), 166122–166137. doi:10.1109/ACCESS.2019.2953308.

[21]   S. Rendle, *Context-aware ranking with factorization models,* Springer, 2011.

[22]   G. Adomavicius and A. Tuzhilin, Context-Aware Recommender Systems, in: *Recommender Systems Handbook,* F. Ricci, L. Rokach and B. Shapira, eds, Springer, 2015, pp. 191–226. doi:10.1007/978-1-4899-7637-6_6.

[23]   G. Adomavicius and Y. Kwon, Multi-Criteria Recommender Systems, in: *Recommender Systems Handbook,* F. Ricci, L. Rokach and B. Shapira, eds, Springer, 2015, pp. 847–880. doi:10.1007/978-1-4899-7637-6_25.

[24]   Y. Zheng, B. Mobasher and R.D. Burke, Incorporating Context Correlation into Context-aware Matrix Factorization, in: *Proc. of the IJCAI 2015 Joint Workshop on Constraints and Preferences for Configuration and Recommendation and Intelligent Techniques for Web Personalization co-located with the 24th Int. Joint Conf. on Artificial Intelligence (IJCAI 2015), Buenos Aires, Argentina, July 27, 2015.,* D. Jannach, J. Mengin, B. Mobasher, A. Passerini and P. Viappiani, eds, CEUR Workshop Proceedings, Vol. 1440, CEUR-WS.org, 2015. http://ceur-ws.org/Vol-1440/Paper5.pdf.

[25]   V.W. Anelli, A. Calì, T.D. Noia, M. Palmonari and A. Ragone, Exposing Open Street Map in the Linked Data Cloud, in: *Trends in Applied Knowledge-Based Systems and Data Science - Proc. of 29th Int. Conf. on Industrial Engineering and Other Applications of Applied Intelligent Systems, IEA/AIE 2016, Morioka, Japan, August,* H. Fujita, M. Ali, A. Selamat, J. Sasaki and M. Kurematsu, eds, Lecture Notes in Computer Science, Vol. 9799, Springer, 2016, pp. 344–355. doi:10.1007/978-3-319-42007-3_29.

[26]   T.D. Noia, C. Magarelli, A. Maurino, M. Palmonari and A. Rula, Using Ontology-Based Data Summarization to Develop Semantics-Aware Recommender Systems, in: *The Semantic Web - 15th International Conference, ESWC 2018, Heraklion, Crete, Greece, June 3-7, 2018, Proceedings,* A. Gangemi, R. Navigli, M. Vidal, P. Hitzler, R. Troncy, L. Hollink, A. Tordai and M. Alam, eds, Lecture Notes in Computer Science, Vol. 10843, Springer, 2018, pp. 128–144. doi:10.1007/978-3-319-93417-4_9.

[27]   S. Rendle, C. Freudenthaler, Z. Gantner and L. Schmidt-Thieme, BPR: Bayesian Personalized Ranking from Implicit Feedback, in: *Proceedings of the Twenty-Fifth Conference on Uncertainty in Artificial Intelligence,* UAI '09, AUAI Press, Arlington, Virginia, United States, 2009, pp. 452–461. ISBN ISBN 978-0-9749039-5-8.

[28]   T.D. Noia, R. Mirizzi, V.C. Ostuni, D. Romito and M. Zanker, Linked open data to support content-based recommender systems, in: *I-SEMANTICS 2012 - 8th International Conference on Semantic Systems, I-SEMANTICS '12, Graz, Austria, September 5-7, 2012,* V. Presutti and H.S. Pinto, eds, ACM, 2012, pp. 1–8. doi:10.1145/2362499.2362501.

[29]   S. Rendle, C. Freudenthaler, Z. Gantner and L. Schmidt-Thieme, BPR: Bayesian Personalized Ranking from Implicit Feedback, in: *UAI 2009, Proceedings of the Twenty-Fifth Conference on Uncertainty in Artificial Intelligence, Montreal, QC, Canada, June 18-21, 2009,* J.A. Bilmes and A.Y. Ng, eds, AUAI Press, 2009, pp. 452–461. https://dslpitt.org/uai/displayArticleDetails.jsp?mmnu=1&smnu=2&article_id=1630&proceeding_id=25.

[30]   H. Steck, Evaluation of recommendations: rating-prediction and ranking, in: *Proc. of the 7th ACM Conf. on Recommender systems,* ACM, 2013, pp. 213–220.

[31]   A. Gunawardana and G. Shani, Evaluating Recommender Systems, in: *Recommender Systems Handbook,* F. Ricci, L. Rokach and B. Shapira, eds, Springer, 2015, pp. 265–308. doi:10.1007/978-1-4899-7637-6_8.

[32]   V.W. Anelli, T.D. Noia, E.D. Sciascio, A. Ragone and J. Trotta, Local Popularity and Time in top-N Recommendation, in: *Advances in Information Retrieval - Proc. of 41st European Conf. on IR Research, ECIR 2019, Cologne, Germany, Part I,* Vol. 11437, L. Azzopardi, B. Stein, N. Fuhr, P. Mayr, C. Hauff and D. Hiemstra, eds, Springer, 2019, pp. 861–868. doi:10.1007/978-3-030-15712-8_63.

[33]   H. Paulheim and J. Fürnkranz, Unsupervised generation of data mining features from linked open data, in: *2nd International Conference on Web Intelligence, Mining and Semantics, WIMS '12, Craiova, Romania, June 6-8, 2012,* D.D. Burdescu, R. Akerkar and C. Badica, eds, ACM, 2012, pp. 31:1–31:12. doi:10.1145/2254129.2254168.

[34]   V.W. Anelli, T.D. Noia, E.D. Sciascio, A. Ragone and J. Trotta, The importance of being dissimilar in recommendation, in: *Proc. of the 34th ACM/SIGAPP Symposium on Applied Comput-*

ing, SAC 2019, Limassol, Cyprus, C. Hung and G.A. Papadopoulos, eds, ACM, 2019, pp. 816–821. doi:10.1145/3297280.3297360.

[35] P. Cremonesi, Y. Koren and R. Turrin, Performance of recommender algorithms on top-n recommendation tasks, in: *Proceedings of the 2010 ACM Conference on Recommender Systems, RecSys 2010, Barcelona, Spain, September 26-30, 2010*, X. Amatriain, M. Torrens, P. Resnick and M. Zanker, eds, ACM, 2010, pp. 39–46. doi:10.1145/1864708.1864721.

[36] V.W. Anelli, T.D. Noia, E.D. Sciascio, C. Pomo and A. Ragone, On the discriminative power of hyperparameters in cross-validation and how to choose them, in: *Proc. of the 13th ACM Conf. on Recommender Systems, RecSys 2019, Copenhagen, Denmark*, T. Bogers, A. Said, P. Brusilovsky and D. Tikk, eds, ACM, 2019, pp. 447–451. doi:10.1145/3298689.3347010.

[37] P.G. Campos, F. Díez and I. Cantador, Time-aware recommender systems: a comprehensive survey and analysis of existing evaluation protocols, *User Model. User-Adapt. Interact.* **24**(1–2) (2014), 67–119. doi:10.1007/s11257-012-9136-x.

[38] V.W. Anelli, V. Bellini, T.D. Noia, W.L. Bruna, P. Tomeo and E.D. Sciascio, An Analysis on Time- and Session-aware Diversification in Recommender Systems, in: *Proc. of the 25th Conf. on User Modeling, Adaptation and Personalization, UMAP 2017, Bratislava, Slovakia 2017*, M. Bieliková, E. Herder, F. Cena and M.C. Desmarais, eds, ACM, 2017, pp. 270–274. doi:10.1145/3079628.3079703.

[39] P. Covington, J. Adams and E. Sargin, Deep Neural Networks for YouTube Recommendations, in: *Proceedings of the 10th ACM Conference on Recommender Systems, Boston, MA, USA, September 15-19, 2016*, S. Sen, W. Geyer, J. Freyne and P. Castells, eds, ACM, 2016, pp. 191–198. doi:10.1145/2959100.2959190.

[40] G.E. Hinton and R.R. Salakhutdinov, Reducing the Dimensionality of Data with Neural Networks, *Science (New York, N.Y.)* **313** (2006), 504–7. doi:10.1126/science.1127647.

[41] X. Glorot and Y. Bengio, Understanding the difficulty of training deep feedforward neural networks, in: *Proceedings of the Thirteenth International Conference on Artificial Intelligence and Statistics, AISTATS 2010, Chia Laguna Resort, Sardinia, Italy, May 13-15, 2010*, Y.W. Teh and D.M. Titterington, eds, JMLR Proceedings, Vol. 9, JMLR.org, 2010, pp. 249–256. `http://proceedings.mlr.press/v9/glorot10a.html`.

[42] T. Mikolov, I. Sutskever, K. Chen, G.S. Corrado and J. Dean, Distributed Representations of Words and Phrases and their Compositionality, in: *Advances in Neural Information Processing Systems 26: 27th Annual Conference on Neural Information Processing Systems 2013. Proceedings of a meeting held December 5-8, 2013, Lake Tahoe, Nevada, United States*, C.J.C. Burges, L. Bottou, Z. Ghahramani and K.Q. Weinberger, eds, 2013, pp. 3111–3119. `http://papers.nips.cc/paper/5021-distributed-representations-of-words-and-phrases-and-their-compositionality`.

[43] H. Steck, Evaluation of Recommendations: Rating-prediction and Ranking, in: *Proceedings of the 7th ACM Conference on Recommender Systems*, RecSys '13, ACM, New York, NY, USA, 2013, pp. 213–220. ISBN ISBN 978-1-4503-2409-0.

[44] K. Järvelin and J. Kekäläinen, IR evaluation methods for retrieving highly relevant documents, *SIGIR Forum* **51**(2) (2017), 243–250. doi:10.1145/3130348.3130374.

[45] D.M. Fleder and K. Hosanagar, Recommender systems and their impact on sales diversity, in: *Proceedings 8th ACM Conference on Electronic Commerce (EC-2007), San Diego, California, USA, June 11-15, 2007*, J.K. MacKie-Mason, D.C. Parkes and P. Resnick, eds, ACM, 2007, pp. 192–199. doi:10.1145/1250910.1250939.

[46] R. Pan, Y. Zhou, B. Cao, N.N. Liu, R.M. Lukose, M. Scholz and Q. Yang, One-Class Collaborative Filtering, in: *Proceedings of the 8th IEEE International Conference on Data Mining (ICDM 2008), December 15-19, 2008, Pisa, Italy*, IEEE Computer Society, 2008, pp. 502–511. doi:10.1109/ICDM.2008.16.

[47] Y. Hu, Y. Koren and C. Volinsky, Collaborative Filtering for Implicit Feedback Datasets, in: *Proceedings of the 8th IEEE International Conference on Data Mining (ICDM 2008), December 15-19, 2008, Pisa, Italy*, IEEE Computer Society, 2008, pp. 263–272. doi:10.1109/ICDM.2008.22.

[48] Y. Zhang, M. Zhang, Y. Zhang, G. Lai, Y. Liu, H. Zhang and S. Ma, Daily-Aware Personalized Recommendation based on Feature-Level Time Series Analysis, in: *Proceedings of the 24th International Conference on World Wide Web, WWW 2015, Florence, Italy, May 18-22, 2015*, A. Gangemi, S. Leonardi and A. Panconesi, eds, ACM, 2015, pp. 1373–1383. doi:10.1145/2736277.2741087.

[49] B. Abdollahi and O. Nasraoui, Explainable Matrix Factorization for Collaborative Filtering, in: *Proceedings of the 25th International Conference on World Wide Web, WWW 2016, Montreal, Canada, April*

11-15, 2016, Companion Volume, J. Bourdeau, J. Hendler, R. Nkambou, I. Horrocks and B.Y. Zhao, eds, ACM, 2016, pp. 5–6. doi:10.1145/2872518.2889405.

[50]   B. Abdollahi and O. Nasraoui, Explainable Restricted Boltzmann Machines for Collaborative Filtering, *CoRR* **abs/1606.07129** (2016). http://arxiv.org/abs/1606.07129.

[51]   A. Rana and D. Bridge, Explanation Chains: Recommendations by Explanation, in: *Proceedings of the Poster Track of the 11th ACM Conference on Recommender Systems (RecSys 2017), Como, Italy, August 28, 2017.*, D. Tikk and P. Pu, eds, CEUR Workshop Proceedings, Vol. 1905, CEUR-WS.org, 2017. http://ceur-ws.org/Vol-1905/recsys2017_poster4.pdf.

[52]   M. Vlachos, C. Duenner, R. Heckel, V.G. Vassiliadis, T. Parnell and K. Atasu, Addressing Interpretability and Cold-Start in Matrix Factorization for Recommender Systems, *IEEE Transactions on Knowledge and Data Engineering* (2018).

[53]   L. Hu, S. Jian, L. Cao and Q. Chen, Interpretable Recommendation via Attraction Modeling: Learning Multilevel Attractiveness over Multimodal Movie Contents, in: *Proceedings of the Twenty-Seventh International Joint Conference on Artificial Intelligence, IJCAI 2018, July 13-19, 2018, Stockholm, Sweden.*, J. Lang, ed., ijcai.org, 2018, pp. 3400–3406. doi:10.24963/ijcai.2018/472.

[54]   G. Peake and J. Wang, Explanation Mining: Post Hoc Interpretability of Latent Factor Models for Recommendation Systems, in: *Proceedings of the 24th ACM SIGKDD International Conference on Knowledge Discovery & Data Mining, KDD 2018, London, UK, August 19-23, 2018*, Y. Guo and F. Farooq, eds, ACM, 2018, pp. 2060–2069. doi:10.1145/3219819.3220072.

[55]   A. Dhurandhar, S. Oh and M. Petrik, Building an Interpretable Recommender via Loss-Preserving Transformation, *CoRR* **abs/1606.05819** (2016). http://arxiv.org/abs/1606.05819.

[56]   S. Rendle, Factorization Machines, in: *ICDM 2010, The 10th IEEE International Conference on Data Mining, Sydney, Australia, 14-17 December 2010*, G.I. Webb, B. Liu, C. Zhang, D. Gunopulos and X. Wu, eds, IEEE Computer Society, 2010, pp. 995–1000. doi:10.1109/ICDM.2010.127.

[57]   Y. Koren, Factorization meets the neighborhood: a multifaceted collaborative filtering model, in: *Proceedings of the 14th ACM SIGKDD International Conference on Knowledge Discovery and Data Mining, Las Vegas, Nevada, USA, August 24-27, 2008*, Y. Li, B. Liu and S. Sarawagi, eds, ACM, 2008, pp. 426–434. doi:10.1145/1401890.1401944.

[58]   S. Rendle and L. Schmidt-Thieme, Pairwise interaction tensor factorization for personalized tag recommendation, in: *Proceedings of the Third International Conference on Web Search and Web Data Mining, WSDM 2010, New York, NY, USA, February 4-6, 2010*, B.D. Davison, T. Suel, N. Craswell and B. Liu, eds, ACM, 2010, pp. 81–90. doi:10.1145/1718487.1718498.

[59]   S. Rendle, C. Freudenthaler and L. Schmidt-Thieme, Factorizing personalized Markov chains for next-basket recommendation, in: *Proceedings of the 19th International Conference on World Wide Web, WWW 2010, Raleigh, North Carolina, USA, April 26-30, 2010*, M. Rappa, P. Jones, J. Freire and S. Chakrabarti, eds, ACM, 2010, pp. 811–820. doi:10.1145/1772690.1772773.

[60]   I. Fernández-Tobías, I. Cantador, P. Tomeo, V.W. Anelli and T.D. Noia, Addressing the user cold start with cross-domain collaborative filtering: exploiting item metadata in matrix factorization, *User Model. User-Adapt. Interact.* **29**(2) (2019), 443–486.

[61]   X. He and T. Chua, Neural Factorization Machines for Sparse Predictive Analytics, in: *Proceedings of the 40th International ACM SIGIR Conference on Research and Development in Information Retrieval, Shinjuku, Tokyo, Japan, August 7-11, 2017*, N. Kando, T. Sakai, H. Joho, H. Li, A.P. de Vries and R.W. White, eds, ACM, 2017, pp. 355–364. doi:10.1145/3077136.3080777.

[62]   J. Xiao, H. Ye, X. He, H. Zhang, F. Wu and T. Chua, Attentional Factorization Machines: Learning the Weight of Feature Interactions via Attention Networks, in: *Proceedings of the Twenty-Sixth International Joint Conference on Artificial Intelligence, IJCAI 2017, Melbourne, Australia, August 19-25, 2017*, C. Sierra, ed., ijcai.org, 2017, pp. 3119–3125. doi:10.24963/ijcai.2017/435.

[63]   S. Rendle, Z. Gantner, C. Freudenthaler and L. Schmidt-Thieme, Fast context-aware recommendations with factorization machines, in: *Proceeding of the 34th International ACM SIGIR Conference on Research and Development in Information Retrieval, SIGIR 2011, Beijing, China, July 25-29, 2011*, W. Ma, J. Nie, R.A. Baeza-Yates, T. Chua and W.B. Croft, eds, ACM, 2011, pp. 635–644. doi:10.1145/2009916.2010002.

Knowledge Graphs for eXplainable Artificial Intelligence: Foundations, Applications and Challenges   125
I. Tiddi et al. (Eds.)
IOS Press, 2020
© 2020 Akademische Verlagsgesellschaft AKA GmbH, Berlin. All rights reserved.
doi:10.3233/SSW200015

Differentiable Reasoning on Large Knowledge Bases and Natural Language

Pasquale MINERVINI [a], Matko BOŠNJAK [a], Tim ROCKTÄSCHEL [a,b],
Sebastian RIEDEL [a,b], and Edward GREFENSTETTE [a,b]

[a] *UCL Centre for Artificial Intelligence, University College London*
[b] *Facebook AI Research*

Abstract. Reasoning with knowledge expressed in natural language and Knowledge Bases (KBs) is a major challenge for Artificial Intelligence, with applications in machine reading, dialogue, and question answering. General neural architectures that jointly learn representations and transformations of text are very data-inefficient, and it is hard to analyze their reasoning process. These issues are addressed by end-to-end differentiable reasoning systems such as Neural Theorem Provers (NTPs), although they can only be used with small-scale symbolic KBs. In this paper we first propose Greedy NTPs (GNTPs), an extension to NTPs addressing their complexity and scalability limitations, thus making them applicable to real-world datasets. This result is achieved by dynamically constructing the computation graph of NTPs and including only the most promising proof paths during inference, thus obtaining orders of magnitude more efficient models. [1]Then, we propose a novel approach for jointly reasoning over KBs and textual mentions, by embedding logic facts and natural language sentences in a shared embedding space. We show that GNTPs perform on par with NTPs at a fraction of their cost while achieving competitive link prediction results on large datasets, providing explanations for predictions, and inducing interpretable models.

Keywords. Neuro-Symbolic Reasoning, Representation Learning, eXplainable AI

1. Introduction

The main focus of Artificial Intelligence is building systems that exhibit intelligent behavior [38]. Notably, Natural Language Understanding (NLU) and Machine Reading (MR) aim at building models and systems with the ability to read text, extract meaningful knowledge, and reason with it [11,16,27,60]. This ability facilitates both the synthesis of new knowledge and the possibility to verify and update a given assertion. Traditionally, automated reasoning applied to text requires natural language processing tools that compile it into the structured form of a KB [50]. However, the compiled KBs tend to be incomplete, ambiguous, and noisy, impairing the application of standard deductive reasoners [28].

A rich and broad literature in MR has approached this problem within a variety of frameworks, including Natural Logic [40], Semantic Parsing [6], Natural Language

---

[1]Source code and datasets are available online at `https://github.com/uclnlp/gntp`. This is an extended version of [45], selected for an oral presentation at AAAI 2020.

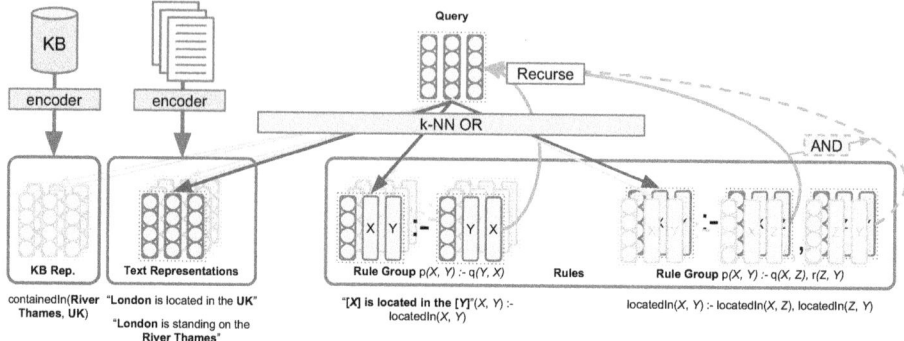

Figure 1. Overall architecture of GNTPs. The two main contributions lie in *i)* the significantly faster inference mechanism, sped up by the k-NN OR component, and *ii)* the text encoder.

Inference and Recognizing Textual Entailment [9,18], and Question Answering [27]. Nonetheless, such methods suffer from several limitations. They rely on significant amounts of annotated data to suitably approximate the implicit distribution from which the data is drawn. In practice, this makes them unable to generalize well in the absence of a sufficient quantity of training data or appropriate priors on model parameters [17]. Orthogonally, even when accurate, such methods cannot explain given predictions [39].

A promising strategy for overcoming these issues consists of combining *neural models* and *symbolic reasoning*, given their complementary strengths and weaknesses [12,17,54,59,63]. While symbolic models can generalize well from a small number of examples, they are brittle and prone to failure when the observations are noisy or ambiguous, or when the properties of the domain are unknown or hard to formalize, all of which being the case for natural language [21,52]. Contrarily, neural models are robust to noise and ambiguity but not easily interpretable, making them unable to provide explanations or incorporating background knowledge [24].

Recent work in neuro-symbolic systems has made progress towards end-to-end differentiable reasoning models that can be trained via backpropagation while maintaining interpretability and generalization, thereby inheriting the best of both worlds. Among such systems, NTPs [44,54] are end-to-end differentiable deductive reasoners based on Prolog's backward chaining algorithm, where discrete unification between atoms is replaced by a differentiable operator computing the similarities between their embedding representations.

NTPs are especially interesting since they allow learning *interpretable rules* from data, by back-propagating the prediction errors to the rule representations. Furthermore, the proving process in NTPs is *explainable* – the proof path associated with the largest proof score denotes which rules and facts are used in the reasoning process. However, NTPs have only been successfully applied to learning tasks involving very small datasets, since their computational complexity makes them unusable on larger, real-world KBs. Furthermore, most human knowledge is not available in KBs, but in natural language texts which are difficult to reason over automatically.

In this paper we address these issues by proposing: *i)* two efficiency improvements for significantly reducing the time and space complexity of NTPs by reducing the number of candidate proof paths and introducing an attention mechanism for rule induction, and *ii)* an extension of NTPs towards natural language, jointly embedding predicates and textual surface patterns in a shared space by using an end-to-end differentiable reading component.

2. End-to-end Differentiable Proving

NTPs [54] recursively build a neural network enumerating all the possible proof paths for proving a query (or *goal*) on a given KB, and aggregate all their proof scores via max pooling. They do so by relying on three modules—a *unification module*, which compares sub-symbolic representations of logic atoms, and mutually recursive *or* and *and modules*, which jointly enumerate all possible proof paths, before the final aggregation selects the highest-scoring one.

In the following, we briefly overview these modules, and the training process used for learning the model parameters from data. We assume the existence of a function-free Datalog KB $\mathfrak{K}$ containing *ground facts* in the form $[\text{p}, \text{A}, \text{B}]$ [2], representing the logical atom $\text{p}(\text{A}, \text{B})$ where p is a relation type, and A, B are its arguments. [3] It also contains *rules* in the form H :– B such as $[\text{p}, \text{X}, \text{Y}] :– [[\text{q}, \text{X}, \text{Z}], [\text{r}, \text{Z}, \text{Y}]]$, denoting the rule $\text{p}(\text{X}, \text{Y}) :– \text{q}(\text{X}, \text{Z}), \text{r}(\text{Z}, \text{Y})$, meaning that $\text{q}(\text{X}, \text{Z}), \text{r}(\text{Z}, \text{Y})$ implies $\text{p}(\text{X}, \text{Y})$, where X, Y, Z are universally quantified variables.

Unification Module. In the backward chaining reasoning algorithm, *unification* is the operator that matches two logic atoms, such as locatedIn(LONDON, UK) and situatedIn(X, Y). Discrete unification checks for equality between the elements composing the two atoms (*e.g.* locatedIn $\neq$ situatedIn), and binds variables to symbols via substitutions (*e.g.* $\{\text{X}/\text{LONDON}, \text{Y}/\text{UK}\}$). In NTPs, unification matches two atoms by comparing their *embedding representations* via a differentiable similarity function – a Gaussian kernel – which enables matching different symbols with similar semantics.

More formally, $\text{unify}_\theta(\text{H}, \text{G}, \text{S}) = S'$ creates a neural network module that matches two atoms H and G by comparing their embedding vectors. For instance, given a goal $G = [\text{locatedIn}, \text{LONDON}, \text{UK}]$, a fact $H = [\text{situatedIn}, \text{X}, \text{Y}]$, and a proof state $S = (S_\psi, S_\rho)$ consisting of a set of substitutions S_ψ and a proof score S_ρ, the unify module compares the embedding representations of locatedIn and situatedIn with a Gaussian kernel k, updates the variable binding substitution set $S'_\psi = S_\psi \cup \{\text{X}/\text{LONDON}, \text{Y}/\text{UK}\}$, and calculates the new proof score $S'_\rho = \min \left(S_\rho, k\left(\boldsymbol{\theta}_{\text{locatedIn:}}, \boldsymbol{\theta}_{\text{situatedIn:}}\right)\right)$ and proof state $S' = (S'_\psi, S'_\rho)$.

OR Module. The or module computes the unification between a goal and all facts and rule heads in a KB, and then recursively invokes the and module on the corresponding rule bodies. Formally, for each rule H :– B [4] in a KB $\mathfrak{K}$, $\text{or}_\theta^{\mathfrak{K}}(\text{G}, d, S)$ unifies the goal G with the rule head H, and invokes the and module to prove atoms in the body B, keeping track of the maximum proof depth d:

$$\text{or}_\theta^{\mathfrak{K}}(G, d, S) = [S' \mid H :– B \in \mathfrak{K}, S' \in \text{and}_\theta^{\mathfrak{K}}(B, d, \text{unify}_\theta(H, G, S))] \qquad (1)$$

---

[2]For consistency, we use the same notation as [54].

[3]We consider binary predicates, without loss of generality.

[4]Facts are seen as rules with no body and variables, *i.e.* F :– [].

For example, given a goal G = [situatedIn, Q, UK] and a rule H :– B with H = [locatedIn, X, Y] and B = [[locatedIn, X, Z], [locatedIn, Z, Y]], the model would unify the goal G with the rule head H, and invoke the and modules to prove the sub-goals in the rule body B.

AND Module. The and module recursively proves a list of sub-goals in a rule body. Given the first sub-goal B and the following sub-goals $\mathbb{B}$, the $\text{and}_\theta^{\mathfrak{K}}(B : \mathbb{B}, d, S)$ module will substitute variables in B with constants according to the substitutions in S, and invoke the or module on B. The resulting state is used to prove the atoms in $\mathbb{B}$, by recursively invoking the and module:

$$\text{and}_\theta^{\mathfrak{K}}(B : \mathbb{B}, d, S) = [S'' \mid d > 0, S'' \in \text{and}_\theta^{\mathfrak{K}}(\mathbb{B}, d, S'), S' \in \text{or}_\theta^{\mathfrak{K}}(\text{sub}(B, S_\psi), d-1, S)] \quad (2)$$

For example, when invoked on the rule body B of the example mentioned above, the and module will substitute variables with constants for the sub-goal [locatedIn, X, Z] and invoke the or module, whose resulting state will be the basis of the next invocation of and module on [locatedIn, Z, Y].

Proof Aggregation. After building a neural network that evaluates all the possible proof paths of a goal G on a KB $\mathfrak{K}$, NTPs select the proof path with the largest proof score:

$$\text{ntp}_\theta^{\mathfrak{K}}(G, d) = \max_S S_\rho \quad \text{with} \quad S \in \text{or}_\theta^{\mathfrak{K}}(G, d, (\varnothing, 1)) \quad (3)$$

where $d \in \mathbb{N}$ is a predefined maximum proof depth. The initial proof state is set to $(\varnothing, 1)$ corresponding to an empty substitution set and to a proof score of 1.

Training. In NTPs, embedding representations are learned by minimizing a cross-entropy loss $\mathscr{L}^{\mathfrak{K}}(\boldsymbol{\theta})$ on the final proof score, by iteratively masking facts in the KB and trying to prove them using other available facts and rules.

Negative examples are obtained via a corruption process, denoted by corrupt$(\cdot)$, by modifying the subject and object of triples in the KB [49]:

$$\mathscr{L}^{\mathfrak{K}}(\boldsymbol{\theta}) = - \sum_{F :- [] \in \mathfrak{K}} \log \text{ntp}_\theta^{\mathfrak{K} \backslash F}(F, d) - \sum_{\tilde{F} \sim \text{corrupt}(F)} \log[1 - \text{ntp}_\theta^{\mathfrak{K}}(\tilde{F}, d)] \quad (4)$$

NTPs can also learn *interpretable rules*. [54] shows that it is possible to learn rules from data by specifying *rule templates*, such as H :– B with H = $[\boldsymbol{\theta}_{p:}, X, Y]$ and B = $[[\boldsymbol{\theta}_{q:}, X, Z], [\boldsymbol{\theta}_{r:}, Z, Y]]$.

Parameters $\boldsymbol{\theta}_{p:}, \boldsymbol{\theta}_{q:}, \boldsymbol{\theta}_{r:} \in \mathbb{R}^k$, denoting rule-predicate embeddings, can be learned from data by minimizing the loss in Eq. 4, and decoded by searching the closest representation of known predicates.

3. Efficient Differentiable Reasoning on Large-Scale KBs

NTPs are capable of deductive reasoning, and the proof paths with the highest score can provide human-readable explanations for a given prediction. However, enumerating and scoring all bounded-depth proof paths for a given goal, as given in Eq. 3, is computationally intractable. For each goal and sub-goal G, this process requires to unify G with the representations of *all* rule heads and facts in the KB, which quickly becomes computationally prohibitive even for moderately sized KBs. Furthermore, the expansion of a rule like $p(X, Y) :- q(X, Z), r(Z, Y)$ via backward chaining causes an increase of the sub-goals to prove, both because all atoms in the body need to be proven, and because Z is a free variable with many possible bindings [54]. We consider two problems – given a sub-goal G such as $[p, A, B]$, we need to efficiently select *i)* the k_f *facts* that are most likely to prove a sub-goal G, and *ii)* the k_r *rules* to expand to reach a high-scoring proof state.

Fact Selection.   Unifying a sub-goal G with all facts in the KB $\mathfrak{K}$ may not be feasible in practice. The number of facts in a real-world KB can be in the order of millions or billions. For instance, Freebase contains over 637×10^6 facts, while the Google Knowledge Graph contains more than 18×10^9 facts [49]. Identifying the facts $F \in \mathfrak{K}$ that yield the maximum proof score for a sub-goal G reduces to solving the following optimization problem:

$$\mathtt{ntp}_{\boldsymbol{\theta}}^{\mathfrak{K}}(G, 1) = \max_{F :- [] \in \mathfrak{K}} S_{\rho}^{F} = S_{\rho}^{\star} \quad \text{with} \quad S^{F} = \mathtt{unify}_{\boldsymbol{\theta}}(F, G, (\varnothing, 1)) \tag{5}$$

Hence, the fact $F \in \mathfrak{K}$ that yields the maximum proof score for a sub-goal G is the fact F that yields the maximum unification score with G. Recall that the unification score between a fact F and a goal G is given by the similarity of their embedding representations $\boldsymbol{\theta}_{F:}$ and $\boldsymbol{\theta}_{G:}$, computed via a Gaussian kernel $k(\boldsymbol{\theta}_F, \boldsymbol{\theta}_G)$. Given a goal G, NTPs will compute the unification score between G and every fact $F \in \mathfrak{K}$ in the KB. This is problematic, since computing the similarity between the representations of the goal G and every fact $F \in \mathfrak{K}$ is computationally prohibitive – the number of comparisons is $\mathcal{O}(|\mathfrak{K}|n)$, where n is the number of (sub-)goals in the proving process. However, $\mathtt{ntp}_{\boldsymbol{\theta}}^{\mathfrak{K}}(G, d)$ only returns the single largest proof score. This means that, at inference time, we only need the largest proof score for returning the correct output. Similarly, during training, the gradient of the proof score with respect to the parameters $\boldsymbol{\theta}$ can also be calculated exactly by using the single largest proof score:

$$\frac{\partial \mathtt{ntp}_{\boldsymbol{\theta}}^{\mathfrak{K}}(G, 1)_{\rho}}{\partial \boldsymbol{\theta}} = \frac{\partial \max_{F \in \mathfrak{K}} S_{\rho}^{F}}{\partial \boldsymbol{\theta}} = \frac{\partial S_{\rho}^{\star}}{\partial \boldsymbol{\theta}} \quad \text{with} \quad S_{\rho}^{\star} = \max_{F \in \mathfrak{K}} S_{\rho}^{F}$$

In this paper, we propose to efficiently compute $S^{\star}$, the highest unification score between a given sub-goal G and a fact $F \in \mathfrak{K}$, by casting it as a Nearest Neighbour Search (NNS) problem. This is feasible since the Gaussian kernel used by NTPs is a monotonic transformation of the negative Euclidean distance.

Identifying $S^{\star}$ permits to reduce the number of neural network sub-structures needed for the comparisons between each sub-goal and facts from $\mathcal{O}(|\mathfrak{K}|)$ to $\mathcal{O}(1)$. We use the exact and approximate NNS framework proposed by [30] for efficiently searching $\mathfrak{K}$ for the best supporting facts for a given sub-goal. Specifically we use the exact L2-nearest neighbor search and, for the sake of efficiency, we update the search index every 10 batches, assuming that the small updates made by stochastic gradient descent do not necessarily invalidate previous search indexes.

Rule Selection.   We use a similar idea for selecting which rules to activate for proving a given goal G. We empirically notice that unifying G with the closest rule heads, such as G = [locatedIn, LONDON, UK] and H = [situatedIn, X, Y], is more likely to generate high-scoring proof states. This is a trade-off between symbolic reasoning, where proof paths are expanded only when the heads exactly match with the goals, and differentiable reasoning, where all proof paths are explored.

This prompted us to implement a heuristic that dynamically selects rules among rules sharing the same template during both inference and learning. In our experiments, this heuristic for selecting proof paths was able to recover valid proofs for a goal when they exist, while drastically reducing the computational complexity of the differentiable proving process.

More formally, we generate a partitioning $\mathfrak{P} \in 2^{\mathfrak{K}}$ of the KB $\mathfrak{K}$, where each element in $\mathfrak{P}$ groups all facts and rules in $\mathfrak{K}$ sharing the same template, or high-level structure – *e.g.* an element of $\mathfrak{P}$ contains all rules with structure $\boldsymbol{\theta}_{p:}(X,Y) :\!- \boldsymbol{\theta}_{q:}(X,Z), \boldsymbol{\theta}_{r:}(Z,Y)$, with $\boldsymbol{\theta}_{p:}, \boldsymbol{\theta}_{q:}, \boldsymbol{\theta}_{r:} \in \mathbb{R}^k$. [5] We then redefine the or operator as follows:

$$\text{or}_{\boldsymbol{\theta}}^{\mathfrak{K}}(G, d, S) = [S' \mid H :\!- B \in \mathcal{N}_{\mathfrak{P}}(G), \mathscr{P} \in \mathfrak{P}, S' \in \text{and}_{\boldsymbol{\theta}}^{\mathfrak{K}}(B, d, \text{unify}_{\boldsymbol{\theta}}(H, G, S))]$$

where, instead of unifying a sub-goal G with all rule heads, we constrain the unification to only the rules where heads are in the neighborhood $\mathcal{N}_{\mathfrak{P}}(G)$ of G.

Learning to Attend Over Predicates.   Although NTPs can be used for *learning inter- pretable rules* from data, the solution proposed by [54] can be quite inefficient, as the number of parameters associated to rules can be quite large. For instance, the rule H :- B, with $H = [\boldsymbol{\theta}_{p:}, X, Y]$ and $B = [[\boldsymbol{\theta}_{q:}, X, Z], [\boldsymbol{\theta}_{r:}, Z, Y]]$, where $\boldsymbol{\theta}_{p:}, \boldsymbol{\theta}_{q:}, \boldsymbol{\theta}_{r:} \in \mathbb{R}^k$, introduces $3k$ parameters in the model, where k denotes the embedding size, and it may be computa- tionally inefficient to learn each of the embedding vectors if k is large.

We propose using an *attention mechanism* [3] for attending over known predicates for defining the rule-predicate embeddings $\boldsymbol{\theta}_{p:}, \boldsymbol{\theta}_{q:}, \boldsymbol{\theta}_{r:}$. Let $\mathscr{R}$ be the set of known predicates, and let $R \in \mathbb{R}^{|\mathscr{R}| \times k}$ be a matrix representing the embeddings for the predicates in $\mathscr{R}$. We define $\boldsymbol{\theta}_{p:}$ as $\boldsymbol{\theta}_{p:} = \text{softmax}(\mathbf{a}_{p:})^{\top} R$. where $\mathbf{a}_{p:} \in \mathbb{R}^{|\mathscr{R}|}$ is a set of trainable *attention weights* associated with the predicate p. This sensibly improves the parameter efficiency of the model in cases where the number of known predicates is low, *i.e.* $|\mathscr{R}| \ll k$, by introducing $c|\mathscr{R}|$ parameters for each rule rather than ck, where c is the number of trainable predicate embeddings in the rule.

4. Jointly Reasoning on Knowledge Bases and Natural Language

In this section, we show how GNTPs can jointly reason over KBs and natural language corpora. In the following, we assume that our KB $\mathfrak{K}$ is composed of facts, rules, and *textual mentions*. A fact is composed of a predicate symbol and a sequence of arguments, *e.g.* [locationOf, LONDON, UK]. On the other hand, a *mention* is a textual pattern between two co-occurring entities in the KB [56], such as "LONDON *is located in the* UK".

---

[5]Grouping rules with the same structure together makes allows parallel inference to be implemented very efficiently on GPU. This optimization is also present in [54].

We represent mentions jointly with facts and rules in $\mathfrak{K}$ by considering each textual surface pattern linking two entities as a new predicate, and embedding it in a d-dimensional space by means of an end-to-end differentiable reading component. For instance, the sentence "United Kingdom borders with Ireland" can be translated into the following mention: $[[\,[\text{arg1}],\text{borders},\text{with},[\text{arg2}]\,],\text{UK},\text{IRELAND}]$, by first identifying sentences or paragraphs containing KB entities, and then considering the textual surface pattern connecting such entities as an extra relation type. While predicates in $\mathscr{R}$ are encoded by a look-up operation to a predicate embedding matrix $R \in \mathbb{R}^{|\mathscr{R}| \times k}$, textual surface patterns are encoded by an $\text{encode}_{\boldsymbol{\theta}} : \mathscr{V}^* \to \mathbb{R}^k$ module, where $\mathscr{V}$ is the vocabulary of words and symbols occurring in textual surface patterns.

More formally, given a textual surface pattern $t \in \mathscr{V}^*$ (an example of surface pattern is $t = [[\text{arg1}],\text{borders},\text{with},[\text{arg2}]]$), the $\text{encode}_{\boldsymbol{\theta}}$ module first encodes each token w in t by means of a token embedding matrix $V \in \mathbb{R}^{|\mathscr{V}| \times k'}$, resulting in a pattern matrix $W_t \in \mathbb{R}^{|t| \times k'}$. Then, the module produces a textual surface pattern embedding vector $\boldsymbol{\theta}_{t:} \in \mathbb{R}^k$ from W_t by means of an end-to-end differentiable encoder. For assessing whether a simple encoder architecture can already provide benefits to the model, we use an $\text{encode}_{\boldsymbol{\theta}}$ module that aggregates the embeddings of the tokens composing a textual surface pattern via mean pooling: $\text{encode}_{\boldsymbol{\theta}}(t) = \frac{1}{|t|} \sum_{w \in t} V_{w:} \in \mathbb{R}^k$. Albeit the encoder can be implemented by using other differentiable architectures, for this work we opted for a simple but still very effective Bag of Embeddings model [2,61] showing that, even in this case, the model achieves very accurate results.

5. Related Work

Differentiable Memory Models. A notable corpus of literature aims at addressing the limitations of neural architectures in terms of generalization and reasoning abilities. A line of research consists of enriching neural network architectures with a differentiable *external memory* [22,23,31,32,55]. The underlying idea is that a neural network can learn to represent and manipulate complex data structures, thus disentangling the algorithmic part of the process from the representation of the inputs. By doing so, it becomes possible to train such models from enriched supervision signals, such as from *program traces* rather than simple input-output pairs.

Differentiable Program Interpreters. A related field is *differentiable interpreters*—program interpreters where declarative or procedural knowledge is compiled into a neural network architecture [8,17,54]. This family of models allows imposing strong inductive biases on the models by partially defining the program structure used for constructing the network, *e.g.*, in terms of instruction sets or rules. A major drawback of differentiable interpreters, however, is their computational complexity, so far deeming them unusable except for smaller learning problems. [51] use an approximate nearest neighbor data structures for sparsifying read operations in memory networks.

Neural Module Networks. This work is also related to neural module networks [1], which are composed by collections of jointly trained neural modules. NTPs are a recursive composition of or and and modules, following from the backward-chaining reasoning algorithm, and jointly trained on downstream reasoning tasks. [26] extend neural module networks to question answering, by implementing differentiable reusable modules for

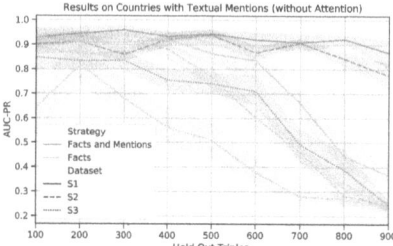
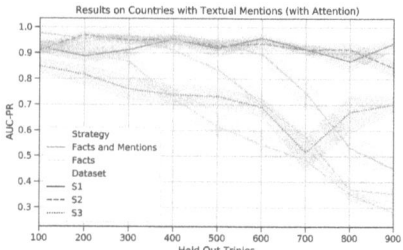

Figure 2. GNTPs on Countries with generated mentions. We replaced a varying number of relations with textual mentions and integrated them by encoding the mentions using a text encoder (*Facts and Mentions*) and by simply adding them to the KB (*Facts*). Two figures contrast the effects of rule learning without attention (left) and with it (right).

Predicate Name	Mentions
`locatedIn`(a,b)	a is located in b, a is situated in b, a is placed in b, a is positioned in b, a is sited in b, a can be found in b, a is still in b, a is localized in b, a is present in b, a is contained in b, a is found in b, a was located in b, a was situated in b, a was placed in b, a was positioned in b, a was sited in b, a was currently in b, a used to be found in b, a was still in b, a was localized in b, a was present in b, a was contained in b, a was found in b
`neighborOf`(a,b)	a is adjacent to b, a borders with b, a is butted against b, a neighbors b, a is a neighbor of b, a is a neighboring country of b, a is a neighboring state to b, a was adjacent to b, a borders b, a was butted against b, a neighbors with b, a was a neighbor of b, a was a neighboring country of b, a was a neighboring state to b

Table 1. Mentions used for replacing a varying number of training triples in the Countries S1, S2, and S3 datasets.

operations such as arithmetic, sorting, and counting. [29] extend this idea by implementing four neural modules, namely `find`, `relocate`, `compare`, and `no-op`, coordinated by a Recurrent Neural Network (RNN), for executing natural language reasoning tasks.

Reasoning over Text and Knowledge Bases.   [53] pioneered the idea of jointly embedding KB facts and textual mentions in shared embedding space, by considering mentions as additional relations in a KB factorization setting, and more elaborate mention encoders were investigated by [42].

Our work is also related to path encoding models [11] and random walk approaches [20,37], both of which lack a rule induction mechanisms, and to approaches combining observable and latent features of the graph [46,48]. Lastly, our work is related to [63], a scalable rule induction approach for KB completion, but has not been applied to textual surface patterns.

6. Experiments

6.1. Datasets and Evaluation Protocols.

We report the results of experiments on benchmark datasets—Countries [7], Nations, UMLS, and Kinship [33]—following the same evaluation protocols as [54].

Countries   Countries is a dataset introduced by [7] for testing reasoning capabilities of neural link prediction models. It consists of 244 countries, 5 regions (*e.g.* EUROPE), 23 sub-regions (*e.g.* WESTERN EUROPE, NORTH AMERICA), and 1158 facts about the

Table 2. Examples of the clauses used for Freebase (FB122) and WordNet (WN18).

/people/person/languages(X,Z) :− /people/person/nationality(X,Y),/location/country/official_language(Y,Z)
/location/contains(X,Z) :− /country/administrative_divisions(X,Y),/administrative_division/capital(Y,Z)
/location/location/contains(X,Y) :− /location/country/capital(X,Y)

_hyponym(Y,X) :− _hypernym(X,Y)	_hypernym(Y,X) :− _hyponym(X,Y)
_part_of(Y,X) :− _has_part(X,Y)	_has_part(Y,X) :− _part_of(X,Y)

neighborhood of countries and the location of countries and sub-regions. As in [54], we randomly split countries into a training set of 204 countries (train), a development set of 20 countries (validation), and a test set of 20 countries (test), such that every validation and test country has at least one neighbor in the training set. Subsequently, three different task datasets are created, namely **S1**, **S2**, and **S3**. For all tasks, the goal is to predict locatedIn(c,r) for every test country c and all five regions r, but the access to training atoms in the KB varies.

S1: All ground atoms locatedIn(c,r), where c is a test country and r is a region, are removed from the KB. Since information about the sub-region of test countries is still contained in the KB, this task can be solved by using the transitivity rule:

$$\text{locatedIn}(X,Y) :- \text{locatedIn}(X,Z), \text{locatedIn}(Z,Y).$$

S2: In addition to **S1**, all ground atoms locatedIn(c,s) are removed where c is a test country and s is a sub-region. The location of countries in the test set needs to be inferred from the location of its neighboring countries:

$$\text{locatedIn}(X,Y) :- \text{neighborOf}(X,Z), \text{locatedIn}(Z,Y).$$

This task is more difficult than **S1**, as neighboring countries might not be in the same region, so the rule above will not always hold.

S3: In addition to **S2**, also all ground atoms locatedIn(c,r) are removed where r is a region and c is a country from the training set training that has a country from the validation or test sets as a neighbor. The location of test countries can for instance be inferred using the rule:

$$\text{locatedIn}(X,Y) :- \text{neighborOf}(X,Z), \text{neighborOf}(Z,W), \text{locatedIn}(W,Y).$$

Countries with Mentions   We generated a set of variants of Countries S1, S2, and S3, by randomly replacing a varying number of training set triples with mentions. The employed mentions are outlined in Table 1.

Nations and UMLS   Furthermore, we consider the Nations, and the Unified Medical Language System (UMLS) datasets [36]. UMLS contains 49 predicates, 135 constants and 6529 true facts, while Nations contains 56 binary predicates, 111 unary predicates, 14 constants and 2565 true facts. We follow the protocol used by [54] and split every dataset into training, development, and test facts, with a 80%/10%/10% ratio. For evaluation, we take a test fact and corrupt its first and second argument in all possible ways such that the corrupted fact is not in the original KB. Subsequently, we predict a ranking of the test fact and its corruptions to calculate Mean Reciprocal Rank (MRR) and HITS@m.

WordNet and Freebase   Furthermore, since GNTPs allows to experiment on significantly larger datasets, we also report results on the WN18 [5], WN18RR [15] and FB122 [25] datasets.

We also evaluate the proposed method on WordNet (WN18) and Freebase (FB122) jointly with the set of rules released by [25]. WordNet [43] is a lexical knowledge base for the English language, where entities correspond to word senses, and relationships define lexical relations between them. The WN18 dataset consists of a subset of WordNet, containing 40,943 entities, 18 relation types, and 151,442 triples.

We also consider WN18RR [15], a dataset derived from WN18 where predicting missing links is sensibly harder.

Freebase [4] is a large knowledge graph that stores general facts about the world. The FB122 dataset is a subset of Freebase regarding the topics of *people*, *location* and *sports*, and contains 9,738 entities, 122 relation types, and 112,476 triples.

For both data sets, we used the fixed training, validation, test sets and rules provided by [25]; a subset of the rules is shown in Table 2. Note that a subset of the test triples can be inferred by deductive logic inference.

For such a reason, following [25], we also partition the test set in two subsets, namely Test-I and Test-II: Test-I contains triples that *cannot* be inferred by deductive logic inference, while Test-II contains all remaining test triples.

Metrics   Results are reported in terms of the Area Under the Precision-Recall Curve (AUC-PR) [13], MRR, and HITS@m [5].

Hyper-parameters   For each experiment, the best hyperparameters were selected via cross-validation. We use Adam [35] for minimizing the loss function in Eq. 4. We searched for the best learning rates in $\{0.001, 0.005, 0.01, 0.05, 0.1\}$, for the best L2 regularization weights in $\{0.001, 0.0001\}$. For Freebase and WordNet, we fixed the batch size to 1000, while for Countries, UMLS, Kinship, and Nations we searched the best batch size in $\{10, 20, 50, 100\}$. About GNTPs-specific hyperparameters, we searched for the best number of rules k_r and facts k_f to unify with in $\{1, 3, 5\}$.

Due to time and computational constraints, the embedding size of entities and relation types was set to 100, the number of epochs was also set to 100, while the maximum proof depth d was fixed to 2.

In all experiments, we observed a quick convergence of the model already in the first 20-30 epochs. On FB122, we found it useful to pre-train rules first (95 epochs), without updating any entity or relation embeddings, and then training the entity embeddings jointly with the rules (5 epochs). This forces GNTPs to learn a good rule-based model of the domain before fine-tuning its representations.

Baselines.   On benchmark datasets, we compare GNTPs with NTPs and two other neuro-symbolic reasoning systems, MINERVA [10], which employs a reinforcement learning algorithm to reach answers by traversing the KB graph, and NeuralLP [63], which compiles inference tasks in a sequence of differentiable operations. In addition, we consider DistMult [62] and ComplEx [58], two state-of-the-art black-box neural link predictors suited for large datasets.

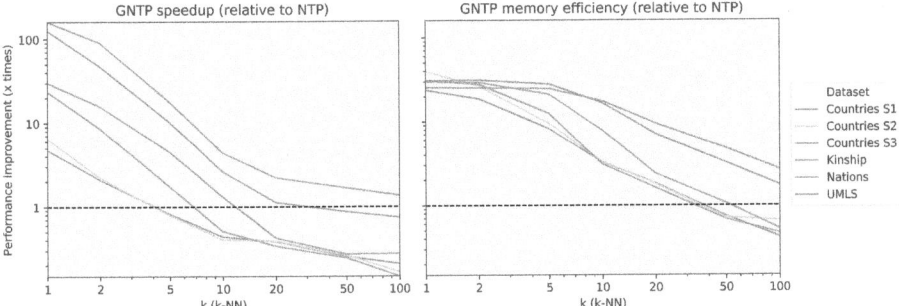

Figure 3. Run-time and memory performance of GNTP in comparison with NTP Run-time speedup calculated as the ratio of examples per second of GNTP and NTP. Memory efficiency calculated as a ratio of the memory use of NTP and GNTP. Dashed line denotes equal performance – above it (green) GNTP performs better, below it (red) performs worse.

6.2. Run-Time Evaluation.

To assess the benefits of GNTPs in terms of computational complexity and range of applications, we conduct two experiments, comparing GNTPs to NTPs on both small and large datasets.

First, we compare GNTP to NTP with respect to time and memory performance during training on smaller datasets. In these experiments, we vary the n of the NNS to assess the computational demands by increasing n. We compare two quantities: the average number of examples (queries) per second by running 10 training batches with a maximum batch to fit the memory of NVIDIA GeForce GTX 1080 Ti, for all models, and the the maximum memory usage of both models on a CPU, over 10 training batches with same batch sizes. The comparison is done on a CPU to ensure that we include the size of the NNS index in GNTP measures and as a fail-safe, in case the model does not fit on the GPU memory.

The results, presented in Fig. 3, demonstrate that, compared to NTP, GNTP is considerably more efficient. In particular, we observe that GNTP yields significant speedups of an order of magnitude for smaller datasets (Countries S1 and S2), and more than two orders of magnitude for larger datasets (Kinship and Nations). Interestingly, with the increased size of the dataset, GNTP consistently achieves higher speedups, when compared to NTP. Similarly, GNTP is more memory efficient, with savings bigger than an order of magnitude, making them readily applicable to larger datasets, even when augmented with textual surface forms.

Second, we measure the time needed for each training epoch varying the number of unified facts and rules during inference on the best hyperparameters we found for the WN18 dataset. Results, outlined in Fig. 4, show that learning on WN18 quickly becomes infeasible by increasing the number of unified facts and rules. NTPs are a special case of GNTPs where, during the forward pass, there is no pruning of the proof paths.

From Fig. 4 we can see that even for KBs a fraction the size of WordNet and Freebase, NTPs rapidly run out of memory, deeming them inapplicable to reasonably sized KBs. Instead, sensible pruning of proof paths in GNTPs drastically increases the efficiency of both the learning and the inference process, allowing to train on large KBs like WordNet.

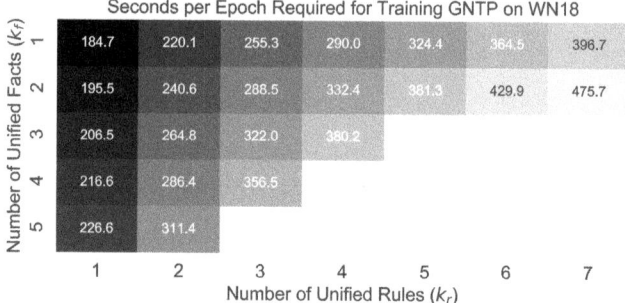

Figure 4. Number of seconds per epoch required for training on the WN18 dataset using batches of 1000 examples on a GPU. Missing entries denote out-of-memory errors.

Table 3. Comparison of GNTPs, NTPs, NeuralLP [63], and MINERVA [10] (from [10]) on benchmark datasets, with and without attention.

Datasets	Metrics	NTP [7]	GNTP Standard	GNTP Attention	NeuralLP	MINERVA	Rules Learned by GNTP
Countries	S1	90.83 ± 15.4	99.98 ± 0.05	**100.0 ± 0.0**	100.0 ± 0.0	100.0 ± 0.0	located(X,Y) :- located(X,Z), located(Z,Y)
	S2	87.40 ± 11.7	90.82 ± 0.88	**93.48 ± 3.29**	75.1 ± 0.3	92.36 ± 2.41	neighbor(X,Y) :- neighbor(X,Z), located(Z,Y)
	S3	56.68 ± 17.6	87.70 ± 4.79	**91.27 ± 4.02**	92.20 ± 0.2	95.10 ± 1.20	neighbor(X,Y) :- neighbor(Y,X)
Kinship	MRR	0.35	0.719	**0.759**	0.619	0.720	term0(X, Y) :- term0(Y, X)
	HITS@1	0.24	0.586	**0.642**	0.475	0.605	term4(X, Y) :- term4(Y, X)
	HITS@3	0.37	0.815	**0.850**	0.707	0.812	term13(X,Y) :- term13(X, Z), term10(Z, Y)
	HITS@10	0.57	0.958	**0.959**	0.912	0.924	term2(X,Y) :- term4(X, Z), term7(Z, Y)
Nations	MRR	0.61	**0.658**	0.645	—	—	commonbloc1(X, Y) :- relngo(Y, X)
	HITS@1	0.45	**0.493**	0.490	—	—	timesincewar(X,Y) :- independence(X,Y)
	HITS@3	0.73	**0.781**	0.736	—	—	unweightedunvote(X,Y) :- relngo(X,Y)
	HITS@10	0.87	**0.985**	0.975	—	—	ngo(X, Y) :- independence(Y, X)
UMLS	MRR	0.80	0.841	**0.857**	0.778	0.825	isa(X,Y) :- isa(X,Z), isa(Z,Y)
	HITS@1	0.70	0.732	**0.761**	0.643	0.728	complicates(X,Y) :- affects(X,Y)
	HITS@3	0.88	**0.941**	0.947	0.869	0.900	affects(X, Y) :- affects(X, Z), affects(Z, Y)
	HITS@10	0.95	**0.986**	0.983	0.962	0.968	process_of(X,Y) :- affects(X,Y)

6.3. Link Prediction Results.

We compare GNTPs and NTPs on a set of link prediction benchmarks, also used in [54]. Results, presented in Table 3, show that GNTPs achieves better or on-par results in comparison with NTPs and baselines MINERVA [10] and NeuralLP [10], consistently through all benchmark datasets. We can also see that models learned by GNTPs are *interpretable*: in Table 3 we show the decoded rules learned by the model, and learn about the domain at hand. For instance, we can see that on UMLS, a biomedical KB, the isa and affects relation are transitive.

6.4. Experiments with Generated Mentions.

For evaluating different strategies of integrating textual surface patterns, in the form of mentions, in NTPs, we proceeded as follows. We replaced a varying number of training set triples from each of the Countries S1-S3 datasets with human-generated textual mentions. For instance, the fact neighborOf(UK, IRELAND) may be replaced by the textual mention "UK is neighboring with IRELAND". The entities UK and

Table 4. Link prediction results on the Test-I, Test-II and Test-ALL on FB122. Note that KALE, *ASR* methods, and KBLR have access to a set of rules provided by [25], while neural link predictors and GNTPs do not. Test-II (6,186 triples) denotes a subset of FB122 that can be inferred via logic rules, while Test-I (5,057 triples) denotes all other test triples. We can see that, even without providing any rule to the model, GNTPs yields better ranking results in comparison with neural link prediction models—since it is able to learn such rules from data—and it is comparable with models that can leverage the provided rules.

		Test-I				Test-II				Test-ALL			
		Hits@N (%)			MRR	Hits@N (%)			MRR	Hits@N (%)			MRR
		3	5	10		3	5	10		3	5	10	
With Rules	KALE-Pre [25]	35.8	41.9	49.8	0.291	82.9	86.1	89.9	0.713	61.7	66.2	71.8	0.523
	KALE-Joint [25]	38.4	44.7	52.2	0.325	79.7	84.1	89.6	0.684	61.2	66.4	72.8	0.523
	ASR-DistMult [47]	36.3	40.3	44.9	0.330	98.0	99.0	99.2	0.948	70.7	73.1	75.2	0.675
	ASR-ComplEx [47]	37.3	41.0	45.9	**0.338**	99.2	99.3	99.4	**0.984**	71.7	73.6	75.7	0.698
	KBLR [19]	–	–	–	–	–	–	–	–	74.0	77.0	79.7	0.702
Without Rules	TransE [5]	36.0	41.5	48.1	0.296	77.5	82.8	88.4	0.630	58.9	64.2	70.2	0.480
	DistMult [62]	36.0	40.3	45.3	0.313	92.3	93.8	94.7	0.874	67.4	70.2	72.9	0.628
	ComplEx [58]	**37.0**	**41.3**	**46.2**	**0.329**	91.4	91.9	92.4	**0.887**	67.3	69.5	71.9	**0.641**
	GNTPs	33.7	36.9	41.2	0.313	98.2	99.0	99.3	0.977	69.2	71.1	73.2	0.678

IRELAND become the arguments, while the text between them is treated as a new logic predicate, forming a new fact "X is neighboring with Y"(UK, IRELAND).

Then, we evaluate two ways of integrating textual mentions in GNTPs: *i)* adding them as facts to the KB, and *ii)* parsing the mention by means of an encoder. The results, presented in Fig. 2, show that the proposed encoding module yields consistent improvements of the ranking accuracy in comparison to simply adding the mentions as facts to the KB. This is especially evident in cases where the number of held-out facts is higher, as it is often the case in real-world use cases, where there is an abundance of text but the KBs are sparse and incomplete [49]. GNTPs are extremely efficient at learning rules involving both *logic atoms and textual mentions*.

For instance, by analyzing the learned models and their explanations, we can see that GNTPs learn rules such as:

neighborOf(X, Y) :– "Y is a neighboring state to X"(X, Y)
locatedIn(X, Y) :– "X is a neighboring state to Z"(X, Z), "Z is located in Y"(Z, Y)

and leverage them during their reasoning process, providing human-readable explanations for a given prediction.

6.5. Results on Freebase and WordNet

Link prediction results for FB122 are summarized in Table 4. The FB122 dataset proposed by [25] is fairly large scale: it comprises 91,638 triples, 9,738 entities, and 122 relations, as well as 47 rules that can be leveraged by models for link prediction tasks. For such a reason, we consider a series of models that can leverage the presence of such rules, namely KALE [25], DistMult and ComplEx using Adversarial Sets (*ASR*) [47]—a method for incorporating rules in neural link predictors via adversarial training—and the recently

---

[7]Results reported in [54] were calculated with an incorrect evaluation function, causing artificially better results. We corrected the issues, and recalculated the results.

Table 5. Explanations, in terms of rules and supporting facts, for the queries in the validation set of WN18 provided by GNTPs by looking at the proof paths yielding the largest proof scores.

Query	Score S_ρ	Proofs / Explanations
	0.995	part_of(X, Y) :− has_part(Y, X)
part_of(CONGO.N.03, AFRICA.N.01)		has_part(AFRICA.N.01, CONGO.N.03)
	0.787	part_of(X, Y) :− instance_hyponym(Y, X)
		instance_hyponym(AFRICAN_COUNTRY.N.01, CONGO.N.03)
hyponym(EXTINGUISH.V.04, DECOUPLE.V.03)	0.987	hyponym(X, Y) :− hypernym(Y, X)
		hypernym(DECOUPLE.V.03, EXTINGUISH.V.04)
has_part(TEXAS.N.01, ODESSA.N.02)	0.961	has_part(X, Y) :− part_of(Y, X)
		part_of(ODESSA.N.02, TEXAS.N.01)

proposed KBLR [19]. Note that, unlike these methods, GNTPs do not have access to such rules and need to learn them from data.

Table 4 shows that GNTP, whilst not having access to rules, performs significantly better than neural link predictors, and on-par with methods that have access to all rules. In particular, we can see that on Test-II, a subset of FB122 directly related to logic rules, GNTP yields competitive results. GNTP is able to induce rules accurately describing the domain and use them during inference for identifying missing links, such as:

timeZone(X, Y) :− containedBy(X, Z), timeZone(Z, Y)
nearbyAirports(X, Y) :− containedBy(X, Z), contains(Z, Y)
children(X, Y) :− parents(Y, X)
spouse(X, Y) :− spouse(Y, X)

We also evaluate GNTP on WN18 [5] and WN18RR [15]. In terms of ranking accuracy, GNTPs is comparable to state-of-the-art models, such as ComplEx and KBLR. In [19] authors report a 94.2 MRR for ComplEx and 93.6 MRR for KBLR, while NeuralLP [63] achieves 94.0, with hits@10 equal to 94.5. GNTP achieves 94.2 MRR and 94.31, 94.41, 94.51 hits@3, 5, 10, which is on par with state-of-the-art neural link prediction models, while being interpretable via proof paths. Table 5 shows an excerpt of validation triples together with their GNTP proof scores and associated proof paths for WN18. On WN18RR, GNTP with MRR of 43.4 performs close to ComplEx [15] (44.0 MRR) but lags behind NeuralLP (46.3 MRR).

We can see that GNTPs is capable of learning and utilizing rules, such as has_part(X, Y) :− part_of(Y, X), and hyponym(X, Y) :− hypernym(Y, X). Interestingly, GNTP is able to find non-trivial explanations for a given fact, based on the similarity between entity representations. For instance, it can explain that CONGO is part of AFRICA by leveraging the semantic similarity with AFRICAN_COUNTRY.

7. Conclusions, Limitations, and Future Work

NTPs combine the strengths of rule-based and neural models but, so far, they were unable to reason over large KBs and natural language. In this paper, we overcome such limitations by considering only the subset of proof paths associated with the largest proof scores during the construction of a dynamic computation graph.

The proposed model, GNTP, is more computationally efficient by several orders of magnitude, while achieving similar or better predictive performance than NTPs. GNTPs enable end-to-end differentiable reasoning on large KBs and natural language texts, by embedding logic atoms and textual mentions in the same embedding space. Furthermore, GNTPs are interpretable and can provide explanations in terms of logic proofs at scale.

Limitations and Future Work.   There are several exciting research directions for extending this work. For instance, at the moment of this writing, the expressiveness of GNTPs is still fairly limited. Case in point, GNTPs supports only function-free Horn clauses, leaving negation, logical or, and function operators out of the scope of the model. Other than increasing the expressiveness of the model with the negation and the or operators, it would be interesting to support a wider range of operators and predicates, such as arithmetic operators and neural predicates. Arithmetic operators can be used to expand the reasoning process with either predefined function set, or via learned operators, such as Neural Arithmetic Logic Units [57] and Neural Arithmetic Units [41]. Neural predicates, on the other hand, could provide means of learning the computation on different types of modalities. This would enable the model to use *e.g.* perceptual, speech or language information, and encoding it in the KB, as well as to induce relationships between such objects.

Though far more efficient than NTPs, GNTPs still leave further opportunities for improvement. The rule selection process in GNTPs is a heuristic parameterless process, based on local information. Given a goal, during the proving process, the model only considers the top-k rules, selected based on the similarity between the learned representations of rule heads and the goal. This may lead to sub-optimal choices of the set of rules for each goal and sub-goal. A more principled way to deal with this issue could consist of learning a *rule selection policy* that, conditioned on a goal, can learn to select a rule or a fact that maximizes the final proof score. Interestingly, such a policy could be learned jointly with the model parameters, enabling learning representations of entities and relations in the KB at the same time as the policy itself.

When it comes to learning efficiency, [14] note that NTPs do not learn rules efficiently. During training, the model only returns the highest-scoring proof score for any given training query and updates the corresponding proof path via gradient-based optimization. This implies incredibly sparse gradient-based updates, since the highest-scoring proof score depends only on the value of the unification score between two sub-symbolic representations, which are the only ones receiving gradient updates. This can be an issue since it limits the exploration of the rule space to modifying one rule at a time. To resolve this issue, [14] propose to modify the rule aggregation mechanism in NTPs to consider the top-k highest-scoring proofs. [17] make a related observation, noting that aggregating scores in a proof path via minimum or maximum operations lead to sparse gradients in comparison with other soft operators, adversely affecting the rule induction process.

Finally, GNTPs are not designed to explicitly acquire, incorporate, and express uncertainty, which can be of crucial importance in critical reasoning tasks. An extension of this model could allow users to express the uncertainty associated with a rule or a fact, akin to DeepProbLog programs and Bayesian Logic Programs [34], and possibly let the model learn the uncertainty of rules and facts from data.

References

[1]   Jacob Andreas, Marcus Rohrbach, Trevor Darrell, and Dan Klein. Neural module networks. In *CVPR*, pages 39–48. IEEE Computer Society, 2016.

[2]   Sanjeev Arora, Yingyu Liang, and Tengyu Ma. A simple but tough-to-beat baseline for sentence embeddings. In *ICLR*, 2017.

[3]   Dzmitry Bahdanau, Kyunghyun Cho, and Yoshua Bengio. Neural Machine Translation by Jointly Learning to Align and Translate. In *ICLR*, 2015.

[4]   Kurt D. Bollacker, Robert P. Cook, and Patrick Tufts. Freebase: A Shared Database of Structured General Human Knowledge. In *AAAI*, pages 1962–1963, 2007.

[5]   Antoine Bordes, Nicolas Usunier, Alberto García-Durán, Jason Weston, and Oksana Yakhnenko. Translating Embeddings for Modeling Multi-relational Data. In *NIPS*, pages 2787–2795, 2013.

[6]   Johan Bos. Wide-coverage semantic analysis with boxer. In *STEP*. Association for Computational Linguistics, 2008.

[7]   Guillaume Bouchard, Sameer Singh, and Théo Trouillon. On approximate reasoning capabilities of low-rank vector spaces. In *AAAI Spring Symposia*. AAAI Press, 2015.

[8]   Matko Bošnjak, Tim Rocktäschel, Jason Naradowsky, and Sebastian Riedel. Programming with a Differentiable Forth Interpreter. In *ICML*, volume 70, pages 547–556, 2017.

[9]   Samuel R Bowman, Gabor Angeli, Christopher Potts, and Christopher D Manning. A large annotated corpus for learning natural language inference. In *EMNLP*, 2015.

[10] Rajarshi Das, Shehzaad Dhuliawala, Manzil Zaheer, Luke Vilnis, Ishan Durugkar, Akshay Krishnamurthy, Alexander J. Smola, and Andrew McCallum. Go for a Walk and Arrive at the Answer: Reasoning Over Paths in Knowledge Bases using Reinforcement Learning. In *ICLR*, 2018.

[11] Rajarshi Das, Arvind Neelakantan, David Belanger, and Andrew McCallum. Chains of Reasoning over Entities, Relations, and Text using Recurrent Neural Networks. In *EACL*, pages 132–141, 2017.

[12] Artur S. d'Avila Garcez, Tarek R. Besold, Luc De Raedt, Peter Földiák, Pascal Hitzler, Thomas Icard, Kai-Uwe Kühnberger, Luís C. Lamb, Risto Miikkulainen, and Daniel L. Silver. Neural-symbolic learning and reasoning: Contributions and challenges. In *AAAI Spring Symposia*, 2015.

[13] Jesse Davis and Mark Goadrich. The relationship between Precision-Recall and ROC curves. In *ICML*, volume 148, 2006.

[14] Michiel de Jong and Fei Sha. Neural theorem provers do not learn rules without exploration. *arXiv preprint arXiv:1906.06805*, 2019.

[15] Tim Dettmers, Pasquale Minervini, Pontus Stenetorp, and Sebastian Riedel. Convolutional 2D Knowledge Graph Embeddings. In *AAAI*, 2018.

[16] Oren Etzioni, Michele Banko, and Michael J. Cafarella. Machine reading. In *AAAI*, pages 1517–1519. AAAI Press, 2006.

[17] Richard Evans and Edward Grefenstette. Learning Explanatory Rules from Noisy Data. *JAIR*, 61:1–64, 2018.

[18] Yaroslav Fyodorov, Yoad Winter, and Nissim Francez. A Natural Logic Inference System. In *Proceedings of the of the 2nd Workshop on Inference in Computational Semantics*, 2000.

[19] Alberto García-Durán and Mathias Niepert. KBlrn: End-to-End Learning of Knowledge Base Representations with Latent, Relational, and Numerical Features. In *UAI*, pages 372–381, 2018.

[20] Matt Gardner, Partha Pratim Talukdar, Jayant Krishnamurthy, and Tom M. Mitchell. Incorporating Vector Space Similarity in Random Walk Inference over Knowledge Bases. In *EMNLP*, pages 397–406, 2014.

[21] Marta Garnelo and Murray Shanahan. Reconciling deep learning with symbolic artificial intelligence: representing objects and relations. *Current Opinion in Behavioral Sciences*, 29:17 – 23, 2019.

[22] Alex Graves, Greg Wayne, and Ivo Danihelka. Neural Turing Machines. *CoRR*, abs/1410.5401, 2014.

[23] Edward Grefenstette, Karl Moritz Hermann, Mustafa Suleyman, and Phil Blunsom. Learning to Transduce with Unbounded Memory. In *NIPS*, pages 1828–1836, 2015.

[24] Riccardo Guidotti, Anna Monreale, Salvatore Ruggieri, Franco Turini, Fosca Giannotti, and Dino Pedreschi. A Survey of Methods for Explaining Black Box Models. *ACM CSUR*, 51(5):93:1–93:42, 2018.

[25] Shu Guo, Quan Wang, Lihong Wang, Bin Wang, and Li Guo. Jointly Embedding Knowledge Graphs and Logical Rules. In *EMNLP*, pages 192–202, 2016.

[26] Nitish Gupta, Kevin Lin, Dan Roth, Sameer Singh, and Matt Gardner. Neural module networks for reasoning over text. *CoRR*, abs/1912.04971, 2019.

[27] Karl Moritz Hermann, Tomas Kocisky, Edward Grefenstette, Lasse Espeholt, Will Kay, Mustafa Suleyman, and Phil Blunsom. Teaching Machines to Read and Comprehend. In *NIPS*, pages 1693–1701, 2015.

[28] Zhisheng Huang, Frank van Harmelen, and Annette ten Teije. Reasoning with Inconsistent Ontologies. In *IJCAI*, pages 454–459, 2005.

[29]   Yichen Jiang and Mohit Bansal. Self-assembling modular networks for interpretable multi-hop reasoning. In *EMNLP/IJCNLP (1)*, pages 4473–4483. Association for Computational Linguistics, 2019.

[30]   Jeff Johnson, Matthijs Douze, and Hervé Jégou. Billion-scale similarity search with gpus. *arXiv preprint arXiv:1702.08734*, 2017.

[31]   Armand Joulin and Tomas Mikolov. Inferring Algorithmic Patterns with Stack-Augmented Recurrent Nets. In *NIPS*, 2015.

[32]   Lukasz Kaiser and Ilya Sutskever. Neural GPUs Learn Algorithms. In *ICLR*, 2016.

[33]   Charles Kemp, Joshua B. Tenenbaum, Thomas L. Griffiths, Takeshi Yamada, and Naonori Ueda. Learning Systems of Concepts with an Infinite Relational Model. In *AAAI*, pages 381–388, 2006.

[34]   Kristian Kersting and Luc De Raedt. Basic principles of learning bayesian logic programs. In *Probabilistic Inductive Logic Programming*, volume 4911 of *Lecture Notes in Computer Science*, pages 189–221. Springer, 2008.

[35]   Diederik P. Kingma and Jimmy Ba. Adam: A Method for Stochastic Optimization. In *ICLR*, 2015.

[36]   Stanley Kok and Pedro M. Domingos. Statistical Predicate Invention. In *ICML*, volume 227, pages 433–440, 2007.

[37]   Ni Lao, Tom M. Mitchell, and William W. Cohen. Random Walk Inference and Learning in A Large Scale Knowledge Base. In *EMNLP*, pages 529–539, 2011.

[38]   Hector J. Levesque. On our best behaviour. *Artificial Intelligence*, 212:27–35, 2014.

[39]   Zachary C. Lipton. The mythos of model interpretability. *Commun. ACM*, 61(10):36–43, 2018.

[40]   Bill MacCartney and Christopher D. Manning. Natural logic for textual inference. In *ACL-PASCAL@ACL*, pages 193–200. ACL, 2007.

[41]   Andreas Madsen and Alexander Rosenberg Johansen. Neural arithmetic units. *CoRR*, abs/2001.05016, 2020.

[42]   Andrew McCallum, Arvind Neelakantan, and Patrick Verga. Generalizing to Unseen Entities and Entity Pairs with Row-less Universal Schema. In *EACL*, pages 613–622, 2017.

[43]   George A. Miller. WordNet: A Lexical Database for English. *Communications of the ACM*, 38(11):39–41, 1995.

[44]   Pasquale Minervini, Matko Bosnjak, Tim Rocktäschel, and Sebastian Riedel. Towards neural theorem proving at scale. *CoRR*, abs/1807.08204, 2018.

[45]   Pasquale Minervini, Matko Bosnjak, Tim Rocktäschel, Sebastian Riedel, and Edward Grefenstette. Differentiable reasoning on large knowledge bases and natural language. *CoRR*, abs/1912.10824, 2019.

[46]   Pasquale Minervini, Claudia d'Amato, Nicola Fanizzi, and Floriana Esposito. Leveraging the schema in latent factor models for knowledge graph completion. In *SAC*, pages 327–332. ACM, 2016.

[47]   Pasquale Minervini, Thomas Demeester, Tim Rocktäschel, and Sebastian Riedel. Adversarial Sets for Regularising Neural Link Predictors. In *UAI*, 2017.

[48]   Maximilian Nickel, Xueyan Jiang, and Volker Tresp. Reducing the rank in relational factorization models by including observable patterns. In *NIPS*, pages 1179–1187, 2014.

[49]   Maximilian Nickel, Kevin Murphy, Volker Tresp, and Evgeniy Gabrilovich. A Review of Relational Machine Learning for Knowledge Graphs. *Proceedings of the IEEE*, 104(1):11–33, 2016.

[50]   Christina Niklaus, Matthias Cetto, André Freitas, and Siegfried Handschuh. A Survey on Open Information Extraction. In *CICLing*, 2018.

[51]   Jack W. Rae, Jonathan J. Hunt, Ivo Danihelka, Timothy Harley, Andrew W. Senior, Gregory Wayne, Alex Graves, and Tim Lillicrap. Scaling memory-augmented neural networks with sparse reads and writes. In *NIPS*, pages 3621–3629, 2016.

[52]   Luc De Raedt, Paolo Frasconi, Kristian Kersting, and Stephen Muggleton, editors. *Probabilistic Inductive Logic Programming - Theory and Applications*, volume 4911 of *LNCS*. Springer, 2008.

[53]   Sebastian Riedel, Limin Yao, Andrew McCallum, and Benjamin M. Marlin. Relation extraction with matrix factorization and universal schemas. In *HLT-NAACL*, pages 74–84. ACL, 2013.

[54]   Tim Rocktäschel and Sebastian Riedel. End-to-end Differentiable Proving. In *NIPS*, pages 3791–3803, 2017.

[55]   Sainbayar Sukhbaatar, Arthur Szlam, Jason Weston, and Rob Fergus. End-To-End Memory Networks. In *NIPS*, pages 2440–2448, 2015.

[56]   Kristina Toutanova, Danqi Chen, Patrick Pantel, Hoifung Poon, Pallavi Choudhury, and Michael Gamon. Representing Text for Joint Embedding of Text and Knowledge Bases. In *EMNLP*, pages 1499–1509, 2015.

[57]   Andrew Trask, Felix Hill, Scott E. Reed, Jack W. Rae, Chris Dyer, and Phil Blunsom. Neural arithmetic

logic units. In *NeurIPS*, pages 8046–8055, 2018.

[58]   Théo Trouillon, Johannes Welbl, Sebastian Riedel, Éric Gaussier, and Guillaume Bouchard. Complex Embeddings for Simple Link Prediction. In *ICML*, volume 48, pages 2071–2080, 2016.

[59]   Leon Weber, Pasquale Minervini, Jannes Münchmeyer, Ulf Leser, and Tim Rocktäschel. Nlprolog: Reasoning with weak unification for question answering in natural language. In *ACL (1)*, pages 6151–6161. Association for Computational Linguistics, 2019.

[60]   Jason Weston, Antoine Bordes, Sumit Chopra, and Tomas Mikolov. Towards AI-Complete Question Answering: A Set of Prerequisite Toy Tasks. *CoRR*, abs/1502.05698, 2015.

[61]   Lyndon White, Roberto Togneri, Wei Liu, and Mohammed Bennamoun. How well sentence embeddings capture meaning. In *ADCS*, 2015.

[62]   Bishan Yang, Wen-tau Yih, Xiaodong He, Jianfeng Gao, and Li Deng. Embedding Entities and Relations for Learning and Inference in Knowledge Bases. In *ICLR*, 2015.

[63]   Fan Yang, Zhilin Yang, and William W. Cohen. Differentiable Learning of Logical Rules for Knowledge Base Reasoning. In *NIPS*, pages 2316–2325, 2017.

Knowledge Graphs for eXplainable Artificial Intelligence: Foundations, Applications and Challenges 143
I. Tiddi et al. (Eds.)
IOS Press, 2020
© *2020 Akademische Verlagsgesellschaft AKA GmbH, Berlin. All rights reserved.*
doi:10.3233/SSW200016

Neuro-Symbolic Architectures for Context Understanding

Alessandro OLTRAMARI [a], Jonathan FRANCIS [a,b], Cory HENSON [a], Kaixin MA [b1],
and Ruwan WICKRAMARACHCHI [c1]

[a] *Intelligent IoT, Bosch Research and Technology Center (Pittsburgh, PA, USA)*
[b] *Language Technologies Institute, School of Computer Science, Carnegie Mellon University (Pittsburgh, PA, USA)*
[c] *Artificial Intelligence Institute, University of South Carolina (Columbia, SC, USA)*

Abstract. Computational context understanding refers to an agent's ability to fuse disparate sources of information for decision-making and is, therefore, generally regarded as a prerequisite for sophisticated machine reasoning capabilities, such as in artificial intelligence (AI). *Data-driven* and *knowledge-driven* methods are two classical techniques in the pursuit of such machine sense-making capability. However, while data-driven methods seek to model the statistical regularities of events by making observations in the real-world, they remain difficult to interpret and they lack mechanisms for naturally incorporating external knowledge. Conversely, knowledge-driven methods, combine structured knowledge bases, perform symbolic reasoning based on axiomatic principles, and are more interpretable in their inferential processing; however, they often lack the ability to estimate the statistical salience of an inference. To combat these issues, we propose the use of *hybrid* AI methodology as a general framework for combining the strengths of both approaches. Specifically, we inherit the concept of *neuro-symbolism* as a way of using knowledge-bases to guide the learning progress of deep neural networks. We further ground our discussion in two applications of neuro-symbolism and, in both cases, show that our systems maintain interpretability while achieving comparable performance, relative to the state-of-the-art.

Keywords. Context Understanding, Knowledge Graphs, Representation Learning, Commonsense, Question Answering, Machine Learning, Artificial Intelligence, eXplainable AI

1. Explainability through Context Understanding

Context understanding is a natural property of human cognition, that supports our decision-making capabilities in complex sensory environments. Humans are capable of fusing information from a variety of modalities—e.g., auditory, visual—in order to perform different tasks, ranging from the operation of a motor vehicle to the generation of logical inferences based on commonsense. Allen Newell and Herbert Simon described this *sense-making capability* in their theory of cognition [30,31]: through sensory stim-

---

[0] All authors contributed equally to the chapter.
[1] Work done during an internship at Bosch Research & Technology Center Pittsburgh.

uli, humans accumulate experiences, generalize, and reason over them, storing the resulting knowledge in memory; the dynamic combination of live experience and distilled knowledge during task-execution, enables humans to make time-effective decisions and evaluate how good or bad a decision was by factoring in external feedback.

Endowing machines with this sense-making capability has been one of the long-standing goals of Artificial Intelligence (AI) practice and research, both in industry and academia. *Data-driven* and *knowledge-driven* methods are two classical techniques in the pursuit of such machine sense-making capability. Sense-making is not only a key for improving machine autonomy, but is a precondition for enabling seamless interaction with humans. Humans communicate effectively with each other, thanks to their shared mental models of the physical world and social context [16]. These models foster reciprocal trust by making contextual knowledge transparent; they are also crucial for explaining how decision-making unfolds. In a similar fashion, we can assert that 'explainable AI' is a byproduct or an *affordance* of computational context understanding and is predicated on the extent to which humans can introspect the decision processes that enable machine sense-making [20].

2. Context Understanding through Neuro-symbolism

From the definitions of 'explainable AI' and 'context understanding,' in the previous section, we can derive the following corollary:

> *The explainability of AI algorithms is related to how context is processed, computationally, based on the machine's perceptual capabilities and on the external knowledge resources that are available.*

Along this direction, the remainder of this chapter explores two concrete scenarios of context understanding, realized by *neuro-symbolic architectures*—i.e., hybrid AI frameworks that instruct machine perception (based on deep neural networks) with knowledge graphs[2]. These examples were chosen to illustrate the general applicability of neuro-symbolism and its relevance to contemporary research problems.

Specifically, section 3.1 considers context understanding for autonomous vehicles: we describe how a knowledge graph can be built from a dataset of urban driving situations and how this knowledge graph can be translated into a continuous vector-space representation. This embedding space can be used to estimate the semantic similarity of visual scenes by using neural networks as powerful, non-linear function approximators. Here, models may be trained to make danger assessments of the visual scene and, if necessary, transfer control to the human in complex scenarios. The ability to make this assessment is an important capability for autonomous vehicles, when we consider the negative ramifications for a machine to remain invariant to changing weather conditions, anomalous behavior of dynamic obstacles on the road (e.g., other vehicles, pedestrians), varied lighting conditions, and other challenging circumstances. We suggest neuro-symbolic fusion as one solution and, indeed, our results show that our embedding space preserves the semantic properties of the conceptual elements that make up visual scenes.

---

[2]Although inspired by the human capability of fusing perception and knowledge, the neuro-symbolic architectures we illustrate in this chapter do not commit on replicating the mechanisms of human context understanding—this being the scientific tenet of cognitive architecture research (see, e.g., [19,3]).

In section 3.2, we describe context understanding for language tasks. Here, models are supplied with three separate modalities: external commonsense knowledge, unstructured textual context, and a series of answer candidates. In this task, models are tested on their ability to fuse together these disparate sources of information for making the appropriate logical inferences. We designed methods to extract adequate semantic structures (i.e., triples) from two comprehensive commonsense knowledge graphs, `ConceptNet` [22] and `Atomic` [37], and to inject this external context into language models. In general, open-domain linguistic context is useful for different tasks in Natural Language Processing (NLP), including: information-extraction, text-classification, extractive and abstractive summarization, and question-answering (QA). For ease of quantitative evaluation, we consider a QA task in section 3.2. In particular, the task is to select the correct answer from a pool of candidates, given a question that specifically requires commonsense to resolve. For example, the question, *If electrical equipment won't power on, what connection should be checked?* is associated with 'company', 'airport', 'telephone network', 'wires', and 'freeway'(where 'wires' is the correct answer choice). We demonstrate that our proposed hybrid architecture out-performs the state-of-the-art neural approaches that do not utilize structured commonsense knowledge bases. Furthermore, we discuss how our approach maintains explainability in the model's decision-making process: the model has the joint task of learning an attention distribution over the commonsense knowledge context which, in turn, depends on the knowledge triples that were conceptually most salient for selecting the correct answer candidate, downstream. Fundamentally, the goal of this project is to make human interaction with chatbots and personal assistants more robust. For this to happen, it is crucial to equip intelligent agents with a shared understanding of general contexts, i.e., commonsense. Conventionally, machine commonsense had been computationally articulated using symbolic languages—Cyc being one of the most prominent outcomes of this approach [26]. However, symbolic commonsense representations are neither scalable nor comprehensive, as they depend heavily on the knowledge engineering experts that encode them. In this regard, the advent of deep learning and, in particular, the possibility of fusing symbolic knowledge into sub-symbolic (neural) layers, has recently led to a revival of this AI research topic.

3. Applications of Neuro-symbolism

3.1. Application I: Learning a Knowledge Graph Embedding Space for Context Understanding in Automotive Driving Scenes

3.1.1. Introduction

Recently, there has been a significant increase in the investment for autonomous driving (AD) research and development, with the goal of achieving full autonomy in the next few years. Realizing this vision requires robust ML/AI algorithms that are trained on massive amounts of data. Thousands of cars, equipped with various types of sensors (e.g., LIDAR, RGB, RADAR), are now deployed around the world to collect this heterogeneous data from real-world driving scenes. The primary objective for AD is to use these data to optimize the vehicle's *perception pipeline* on such tasks as: 3D object detection, obstacle tracking, object trajectory forecasting, and learning an ideal driving policy. Fundamental to all of these tasks will be the vehicle's context understanding capability, which requires knowledge of the time, location, detected objects, participating events, weather, and various other aspects of a driving scene. Even though state-of-the-art AI technologies are used for this purpose, their current effectiveness and scalability are insufficient to achieve full autonomy. Humans naturally exhibit context understanding behind the wheel, where the decisions we make are the result of a continuous evaluation of perceptual cues combined with background knowledge. For instance, human drivers generally know which area of a neighborhood might have icy road conditions on a frigid winter day, where flooding is more frequent after a heavy rainfall, which streets are more likely to have kids playing after school, and which intersections have poor lighting. Currently, this type of common knowledge is not being used to assist self-driving cars and, due to the sample-inefficiency of current ML/AI algorithms, vehicle models cannot effectively learn these phenomena through statistical observation alone.

On March 18, 2018, Elaine Herzberg's death was reported as the first fatality incurred from a collision with an autonomous vehicle[3]. An investigation into the collision, conducted by The National Transportation Safety Board (NTSB), remarks on the shortcomings of current AD and context understanding technologies. Specifically, NTSB found that the autonomous vehicle incorrectly classified Herzberg as an unknown object, a vehicle, and then a bicycle within the complex scene as she walked across the road. Further investigation revealed that the system design did not include consideration for pedestrians walking outside of a crosswalk, or jaywalking [1]. Simply put, the current AD technology lacks fundamental understanding of the characteristics of objects and events within common scenes; this suggests that more research is required in order to achieve the vision of autonomous driving.

Knowledge Graphs (KGs) have been successfully used to manage heterogeneous data within various domains. They are able to integrate and structure data and metadata from multiple modalities into a unified semantic representation, encoded as a graph. More recently, KGs are being translated into latent vector space representations, known as Knowledge Graph Embeddings (KGEs), that have been shown to improve the performance of machine learning models when applied to certain downstream tasks, such as classification [9,43]. Given a KG as a set of triples, KGE algorithms learn to create a latent representation of the KG entities and relations as continuous KGE vectors. This encoding allows KGEs to be easily manipulated and integrated with machine learning algorithms. Motivated by the shortcomings of current context understanding technologies, along with the promising outcomes of KGEs, our research focuses on the generation and evaluation of KGEs on AD data. Before directly applying KGEs on critical AD applications, however, we evaluate the intrinsic quality of KGEs across multiple metrics and KGE algorithms [45]. Additionally, we present an early investigation of using KGEs for a selected use-case from the AD domain.

3.1.2. Scene Knowledge Graphs

Dataset. To promote and enable further research on autonomous driving, several benchmark datasets have been made publicly available by companies in this domain [18]. NuScenes is a benchmark dataset of multimodal vehicular data, recently released by Aptiv [8] and used for our experiments. NuScenes consists of a collection of 20-second

---

[3]https://www.nytimes.com/2018/03/19/technology/uber-driverless-fatality.html

driving scenes, with ~40 sub-scenes sampled per driving scene (i.e., one every 0.5 seconds). In total, NuScenes includes 850 driving scenes and 34,149 sub-scenes. Each sub-scene is annotated with detected objects and events, each defined within a taxonomy of 23 object/event categories.

Scene Ontology. In autonomous driving, a scene is defined as an observable volume of time and space [14]. On the road, a vehicle may encounter many different situations—such as merging onto a divided highway, stopping at a traffic light, and overtaking another vehicle—all of which are considered as common driving scenes. A scene encapsulates all relevant information about a particular situation, including data from vehicular sensors, objects, events, time and location. A scene can also be divided into a sequence of sub-scenes. As an example, a 20-second drive consisting primarily of the vehicle merging into a highway could be considered as a scene. In addition, all the different situations the vehicle encounters within these 20 seconds can also be represented as (sub-)scenes. In this case, a scene may be associated with a time interval and spatial region while a sub-scene may be associated with a specific timestamp and a set of spatial coordinates. This semantic representation of a scene is formally defined in the Scene Ontology (see figure 1(a), depicted in Protege[4]). To enable the generation of a KG from the data within NuScenes, the Scene Ontology is extended to include all the concepts (i.e., objects and event categories) found in the NuScenes dataset.

(a) (b)

Figure 1. Scene Ontology: (a) formal definition of a *Scene*, and (b) a subset of *Features-of-Interests* and *events* defined within a taxonomy.

Generating Knowledge Graphs. The Scene Ontology identifies *events* and *features-of-interests* (FoIs) as top-level concepts. An *event* or a *FoI* may be associated with a *Scene* via the *includes* relation. *FoIs* are associated with *events* through the *isParticipantOf* relation. Figure 1(b) shows a subset of the *FoIs* and *events* defined by the Scene Ontology.

---

[4]https://protege.stanford.edu/

In generating the scenes' KG, each scene and sub-scene found in NuScenes is annotated using the Scene Ontology. Table 1 shows some basic statistics of the generated KG.

# of triples	5.95M
# of entities	2.11M
# of relations	11

Table 1. Statistics of the scene KG generated from the NuScenes dataset

3.1.3. Knowledge Graph Embeddings

KGE Algorithms. KGE algorithms enable the ability to easily feed knowledge into ML algorithms and improve the performance of learning tasks, by translating the knowledge contained in knowledge graphs into latent vector space representation of KGEs [29]. To select candidate KGE algorithms for our evaluation, we referred to the classification of KGE algorithms provided by Wang et al. [44]. In this work, KGE algorithms are classified into two primary categories: (1) Transitional distance-based algorithms and (2) Semantic matching-based models. Transitional distance-based algorithms define the scoring function of the model as a distance-based measure, while semantic matching-based algorithms define it as a similarity measure. Here, entity and relation vectors interact via addition and subtraction in the case of Transitional distance-based models; in semantic matching-based models, the interaction between entity and relation vectors is captured by multiplicative score functions [39].

Initially, for our study we had selected one algorithm from each class: TransE [6] to represent the transitional distance-based algorithms and RESCAL [33] to represent the semantic matching-based algorithms. However, after experimentation, RESCAL did not scale well for handling large KGs in our experiments. Therefore, we also included HolE [32]—an efficient successor of RESCAL—in the evaluation. A brief summary of each algorithm is provided for each model, below:

TransE: the TransE model is often considered to be the most-representative of the class of transitional distance-based algorithms [44]. Given a triple *(h, r, t)* from the KG, TransE encodes *h*, *r* and *t* as vectors, with *r* represented as a transition vector from *h* to *t*: $\mathbf{h} + \mathbf{r} \approx \mathbf{t}$. Since both entities and relations are represented as vectors, TransE is one of the most efficient KGE algorithms, with $\mathcal{O}(nd + md)$ space complexity and $\mathcal{O}(n_t d)$ time complexity (n_t is the number of training triples).

RESCAL: RESCAL is capable of generating an expressive knowledge graph embedding space, due to its ability to capture complex patterns over multiple hops in the KG. RESCAL encodes relations as matrices and captures the interaction between entities and relations using a bi-linear scoring function. Though the use of a matrix to encode each relation yields improved expressivity, it also limits RESCAL's ability to scale with large KGs. It has $\mathcal{O}(nd + md^2)$ space complexity and $\mathcal{O}(n_t d^2)$ time complexity.

HolE: HolE is a more efficient successor of RESCAL, addressing its space and time complexity issues, by encoding relations as vectors without sacrificing the expressivity of the model. By using circular correlation operation [32], it captures the pairwise interaction of entities as composable vectors. This optimization yields $\mathscr{O}(nd + md)$ space complexity and $\mathscr{O}(n_t d \log d)$ time complexity.

Visualizing KGEs. In order to visualize the generated KGE, a "mini" KG from the NuScenes-mini dataset was created. Specifically, 10 scenes were selected (along with their sub-scenes) to generate the KG, and the TransE algorithm was used to learn the embeddings. When training the KGEs, we chose the dimension of the vectors to be 100. To visualize the embeddings in 2-dimensional (2D) space, the dimensions are reduced using the t-Distributed Stochastic Neighbor Embedding (t-SNE) [25] projection. Figure 2 shows the resulting embeddings of the NuScenes dataset. To denote interesting patterns that manifest in the embeddings, instances of *Car* (a *FoI*) and the *events* in which they participate are highlighted. In this image, events such as *parked car*, *moving car*, and *stopped car* are clustered around entities of type *Car*. This shows that the *isParticipantOf* relations defined in the KG are maintained within the KG embeddings.

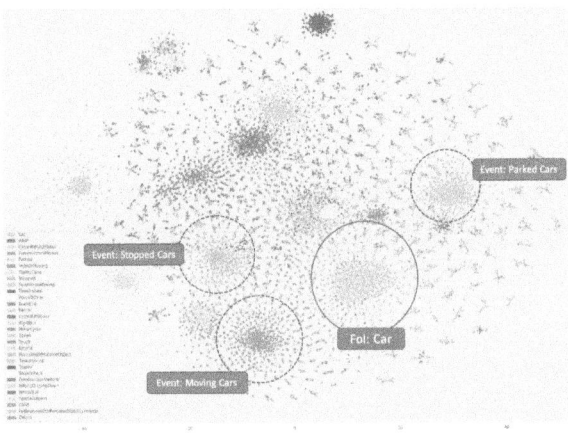

Figure 2. 2D visualizations of KGEs of NuScenes instances generated from the TransE algorithm.

3.1.4. Intrinsic Evaluation

Here, we deviate slightly from the prior work in evaluating KGE algorithms, which evaluate KGEs based downstream task performance. Instead, we focus on an evaluation that uses only metrics that quantify the *intrinsic* quality of KGEs [2]: categorization measure, coherence measure, and semantic transition distance. Categorization measures how well instances of the same type cluster together. To quantify this quality, all vectors of the same type are averaged together and the cosine similarity is computed between the averaged vector and the typed class. The Coherence measure quantifies the proportion of neighboring entities that are of the same type; the evaluation framework proposes that, if a set of entities are typed by the class, those entities should form a cluster in the embedding space with the typed class as the centroid. Adapted from the word embedding literature, *Semantic Transitional Distance* captures the relational semantics of the KGE: if a triple (h, r, t) is correctly represented in the embedding space, the transition distance between the vectors representing $(\mathbf{h} + \mathbf{r})$ should be close to $\mathbf{t}$. This is quantified by computing the cosine similarity between $(\mathbf{h} + \mathbf{r})$ and $\mathbf{t}$.

Results. Evaluation results are reported with respect to each algorithm and metric. Figure 3 shows the evaluation results of categorization measure, coherence measure, and semantic transitional distance—for each KGE algorithm. The NuScenes KG, generated from the NuScenes-trainval dataset, is large in terms of both the number of triples and number of entities (see Table 1). Hence, RESCAL did not scale well to this dataset. For this reason, we only report the evaluation results for TransE and HolE. When considering the KGE algorithms, TransE's performance is consistently better across metrics, compared to HolE's performance. However, it is interesting to note that HolE significantly outperforms TransE for some classes/relations. When considering the evaluation metrics, it is evident that the categorization measure and semantic transitional distance are able to capture the quality of type semantics and relational semantics, respectively. The value of the coherence measure, however, is zero for HoLE in most cases and close to zero for TransE in some cases. In our experimental setting, the poor performance with respect to the coherence measure may suggest that it may not be a good metric for evaluating KGEs in the AD domain.

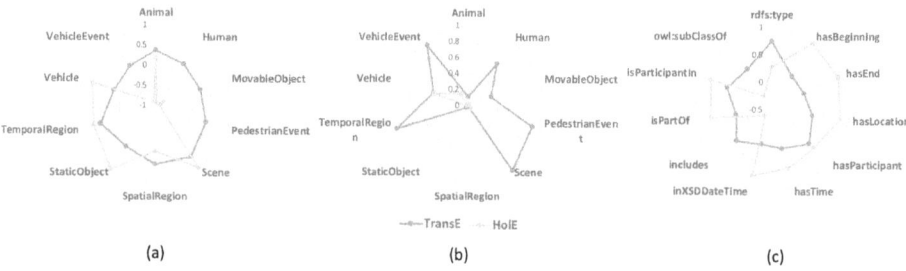

Figure 3. Evaluation results of the NuScenes dataset: (a) Categorization measure, (b) Coherence measure, and (c) Semantic transitional distance

3.1.5. A use-case from the AD domain

We report preliminary results from our investigation into using KGEs for a use-case in the AD domain. More specifically, we apply KGEs for computing scene similarity. In this case, the goal is to find (sub-)scenes that are characteristically similar, using the learned KGEs. Given a set of scene pairs, we choose the pair with the highest cosine similarity as the most similar. Figure 4 shows an illustration of the two most similar sub-scenes, when the list of pairs include sub-scenes from different scenes. An interesting observation is that the black string of objects in sub-scene (a) are *Barriers* (*a Static Object*), and the orange string of objects in sub-scene (b) are *Stopped Cars*. This example suggests that the KGE-based approach could identify sub-scenes that share similar characteristics even though the sub-scenes are visually dissimilar.

3.1.6. Discussion

We presented an investigation of using KGEs for AD context understanding, along with an evaluation of the intrinsic quality of KGEs. The evaluation suggests that KGEs are specifically able to capture the semantic properties of a scene knowledge graph (e.g., *isParticipantOf* relation between objects and events). More generally, KGE algorithms are capable of translating semantic knowledge, such as type and relational semantics to

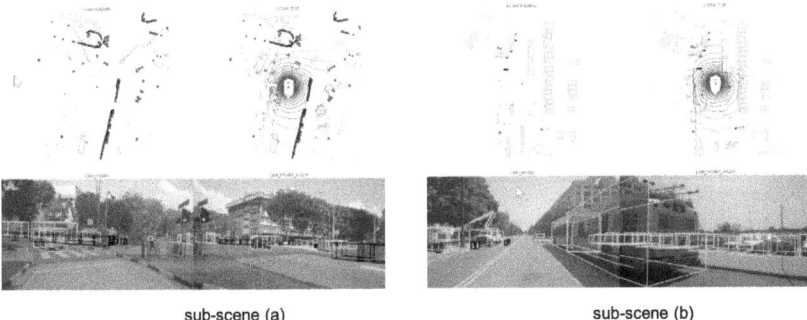

sub-scene (a)   sub-scene (b)

Figure 4. Results of scene similarity: Most similar sub-scenes computed using KGEs trained on NuScenes KG

KGEs. When considering the different KGE algorithms, we report that the transitional distance-based algorithm, TransE, shows consistent performance across multiple quantitative KGE-quality metrics. Our evaluation further suggests that some quality metrics currently in use, such as the coherence measure, may not be effective in measuring the quality of the type semantics from KGEs, in the AD domain. Finally, in applying the learned KGEs to a use-case of importance in the AD domain, we shed some light on the effectiveness of leveraging KGEs in capturing AD scene similarity.

3.2. Application II: Neural Question-Answering using Commonsense Knowledge Bases

3.2.1. Introduction

Recently, many efforts have been made towards building challenging question-answering (QA) datasets that, by design, require models to synthesize external commonsense knowledge and leverage more sophisticated reasoning mechanisms [41,49,34,47,48]. Two directions of work that try to solve these tasks are: purely *data-oriented* and purely *knowledge-oriented* approaches. The data-oriented approaches generally propose to pre-train language models on large linguistic corpora, such that the model would implicitly acquire "commonsense" through its statistical observations. Indeed, large pre-trained language models have achieved promising performance on many commonsense reasoning benchmarks [11,35,46,23]. The main downsides of this approach are that models are difficult to interpret and that they lack mechanisms for incorporating explicit commonsense knowledge. Conversely, purely knowledge-oriented approaches combine structured knowledge bases and perform symbolic reasoning, on the basis of axiomatic principles. Such models enjoy the property of interpretability, but often lack the ability to estimate the statistical salience of an inference, based on real-world observations. Hybrid models are those that attempt to fuse these two approaches, by extracting knowledge from structured knowledge bases and using the resulting information to guide the learning paradigm of statistical estimators, such as deep neural network models.

Different ways of injecting knowledge into models have been introduced, such as attention-based gating mechanisms [5], key-value memory mechanisms [28,27], extrinsic scoring functions [50], and graph convolution networks [17,21]. Our approach is to combine the powerful pre-trained language models with structured knowledge, and we extend previous approaches by taking a more fine-grained view of commonsense.

The subtle differences across the various knowledge types have been discussed at length in AI by philosophers, computational linguists, and cognitive psychologists [10]. At the high level, we can identify *declarative commonsense*, whose scope encompasses factual knowledge, e.g., 'the sky is blue' and 'Paris is in France'; *taxonomic knowledge*, e.g., 'football players are athletes' and 'cats are mammals'; *relational knowledge*, e.g., 'the nose is part of the skull' and 'handwriting requires a hand and a writing instrument'; *procedural commonsense*, which includes prescriptive knowledge, e.g., 'one needs an oven before baking cakes' and 'the electricity should be off while the switch is being repaired' [15]; *sentiment knowledge*, e.g., 'rushing to the hospital makes people worried' and 'being in vacation makes people relaxed'; and *metaphorical knowledge* which includes idiomatic structures, e.g., 'time flies' and 'raining cats and dogs'. We believe that it is important to identify the most appropriate commonsense knowledge type required for specific tasks, in order to get better downstream performance. Once the knowledge type is identified, we can then select the appropriate knowledge base(s), the corresponding knowledge-extraction pipeline, and the suitable neural injection mechanisms.

In this work, we conduct a comparison study of different knowledge bases and knowledge-injection methods, on top of pre-trained neural language models; we evaluate model performance on a multiple-choice QA dataset, which explicitly requires commonsense reasoning. In particular, we used ConceptNet [22] and the recently-introduced ATOMIC [37] as our external knowledge resources, incorporating them in the neural computation pipeline using the *Option Comparison Network* (OCN) model mechanism [36]. We evaluate our models on the CommonsenseQA [42] dataset; an example question from the CommonsenseQA task is shown in Table 2. Our experimental results and analysis suggest that attention-based injection is preferable for knowledge-injection and that the degree of domain overlap, between knowledge-base and dataset, is vital to model success.[5]

Question:
A revolving door is convenient for two direction travel, but it also serves as a security measure at a what?
Answer choices:
A. Bank*; B. Library; C. Department Store; D. Mall; E. New York;

Table 2. An example from the CommonsenseQA dataset; the asterisk (*) denotes the correct answer.

3.2.2. Dataset

CommonsenseQA is a multiple-choice QA dataset that specifically measure commonsense reasoning [42]. This dataset is constructed based on ConceptNet (see section 3.2.3 for more information about this knowledge base). Specifically, a source concept is first extracted from ConceptNet, along with 3 target concepts that are connected to the source concept, i.e., a sub-graph. Crowd-workers are then asked to generate questions, using the source concept, such that only one of the target concepts can correctly answer the question. Additionally, 2 more "distractor" concepts are selected by crowd-workers, so that each question is associated with 5 answer-options. In total, the dataset contains 12,247

---

[5]From a terminological standpoint, 'domain overlap' here should be interpreted as the overlap, between question types in the targeted datasets and types of commonsense represented in the knowledge bases under consideration.

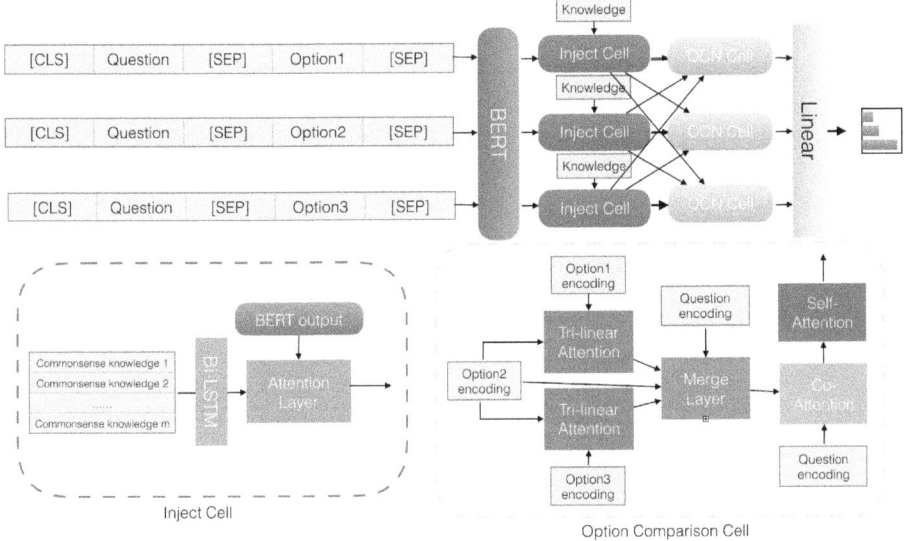

Figure 5. Option Comparison Network with Knowledge Injection

questions. For `CommonsenseQA`, we evaluate models on the development-set only, since test-set answers are not publicly available.

3.2.3. Knowledge bases

The first knowledge-base we consider for our experiments is `ConceptNet` [22]. `ConceptNet` contains over 21 million edges and 8 million nodes (1.5 million nodes in the partition for the English vocabulary), from which one may generate triples of the form $(C1, r, C2)$, wherein the natural-language concepts $C1$ and $C2$ are associated by commonsense relation r, e.g., *(dinner, AtLocation, restaurant)*. Thanks to its coverage, `ConceptNet` is one of the most popular semantic networks for commonsense. `ATOMIC` [37] is a knowledge-base that focuses on procedural knowledge. Triples are of the form *(Event, r, {Effect|Persona|Mental-state})*, where head and tail are short sentences or verb phrases and r represents an *if-then* relation type: *(X compliments Y, xIntent, X wants to be nice)*. Since the `CommonsenseQA` dataset is open-domain and requires general commonsense, we think these knowledge-bases are most appropriate for our investigation.

3.2.4. Model architecture

The model class we select is that of the *Bidirectional Encoder Representations with Transformer* (BERT) model [11], as it has been applied to numerous QA tasks and has achieved very promising performance, particularly on the `CommonsenseQA` dataset. When utilizing BERT on multiple-choice QA tasks, the standard approach is to concatenate the question with each answer-option, in order to generate a list of tokens which is then fed into BERT encoder; a linear layer is added on top, in order to predict the answer. One aspect of this strategy is that each answer-option is encoded independently, which limits the model's ability to find correlations between answer-options and with respect to the original question context. To address this issue, the *Option Comparison Network*

(OCN) [36] was introduced to explicitly model the pairwise answer-option interactions, making OCN better-suited for multiple-choice QA task structures. The OCN model uses BERT as its base encoder: the question/option encoding is produced by BERT and further processed in an Option Comparison Cell, before being fed into linear layer. The Option Comparison Cell is illustrated in the bottom right of figure 5. We re-implemented OCN while keeping BERT as its upstream encoder (we refer an interested reader to [36,24] for more details).

3.2.5. Knowledge elicitation

ConceptNet. We identify `ConceptNet` relations that connect questions to the answer-options. The intuition is that these relation paths would provide explicit evidence that would help the model find the answer. Formally, given a question Q and an answer-option O, we find all `ConceptNet` relations *(C1, r, C2)*, such that $C1 \in Q$ and $C2 \in O$, or vice versa. This rule works well for single-word concepts. However, a large number of concepts in `ConceptNet` are actually phrases, where finding exactly matching phrases in Q/O is more challenging. To fully utilize phrase-based relations, we relaxed the exact-match constraint to the following:

$$\frac{\text{\# words in C} \cap \text{S}}{\text{\# words in C}} > 0.5 \tag{1}$$

Here, the sequence S represents Q or O, depending on which sequence we try to match the concept C to. Additionally, when the part-of-speech (POS) tag for a concept is available, we make sure it matches the POS tag of the corresponding word in Q/O. Table 3 shows the extracted `ConceptNet` triples for the `CommonsenseQA` example in Table 2. It is worth noting that we are able to extract the original `ConceptNet` sub-graph that was used to create the question, along with some extra triples. Although not perfect, the bold `ConceptNet` triple provides clues that could help the model resolve the correct answer.

Options	Extracted `ConceptNet` triples
Bank	(revolving door *AtLocation* bank) **(bank RelatedTo security)**
Library	(revolving door *AtLocation* library)
Department Store	(revolving door *AtLocation* store) (security IsA department)
Mall	(revolving door *AtLocation* mall)
New York	(revolving door *AtLocation* New York)

Table 3. Extracted `ConceptNet` relations for sample shown in Table 2.

ATOMIC. We observe that many questions in the `CommonsenseQA` task ask about which event is likely to occur, given a condition. Superficially, this particular question type seems well-suited for `ATOMIC`, whose focus is on procedural knowledge. Thus, we could frame our goal as evaluating whether `ATOMIC` can provide relevant knowledge to help answer these questions. However, one challenge of extracting knowledge from this resource is that heads and tails of knowledge triples in `ATOMIC` are short sentences or verb phrases, while rare words and person-references are reduced to blanks and PersonX/PersonY, respectively.

3.2.6. Knowledge injection

Given previously-extracted knowledge triples, we need to integrate them with the OCN component of our model. Inspired by [5], we propose to use attention-based injection. For ConceptNet knowledge triples, we first convert concept-relation entities into tokens from our lexicon, in order to generate a pseudo-sentence. For example, *"(book, AtLocation, library)"* would be converted to "book at location library." Next, we used the knowledge injection cell to fuse the commonsense knowledge into BERT's output, before feeding the fused output into the OCN cell. Specifically, in a knowledge-injection cell, a Bi-LSTM layer is used to encode these pseudo-sentences, before computing the attention with respect to BERT output, as illustrated in bottom left of figure 5.

3.2.7. Knowledge pre-training

Pre-training large-capacity models (e.g., BERT, GPT [35], XLNet [46]) on large corpora, then fine-tuning on more domain-specific information, has led to performance improvements on various tasks. Inspired by this, our goal in this section is to observe the effect of pre-training BERT on commonsense knowledge and refining the model on task-specific content from the CommonsenseQA dataset. Essentially, we would like to test if pre-training on our external knowledge resources can help the model acquire commonsense. For the ConceptNet pre-training procedure, pre-training BERT on pseudo-sentences formulated from ConceptNet knowledge triples does not provide much gain on performance. Instead, we trained BERT on the *Open Mind Common Sense* (OMCS) corpus [40], the originating corpus that was used to create ConceptNet. We extracted about 930K English sentences from OMCS and randomly masked out 15% of the tokens; we then fine-tuned BERT, using a masked language model objective, where the model's objective is to predict the masked tokens, as a probability distribution over the entire lexicon. Finally, we load this fine-tuned model into OCN framework proceed with the downstream CommonsenseQA task. As for pre-training on ATOMIC, we follow previous work's pre-processing steps to convert ATOMIC knowledge triples into sentences [7]; we created special tokens for 9 types of relations as well as blanks. Next, we randomly masked out 15% of the tokens, only masking out tail-tokens; we used the same OMCS pre-training procedure.

Models	Dev Acc
BERT + OMCS pre-train(*)	68.8
RoBERTa + CSPT(*)	**76.2**
OCN	64.1
OCN + CN injection	67.3
OCN + OMCS pre-train	65.2
OCN + ATOMIC pre-train	61.2
OCN + OMCS pre-train + CN inject	**69.0**

Table 4. Results on CommonsenseQA; the asterisk (*) denotes results taken from leaderboard.

3.2.8. Results

For all of our experiments, we run 3 trials with different random seeds and we report average scores tables 4 and 5. Evaluated on `CommonsenseQA`, `ConceptNet` knowledge-injection provides a significant performance boost (+2.8%), compared to the OCN baseline, suggesting that explicit links from question to answer-options help the model find the correct answer. Pre-training on OMCS also provides a small performance boost to the OCN baseline. Since both `ConceptNet` knowledge-injection and OMCS pre-training are helpful, we combine both approaches with OCN and we are able to achieve further improvement (+4.9%). Finally, to our surprise, OCN pre-trained on `ATOMIC` yields a significantly lower performance.

Models	AtLoc.(596)	Cau.(194)	Cap.(109)	Ant.(92)	H.Pre.(46)	H.Sub.(39)	C.Des.(28)	Des.(27)
OCN	64.9	66.5	65.1	55.4	69.6	64.1	57.1	66.7
+CN inj,	67.4(+2.5)	70.6(+4.1)	66.1(+1.0)	60.9(+5.5)	73.9(+4.3)	66.7(+2.6)	64.3(+7.2)	77.8(+11.1)
+OMCS	68.8(+3.9)	63.9(-2.6)	62.4(-2.7)	60.9(+5.5)	71.7(+2.1)	59.0(-5.1)	64.3(+7.2)	74.1(+7.4)
+ATOMIC	62.8(-2.1)	66.0(**-0.5**)	60.6(-4.5)	52.2(-3.2)	63.0(-6.6)	56.4(-7.7)	60.7(**+3.6**)	74.1(**+7.4**)
+OMCS+CN	71.6(+6.7)	71.6(+5.1)	64.2(+0.9)	59.8(+4.4)	69.6(+0.0)	69.2(+5.1)	75.0(+17.9)	70.4(+3.7)

Table 5. Accuracies for each `CommonsenseQA` question type: **AtLoc.** means *AtLocation*, **Cau.** means Causes, **Cap.** means *CapableOf*, **Ant.** means *Antonym*, **H.Pre.** means *HasPrerequiste*, **H.Sub** means *HasSubevent*, **C.Des.** means *CausesDesire*, and **Des.** means *Desires*. Numbers beside types denote the number of questions of that type.

3.2.9. Error Analysis

To better understand when a model performs better or worse with knowledge-injection, we analyzed model predictions by question type. Since all questions in `CommonsenseQA` require commonsense reasoning, we classify questions based on the `ConceptNet` relation between the question concept and correct answer concept. The intuition is that the model needs to capture this relation in order to answer the question. The accuracies for each question type are shown in Table 5. Note that the number of samples by question type is very imbalanced. Thus due to the limited space, we omitted the long tail of the distribution (about 7% of all samples). We can see that with `ConceptNet` relation-injection, all question types got performance boosts—for both the OCN model and OCN model that was pre-trained on OMCS—suggesting that external knowledge is indeed helpful for the task. In the case of OCN pre-trained on `ATOMIC`, although the overall performance is much lower than the OCN baseline, it is interesting to see that performance for the "Causes" type is not significantly affected. Moreover, performance for "CausesDesire" and "Desires" types actually got much better. As noted by [37], the "Causes" relation in `ConceptNet` is similar to "Effects" and "Reactions" in `ATOMIC`; and "CausesDesire" in `ConceptNet` is similar to "Wants" in `ATOMIC`. This result suggests that models with knowledge pre-training perform better on questions that fit the knowledge domain, but perform worse on others. In this case, pre-training on `ATOMIC` helps the model do better on questions that are similar to `ATOMIC` relations, even though overall performance is inferior. Finally, we noticed that questions of type "Antonym" appear to be the hardest ones. Many questions that fall into this category contain negations, and we hypothesize that the models still lack the ability to reason over negation sentences, suggesting another direction for future improvement.

3.2.10. Discussion

Based on our experimental results and error analysis, we see that external knowledge is only helpful when there is alignment between questions and knowledge-base types. Thus, it is crucial to identify the question type and apply the best-suited knowledge. In terms of knowledge-injection methods, attention-based injection seems to be the better choice for pre-trained language models such as BERT. Even when alignment between knowledge-base and dataset is sub-optimal, the performance would not degrade. On the other hand, pre-training on knowledge-bases would shift the language model's weight distribution toward its own domain, greatly. If the task domain does not fit knowledge-base well, model performance is likely to drop. When the domain of the knowledge-base aligns with that of the dataset perfectly, both knowledge-injection methods bring performance boosts and a combination of them could bring further gain.

We have presented a survey on two popular knowledge bases (ConceptNet and ATOMIC) and recent knowledge-injection methods (attention and pre-training), on the CommonsenseQA task. We believe it is worth conducting a more comprehensive study of datasets and knowledge-bases and putting more effort towards defining an auxiliary neural learning objectives, in a multi-task learning framework, that classifies the type of knowledge required, based on data characteristics. In parallel, we are also interested in building a *global commonsense knowledge base* by aggregating ConceptNet, ATOMIC, and potentially other resources like FrameNet [4] and MetaNet [12], on the basis of a shared-reference ontology (following the approaches described in [13] and [38]): the goal would be to assess whether injecting knowledge structures from a semantically-cohesive lexical knowledge base of commonsense would guarantee stable model accuracy across datasets.

4. Conclusion

We illustrated two projects on computational context understanding through neuro-symbolism. The first project (section 3.1) concerned the use of knowledge graphs to learning an embedding space for characterizing visual scenes, in the context of autonomous driving. The second application (section 3.2) focused on the extraction and integration of knowledge, encoded in commonsense knowledge bases, for guiding the learning process of neural language models in question-answering tasks. Although diverse in scope and breadth, both projects adopt a hybrid approach to building AI systems, where deep neural networks are enhanced with knowledge graphs. For instance, in the first project we demonstrated that scenes that are visually different can be discovered as sharing similar semantic characteristics by using knowledge graph embeddings; in the second project we showed that a language model is more accurate when it includes specialized modules to evaluate questions and candidate answers on the basis of a common knowledge graph. In both cases, *explainability* emerges as a property of the mechanisms that we implemented, through this combination of data-driven algorithms with the relevant knowledge resources.

We began the chapter by alluding to the way in which humans leverage a complex array of cognitive processes, in order to understand the environment; we further stated that one of the greatest challenges in AI research is learning how to endow machines with similar sense-making capabilities. In these final remarks, it is important to emphasize again (see *footnote #3*) that the capability we describe here need only follow from satisfying the functional requirements of context understanding, rather than concerning ourselves with how those requirements are specifically implemented in humans versus machines. In other words, our hybrid AI approach stems from the complementary nature of perception and knowledge, but does not commit to the notion of replicating human cognition in the machine: as knowledge graphs can only capture a stripped-down representation of what we know, deep neural networks can only approximate how we perceive the world and learn from it. Certainly, human knowledge (encoded in machine-consumable format) abounds in the digital world, and our work shows that these knowledge bases can be used to instruct ML models and, ultimately, enhance AI systems.

References

[1]   'inadequate safety culture' contributed to uber automated test vehicle crash - ntsb calls for federal review process for automated vehicle testing on public roads. `https://ntsb.gov/news/press-releases/Pages/NR20191119c.aspx`. (Accessed on 11/26/2019).

[2]   Faisal Alshargi, Saeedeh Shekarpour, Tommaso Soru, and Amit Sheth. Metrics for evaluating quality of embeddings for ontological concepts. In *AAAI 2019 Spring Symposium on Combining Machine Learning with Knowledge Engineering (AAAI-MAKE)*, 2019.

[3]   John R Anderson. *How can the human mind occur in the physical universe?*, volume 3. Oxford University Press, 2009.

[4]   Collin F Baker, Charles J Fillmore, and John B Lowe. The berkeley framenet project. In *Proceedings of the 17th international conference on Computational linguistics-Volume 1*, pages 86–90. Association for Computational Linguistics, 1998.

[5]   Lisa Bauer, Yicheng Wang, and Mohit Bansal. Commonsense for generative multi-hop question answering tasks. In *Proceedings of the 2018 Conference on Empirical Methods in Natural Language Processing*, pages 4220–4230, Brussels, Belgium, October-November 2018. Association for Computational Linguistics.

[6]   Antoine Bordes, Nicolas Usunier, Alberto Garcia-Duran, Jason Weston, and Oksana Yakhnenko. Translating embeddings for modeling multi-relational data. In *Advances in Neural Information Processing Systems*, pages 2787–2795, 2013.

[7]   Antoine Bosselut, Hannah Rashkin, Maarten Sap, Chaitanya Malaviya, Asli Celikyilmaz, and Yejin Choi. COMET: Commonsense transformers for automatic knowledge graph construction. In *Proceedings of the 57th Annual Meeting of the Association for Computational Linguistics*, pages 4762–4779, Florence, Italy, July 2019. Association for Computational Linguistics.

[8]   Holger Caesar, Varun Bankiti, Alex H. Lang, Sourabh Vora, Venice Erin Liong, Qiang Xu, Anush Krishnan, Yu Pan, Giancarlo Baldan, and Oscar Beijbom. nuscenes: A multimodal dataset for autonomous driving. *arXiv preprint arXiv:1903.11027*, 2019.

[9]   Muhao Chen, Yingtao Tian, Mohan Yang, and Carlo Zaniolo. Multilingual knowledge graph embeddings for cross-lingual knowledge alignment. In *Proceedings of the 26th International Joint Conference on Artificial Intelligence*, pages 1511–1517. AAAI Press, 2017.

[10] Ernest Davis. *Representations of commonsense knowledge*. Morgan Kaufmann, 2014.

[11] Jacob Devlin, Ming-Wei Chang, Kenton Lee, and Kristina Toutanova. BERT: Pre-training of deep bidirectional transformers for language understanding. In *Proceedings of the 2019 Conference of the North American Chapter of the Association for Computational Linguistics: Human Language Technologies, Volume 1 (Long and Short Papers)*, pages 4171–4186, Minneapolis, Minnesota, June 2019. Association for Computational Linguistics.

[12] Ellen Dodge, Jisup Hong, and Elise Stickles. Metanet: Deep semantic automatic metaphor analysis. In *Proceedings of the Third Workshop on Metaphor in NLP*, pages 40–49, 2015.

[13] Aldo Gangemi, Nicola Guarino, Claudio Masolo, and Alessandro Oltramari. Interfacing wordnet with dolce: towards ontowordnet. *Ontology and the Lexicon: A Natural Language Processing Perspective*, pages 36–52, 2010.

[14] Cory Henson, Stefan Schmid, Tuan Tran, and Antonios Karatzoglou. Using a knowledge graph of scenes to enable search of autonomous driving data. In *Proceedings of the 2019 International Semantic Web Conference (ISWC 2019)*, 2019.

[15] Jerry R Hobbs, William Croft, Todd Davies, Douglas Edwards, and Kenneth Laws. Commonsense metaphysics and lexical semantics. *Computational linguistics*, 13(3-4):241–250, 1987.

[16] Philip N Johnson-Laird. Mental models, deductive reasoning, and the brain. *The cognitive neurosciences*, 65:999–1008, 1995.

[17] Thomas N. Kipf and Max Welling. Semi-supervised classification with graph convolutional networks. *CoRR*, abs/1609.02907, 2016.

[18] Charles-Éric Noël Laflamme, François Pomerleau, and Philippe Giguère. Driving datasets literature review. *arXiv preprint arXiv:1910.11968*, 2019.

[19] John E Laird, Christian Lebiere, and Paul S Rosenbloom. A standard model of the mind: Toward a common computational framework across artificial intelligence, cognitive science, neuroscience, and robotics. *Ai Magazine*, 38(4):13–26, 2017.

[20] William F Lawless, Ranjeev Mittu, Donald Sofge, and Laura Hiatt. Artificial intelligence, autonomy, and human-machine teams: Interdependence, context, and explainable ai. *AI Magazine*, 40(3), 2019.

[21] Bill Yuchen Lin, Xinyue Chen, Jamin Chen, and Xiang Ren. Kagnet: Knowledge-aware graph networks for commonsense reasoning. *ArXiv*, abs/1909.02151, 2019.

[22] Hugo Liu and Push Singh. Conceptnet—a practical commonsense reasoning tool-kit. *BT technology journal*, 22(4):211–226, 2004.

[23] Yinhan Liu, Myle Ott, Naman Goyal, Jingfei Du, Mandar Joshi, Danqi Chen, Omer Levy, Mike Lewis, Luke Zettlemoyer, and Veselin Stoyanov. Roberta: A robustly optimized BERT pretraining approach. *CoRR*, abs/1907.11692, 2019.

[24] Kaixin Ma, Jonathan Francis, Quanyang Lu, Eric Nyberg, and Alessandro Oltramari. Towards generalizable neuro-symbolic systems for commonsense question answering. In *Proceedings of the First Workshop on Commonsense Inference in Natural Language Processing*, pages 22–32, Hong Kong, China, November 2019. Association for Computational Linguistics.

[25] Laurens van der Maaten and Geoffrey Hinton. Visualizing data using t-sne. *Journal of machine learning research*, 9(Nov):2579–2605, 2008.

[26] Cynthia Matuszek, Michael Witbrock, John Cabral, and John DeOliveira. An introduction to the syntax and content of cyc. *UMBC Computer Science and Electrical Engineering Department Collection*, 2006.

[27] Todor Mihaylov and Anette Frank. Knowledgeable reader: Enhancing cloze-style reading comprehension with external commonsense knowledge. In *Proceedings of the 56th Annual Meeting of the Association for Computational Linguistics (Volume 1: Long Papers)*, pages 821–832, Melbourne, Australia, July 2018. Association for Computational Linguistics.

[28] Alexander Miller, Adam Fisch, Jesse Dodge, Amir-Hossein Karimi, Antoine Bordes, and Jason Weston. Key-value memory networks for directly reading documents. In *Proceedings of the 2016 Conference on Empirical Methods in Natural Language Processing*, pages 1400–1409, Austin, Texas, November 2016. Association for Computational Linguistics.

[29] Erik B Myklebust, Ernesto Jimenez-Ruiz, Jiaoyan Chen, Raoul Wolf, and Knut Erik Tollefsen. Knowledge graph embedding for ecotoxicological effect prediction. In *International Semantic Web Conference*, pages 490–506. Springer, 2019.

[30] Allen Newell. *Unified theories of cognition*. Harvard University Press, 1994.

[31] Allen Newell, Herbert Alexander Simon, et al. *Human problem solving*, volume 104. Prentice-hall Englewood Cliffs, NJ, 1972.

[32] Maximilian Nickel, Lorenzo Rosasco, and Tomaso Poggio. Holographic embeddings of knowledge graphs. In *Thirtieth AAAI Conference on Artificial Intelligence*, 2016.

[33] Maximilian Nickel, Volker Tresp, and Hans-Peter Kriegel. A three-way model for collective learning on multi-relational data. In *Proceedings of the 28th International Conference on International Conference on Machine Learning*, pages 809–816. Omnipress, 2011.

[34] Simon Ostermann, Michael Roth, Ashutosh Modi, Stefan Thater, and Manfred Pinkal. SemEval-2018 task 11: Machine comprehension using commonsense knowledge. In *Proceedings of The 12th International Workshop on Semantic Evaluation*, pages 747–757, New Orleans, Louisiana, June 2018. Association for Computational Linguistics.

[35] Alec Radford, Jeff Wu, Rewon Child, David Luan, Dario Amodei, and Ilya Sutskever. Language models are unsupervised multitask learners. 2019.

[36] Qiu Ran, Peng Li, Weiwei Hu, and Jie Zhou. Option comparison network for multiple-choice reading comprehension. *CoRR*, abs/1903.03033, 2019.

[37] Maarten Sap, Ronan Le Bras, Emily Allaway, Chandra Bhagavatula, Nicholas Lourie, Hannah Rashkin, Brendan Roof, Noah A Smith, and Yejin Choi. Atomic: An atlas of machine commonsense for if-then reasoning. In *Proceedings of the AAAI Conference on Artificial Intelligence*, volume 33, pages 3027–3035, 2019.

[38] Jan Scheffczyk, Collin F Baker, and Srini Narayanan. Reasoning over natural language text by means of framenet and ontologies. *Ontology and the lexicon: A natural language processing perspective*, pages 53–71, 2010.

[39] Aditya Sharma, Partha Talukdar, et al. Towards understanding the geometry of knowledge graph embeddings. In *Proceedings of the 56th Annual Meeting of the Association for Computational Linguistics (Volume 1: Long Papers)*, pages 122–131, 2018.

[40] Push Singh, Thomas Lin, Erik T. Mueller, Grace Lim, Travell Perkins, and Wan Li Zhu. Open mind common sense: Knowledge acquisition from the general public. In *On the Move to Meaningful Internet Systems, 2002 - DOA/CoopIS/ODBASE 2002 Confederated International Conferences DOA, CoopIS and ODBASE 2002*, pages 1223–1237, Berlin, Heidelberg, 2002. Springer-Verlag.

[41] Kai Sun, Dian Yu, Jianshu Chen, Dong Yu, Yejin Choi, and Claire Cardie. Dream: A challenge dataset and models for dialogue-based reading comprehension. *Transactions of the Association for Computational Linguistics*, 7:217–231, 2019.

[42] Alon Talmor, Jonathan Herzig, Nicholas Lourie, and Jonathan Berant. CommonsenseQA: A question answering challenge targeting commonsense knowledge. In *Proceedings of the 2019 Conference of the North American Chapter of the Association for Computational Linguistics: Human Language Technologies, Volume 1 (Long and Short Papers)*, pages 4149–4158, Minneapolis, Minnesota, June 2019. Association for Computational Linguistics.

[43] Hongwei Wang, Fuzheng Zhang, Miao Zhao, Wenjie Li, Xing Xie, and Minyi Guo. Multi-task feature learning for knowledge graph enhanced recommendation. In *The World Wide Web Conference*, pages 2000–2010. ACM, 2019.

[44] Quan Wang, Zhendong Mao, Bin Wang, and Li Guo. Knowledge graph embedding: A survey of approaches and applications. *IEEE Transactions on Knowledge and Data Engineering*, 29(12):2724–2743, 2017.

[45] Ruwan Wickramarachchi, Cory Henson, and Amit Sheth. An evaluation of knowledge graph embeddings for autonomous driving data: Experience and practice. In *AAAI 2020 Spring Symposium on Combining Machine Learning and Knowledge Engineering in Practice (AAAI-MAKE 2020)*, 2020.

[46] Zhilin Yang, Zihang Dai, Yiming Yang, Jaime Carbonell, Ruslan Salakhutdinov, and Quoc V. Le. Xlnet: Generalized autoregressive pretraining for language understanding, 2019. cite arxiv:1906.08237Comment: Pretrained models and code are available at https://github.com/zihangdai/xlnet.

[47] Rowan Zellers, Yonatan Bisk, Roy Schwartz, and Yejin Choi. SWAG: A large-scale adversarial dataset for grounded commonsense inference. In *Proceedings of the 2018 Conference on Empirical Methods in Natural Language Processing*, pages 93–104, Brussels, Belgium, October-November 2018. Association for Computational Linguistics.

[48] Rowan Zellers, Ari Holtzman, Yonatan Bisk, Ali Farhadi, and Yejin Choi. HellaSwag: Can a machine really finish your sentence? In *Proceedings of the 57th Annual Meeting of the Association for Computational Linguistics*, pages 4791–4800, Florence, Italy, July 2019. Association for Computational Linguistics.

[49] Sheng Zhang, Xiaodong Liu, Jingjing Liu, Jianfeng Gao, Kevin Duh, and Benjamin Van Durme. Record: Bridging the gap between human and machine commonsense reading comprehension. *CoRR*, abs/1810.12885, 2018.

[50] Wanjun Zhong, Duyu Tang, Nan Duan, Ming Zhou, Jiahai Wang, and Jian Yin. Improving question answering by commonsense-based pre-training. *CoRR*, abs/1809.03568, 2018.

Knowledge Graphs for eXplainable Artificial Intelligence: Foundations, Applications and Challenges   161
I. Tiddi et al. (Eds.)
IOS Press, 2020
© 2020 Akademische Verlagsgesellschaft AKA GmbH, Berlin. All rights reserved.
doi:10.3233/SSW200017

Knowledge Representation and Reasoning Methods to Explain Errors in Machine Learning

Marjan ALIREZAIE [a], Martin LÄNGKVIST [a], and Amy LOUTFI [a]

[a] *Center for Applied Autonomous Sensor Systems, Örebro University, Örebro, Sweden*

Abstract. In this chapter we focus the use of knowledge representation and reasoning (KRR) methods as a guide to machine learning algorithms whereby relevant contextual knowledge can be leveraged upon. In this way, the learning methods improve performance by taking into account causal relationships behind errors. Performance improvement can be obtained by focusing the learning task on aspects that are particularly challenging (or prone to error), and then using added knowledge inferred by the reasoner as a means to provide further input to learning algorithms. Said differently, the KRR algorithms guide the learning algorithms, feeding it labels and data in order to iteratively reduce the errors calculated by a given cost function. This closed loop system comes with the added benefit that errors are also made more understandable to the human, as it is the task of the KRR system to contextualize the errors from the ML algorithm in accordance with its knowledge model. This represents a type of explainable AI that is focused on interpretability. This chapter will discuss the benefits of using KRR methods with ML methods in this way, and demonstrate an approach applied to satellite data for the purpose of improving classification and segmentation task.

Keywords. Machine Learning, Knowledge Representation and Reasoning, Error Explanation, eXplainable AI

1. Introduction

Machine learning (ML) models are trained iteratively by optimizing a cost function that measures the training errors during learning, and adapts the values of the model's parameters to minimize these errors. Apart from training errors, machine learning practitioners are also concerned with out-of-sample or generalization errors which are found on new data set (i.e., test data) fed to the trained model [4]. Training and test errors which are related to the under-fitting and over-fitting problems in statistical learning, determine the state or the performance of a learning model [19]. More specifically, a ML model is said to be over-fit if its training error is low (i.e., the model fits very well to the given training data), however its testing (out-of-sample) error is high (i.e., the model imperfectly generalizes). On the other hand, an under-fit model has high values for both training and test errors (i.e., the model does not fit well even to the training data). The trade-off between over-fitting and under-fitting problems allows the machine learning practitioners to understand the behavior of a learning model and ways to increase its performance.

Depending on the learning method, there are a number of solutions offered to deal with the aforementioned problems. For instance, adding more features of data can be an alternative to improve the under-fitting problem while feature reduction, regularization (in case of neural networks) and including more training data are recommended to deal with the over-fitting problem [19].

The aforementioned solutions in error handling have been effective [30], and we see acceptable performance from different types of ML models including deep learning methods in different areas such as machine vision [18], agriculture [21], health and diagnostics [10,24].

Although the algorithms enable machines to learn from their errors, the process of understanding why the algorithm has failed is often the task of the human who, using domain knowledge and contextual information, can explain the likely reason(s) behind the errors. Nevertheless, the human-generated explanations can only provide a better insight on how to refine the data set such that the model can better adjust its parameters. One might consider to automate the process to refine or add to the training data based on ML performance and contextual knowledge. In this way, the learning methods, may *learn both from their mistakes* by also taking into account the causes behind them.

Indeed, one of the hallmarks of explainable AI according to [29] is an umbrella term to refer to a collection of techniques aimed to make ML methods explainable, interpretable, transparent or comprehensible. Enabling ML methods to explain their errors in terms of their causes might be seen as a different solution to improve the performance of machine learning methods. This chapter will focus on the comprehensibility of ML methods for the purpose of the human but also for the purpose of improving the learning algorithm per se. More precisely, this chapter by focusing on specific use case about segmentation of satellite imagery data, will show how Knowledge Representation and Reasoning (KRR) techniques can be a tool to facilitate the process of adding a layer of comprehensibility that can be utilized by ML algorithms to improve performance.

We start with a brief introduction to knowledge representation and reasoning and its applications in machine learning and explainable AI in Section 2. In Section 3 we focus on different steps involved in the process of learning from errors. This section is followed by a case study in Section 4 which gives the overview of a developed system based on error explanation in classification and segmentation of satellite imagery data. We end the chapter with a discussion and possible directions for future work.

2. Knowledge Representation & Reasoning, Machine Learning, Explainable AI

2.1. Knowledge Representation & Reasoning (KRR)

In the area of AI, knowledge representation and reasoning (KRR) methods are applied to enable machines to understand a context and infer implicit information about the context. More specifically, knowledge representation (KR) methods are used to model a context in the form of its concepts, rules and constraints. By modeling a context we refer to a process during which a formal representation of the given context is created. A formal representation relies on formal languages which are understood by machines and define (contextual) concepts based on their relations. In other words, each concept finds its meaning based on its properties that are connected to the other ones. For example, the concept container is defined in an ontology as an object which is used to hold different substances (such as water or food) as another concept, and can be specialized into other concepts (sub-concepts) including bowls and cups. Ontologies are an example of such formal representation models suggested by the Semantic Web community in 2001 [6] to represent the human knowledge available on the traditional Web. Due to their formal languages (i.e, Description Logic based languages), ontologies are understandable for machines [31]. In other words, using ontologies, computer systems are able to understand the meaning of concepts based on their relations with the rest of the context.

Given the contextual model, a reasoning method can be applied to infer more information about the context based on implicitly defined concepts. For instance, given an ontology whereby a container is defined as a tool to hold a substance, and cup is defined as a container (see the following axioms in Description Logic), a machine or any computational agent equipped with a reasoner is able to infer that a cup observed in a given scene can also be used to hold a substance:

$$\texttt{Container} \sqsubseteq \forall \texttt{holds. Substance} \qquad (1)$$

$$\texttt{Cup} \sqsubseteq \texttt{Container} \qquad (2)$$

$$(1) \ \& \ (2) \ \Rightarrow \ \texttt{Cup} \sqsubseteq \forall \texttt{holds. Substance}$$

2.2. Explainable Artificial Intelligence in Machine Learning

With the increasing interest in machine learning techniques, and in particular in deep learning methods, research on integration of knowledge representation and reasoning (KRR) systems with learning methods has recently made considerable progress. Such integrations are increasingly deemed as a solution to address problems concerned with explainable Artificial Intelligence (XAI) [15], and are used to provide better insights into the learning process [12].

The insights which are in the form of explanations become necessary when not only the precision but also the reliability of the learning methods matters specially in crucial decision-making processes (e.g., in people's safety or health). Explanations are provided for different targets ranging from human users to computational systems. Depending on many factors including type of users, we can categorize the explanations into three types as follows:

- **Justification**: explains why and how a learning process ends up with its output.
- **Feature explanation**: explains feature(s) of data extracted to be used in a learning process.
- **Error explanation**: explains the errors as well as the reason behind the errors that a learning process commits.

2.2.1. KRR and Transparency in Machine Learning

The main focus of research efforts in explainable AI is to provide transparency for the sake of interpretation (for human user) as a reliability support in neural-based classifiers.

As discussed in the work done by Xie et al., 2017, in neural-symbolic systems where the learning is based on a connectionist approach, one way of interpreting the learning process is to explain the classification outputs using the concepts related to the classifier's decision [34]. However, there is a limited body of work where symbolic techniques are used to explain the conclusions. The work presented by Hendricks et al., 2016 introduces a learning system based on a Long-Term Convolutional Network (LTCN) [11] that provides explanations over the decisions of the classifier [16]. An explanation is in the form of a justification text. In order to generate the text, the authors have proposed a loss function upon sampled concepts that, by enforcing global sentence constraints, helps the system to construct sentences based on discriminating features of the objects found in the scene. However, no specific symbolic representation was provided, and the features related to the objects are taken from the sentences that are already available for each image in the (CUB data set [32]).

With focus on the knowledge model, Sarker et al,. 2016 proposed a system that explains the classifier's outputs based on the background knowledge [28]. The key tool of the system, called DL-Learner, works in parallel with the classifier and accepts the same data as input. Using the Suggested Upper Merged Ontology (SUMO)[1] as the symbolic knowledge model, the DL-Learner is also able to categorize the images by reasoning upon the objects together with the concepts defined in the ontology. The compatibility between the output of the DL-Learner and the classifier can be seen as a reliability support and at the same time as an interpretation of the classification process.

2.2.2. KRR and Improvement of Learning

KRR methods can also associate learning methods to improve the results. Icarte et al., 2017, introduced a general-purpose knowledge model called the ConceptNet Ontology [17] which contains knowledge about affordances of objects. In this work, the integration of the symbolic model and a sentence-based image retrieval process based on deep learning is used to improve the performance of the learning process by retrieving more meaningful explanations for each image. The knowledge about different concepts, such as their affordances and their relations with other objects, is aligned with objects derived from the deep learning method.

The method of enriching the data by providing information as additional channels for training a CNN-based network has been done before. Liu et al., 2018 and Zhenyi et al., 2018, have explained how to augment the input data by adding two additional channels that represent the i and j coordinates in the image to obtain the location information [25,33].

Although in these works the role of symbolic knowledge represented by ontologies has been emphasized, they are limited in terms of the symbolic representation models. More specifically, the concepts and their relations in ontologies are simplified, limiting the richness of deliberation in an eventual reasoning process, especially for visual imagery data.

2.2.3. KRR and Error Explanation

Reliability of computational systems grows by enabling them to present more human-like behaviors. Learning from mistakes is one of the features that we expect to see from an intelligent agent. As explained above, machine learning algorithms seem to learn from their errors. However, there is a difference between such learning process and how humans tend to deal with their errors. We as humans are able to learn from our errors by investigating the mistake and understanding the reason behind it in order to ensure that

---

[1]http://www.adampease.org/OP/

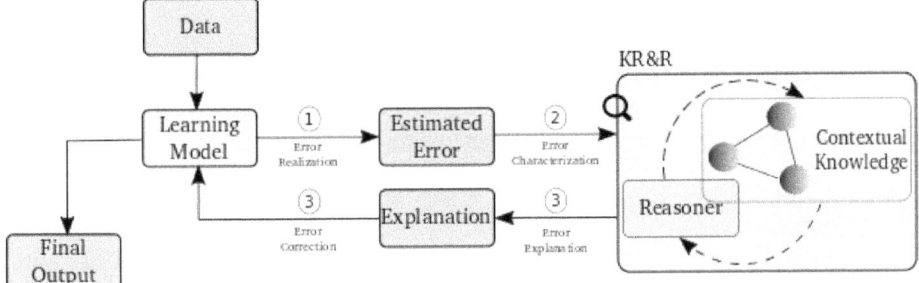

Figure 1. General flow of steps in error explanation process.

we will not make the same mistake in the future. Ability of a system in explaining its errors to itself may lead to an improvement in the learning process. To include the reason behind the errors, the explanations may be based on features of data related to the context and not necessarily those features used (extracted) during the feature extraction phase of the learning process. In the literature, improving the performance by learning and reasoning about mistakes has not been widely explored. Error explanation relying on contextual knowledge has been addressed in [3] and [2] where the knowledge representation and reasoning technique plays the role of a semantic referee to guide an imagery data classifier in dealing with its errors caused by the spatial structure of the environment (outdoor-area). We will go through the details in the following sections.

3. Learning From Errors

As shown in Fig. 1, learning from errors is a process which is composed of several steps including:

- Error Realization
- Error Characterization
- Error Explanation
- Improve Learning

Each step is explained in the following sections.

3.1. Error Realization

In binary classification there are two types of classification errors: false positives (type 1 error) and false negatives (type 2 error). For multi-class classification, when using the top-1 error rate there is a misclassification if the correct class is not the highest predicted class and for top-5 error rate if the correct class is not in the top 5 highest predicted classes. The most likely reason for a poor classification performance for both binary and multi-class classification is that there is an issue with the data set or that the model is not trained properly and is either underfit or overfit. The latter is solved by adjusting the number of data features, model complexity, regularization, optimization, data pre-processing, training time, etc., and will not be covered here. Assuming that the data scientist has performed these adjustments and correctly trained a model that is not suffering from a high bias or high variance, there are still sources of errors that can cause the classifier to make misclassifications. A common approach for discovering the underlying causes of a classifier's errors is to perform an error analysis by manually examining misclassified samples from the validation set. This can give a direction for which type of error is the most common in the data that should be addressed first. There are many sources of errors that are unique for each model and data set.

Mislabeled Data Data is usually manually labeled by humans. Errors in the annotations can be caused by a variety of factors, e.g., labeling fatigue, typing mistakes, inexperience or incorrect knowledge about the data. A proposed method for finding mislabeled training data is to use nearest neighbor search on the training data for misclassified validation samples [20].

Class ambiguity Sometimes there are cases where the data can belong to several classes, e.g., a hand-written 1 that also looks like a 7. The common practice of the annotator is to label each data sample as one, and only one class. For some cases when the demarcation is unclear, a method that allows for multi-class annotation, using the classification certainty, or introducing an unclear/unknown class can be used.

Class imbalance Data class imbalance has a detrimental effect on the classification performance [7]. Methods for compensating for prior class probabilities can be data-based, by undersampling (removing data from the majority classes) and oversampling (replicating data from the minority classes), or classifier-based, by thresholding (adjusting the decision boundary for each class) or cost-sensitive learning (weighting the cost for each class based on the class prevalence).

Concept drift A model that has been trained on data that changes over time can produce errors that are caused by concept drift [13]. The solution to reduce these errors is either to re-train the model or use models that can handle domain-adaptation [9].

Faulty learning Occasionally, the classifier fails to capture the correct class properties and can be discovered when performing an error analysis. For example, if we want a dog/cat classifier and train it on only black cats and white dogs, it will most likely focus on the color property of the classes and misclassify an unseen black dog as a cat.

Incomplete knowledge Similarly to class ambiguity, another case is when there are data samples that look very similar to each other but are differently annotated. This can happen when there is incomplete knowledge and the annotator knows more about the data than is actually present in the data itself and can use common sense and prior knowledge. For example, a building with a gray roof might look very similar to a road or parking lot but an annotator might be able to correctly label it as a building because we see that it casts a shadow and we know that buildings are tall and tall objects cast shadows. Due to the classifier's limited field of perception and inability to infer the height of the object, the building will be misclassified.

3.2. Error Characterization

Error characterization is the process of conceptualizing data by extracting its features related to its context (i.e., contextual features). This process is independent of the learning method, meaning that, the features of data at this step are not necessarily the same as those ones that are considered by the learning method during its feature selection phase. As shown in Fig. 1, the error characterization step relies on the knowledge representation and reasoning module. The assumption is that the contextual features of data are represented in the given knowledge model. As we said above, a knowledge model is a formal representation that provides meaning for any concept related to the domain, based on their characteristics such as their affordances, their spatial relations with the environment, their shape, etc. Depending on the context and domain of work, the error characterization process may involve different types of reasoning (such as thematic, spatial or temporal reasoning) or other analysis process (such as geometrical processing) to maximize the amount of features that it can extract.

3.3. Error Explanation

Given the knowledge model of the domain and the set of extracted contextual features of the data labeled as error. Depending on the content of the knowledge model, the reasoner which receives the extracted contextual features may be able to infer the best possible concept in the knowledge model, compatible with the given feature set. This inference process may continue to include more information about the inferred concept. This information may reveal more constraints about the error-related concept or its relation with the other concepts in the domain.

The reasoner generates a formal explanation about the error data based on what it has inferred as long as it can ensure that the inferred information is generic and not specific for the given instance of error data. In other words, the generated explanation by the reasoner can disclose the general characteristic of the situation in which the error under study is identified.

3.4. Improving learning

The learning model only relies on data. The more diverse and larger the data set, the more precise the learning output will be. In order to inform the learning model about the circumstances under which it made the mistake, the reasoner requires to send feedback to the learning model through a new channel of data. This explained circumstance can also include the cause behind the errors, meaning that the same circumstance will cause the same mistake for the learning model.

By translating the generated explanation that explain the error-related situation into a data format understandable by the learning method, the reasoner may provide new channels of data for the learning process. In other words, the inferred explanation can play the role of new and unseen data for the learning model and enforce it to fix the error and subsequently avoid making the same mistake in next learning iterations.

4. Case Study: XAI for Satellite Images

Error explanation as a solution has been applied in the domain of satellite image segmentation to tackle the misclassification problem [3,2]. The focus in this research has been on the development of a reasoner relying on ontological knowledge to assist a neural network classifier for satellite image segmentation task. This assistance is in particular about representing errors and extracting their features which are eventually used in correcting misclassification. This method depicted in Fig. 2[2] plays the role of a semantic referee in interaction with an imagery data classifier.

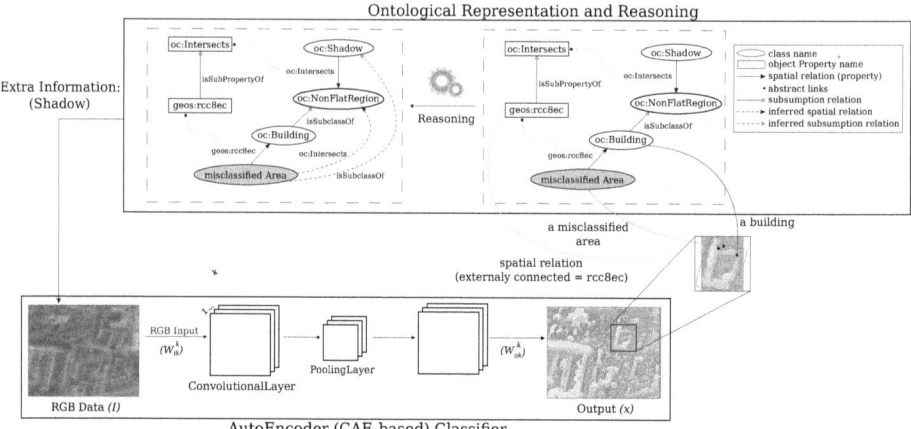

Figure 2. An example representing how the semantic referee (top layer) is used to improve the semantic segmentation task of the convolutional encoder-decoder classifier (bottom layer). The improvement is achieved by enabling the classifier to learn the reasons behind its mistakes (misclassifications). The semantic referee reasons about the mistakes based on ontological concepts and provides additional information back to the classifier that prevents the classifier from making the same misclassifications.

The classifier used in the semantic referee is a deep convolutional network with an encoder-decoder structure that provides the semantic segmentation of the input image. To deal with the misclassification, the semantic referee reasons about the errors based on their geometrical and spatial properties as well as the ontological knowledge about the domain of work (i.e., cities). The reasoner results in the best possible concept which is inferred from the ontology and is matching the errors in terms of its features. The inferred concept related to the misclassified data is then given to the classifier as a feedback from the referee to prevent the classifier from making the same mistake. The feedback from the semantic referee is seen as an additional source or channel of data which requires to be represented in a format understandable for the classifier. The acceptable format is a 2-D matrix with the same size as the RGB input. The additional data channels generated by the reasoner contains information about shadow estimation, elevation estimation, and reports on discovered inconsistencies. More specifically, the classifier can continue to learn using 6 data channels instead of the original 3 RGB channels. The closure of this loop between the semantic referee and the classifier is when the classification accuracy on the validation data converges.

4.1. Ontological Knowledge Model

As we mentioned, the reasoner relies on ontological knowledge representing the domain of work. The domain is outdoor environment with urban structures. The publicly available ontology used to represent the environment is called OntoCity[3]. This ontol-

---

[2]The figure is borrowed from the paper available at IOS Press through `https://dx.doi.org/10.3233/SW-190362` [3]

[3]https://w3id.org/ontocity/ontocity.owl

ogy whose part of representational details can be found in [1], is an extension of the GeoSPARQL ontology, known as a standard vocabulary for geospatial data [23]. The main idea behind designing OntoCity was to develop a generalized knowledge model for representation of cities in terms of their structural, conceptual and physical aspects.

The direct subclass of the class `geos:Feature` is `oc:CityFeature`. As can be seen, the name of a classes is composed of a prefix indicating the ontology and the name of the class within that ontology. In the aforementioned classes, the two prefixes `oc` and `geos` refer to the two ontologies OntoCity and GeoSPARQL, respectively. The class `oc:CityFeature` represents features in a city. Each feature represents a spatial entity in the form of a polygon with geometrical that shares spatial relations with other features. The axioms of OntoCity given in the following are in description logic (DL) [5]:

```
oc:CityFeature ⊑ geos:Feature ⊓
      ∃ geos:hasGeomtery.geos:Polygon ⊓
      ∃ oc:hasSpatialRelation.oc:CityFeature
```

Spatial relations in OntoCity include the RCC-8 (Region Connection Calculus) relations defined by Cohn et al., 1997 [8] and adopted by GeoSPARQL, with a bit of extension. The extension includes the definition of the relation `oc:intersects` that subsumes several RCC-8 relations including partially overlapping (`geos:rcc8po`) and externally connected (`geos:rcc8ec`). Spatial relations like other types of constraints are used to provide more precise definitions for the features in a given city. In OntoCity, there are different categorization of City features. For instance, the features can be categorized into `oc:PhysicalFeature` or `oc:ConceptualFeature`, that represent features with physical geometry (e.g. a landmark with an absolute elevation value measured from the sea floor), or conceptual geometry (e.g. a rectangular division in a city regardless of their landmarks), respectively.

```
oc:PhysicalFeature ⊑ oc:CityFeature ⊓
      ∃ oc:hasAbsoluteElevationValue.xsd:double
oc:ConceptualFeature ⊑ oc:CityFeature
```

Another categorization of the classes is based on their geometrical shape if it is fixed or dynamic (changing in time). The two classed `oc:FixedGeometryFeature` and `oc:DynamicGeometryFeature` represent features with fixed and dynamic geometries, respectively. Mobility is another property that categorizes the city features into mobile (`oc:MobileFeature`, e.g. a car), or stationary (`oc:StationaryFeature`, e.g. a building):

```
oc:FixedGeometryFeature ⊑ oc:CityFeature
oc:DynamicGeometryFeature ⊑ oc:CityFeature
oc:MobileFeature ⊑ oc:CityFeature
oc:StationaryFeature ⊑ oc:CityFeature
```

Each city feature is a subclasses of the class `oc:CityFeature` and can be specialized into more specific urban element. As shown in the following, a region in a city is defined as a class which is stationary (i.e., non-mobile) with a fixed geometry. Each region can per se be categorized into other types such as flat or non-flat, or likewise, into man-made or natural regions in order to define more precise urban entities:

> oc:Region ⊑ oc:PhysicalFeature ⊓
>   oc:StationaryFeature ⊓
>   oc:FixedGeometryFeature
>
> oc:ManmadeRegion ⊑ oc:Region
>
> oc:NaturalRegion ⊑ oc:Region
>
> oc:FlatRegion ⊑ oc:Region
>
> oc:NonFlatRegion ⊑ oc:Region ⊓
>   ∃ oc:hasRelativeElevationValue.xsd:double ⊓
>   ∃ oc:intersects.oc:Shadow

OntoCity also allows us to define non-flat regions which are regions in a city with a non-zero relative elevation value. Due to its height, a non-flat region is also assumed to cast shadows. As shown in the following set of axioms, the class shadow has been also defined in OntoCity (oc:Shadow) due to its spatial relations with the other city features. The concept shadow is defined as a mobile and non-physical (conceptual) feature with a dynamic geometry in OntoCity. Although the exact shape of shadows and their exact positions depend on many quantitative parameters including the position of the source light and the height value of the casting objects, it is still possible to qualitatively describe shadows in the ontology. As shown in the following, spatial constraints are also involved in the definition of shadow concept to emphasis on existence of the shadow casting object which is a non-flat region:

> oc:Shadow ⊑ oc:ConceptualFeature ⊓
>   oc:DynamicGeometryFeature ⊓
>   oc:MobileFeature ⊓
>   ∃ oc:intersects.oc:NonFlatRegion

Each type of region is defined as a subclass of the class oc:Region. Some of the region types are equivalent to the labels (i.e., classes listed in Table 1) taken into account by the classifier:

> oc:River ⊑ oc:WaterArea ⊑ oc:Region
>
> oc:Road ⊑ oc:PavedArea ⊑ oc:ManmadeRegion
>
> oc:Park ⊑ oc:VegetationArea ⊑ oc:Region
>
> oc:Building ⊑ oc:ManmadeRegion ⊓
>   oc:NonFlatRegion

Each of the region types can be specialized and define more specific concepts. For instance, a railroads is defined as a flat (not high) man-made region which is used as a way (i.e., route) in a city. Given this definition, the main three constraints in the definition of the concept oc:RailRoad are in the form of three subsumption relationship with the concepts oc:ManmadeRegion, oc:FlatRegion and oc:Way as follows:

```
oc:RailRoad ⊑ oc:ManmadeRegion ⊑ oc:Region

oc:RailRoad ⊑ oc:FlatRegion

oc:RailRoad ⊑ oc:Way ⊑ oc:Region
```

The RCC-8 relations are also used to make the definition of region types more precise by adding more spatial relations with their vicinity. For instance, A shore area is a land expected to intersect with (more specifically externally connect to) a an area with large body of water (or a sub class of water area):

```
oc:Shore ⊑ oc:Ground ⊓

    ∃ geos:rcc8ec.oc:WaterArea
```

Likewise, a bridge is a man-made non-flat region that is partially overlapping (referring to the RCC-8 relation geos:rcc8po) at least one other region, the texture of which identifies the bridge type. If the region is a water-area then the overlapping bridge is a water bridge, or if the region is a street, then the bridge is categorized as a street or a pedestrian bridge:

```
oc:Bridge ⊑ oc:ManmadeRegion ⊓

    oc:NonFlatRegion ⊓

    ∃ geos:rcc8po.oc:Region
```

The aforementioned axioms are a subset of general knowledge which is consistent for any city regardless of the location, culture or climate situation (e.g. *"Water bridges cross water areas"*). However, depending on the case study, the background knowledge might be specialized to represent features belonging to a specific environment (e.g. *"in the given region there is no building connected to water areas"*).

The following spatial constraints are valid for the city of Stockholm and are considered as domain-based constraints in special version of OntoCity specialized for this work:

1. Buildings are directly connected to at least a road or a vegetation area (referring to the connected relation in RCC8: geos:rcc8ec relation)
2. Buildings do not intersect with railroads (referring to the negation of the oc:intersects relation)
3. Buildings are not directly connected to water-area (referring to the negation of externally connected relation in RCC8: geos:rcc8ec).
4. Buildings are not directly connected to rail roads (referring to the negation of externally connected relation in RCC8: geos:rcc8ec).
5. Buildings are not contained by roads (referring to the negation of tangential proper part relation in RCC-8: geos:rcc8tpp).
6. Buildings do not contain roads (referring to the negation of tangential proper part inverse relation in RCC-8: geos:rcc8tppi).
7. Railroads are not directly connected to water-area (referring to the negation of the oc:intersects relation).

The class `oc:StockholmBuilding` as the subclass of the class `oc:Building` is given in the following:

> `oc:StockholmBuilding ⊑ oc:Building ⊓`
>
> > `∃ geos:rcc8ec.(oc:VegetationArea⊔oc:Road) ⊓`
> >
> > `∄ oc:intersects.oc:RailRoad ⊓`
> >
> > `∄ geos:rcc8ec.oc:Waterarea ⊓`
> >
> > `∄ geos:rcc8tpp.oc:Road ⊓`
> >
> > `∄ geos:rcc8tppi.oc:Road`

Given a region, a reasoner considers all the spatial constraints used in OntoCity in order to find a valid label (region type) by discarding all the invalid ones w.r.t the neighborhood of the region.

4.2. Data classification

The data to be classified are satellite images of size 4000×8000 pixels each with a pixel-resolution of 0.5 meters from the Swedish capital Stockholm. The ground truth used was provided by Lantmäteriet, the Swedish Mapping, Cadastral and Land Registration Authority.[4]. The 5 classes to classify and their class distribution for each city after the data has been split into 50% training and 50% testing sets can be seen in Table 1.

%	Vegetation	Road	Building	Water	Railroad
Stockholm (train)	7.6	31.3	35.4	23.5	2.2
Stockholm (test)	18.2	36.9	19.7	22.4	2.8

Table 1. Class distribution of the city satellite data used in this work.

A Convolutional Auto-encoder that follows the U-net [27] architecture is implemented in *MATLAB 2018a* and used to perform the semantic segmentation of the satellite images. The satellite data is first divided into patches of size 256×256 and normalized to have 0 mean and unit variance. The U-net model consists of an encoder with 4 layers where each layer performs two convolutions with $64 * L$ filters in the Lth layer and a 2×2 max-pooling operation; followed by two convolutions with 1024 filters and 50% dropout; and finally, a decoder with 4 layers that performs upsampling with a scaling factor of 2, depth concatenation with the output from the encoder at the same layer, and two convolutions. The number of filters in each layer L in the decoder is $512/L$. Each convolution has a filter size of 3×3 and is followed by a ReLu-activation [26]. The classification of each pixel is performed with a convolution with k filters, where k is the number of classes, with filter size 1×1 followed by a *softmax* activation function for the final per-pixel classification.

The model parameters are trained from scratch and were initialized with Xavier initialization [14] and trained using the Adam optimization method [22] with initial learning rate 10^{-4} and minibatch size 20 with early-stopping using a validation set that was randomly drawn from 10% of the training data. In order to deal with the large imbalance in the data set, the loss function uses median frequency class weighting.

---

[4]https://www.lantmateriet.se/

4.3. Semantic Augmentation of Errors

Semantically augmenting the errors refer to error characterization explained in Section 3.2. The output of the classifier is in the form of labeled pixels. In order to conceptualize errors and find their spatial properties, the misclassified pixels carrying the same class label are translated into polygons whose boundaries indicate 2D regions. Each polygon representing a region is also assigned with a probability of classification certainty. Misclassified regions are those with low classification certainty (error realization), where the certainty is calculated based on the ground truth.

Given both the list of classified R and misclassified P regions, the algorithm that the semantic referee is relying on is able to calculates all the possible (RCC-8) qualitative spatial relations between any pairs of (p, r) where $p \in P$ is a misclassified region and $r \in R$ is a classified region in its vicinity. For each pair (p, r), the algorithm calculates the spatial relation q between p and r and also keeps the type of the region r named as t. All the calculates pairs $< q, t >$ are added to the hash-map structure W. The hash-map W will at the end contain all the spatial relations that exist between the misclassified regions for each specific region type. In other words, W is defined to contain the geometrical characteristics of the misclassified regions.

To find the best explanation for the cause behind the misclassification, the semantic referee needs to find a pair $< Q, T >$, where Q is the most observed spatial relation between the misclassified regions and a specific region type T. The pair can be generalized and counted as a representative feature of the misclassified regions. Given the representative pair $< Q, T >$, the algorithm queries OntoCity to find all the spatial features that are at least in one Q relation with the region type T ($\exists T.Q$). By applying the ontological reasoner the query can also be further generalized from type T to its super-classes in OntoCity. The concept (C) as a spatial feature ($C \sqsubseteq$ oc:CityFeature) inferred by the reasoner, is considered as the semantic augmentation for the misclassified regions that are in the given spatial relations with the given region type.

4.4. Feedback from the reasoner to the classifier

To improve the learning process, as already mentioned in Section 3.4, the semantic referee provides the feedback to the classifier in the form of additional information that will be augmented to the original RGB training data. Depending what the reasoner is able to infer, we may define several channels of data. The semantic referee was able to report back to the classifier three concepts related to the misclassified regions including shadow estimation, height estimation and uncertainty information for each pixel of data. Each channel of data is in the form of a matrix the same size as the input RGB. The values for the shadow channel are -1 (not shadow), 0 (no opinion), 1 (shadow). Since elevation difference of regions is one of the main parameters in casting shadows, the semantic referee has assigned the relative elevation value for each region as the average of its pixels' elevation values. Given the elevation value together with the type and the spatial relations of regions in the neighborhood of each misclassified region, the semantic referee is able to localize the shadows as the group of pixels of the misclassified region with the lowest elevation value with respect to the elevation values of the regions intersecting with the misclassified region. The values for this channel are -1 (uncertain), 0 (low height), 1 (medium height), and 2 (high height). Finally, the third channel of data is dedicated to the pixels of those uncertain regions whose spatial relations with their neighborhood were found inconsistent w.r.t OntoCity's constraints. Furthermore, the reasoner may find many uncertain areas whose spatial relations with their neighborhood were inconsistent and violating the constraints defined in OntoCity. The values for this channel are 0 (no opinion) and 1 (uncertain).

Given this information in the form of three new channels of data, the classifier is then re-trained and provides a new semantic segmentation for the reasoner to reason about.

4.5. Empirical Evaluation

4.5.1. Identifying misclassifications

The classification certainty threshold chosen in this work is 70% meaning that the regions whose classification certainty is less than 70% are considered as (likely) misclassified regions. As shown in Table 2, the reasoner which is given the misclassified regions, extracts the spatial relations between the misclassified regions and their neighborhood. Each cell of the table represents number of misclassified regions that are in a spatial relation (given in the column header) with all the regions with a specific type (given in the row header). As we can see, the most observed spatial relations that involves 136 misclassified regions is the pair $< Q=$ `geos:rcc8ec`, $T=$ `oc:Building`$>$.

Type (t) \ Relation (q)	ec	po
`oc:Building`	**136**	3
`oc:Road`	59	0
`oc:Water`	11	0

Table 2. Summary of the inconsistent spatial features of errors in classification of **Stockholm test data**. Each cell value represents the number of misclassified regions involved in the given spatial relations with the given region type, where `ec` and `po` refer to the RCC-8 relations *externally connected* and *partially overlapping*, respectively.

Given the pair $< Q, T >$, the reasoner runs the query $\exists$ `geos:rcc8ec.oc:Building` which is interpreted as "*all the entities that are at least in one* `geos:rcc8ec` *relation with the region type* `oc:Building`". The result is a set of concepts sorted from the most generalized to the most specialized (direct superclass) ones satisfying the constraint given in the query. The satisfactory concept is explained as "*a mobile conceptual feature with a dynamic geometry*" or more specifically a `oc:shadow` (as a direct answer of the query). In OntoCity, the concept shadow is defined based on the spatial constraint: $\exists$ `oc:intersects.oc:NonFlatRegion`, which is found by the reasoner as the generalization of the query $\exists$ `geos:rcc8ec.oc:Building` (where `geos:rcc8ec` $\sqsubseteq$ `oc:intersects` and `oc:Building` $\sqsubseteq$ `oc:NonFlatRegion`) (see Figure 2, top layer).

4.5.2. Visualizing misclassifications

Figure 3 shows some examples of misclassifications. The first row shows a Google Maps screenshot for clarity, second rows shows the data that was used for training and the segmentation, and the third rows shows the semantic segmentation from the classifier. There are some representative misclassifications that can be identified that have been marked with a number: 1) *railroads* that are not connected, 2) *railroads* that are surrounded by non-railroads with no nearby connected railroad, 3) small bodies of *water* with surrounding non-water, 4) *grass* that are in the middle of *roads* or *water* with shadows, and 5) *buildings* that are close to *water* or located in the middle of the *road*. One major source for these errors are due to shadows. *Grass* and *roads* that are covered in shadow change their color values to be darker and look more like *water* or *railroad*. Since *buildings* are often located close to *roads*, many sections of the *road* are likely to be covered in shadows and the road can be segmented into several roads disconnected at the those areas.

Figure 3. Three examples of the output from the classifier (bottom) using the RGB satellite data (middle) with the segmentation. Top row shows the same area from Google Maps for better visualization. The numbers indicate some typical cases of misclassifications, see text for details.

4.5.3. Improving the classifier

Figure 4 shows five examples the classification results before and after using the feedback from the reasoner during training of the classifier. The feedback consists of estimated shadow locations and height information that is used together with the RGB data during training. It can be seen that many of the previous misclassifications without using the reasoner (column 2) have been corrected (column 3) when the reasoner can provide a shadow estimation (column 4) and height information (column 5).

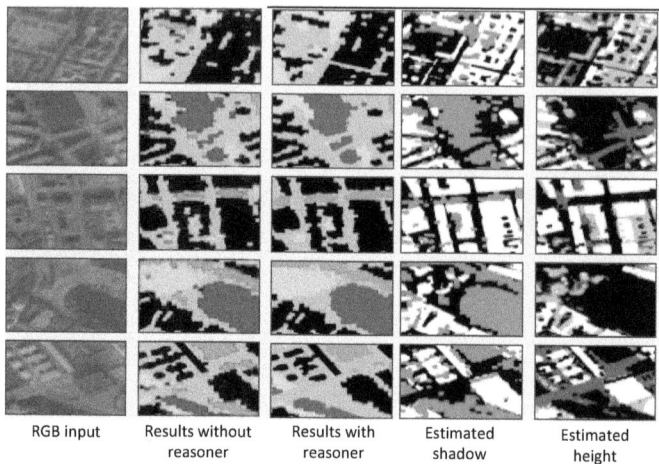

RGB input   Results without   Results with   Estimated   Estimated
                   reasoner   reasoner   shadow   height

Figure 4. RGB input (column 1), predictions from classifier without using the reasoner feedback (column 2) and with using the reasoner feedback (column 3), final shadow estimations from reasoner (column 4, gray=undefined, white=not shadow, black=shadow), and final height estimation from the reasoner (column 5, black=low object, white=tall object).

4.6. Classification results

The confusion matrix before and after using a classifier with reasoner feedback is given in Table 3. The number in parenthesis shows how the result changed when using a semantic referee. The most difficult class to classify is *railroad* and the largest confusion is between *roads* and *railroad*. The semantic referee improved the most for the class *road* (+20%) at the cost of introducing more confusion between the second largest confusion, which was between *vegetation* and *roads*. The reason behind the confusions regarding the class *vegetation* can be related to their wide range of elevation values. The label *vegetation* is not precise enough as it includes trees, lawns, parks, grass on the map and hence their elevation values are not informative enough to help the classifier to differentiate them from roads. The accuracy for *buildings* is already high due to the large amount of buildings in Stockholm and the use of a reasoner did not improve the results for this class. The accuracy for *water* is also high due to the large amount of water in Stockholm and was improved with the reasoner.

5. Conclusion

One way of improving a data classification task is to make data classifiers learn from their mistakes by explaining the reasons behind the mistakes and taking these reasons into account. Error explanation together with justification and feature explanation are techniques recommended to enhance the reliability of decisions made by machines. In

%		Predicted label			
	Vegetation	Road	Building	Water	Railroad
Vegetation	**84.2 (+4.55)**	12.9 (-8.26)	2.3 (+4.13)	0.39 (-0.28)	0.22 (-0.14)
Road	7.4 (+10.9)	**86.4 (-20.0)**	5.8 (+8.23)	0.31 (+0.30)	0.11 (-0.63)
Building	1.2 (+0.61)	8.1 (-2.44)	**90.6 (+1.86)**	0.12 (-0.08)	0.03 (-0.05)
Water	2.3 (+2.85)	2.4 (+3.41)	0.01 (+0.31)	**95.3 (-6.59)**	0.00 (-0.01)
Railroad	11.0 (+13.8)	37.3 (-15.8)	2.6 (+8.0)	0.27 (-0.17)	**48.8 (-5.8)**

Table 3. Confusion matrix [%] for the test set for the classifier that was trained on Stockholm with the use of the reasoner. The numbers in parenthesis show how the result would change compared to a classifier that did not use a reasoner.

these approaches, the reliability is achieved by providing information (i.e., explanation) saying which features of data are selected, discarded or need to be emphasized at different phases of the learning process. The required extra information can be inferred by a symbolic reasoning process applied upon a formally represented domain knowledge.

The reasoning process investigated in this chapter is called semantic referee that is able to find the culprit in confusing the data classifier using ontological knowledge related to the domain of interest. It is worth mentioning that the suggestions made by the semantic referee highly depends on the content of the available ontologies. The richer the ontological knowledge, in terms of spatial constraints, the more meaningful the explanations can be expected from the reasoner. However, the proposed architecture can be viewed as a strength since it allows for different types of classifiers to be coupled onto the reasoning system in a straightforward manner.

A future direction is to look into how the the semantic referee could be integrated into the neural network in such a way that the interaction between the two systems is not limited to only the first and last layers but instead is part of the learning process of the hidden layers of the classifier as well. Another interesting future direction is to explore the reverse process, namely how the classifier can enhance the capabilities of the reasoner.

References

[1] Marjan Alirezaie, Andrey Kiselev, Martin Längkvist, Franziska Klügl, and Amy Loutfi. An ontology-based reasoning framework for querying satellite images for disaster monitoring. *Sensors*, 17(11):2545, 2017.
[2] Marjan Alirezaie, Martin Längkvist, Michael Sioutis, and Amy Loutfi. A symbolic approach for explaining errors in image classification tasks. In *Working Papers and Documents of the IJCAI-ECAI-2018 Workshop on*, 2018.
[3] Marjan Alirezaie, Martin Längkvist, Michael Sioutis, and Amy Loutfi. Semantic referee: A neural-symbolic framework for enhancing geospatial semantic segmentation. *Semantic Web*, (Preprint):1–18, 2019.
[4] Davide Anguita, Alessandro Ghio, Luca Oneto, and Sandro Ridella. In-sample and out-of-sample model selection and error estimation for support vector machines. *IEEE Transactions on Neural Networks and Learning Systems*, 23(9):1390–1406, 2012.
[5] Franz Baader, Diego Calvanese, Deborah McGuinness, Peter Patel-Schneider, Daniele Nardi, et al. *The description logic handbook: Theory, implementation and applications.* Cambridge university press, 2003.
[6] Tim Berners-Lee, James Hendler, and Ora Lassila. The semantic web. *Scientific american*, 284(5):34–43, 2001.

[7]   Mateusz Buda, Atsuto Maki, and Maciej A Mazurowski. A systematic study of the class imbalance problem in convolutional neural networks. *Neural Networks*, 106:249–259, 2018.

[8]   Anthony G Cohn, Brandon Bennett, John Gooday, and Nicholas Mark Gotts. Qualitative spatial representation and reasoning with the region connection calculus. *GeoInformatica*, 1(3):275–316, 1997.

[9]   Hal Daume III and Daniel Marcu. Domain adaptation for statistical classifiers. *Journal of artificial Intelligence research*, 26:101–126, 2006.

[10]   Taye Girma Debelee, Friedhelm Schwenker, Achim Ibenthal, and Dereje Yohannes. Survey of deep learning in breast cancer image analysis. *Evolving Systems*, pages 1–21, 2019.

[11]   Jeffrey Donahue, Lisa Anne Hendricks, Sergio Guadarrama, Marcus Rohrbach, Subhashini Venugopalan, Kate Saenko, and Trevor Darrell. Long-term recurrent convolutional networks for visual recognition and description. In *Proceedings of the IEEE conference on computer vision and pattern recognition*, pages 2625–2634, 2015.

[12]   Derek Doran, Sarah Schulz, and Tarek R Besold. What does explainable ai really mean? a new conceptualization of perspectives. *arXiv preprint arXiv:1710.00794*, 2017.

[13]   João Gama, Indrė Žliobaitė, Albert Bifet, Mykola Pechenizkiy, and Abdelhamid Bouchachia. A survey on concept drift adaptation. *ACM computing surveys (CSUR)*, 46(4):1–37, 2014.

[14]   Xavier Glorot and Yoshua Bengio. Understanding the difficulty of training deep feedforward neural networks. In *Proceedings of the thirteenth international conference on artificial intelligence and statistics*, pages 249–256, 2010.

[15]   David Gunning. Explainable artificial intelligence (xai). *Defense Advanced Research Projects Agency (DARPA), nd Web*, 2, 2017.

[16]   Lisa Anne Hendricks, Zeynep Akata, Marcus Rohrbach, Jeff Donahue, Bernt Schiele, and Trevor Darrell. Generating visual explanations. In *European Conference on Computer Vision*, pages 3–19. Springer, 2016.

[17]   Rodrigo Toro Icarte, Jorge A Baier, Cristian Ruz, and Alvaro Soto. How a general-purpose commonsense ontology can improve performance of learning-based image retrieval. *arXiv preprint arXiv:1705.08844*, 2017.

[18]   Anastasia Ioannidou, Elisavet Chatzilari, Spiros Nikolopoulos, and Ioannis Kompatsiaris. Deep learning advances in computer vision with 3d data: A survey. *ACM Computing Surveys (CSUR)*, 50(2):1–38, 2017.

[19]   Gareth James, Daniela Witten, Trevor Hastie, and Robert Tibshirani. *An introduction to statistical learning*, volume 112. Springer, 2013.

[20]   Mayank Kabra, Alice Robie, and Kristin Branson. Understanding classifier errors by examining influential neighbors. In *Proceedings of the IEEE conference on computer vision and pattern recognition*, pages 3917–3925, 2015.

[21]   Andreas Kamilaris and Francesc X Prenafeta-Boldú. Deep learning in agriculture: A survey. *Computers and electronics in agriculture*, 147:70–90, 2018.

[22]   Diederik P Kingma and Jimmy Ba. Adam: A method for stochastic optimization. *arXiv preprint arXiv:1412.6980*, 2014.

[23]   Manolis Koubarakis, Manos Karpathiotakis, Kostis Kyzirakos, Charalampos Nikolaou, and Michael Sioutis. Data models and query languages for linked geospatial data. In *Reasoning Web International Summer School*, pages 290–328. Springer, 2012.

[24]   Geert Litjens, Thijs Kooi, Babak Ehteshami Bejnordi, Arnaud Arindra Adiyoso Setio, Francesco Ciompi, Mohsen Ghafoorian, Jeroen Awm Van Der Laak, Bram Van Ginneken, and Clara I Sánchez. A survey on deep learning in medical image analysis. *Medical image analysis*, 42:60–88, 2017.

[25]   Rosanne Liu, Joel Lehman, Piero Molino, Felipe Petroski Such, Eric Frank, Alex Sergeev, and Jason Yosinski. An intriguing failing of convolutional neural networks and the coordconv solution. In *Advances in Neural Information Processing Systems*, pages 9605–9616, 2018.

[26]   Vinod Nair and Geoffrey E Hinton. Rectified linear units improve restricted boltzmann machines. In *Proceedings of the 27th international conference on machine learning (ICML-10)*, pages 807–814, 2010.

[27]   Olaf Ronneberger, Philipp Fischer, and Thomas Brox. U-net: Convolutional networks for biomedical image segmentation. In *International Conference on Medical image computing and computer-assisted intervention*, pages 234–241. Springer, 2015.

[28]   Md Kamruzzaman Sarker, Ning Xie, Derek Doran, Michael Raymer, and Pascal Hitzler. Explaining trained neural networks with semantic web technologies: First steps. *arXiv preprint arXiv:1710.04324*, 2017.

[29] Arne Seeliger, Matthias Pfaff, and Helmut Krcmar. Semantic web technologies for explainable machine learning models: A literature review. *PROFILES 2019*, page 30, 2019.

[30] Marina Sokolova and Guy Lapalme. A systematic analysis of performance measures for classification tasks. *Information processing & management*, 45(4):427–437, 2009.

[31] Steffen Staab and Rudi Studer. *Handbook on ontologies*. Springer Science & Business Media, 2010.

[32] Catherine Wah, Steve Branson, Peter Welinder, Pietro Perona, and Serge Belongie. The caltech-ucsd birds-200-2011 dataset. 2011.

[33] Zhenyi Wang and Olga Veksler. Location augmentation for cnn. *arXiv preprint arXiv:1807.07044*, 2018.

[34] Ning Xie, Md Kamruzzaman Sarker, Derek Doran, Pascal Hitzler, and Michael Raymer. Relating input concepts to convolutional neural network decisions. *arXiv preprint arXiv:1711.08006*, 2017.

I. Tiddi et al. (Eds.)
IOS Press, 2020
doi:10.3233/SSW200018

Knowledge-Based Explanations for Transfer Learning

Freddy LÉCUÉ [a,b], Jiaoyan CHEN [c], Jeff Z. PAN [d], and Huajun CHEN [e,f]

[a] *CortAIx Thales, Montreal, Canada*
[b] *Inria, Sophia Antipolis, France*
[c] *Department of Computer Science, University of Oxford, UK*
[d] *Department of Computer Science, The University of Aberdeen, UK*
[e] *College of Computer Science, Zhejiang University, China*
[f] *ZJU-Alibaba Joint Lab on Knowledge Engine, China*

Abstract. Transfer learning aims at building robust prediction models by transferring knowledge gained from one problem to another. In the semantic Web, learning tasks are enhanced with semantic representations. We exploit their semantics to augment transfer learning by dealing with *when to transfer* with semantic measurements and *what to transfer* with semantic embeddings. We further present a general framework that integrates the above measurements and embeddings with existing transfer learning algorithms for higher performance. It has demonstrated to be robust in two real-world applications: bus delay forecasting and air quality forecasting.

Keywords. Explainable Machine Learning, Machine Learning, Transfer Learning, Machine Reasoning

1. Introduction

Transfer learning [25], aims at solving the problem of lacking training data by utilizing data from other related *learning domains*, each of which is referred to as a pair of dataset and prediction task. Transfer Learning plays a critical role in real-world applications of ML as (labelled) data is usually not large enough to train accurate and robust models. Most approaches focus on similarity in raw data distribution with techniques such as dynamic weighting of instances [9] and model parameters sharing [3] (cf. Related Work).

Despite of a large spectrum of techniques [29] in transfer learning, it remains challenging to assess a priori which domain and data set to elaborate from [8]. To deal with such challenges, [7] integrated expert feedback as semantic representation on domain similarity for knowledge transfer while [18] evaluated the graph-based representations of source and target domains. Both studies encode semantics but are limited by the expressivity, which restricts domains interpretability and inhibits a good understanding of transferability. There are also efforts on Markov Logic Networks (MLN) based transfer learning, by using first order [21,22] or second order [11,27] rules as declarative predic-

---

[0] This paper is a long version of paper recently accepted at IJCAI 2019: [16].

tion models. However, these efforts still cannot answer questions like: What ensures a positive domain transfer? Would learning a model from road traffic congestion in London be the best for predicting congestion in Paris? or would an air quality model transfers better?

Towards these challenges, we suggest to encode the semantics of learning tasks and domains with state-of-the-art knowledge representation standard OWL (Web Ontology Language), which is underpinned by Description Logics (DL) [2], and provides a robust foundation to study transferability between source and target learning domains. From knowledge materialization [23], feature selection [28], predictive reasoning [17], stream learning [5] to transfer learning explanation [6], all are examples of inferences tasks where the semantics of data representation are exploited for deriving a priori knowledge from pre-established (certain) statements in ML tasks.

In this study we propose a framework to augment transfer learning by OWL ontology and its reasoning capability, as shown in Figure 1. It deals with *(i) when to transfer* by suitable transferability measurements (i.e., variability of semantic learning task and consistent transferability knowledge), *(ii) what to transfer* by embedding the semantics of learning domains and tasks with transferability vector, consistent vector and variability vector. In addition to expose semantics that drives transfer, a transfer boosting algorithm is developed to integrate the embeddings with existing transfer learning approaches for higher accuracy. Our approach has demonstrated to be robust with high accuracy for transfer learning tasks in real-world applications: *(i)* air quality from Beijing to Hangzhou in China, *(ii)* bus delay from London in UK to Dublin in Ireland and *(iii)* from bus delay in London to air quality in Beijing.

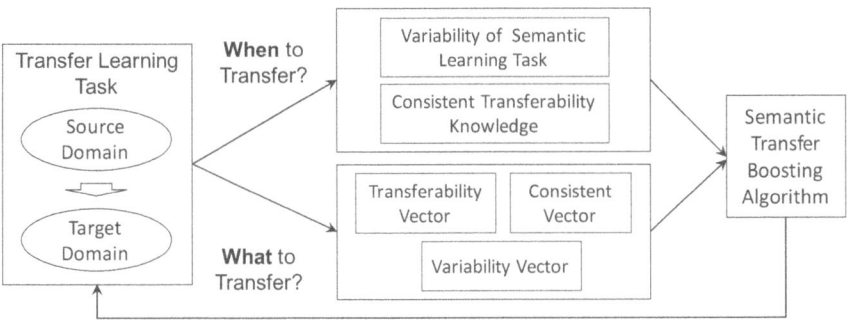

Figure 1. Ontology-based Transfer Learning Augmentation.

2. Background

Ontologies, underpinned by Description Logic (DL), are widely used to model the semantics of data [14]. DL offers reasoning support for most of its expressive families and compatibility to W3C standards e.g., OWL 2. Our work uses DL $\mathcal{EL}^{++}$ [1] to demonstrate the role of semantics, but could be applied with any other DL. The impact will be on decidability, scalability of reasoning. We review basics of (i) DL $\mathcal{EL}^{++}$ and ontology, (ii) ML with ontology, and (iii) transfer learning.

2.1. Description Logics $\mathcal{EL}^{++}$ and Ontology

A signature Σ, noted $(\mathcal{N}_C, \mathcal{N}_R, \mathcal{N}_I)$ consists of 3 disjoint sets of (i) atomic concepts $\mathcal{N}_C$, (ii) atomic roles $\mathcal{N}_R$, and (iii) individuals $\mathcal{N}_I$. Given a signature, the top concept $\top$, the bottom concept $\bot$, an atomic concept A, an individual a, an atomic role expression r, $\mathcal{EL}^{++}$ concept expressions C and D in $\mathcal{C}$ can be composed with the following constructs:

$$\top \mid \bot \mid A \mid C \sqcap D \mid \exists r.C \mid \{a\}$$

A DL ontology is composed of TBox $\mathcal{T}$ and ABox $\mathcal{A}$. $\mathcal{T}$ is a set of concept, role axioms. $\mathcal{EL}^{++}$ supports General Concept Inclusion axioms (GCIs e.g., $C \sqsubseteq D$), Role Inclusion axioms (RIs e.g., $r \sqsubseteq s$). $\mathcal{A}$ is a set of class assertion axioms, e.g., $C(a)$, role assertion axioms, e.g., $R(a, b)$, individual in/equality axioms e.g., $a \neq b$, $a = b$. We consider the ontology's atomic entailment closure (or simply entailment closure, denoted as $\mathcal{G}(\mathcal{T} \cup \mathcal{A})$) as $\{g \mid \mathcal{T} \cup \mathcal{A} \models g\}$, where g represents an atomic class subsumption, an atomic class assertion, or an atomic role assertion entailment, involving only named concepts, named roles and named individuals. Entailment reasoning in $\mathcal{EL}^{++}$ is PTime-Complete.

Example 1. *(TBox and ABox Concept Assertion Axioms)*
Figure 2 presents (i) a TBox $\mathcal{T}$ where Road (1) denotes the concept of "ways which are in a continent", and (ii) concept assertions (8-9) with individuals r_0 and r_1 being roads.

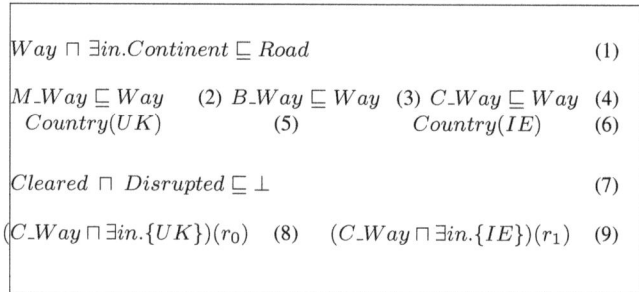

Figure 2. Sample of An Ontology's TBox $\mathcal{T}$ and ABox $\mathcal{A}$.

2.2. Learning Domain and Task

To model the learning domain with ontology, we use Learning Sample Ontology and Target Entailment, as in [6]. A learning domain consists of an LSO set (i.e., dataset) and a target entailment set (i.e., prediction task).

Definition 1. *(Learning Sample Ontology (LSO))*
A learning sample ontology $\mathcal{O} = \langle \langle \mathcal{T}, \mathcal{A} \rangle, S \rangle$ is an ontology $\langle \mathcal{T}, \mathcal{A} \rangle$ annotated by property-value pairs S.

The annotation S in Definition 1 acts as key dimensions to uniquely identify an input sample of ML methods. When the context is clear, we also use LSO to refer to its ontology $\langle \mathcal{T}, \mathcal{A} \rangle$. By using ontology reasoning, we get a complete set of ABox entailments (atomic atomic concept assertions and role assertions, involving only named concepts, named roles and named individuals) for modeling the input sample.

Example 2. (*An LSO in Context of Ireland Traffic*)
Assume an LSO is annotated by property-value pairs $S := \{topic: Road, road : C\_Way, country : UK\}$. Its TBox $\mathcal{T}$ includes static axioms like (1) to (4) and (7), while its ABox $\mathcal{A}$ includes facts e.g., $hasAvgSpeed(r_0, Low)$ that are observed in C_Way in UK.

Definition 2 revisits the concept of *learning domain* in ML and defines *target entailment*. $\mathcal{G}$ denotes a learning domain's entailment closure by default.

Definition 2. (*Learning Domain and Target Entailment*)
A learning domain $\mathcal{D} = \langle \mathbb{O}, \mathcal{G}^{\mathcal{Y}} \rangle$ consists of a set of LSOs $\mathbb{O}$ that share the same TBox $\mathcal{T}$, and target entailments $\mathcal{G}^{\mathcal{Y}}$, each of whose truth in an LSO is to be predicted. Its entailment closure, denoted as $\mathcal{G}(\mathbb{O})$ is defined as $\cup_{\mathcal{O} \in \mathbb{O}} \mathcal{G}(\mathcal{O})$.

Definition 3 revisits supervised learning within a domain. In the training LSO set, a target entailment is true if it is entailed by an LSO, and false otherwise. In the testing LSO set, the truth of a target entailment is to be predicted by the trained model instead of being inferred.

Definition 3. (*Semantic Learning Task*)
Given a learning domain $\mathcal{D} = \langle \mathbb{O}, \mathcal{G}^{\mathcal{Y}} \rangle$, whose LSOs $\mathbb{O}$ are divided into two disjoint sets $\mathbb{O}'$ and $\mathbb{O}''$, a semantic learning task, denoted by $\mathbb{T}$, within $\mathcal{D}$, is defined as: $\langle \mathcal{D}, \mathbb{O}', \mathbb{O}'', f(\cdot) \rangle$ i.e., the task of identifying a function $f(\cdot)$ with $\mathbb{O}'$ and $\mathcal{G}^{\mathcal{Y}}$ to predict the truth of $\mathcal{G}^{\mathcal{Y}}$ in each $\mathcal{O}$ in $\mathbb{O}''$. Here, $\mathbb{O}'$ is called a training LSO set, while $\mathbb{O}''$ is called a testing LSO set.

Example 3. (*Semantic Learning Task*)
Given a learning domain composed of (i) LSOs annotated by $\{topic : Road, country : UK\}$ and (ii) target entailments $Cleared(r_0)$ and $Disrupted(r_0)$, the LSOs are divided into a training set $\mathbb{O}'$ and a testing set $\mathbb{O}''$ according to the type of roads involved, the objective is to identify a function from $\mathbb{O}'$ to predict the condition of road r_0, namely the truth of $Cleared(r_0)$ and $Disrupted(r_0)$ in each LSO in $\mathbb{O}''$.

2.3. Transfer Learning Across Domains

Definition 4 revisits *transfer learning* across two learning domains [25], where the learning domains $\mathcal{D}_S$ and $\mathcal{D}_T$ are called *source domain* and *target domain*. Their entailment closures are denoted as $\mathcal{G}_S$ and $\mathcal{G}_T$.

Definition 4. (*Transfer Learning*)
Given two learning domains $\mathcal{D}_S = \langle \mathbb{O}_S, \mathcal{G}_S^{\mathcal{Y}} \rangle$ and $\mathcal{D}_T = \langle \mathbb{O}_T, \mathcal{G}_T^{\mathcal{Y}} \rangle$, where the LSOs of $\mathcal{D}_T$ are divided into two disjoint sets $\mathbb{O}_T'$ and $\mathbb{O}_T''$, transfer learning from $\mathcal{D}_S$ to $\mathcal{D}_T$ is a task of learning a prediction function $f_{T|S}(\cdot)$ from $\mathbb{O}_S$, $\mathcal{G}_S^{\mathcal{Y}}$, $\mathbb{O}_T'$ and $\mathcal{G}_T^{\mathcal{Y}}$ to predict the truth of $\mathcal{G}_T^{\mathcal{Y}}$ in each LSO in $\mathbb{O}_\beta''$.

Example 4. *(Transfer Learning)*

Assume $\mathcal{D}_T$ is the learning domain in Example 3, $\mathcal{D}_S$ is a learning domain with LSOs annotated by $\{topic : Road, country : IE\}$ and the same target entailments, an example of transfer learning is to identify a function using all the LSOs of Dublin traffic and the training LSOs of London traffic ($\mathbb{O}'_T$) for predicting the traffic condition of road r_0 in each of the testing LSOs of London traffic ($\mathbb{O}''_T$).

The "quality" of a predictive function is measured and analyzed using classic evaluation metrics (e.g., accuracy) [10], denoted as $m(f(\cdot))$. We normalize values into $[0, 1]$ for the sake of readability.

We demonstrate how ontology-based descriptions can drive transfer learning from a source domain $\mathcal{D}_S$ to a target domain $\mathcal{D}_T$. To this end, similarities between domains are first characterized. We adopt the variability of ABox entailments [15] in Definition 5, where (10) reflects *var*iant knowledge between two learning domains while (11) denotes stable (*inv*ariant) knowledge. Other approaches e.g., [12] can also be adapted.

Definition 5. *(Entailment-based Domain Variability)*

Given a source learning domain $\mathcal{D}_S$ and a target learning domain $\mathcal{D}_T$, let $\mathcal{G} = \mathcal{G}_S \cup \mathcal{G}_T$, the variability from $\mathcal{D}_S$ to $\mathcal{D}_T$, denoted as $\nabla(\mathcal{O}_T, \mathcal{O}_S)$ are ABox entailments:

$$\mathcal{G}_{var}^{[S],[T]} = \{g \in \mathcal{G} \mid g \in \mathcal{G}_T \ \vee \ g \notin \mathcal{G}_S\} \tag{10}$$

$$\mathcal{G}_{inv}^{[S],[T]} = \{g \in \mathcal{G} \mid g \in \mathcal{G}_T \ \wedge \ g \in \mathcal{G}_S\} \tag{11}$$

Example 5. *(Entailment-based Domain Variability)*

Let Figure 3 and 4, which capture the contexts in IE and UK, be ontologies of $\mathcal{D}_S$ and $\mathcal{D}_T$ respectively. Table 1 illustrates some variabilities of $\mathcal{D}_S$ and $\mathcal{D}_T$ through ABox entailments. For instance r_1 as a disrupted road in $\mathcal{D}_S$ is new (variant) with respect to knowledge in $\mathcal{D}_T$ and TBox, ABox axioms (1), (9) and (12-15).

$$C\_Way \sqcap \exists adj.(M\_Way \sqcap \exists traffic.Mid) \sqsubseteq Cleared \tag{12}$$

$$D\_Way \sqcap \exists adj.Disrupted \sqsubseteq Disrupted \tag{13}$$

$$(M\_Way \sqcap \exists traffic.Mid)(r_2) \quad (14) \qquad adj(r_1, r_2) \tag{15}$$

Figure 3. Source Domain Ontologies $\mathbb{O}_S$ in Context of IE Traffic.

$$C\_Way \sqcap \exists adj.(M\_Way \sqcap \exists traffic.Mid) \sqsubseteq Disrupted \tag{16}$$

$$(M\_Way \sqcap \exists traffic.Mid)(r_3) \quad (17) \qquad adj(r_0, r_3) \tag{18}$$

$$D\_Way(r_4) \quad (19) \qquad adj(r_4, r_5) \quad (20) \ Disrupted(r_5) \tag{21}$$

Figure 4. Target Domain Ontologies $\mathbb{O}_T$ in Context of UK Traffic.

Ontology Variability	$\nabla(\mathcal{D}_S, \mathcal{D}_T)$	
	variant	*invariant*
$Road(r_3)$		✓
$Cleared(r_1)$	✓	
$Disrupted(r_0)$	✓	

Table 1. Examples for Entailment-based Domain Variability.

3. Transferability

We present (i) variability of semantic learning tasks, (ii) semantic transferability, as a basis for qualifying and quantifying transfer learning (i.e., *when to transfer*), together with (ii) indicators (i.e., *what to transfer*) driving transferability. They have been demonstrated to be pivotal properties. Indeed any change in domains, their transfer function and consistency drastically impact the quality of derived models [19,6].

3.1. Variability of Semantic Learning Tasks

Definition 6 extends the concept of *entailment-based ontology variability* (Definition 5) to capture the learning task variability, where the superscript $(\cdot)^{[\mathcal{Y}_S],[\mathcal{Y}_T]}$ represents using target entailments in (10) and (11).

Definition 6. *(Variability of Semantic Learning Tasks)*
Let $\mathbb{T}_S$ *and* $\mathbb{T}_T$ *be semantic learning tasks of source learning domain* $\mathcal{D}_S$ *and target learning domain* $\mathcal{D}_T$. *The variability of semantic learning tasks* $\nabla(\mathbb{T}_S, \mathbb{T}_T)$ *is defined by* (22), *where* $|\cdot|$ *refers to the cardinality of a set.*

$$\left(\frac{|\mathcal{G}_{var}^{[S],[T]}|}{|\mathcal{G}_{var}^{[S],[T]}| + |\mathcal{G}_{inv}^{[S],[T]}|}, \frac{|\mathcal{G}_{var}^{[\mathcal{Y}_S],[\mathcal{Y}_T]}|}{|\mathcal{G}_{var}^{[\mathcal{Y}_S],[\mathcal{Y}_T]}| + |\mathcal{G}_{inv}^{[\mathcal{Y}_S],[\mathcal{Y}_T]}|} \right) \tag{22}$$

The variability of semantic learning tasks (22), also represented by

$$(\nabla(\mathbb{T}_S, \mathbb{T}_T)|_{\mathbb{O}}, \nabla(\mathbb{T}_S, \mathbb{T}_T)|_{\mathcal{Y}}),$$

with values in $[0, 1]$, captures the variability of source and target domain LSOs as well as the variability of target entailments. The higher values the stronger variability.

(22) is in worst case polynomial time w.r.t size $\mathbb{O}_S$, $\mathbb{O}_T$, $\mathcal{Y}_S$ and $\mathcal{Y}_T$ in $\mathcal{EL}^{++}$. Indeed its evaluation requires (i) ABox entailment, and (ii) basic set theory operations from Definition 5, both in polynomial time [1].

Example 6. *(Variability of Semantic Learning Tasks)*
The variability of learning task between $\mathbb{T}_S$ *and* $\mathbb{T}_T$ *in Example 4 is* $(2/3, 0)$ *as the number of variant and invariant ABox entailments are respectively* 6 *and* 3, *and* $\mathcal{Y}_S = \mathcal{Y}_T$. *i.e., moderate variability of domains, none for target variables.*

Property 1. *(Non-Symmetric Property of Variability)*
The variability of learning tasks is non-symmetric as (22) *exploits the non-symmetric property of Definition 5 to differentiate transfer from* $\mathbb{T}_S$ *to* $\mathbb{T}_T$, *and* $\mathbb{T}_T$ *to* $\mathbb{T}_S$.

3.2. Semantic Transferability

We define *semantic transferability* from a source to a target semantic learning task as the existence of knowledge that are captured as ABox entailments in the source and have positive effects on predictive quality of the prediction function of the target semantic learning task. Such definition identifies *when to transfer* knowledge if any.

Definition 7. *(Semantic ε-Transferability)*
Let $\mathbb{T}_S$, $\mathbb{T}_T$ be source, target semantic learning tasks with entailment closures $\mathcal{G}_S$, $\mathcal{G}_T$. Semantic ε-transferability $\mathbb{T}_S \overset{\varepsilon}{\mapsto} \mathbb{T}_T$ occurs from $\mathbb{T}_S$ to $\mathbb{T}_T$ iff $\exists \mathcal{S} \subseteq \mathbb{O}_S$:

$$m(f_{T|_S}(\cdot)) - m(f_T(\cdot)) > \varepsilon \qquad (23) \qquad\qquad \mathcal{G}_S \neq \mathcal{G}_T \qquad (24)$$

where $f_{T|_S}(\cdot)$ is the predictive function $f_T(\cdot)$ w.r.t. $\mathbb{O}_T \cup \mathcal{S}$. $\mathcal{G}_S$ is the ABox closures of $\mathcal{S}$.

$\mathcal{S}$ is knowledge from $\mathbb{O}_S$, to be used for over-performing the predictive quality of $f_T(\cdot)$ with a $\varepsilon \in (0,1]$ factor (23) while being new with respect to ABox entailments in $\mathcal{G}_T$ (24).

Example 7. *(Semantic ε-Transferability)*
Let $\mathbb{T}_S$, $\mathbb{T}_T$ be semantic learning tasks in $\mathcal{D}_S$, $\mathcal{D}_T$ in Example 4, $\mathcal{S}$ be ABox entailment closure of (12-15) in $\mathcal{O}_S$, and $m(f_{T|_S}(\cdot)) > m(f_T(\cdot))$. Semantic ε-transferability occurs from $\mathbb{T}_S$ to $\mathbb{T}_T$ as (i) an $\varepsilon > 0$, satisfying condition (23), exists, and (ii) (24) is true cf. Table 1 w.r.t. $\mathcal{S}$. Thus, knowledge $\mathcal{S}$ in IE traffic context $(\mathcal{D}_S)$ ensures transferability from $\mathcal{D}_S$ to $\mathcal{D}_T$ for traffic prediction in UK.

ABox entailments $\mathcal{S}$ satisfying Definition 7 are denoted as *transferable knowledge* while those contradicting (23) i.e., $m(f_{T|_S}(\cdot)) - m(f_T(\cdot)) \leq \varepsilon$ are *non-transferable knowledge* as they deteriorate predictive quality of target function $f_T(\cdot)$.

Example 8. *(Transferable Knowledge)*
Consider entailments in $\mathcal{S}$: (i) $Disrupted(r_4)$, derived from (13) (19-21), (ii) $Cleared(r_0)$, derived from (8), (12), (17-18). As part of knowledge $\mathcal{S}$ positively impacting the quality of the prediction task, they are also separate ε-transferable knowledge with max ε: .1, .07 (computation details omitted).

Property 2. *(Non-additive Transferability)*
$\mathcal{S}_1 \cup \mathcal{S}_2$ is not necessarily $(\varepsilon_1 + \varepsilon_2)$-transferable knowledge from $\mathbb{T}_S$ to $\mathbb{T}_T$ if $\mathcal{S}_1 \mid \mathbb{T}_S \overset{\varepsilon_1}{\mapsto} \mathbb{T}_T$ and $\mathcal{S}_2 \mid \mathbb{T}_S \overset{\varepsilon_2}{\mapsto} \mathbb{T}_T$.

The non-additive property of transferable knowledge is due to the characteristics of the evaluation metric $m(\cdot)$ and the predictive function applied $f(\cdot)$, which are not additive.

3.3. Consistent Transferable Knowledge

Transferring knowledge across domains can derive to inconsistency. Definition 8 captures knowledge ensuring transferability while maintaining consistency in the target domain.

Definition 8. *(Consistent Transferable Knowledge)*
Let $\mathcal{S}$ be ABox entailments ensuring $\mathbb{T}_S \overset{\varepsilon}{\mapsto} \mathbb{T}_T$. $\mathcal{S}$ is consistent transferable knowledge from $\mathbb{T}_S$ to $\mathbb{T}_T$ iff $\mathcal{S} \cup \mathbb{O}_T \not\models \bot$.

ABox entailments $\mathcal{S}$ satisfying $\mathcal{S} \cup \mathbb{O}_T \models \bot$ are called inconsistent transferable knowledge. They are interesting ABox entailments as they expose knowledge contradicting the target domain while maintaining transferability.

Example 9. *((In-)Consistent Transferable Knowledge)*
$Disrupted(r_4)$ in $\mathcal{S}$ of Example 8 is consistent transferable knowledge in $\mathbb{T}_T$ as $\{Disrupted(r_4)\} \cup \mathbb{O}_T \not\models \bot$. On contrary $Cleared(r_0)$ and $Disrupted(r_0)$ in $\mathcal{S}$, derived from (16-18) are inconsistent (7). Thus, $Cleared(r_0)$ in $\mathbb{O}_S$ is inconsistent transferable knowledge in $\mathbb{T}_T$.

Evaluating if $\mathcal{S}$ is consistent transferable knowledge is in worst case polynomial time in $\mathcal{EL}^{++}$ w.r.t. size of $\mathcal{S}$ and $\mathbb{O}_T$.

Remark 1. *(On Predictive Quality)*
Although transferable knowledge impacts predictive quality of a learning task, the (in-)consistent-related qualitative impact needs experimental evaluation cf. Section 5.

4. Semantic Transfer Learning

We tackle the problem of transfer learning by (i) computing semantic embeddings (*i.e., how to transfer*) for knowledge transfer, and (ii) determining a strategy to exploit the semantics of the learning tasks (Section 3) in Algorithm 1.

4.1. Semantic Embeddings

The semantics of learning tasks exposes three levels of knowledge which are crucial for transfer learning: variability, transferability, consistency. They are encoded as semantic embeddings through *transferability* (Definition 9), *consistency* (Definition 10), and *variability* (Definition 11) *vectors*.

Definition 9. *(Transferability Vector)*
Let $\mathcal{G} \doteq \{g_1, \ldots, g_m\}$ be all distinct ABox entailments in $\mathbb{O}_S \cup \mathbb{O}_T$. A transferability vector from $\mathbb{T}_S$ to $\mathbb{T}_T$, denoted by $\mathbf{t}(\mathcal{G})$, is a vector of dimension m such that $\forall j \in [1, m]$:

$$t_j \doteq \varepsilon_j \quad \text{if } g_j \text{ is } \varepsilon_j\text{-transferable knowledge, } 0 \quad \text{otherwise} \qquad (25)$$

with $\varepsilon_j \mid \not\exists \varepsilon_j^*, \varepsilon_j < \varepsilon_j^*$ and g is ε_j^*-transferable knowledge.

A transferability vector (Definition 9) is adapting the concept of feature vector [4] in Machine Learning to represent the qualitative transferability from source to target of all ABox entailments. Each dimension captures the best of transferability of a particular ABox entailment.

Example 10. *(Transferability Vector)*
Suppose $\mathcal{G} \doteq \{Disrupted(r_4), Cleared(r_0)\}$. Transferability vector $\mathbf{t}(\mathcal{G})$ is $(.1, .07)$ cf. ε-transferability in Example 8.

A consistency vector (Definition 10) is computed from all entailments by evaluating their (in-)consistency, either 1 or 0, when transferred in the target semantic learning task.

Definition 10. *(Consistency Vector)*
Let $\mathcal{G} \doteq \{g_1, \ldots, g_m\}$ be all distinct ABox entailments in $\mathbb{O}_S \cup \mathbb{O}_T$. A consistency vector from $\mathbb{T}_S$ to $\mathbb{T}_T$, denoted by $\mathbf{c}(\mathcal{G})$, is a vector of dimension m such that $\forall j \in [1, m]$:

$$c_j \doteq 1 \ \ if \ \{c_j\} \cup \mathbb{O}_T \not\models \bot, \ 0 \ \ otherwise \tag{26}$$

Example 11. *(Consistency Vector)*
Consistency vector $\mathbf{c}(\mathcal{G})$ is $(1, 0)$ cf. results from Example 9.

Remark 2. *(Feature / Transferability / Consistency Vector)*
Feature vectors are bounded to only raw data while transferability and consistency vectors, with larger dimensions, embed transferability and consistency of data and its inferred assertions. They ensure a larger, more contextual coverage.

The variability vector (Definition 11) is used as an indicator of semantic variability between the two learning tasks. It is a value in $[0, 1]$ with an emphasis on the domain ontologies and / or label space depending on its parameterization (α, β).

Definition 11. *(Variability Vector)*
Let $\mathcal{G} \doteq \{g_1, \ldots, g_m\}$ be ABox entailments in $\mathbb{O}_S \cup \mathbb{O}_T$. A variability vector $\mathbf{v}(\mathcal{G}, \alpha, \beta)$ from $\mathbb{T}_S$ to $\mathbb{T}_T$ is a vector of dimension m with $\alpha, \beta \in [0, 1]$ such that v_j is defined as:

$$\frac{\alpha(\nabla(\mathbb{T}_S, \mathbb{T}_T)|_{\mathbb{O}}) + \beta(\nabla(\mathbb{T}_S, \mathbb{T}_T)|_{\mathcal{Y}})}{\alpha + \beta}, \ \forall j \in [1, m] \tag{27}$$

Example 12. *(Variability Vector)*
Applying (27) on the variability of semantic learning tasks between $\mathbb{T}_S$ and $\mathbb{T}_T$: $(^2/_3, 0)$ in Example 6 results in $\mathbf{v}(\mathcal{G}, \alpha, \beta) = {^1/_3}$, which represents moderate variability.

We characterize any variability weight above $1/2$ as *inter-domain* transfer learning tasks, and below $1/2$ as *intra-domain* transfer learning tasks.

4.2. Boosting for Semantic Transfer Learning

Algorithm 1 presents a case of extending existing transfer learning methods (TrAdaBoost [9]) by integrating the above semantic embeddings. It aims at learning a predictive function $f_{T|S}(\cdot)$ (line 20) using $\langle \mathbb{T}_S, \mathbb{O}_S \rangle$, $\mathbb{O}_T$ for $\mathbb{T}_T$. The semantic embeddings of all entailments in $\mathcal{G}_S \cup \mathcal{G}_T$ are computed (lines 7-8). Then, their importance / weight $\mathbf{w}$ are iteratively adjusted (line 9) depending on the evaluation of f^t (lines 13-14) when comparing estimated prediction $f^t(\mathbf{e}_i)$ and real values $\mathcal{Y}_T(g_i)$.

The base model (lines 11-12), which can be derived from any weak learner e.g., Logistic Regression, is built on top of all entailments in source, target tasks. However, entailments from the source might be wrongly predicted due to tasks variability (Definition 6 - line 8) $\mathbb{T}_S$, $\mathbb{T}_T$. Thus, we follow the parameterization of γ and γ_t [9] by decreasing the weights of such entailments to reduce their effects (lines 17-19). In the next iteration, the misclassified source entailments, which are dissimilar to the target ones w.r.t. semantic embeddings, will affect the learning process less than the current iteration. Finally, StAdaB returns a binary hypothesis (line 20). Multi-class classification can be easily applied.

Algorithm 1: StAdaB($\langle \mathcal{D}_S, \mathbb{T}_S \rangle, \langle \mathcal{D}_T, \mathbb{T}_T \rangle, \mathbb{O}'_T, \mathcal{G}, \mathbf{L}, N, \alpha, \beta$)

1 **Input:** (i) Source / target learning domains and semantic learning tasks $\langle \mathcal{D}_S, \mathbb{T}_S \rangle, \langle \mathcal{D}_T, \mathbb{T}_T \rangle$, (ii) a training LSO set of the target learning domain $\mathbb{O}'_T$, (iii) all distinct ABox entailments $\mathcal{G} \doteq \{g_1, \ldots, g_m\}$ of $\mathbb{O}_S \cup \mathbb{O}'_T$, (iv) a base Learning algorithm $\mathbf{L}$, (v) max. nb. iterations N, (vi) $\alpha, \beta \in [0, 1]$.

2 **Result:** $f_{T|_S}(\cdot)$: A predictive function utilizing $\langle \mathcal{D}_S \rangle, \mathbb{T}_S$, $\mathbb{O}'_T$ and $\mathcal{G}^{\mathcal{Y}}_T$ for $\mathbb{T}_T$.

3 **begin**

4 $\quad$ % *Initialization of weights for transferability, consistency,*

5 $\quad$ % *and variability vectors of all m ABox entailments in $\mathcal{G}$.*

6 $\quad$ Initialization of $\mathbf{w}^1 \doteq (w_1^1, \cdots, w_{3 \times m}^1)$;

7 $\quad$ % *Computation of semantic embeddings for all $g_i \in \mathcal{G}$.*

8 $\quad$ $\mathbf{e}_i \leftarrow (\mathbf{t}(g_i), \mathbf{c}(g_i), \mathbf{v}(\mathcal{G}, \alpha, \beta)), \forall i \in \{1, \cdots, m\}$;

9 $\quad$ **foreach** $t = 1, 2, ..., N$ **do** % *Weight computation iteration*

10 $\quad\quad$ $\mathbf{p}^t \leftarrow \mathbf{w}^t / \sum_{i=1}^{3m} w_i^t$; % *Probability distribution of $\mathbf{w}^t$.*

11 $\quad\quad$ % *Predictive function f^t over $\mathbb{O}_S \cup \mathbb{O}'_T$.*

12 $\quad\quad$ $(f^t : \mathbf{e}_i \rightarrow \mathcal{Y}_T(\mathbf{e}_i)) \leftarrow \mathbf{L}(\mathbf{e}, \mathbf{p}^t, \mathcal{Y}_T)$;

13 $\quad\quad$ % *Error computation of f^t on $\langle \mathbb{T}_T, \mathbb{O}'_T \rangle$.*

14 $\quad\quad$ $\psi_t \leftarrow \sum_{i|g_i \in \mathcal{G}_T} \frac{w_i^t \cdot |f^t(\mathbf{e}_i) - \mathcal{Y}_T(g_i)|}{\sum_{i|g_i \in \mathcal{G}_T}}$;

15 $\quad\quad$ % *Weights for reducing errors on $\mathbb{T}_T$ over iteration.*

16 $\quad\quad$ $\gamma_t \leftarrow \psi_t/(1 - \psi_t); \quad \gamma \leftarrow 1/(1 + \sqrt{2 \ln(|\mathcal{G}_S|/N)})$;

17 $\quad\quad$ % *Weight update of source and target entailments in $\mathcal{G}$.*

18 $\quad\quad$ % *using $\gamma_t, \gamma,$ and results from previous iteration: w_i^t.*

19 $\quad\quad$ $w_i^{t+1} \leftarrow \begin{cases} w_i^t \cdot \gamma_t^{-|f^t(\mathbf{e}_i) - \mathcal{Y}_T(\mathbf{e}_i)|}, & \text{if } g_i \in \mathcal{G}_T \\ w_i^t \cdot \gamma^{|f^t(\mathbf{e}_i) - \mathcal{Y}_T(\mathbf{e}_i)|}, & \text{else} \end{cases}$

20 $\quad$ **return** *Hypothesis ensemble:*

$$f_{T|_S}(\mathbf{e}) = \begin{cases} 1, & \text{if } \prod_{t=\lceil N/2 \rceil}^N \beta_t^{-f_t(\mathbf{e})} \geq \prod_{t=\lceil N/2 \rceil}^N \beta_t^{-\frac{1}{2}} \\ 0, & \text{else} \end{cases}$$

Figure 5. Algorithm for Transfer Learning.

A brute force approach would consist in generating an exponential number of models with any combination of entailments from source, target. StAdaB reduced its complexity by only evaluating atomic impact and (approximately) computing the optimal combination. As a side effect, StAdaB exposes entailments in the source which are driving transfer learning (cf. final weight assignment of embeddings).

Algorithm 1 solves a classification problem by redefining the features space in line 8. Thus, each entailment is defined with its transferability, consistency and variability effects from source to target domain.

Example 13. *(Boosting for Semantic Transfer Learning)*
Following Algorithm 1 we first obtain a semantic embedding for each entailment. Suppose the entailments set in Example 10, we obtained the stacked embedding $(.1, .07, 1, 0, 1/3)$ according to examples 11 and 12. A model is built on top of the latter entailment and iterated on all $\mathcal{G}_S$ and $\mathcal{G}_T$. Weight of embeddings are adjusted based on their transferability in the target domain (lines 15-19). In case the embedding increases the error, its weight is decreased, otherwise it is increased to impact the model more. The final hypothesis is a set of embeddings with their associated weight in the model. The model construction is then strongly based on the semantic embeddings (variability, consistency) and their transferability.

5. Experimental Results

● **Set-up:** StAdaB is evaluated by two **I**ntra-domain transfer learning cases: (i) air quality forecasting from **B**eijing to **H**angzhou (IBH), (ii) traffic condition prediction from **L**ondon to **D**ublin (ILD), and one **I**nter-domain case: (iii) from traffic condition prediction in **L**ondon to air quality forecasting in **B**eijing (ILB). All tasks are performed with a respective value of .3, .4, .7 for variability $\mathbf{v}(\mathcal{G}, \alpha, \beta)$. We set $\alpha = \beta = 1/2$.

● **Intra-Domain Beijing - Hangzhou (IBH):** Air quality knowledge in Beijing (source) is transferred to Hangzhou (target) for forecasting air quality index, ranging from Good (value 5), Moderate (4), Unhealthy (3), Very Unhealthy (2), Hazardous (1) to Emergent (0). The observations include air pollutants (e.g., $PM_{2.5}$), meteorology elements (e.g., wind speed) and weather condition from 12 stations. The semantics of observations is based on a DL $\mathcal{ALEH}(\mathcal{D})$ ontology, including 48 concepts, 15 roles, 598 axioms. $1,065,600$ RDF triples are generated on a daily basis. 18 (resp. 5) months of observations are used as training (resp. testing). Even though the ontologies are from the same domain, their concept and role similarities are not exact, respectively .81 and .74. For instance, no hazardous air quality concept in Hangzhou.

● **Intra-Domain London - Dublin Bus Delay (ILD):** Bus delay knowledge in London (source) is transferred to Dublin (target) for predicting traffic conditions classified as Free (value 4), Low (3), Moderate (2), Heavy (1), Stopped (0). Source and target domain data (Table 2) include bus location, delay, congestion status, weather conditions. We enrich the data using a DL $\mathcal{EL}^{++}$ domain ontology (55 concepts, 19 roles, $25,456$ axioms). The concept and role similarities among the two ontologies are respectively .73 and .77.

Feature DataSet	City	Size (Mb) per day	#Axioms (10^6) per day	#RDF Triples (10^6) per day
Bus	London	630	91.1	121.3
	Dublin	120	10.8	43.2
Weather	London	6	1.1	2.3
	Dublin	3	0.2	1.1
Incident	London	2.5	0.8	9.6
	Dublin	0.1	0.3	1.2

Table 2.   Datasets of Intra-Domain London Dublin Bus Delay.

- **Inter-Domain London - Beijing (ILB):** Bus delay knowledge in London (source) is transferred to a very different domain: Beijing (target) for forecasting air quality index. Data and ontologies from IBH and ILD are considered. Although they are different domains, they share some common and conflicting knowledge. Inconsistency will then occur, but a much higher level. For instance, both domains have the concepts of City, weather such as Wind but are conflicting on their importance and impact on the targeted variable i.e., bus delay in London and air quality in Beijing. The concept and role similarities among the two ontologies are respectively .23 and .17.

- **Validation:** Accuracy is reported by (i) studying the impact of semantic embeddings, (ii) comparing prediction results with existing approaches on real-world observations using cross-validation. The system is tested on: 16 Intel(R) Xeon(R) CPU E5-2680, 2.80GHz cores and 32GB RAM.

- **Semantic Impact:** Table 3 reports the impact of considering semantics (cf. Sem. vs. Basic) and (in)consistency (cf. Consistency / Inconsistency) in semantic embeddings on Random Forest (RF), Stochastic Gradient Descent (SGD), AdaBoost (AB). "*Basic*" models are models with no semantics attached. "*Plain*" models are modelling and prediction in the target domain i.e., no transfer learning, while "*TL*" refers to transferring entailments from the source. As expected semantics positively boosts accuracy of transfer learning for intra-domain cases (IBH and ILD) with an average improvement of 13.07% across models. More surprisingly it even over-performs in the inter-domain case (ILB) with an improvement of 20.03%. While inconsistency is driving below-baseline accuracy. It is outperformed when considering consistency by 63.55% for intra-domain cases, and by 187.89% for inter-domain cases. Such results confirm that our methods for consistent transferable knowledge and semantic embeddings are effective.

Case	Models	RF		SGD		AB	
		Plain	*TL*	*Plain*	*TL*	*Plain*	*TL*
IBH (Sem.)	*Basic*	.61	.61	.59	.62	.59	.63
	Consistency	.65	.74	.62	.69	.64	.73
	Inconsistency	.56	.64	.52	.60	.49	.63
	Cons. / Incons.	**+16.07%**		**+19.23%**		**+30.61%**	
	Semantic / Basic	**+13.93%**		**+8.18%**		**+12.17%**	
ILD (Sem.)	*Basic*	.68	.71	.57	.62	.63	.69
	Consistency	.75	.78	.65	.71	.75	.82
	Inconsistency	.44	.52	.26	.49	.24	.46
	Cons. / Incons.	**+60.22%**		**+102.86%**		**+152.35%**	
	Semantic / Basic	**+10.07%**		**+14.70%**		**+19.42%**	
ILB (Sem.)	*Basic*	.62	.65	.60	.66	.61	.68
	Consistency	.74	.79	.69	.78	.73	.85
	Inconsistency	.23	.45	.29	.42	.18	.34
	Cons. / Incons.	**+153.96%**		**166.25%**		**+243.46%**	
	Semantic / Basic	**+20.44%**		**+17.33%**		**+22.33%**	

Table 3. Forecasting Accuracy / Improvement over State-of-the-art Models (noted as Basic) with Consistency / Inconsistency (Consistency ratio .8) based Knowledge Transfer.

- **(In-)Consistency Impact:** Figure 6 reports the impact of (in-)consistency on transfer learning by analyzing how the ratio of consistent transferable knowledge in $[0, 1]$ is driving accuracy. Accuracy is reported for methods in Table 3 on intra- (average of IBH and ILD) and inter-domains (ILB). Max. (resp. min.) accuracy is ensured with ratio in $[.9, .7)$ (resp. $[.3, .1)$). The more consistent transferable knowledge the more transfer for $[.9, .1)$. Interestingly having only consistent (resp. inconsistent) transferable knowledge does not ensure best (resp. worst) accuracy. This is partially due to under- (resp. over-) populating the target task with conflicting knowledge, ending up to limit transferability. Experiments show that consistency positively impacts transferability of intra-, inter-domains with similar order of magnitude. This demonstrates the robustness of models supporting semantics when common / conflicting knowledge is shared.

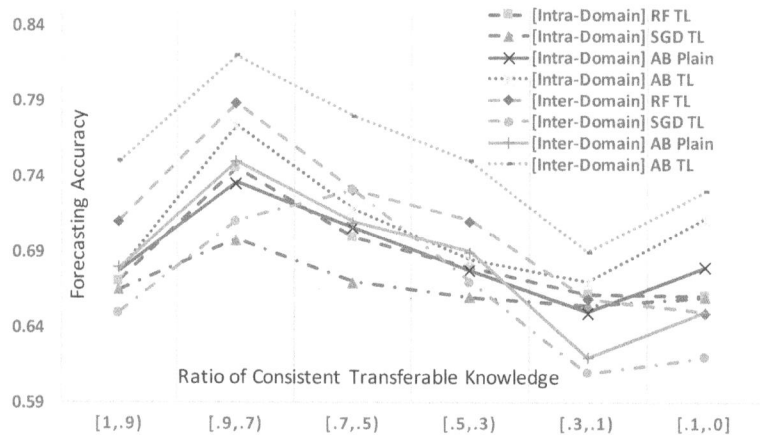

Figure 6. Forecasting Accuracy vs. Semantic Consistency.

• **Baseline:** We compare StAdaB ($\mathbf{L}$ = Logistic Regression, $N = 800$) with (i) Transfer AdaBoost TrAB [9], (ii) Transfer Component Analysis (TCA) [24], (iii) TrSVM [3] and (iv) SemTr [20], which are respectively instance-based, feature-based, parameter-based and semantic-based approaches cf. details in Section 6. We considered intra-domains: IBH, ILD and inter-domains: ILB and ILB* (i.e., ILB with same level of semantic expressivity covered by SemTr). Results report that transfer learning has limitations in the Beijing - Hangzhou context cf. Figure 7(a). Although our approach over-performs other techniques (from 10.29% to 50%), accuracy does not exceed 74%. The latter is due to the context, which is limited by the (i) semantic expressivity and (ii) data availability in Hangzhou. The results show that TrSVM and TCA reach similar results (average difference of 9.1%) in all for cases. However our approach and TrAB tend to maximize the accuracy specially in inter-domains ILB and ILB* in Figures 7(c) and 7(d) as both favor heterogenous domains by design. Interestingly the semantic context of ILB* in Figure 7(d) (i) does not favor SemTr much (+7.46% vs. ILB), (ii) does not have impact for StAdaB compared to ILB, and more surprisingly (iii) does benefit TrAB (+9.15% vs. ILB). This shows that expressivity of semantics is crucial in our approach to benefit from (in-)consistency in transfer learning.

• **Lessons Learnt:** Adding semantics to domains for transfer learning has clearly shown the positive impact on accuracy, specially in context of inter-domains transfer. The ex-

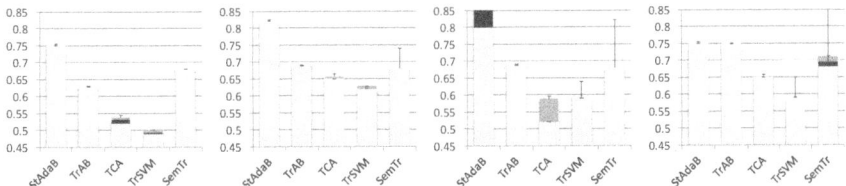

| (a) Intra-Domain IBH | (b) Intra-Domain ILD | (c) Inter-Domains ILB | (d) Inter-Domains ILB* |

Figure 7. Baseline Comparison of Forecasting Accuracy.

pressivity of semantics has also shown positive impacts, specially when (in-)consistency can be derived from the domain logics, although some state-of-the-art approaches benefit from taxonomy-like knowledge structure. Our approach also demonstrates that the more semantic axioms the more robust is the model and hence the higher the accuracy cf. Figure 7(a) vs. 7(b). Data size and axiom numbers are critical as they drive and control the semantics of domain and transfer, which improve accuracy, but not scalability (not reported in the paper). It is worst with more expressive DLs due to consistency checks, and with limited impact on accuracy. Lightweight semantics such as RDF-S or taxonomy-like structures limits the scope of our model given the omission of inconsistency checking cf. Figures 7(c) and 7(d). Sufficient training data in the source domain is required. Indeed logic reasoning could not help if important data or features are not mapped to the ontology. This crucial for the training phase and validation of semantics in transfer learning. In that respect our approach is as robust as other transfer learning approaches, it only differentiate on valuing the transfer-ability at semantic level.

6. Related Work

Transfer learning, a widely studied area in ML [25,29], can be grouped in:

- **Instance-based transfer** which selectively reuses the source domain samples with weights. A typical study is [9]. It computed a degree of influence of each source domain training sample in the target domain. Positive and negative influence is derived by an adaptive boosting algorithm. [26] proposed a selective learning algorithm which selects data points from intermediate domains to obtain smooth transfer between largely distant domains.

- **Model-based transfer** which reuses model parameters. The parameters can be those for features (data representation). For example, [24] introduced a semi-supervised method to learn the transfer components. It spans a subspace of data representation where the source and the target domains aim at being similar. The parameters can also be those describing a prediction model. For example, [13] trained multiple models in source domain and dynamically combined them in the target domain with weights. [3] proposed a hypothesis transfer learning method which selectively shares the hypothesis components learnt by Support Vector Machines.

- **Semantic-based transfer** which incorporates external domain knowledge to boost the above two groups. [20] used semantic nets to select features with similar semantic meaning in both source and target domains. [18] analyzed knowledge graph-structure data to derive similarity in data and features. Note that the semantic representations in these works are lightweight, with no reasoning or inconsistency checking applied. There are efforts on Markov Logic Networks (MLN) based transfer learning, by using first order [21,22] or second order [11,27] rules as declarative prediction models. However, these MLN based approaches do not address the problem of when is feasible to transfer. Our approach uses OWL reasoning to select transferable samples (thus addressing 'when to transfer'); it then enriches the transferred samples with embedded transferability semantics e.g., Consistent Vector. Furthermore, our approach can be used to with different machine learning models and is not limited to rule based models.

7. Conclusion

We addressed the problem of transfer learning in expressive semantics settings. Our approach is exploiting semantic variability, transferability and consistency from source to target domains to compute semantic embeddings. In addition to expose semantics (entailments) which positively drives the transfer, the integration of such embeddings has demonstrated to boost accuracy of state-of-the-art transfer learning approaches. Our approach has been shown to be robust to intra- and inter-domain transfer learning tasks from real-world applications in Dublin, London, Beijing and Hangzhou. In future work we will investigate the limit and the explanation of transferability with expressive semantics.

References

[1] Franz Baader, Sebastian Brandt, and Carsten Lutz. Pushing the el envelope. In *IJCAI*, volume 5, pages 364–369, 2005.

[2] Franz Baader, Diego Calvanese, Deborah McGuinness, Peter Patel-Schneider, Daniele Nardi, et al. *The description logic handbook: Theory, implementation and applications*. Cambridge university press, 2003.

[3] Diana Benavides-Prado, Yun Sing Koh, and Patricia Riddle. Acc-gensvm: Selectively transferring from previous hypotheses. In *Proceedings of the 26th International Joint Conference on Artificial Intelligence*, pages 1440–1446. AAAI Press, 2017.

[4] Christopher M Bishop. *Pattern recognition and machine learning*. springer, 2006.

[5] Jiaoyan Chen, Freddy Lécué, Jeff Pan, and Huajun Chen. Learning from ontology streams with semantic concept drift. 2017.

[6] Jiaoyan Chen, Freddy Lécué, Jeff Z Pan, Ian Horrocks, and Huajun Chen. Knowledge-based transfer learning explanation. In *Sixteenth International Conference on Principles of Knowledge Representation and Reasoning*, 2018.

[7] Jonghyun Choi, Sung Ju Hwang, Leonid Sigal, and Larry S Davis. Knowledge transfer with interactive learning of semantic relationships. In *Thirtieth AAAI Conference on Artificial Intelligence*, 2016.

[8] Wenyuan Dai, Yuqiang Chen, Gui-Rong Xue, Qiang Yang, and Yong Yu. Translated learning: Transfer learning across different feature spaces. In *Advances in neural information processing systems*, pages 353–360, 2009.

[9] Wenyuan Dai, Qiang Yang, Gui-Rong Xue, and Yong Yu. Boosting for transfer learning. In *Proceedings of the 24th international conference on Machine learning*, pages 193–200, 2007.

[10] Jason V Davis, Brian Kulis, Prateek Jain, Suvrit Sra, and Inderjit S Dhillon. Information-theoretic metric learning. In *Proceedings of the 24th international conference on Machine learning*, pages 209–216, 2007.

[11] Jesse Davis and Pedro Domingos. Deep transfer via second-order markov logic. In *Proceedings of the 26th annual international conference on machine learning*, pages 217–224, 2009.

[12] Jérôme Euzenat, Pavel Shvaiko, et al. *Ontology matching*, volume 18. Springer, 2007.

[13] Jing Gao, Wei Fan, Jing Jiang, and Jiawei Han. Knowledge transfer via multiple model local structure mapping. In *Proceedings of the 14th ACM SIGKDD international conference on Knowledge discovery and data mining*, pages 283–291, 2008.

[14] Markus Krötzsch, Maximilian Marx, Ana Ozaki, and Veronika Thost. Attributed description logics: Ontologies for knowledge graphs. In *International Semantic Web Conference*, pages 418–435. Springer, 2017.

[15] Freddy Lécué. Scalable maintenance of knowledge discovery in an ontology stream. In *Twenty-Fourth International Joint Conference on Artificial Intelligence*, 2015.

[16] Freddy Lécu'e, Jiaoyan Chen, Jeff Z Pan, and Huajun Chen. Augmenting transfer learning with semantic reasoning. *arXiv preprint arXiv:1905.13672*, 2019.

[17] Freddy Lécué and Jeff Z Pan. Consistent knowledge discovery from evolving ontologies. In *Twenty-Ninth AAAI Conference on Artificial Intelligence*, 2015.

[18] Jaekoo Lee, Hyunjae Kim, Jongsun Lee, and Sungroh Yoon. Transfer learning for deep learning on graph-structured data. In *Thirty-First AAAI Conference on Artificial Intelligence*, 2017.

[19] Mingsheng Long, Yue Cao, Jianmin Wang, and Michael Jordan. Learning transferable features with deep adaptation networks. In *International Conference on Machine Learning*, pages 97–105, 2015.

[20] Wenlong Lv, Weiran Xu, and Jun Guo. Transfer learning in classification based on semantic analysis. In *Proceedings of 2012 2nd International Conference on Computer Science and Network Technology*, pages 1336–1339. IEEE, 2012.

[21] Lilyana Mihalkova, Tuyen Huynh, and Raymond J Mooney. Mapping and revising markov logic networks for transfer learning. In *Aaai*, volume 7, pages 608–614, 2007.

[22] Lilyana Mihalkova and Raymond J Mooney. Transfer learning from minimal target data by mapping across relational domains. In *Twenty-First International Joint Conference on Artificial Intelligence*, 2009.

[23] Maximilian Nickel, Kevin Murphy, Volker Tresp, and Evgeniy Gabrilovich. A review of relational machine learning for knowledge graphs. *Proceedings of the IEEE*, 104(1):11–33, 2015.

[24] Sinno Jialin Pan, Ivor W Tsang, James T Kwok, and Qiang Yang. Domain adaptation via transfer component analysis. *IEEE Transactions on Neural Networks*, 22(2):199–210, 2010.

[25] Sinno Jialin Pan and Qiang Yang. A survey on transfer learning. *IEEE Transactions on knowledge and data engineering*, 22(10):1345–1359, 2009.

[26] Ben Tan, Yu Zhang, Sinno Jialin Pan, and Qiang Yang. Distant domain transfer learning. In *Thirty-First AAAI Conference on Artificial Intelligence*, 2017.

[27] Jan Van Haaren, Andrey Kolobov, and Jesse Davis. Todtler: Two-order-deep transfer learning. In *Twenty-Ninth AAAI Conference on Artificial Intelligence*, 2015.

[28] Carlos Vicient, David Sánchez, and Antonio Moreno. An automatic approach for ontology-based feature extraction from heterogeneous textualresources. *Engineering Applications of Artificial Intelligence*, 26(3):1092–1106, 2013.

[29] Karl Weiss, Taghi M Khoshgoftaar, and DingDing Wang. A survey of transfer learning. *Journal of Big data*, 3(1):9, 2016.

196   *Knowledge Graphs for eXplainable Artificial Intelligence: Foundations, Applications and Challenges*
I. Tiddi et al. (Eds.)
IOS Press, 2020
© 2020 Akademische Verlagsgesellschaft AKA GmbH, Berlin. All rights reserved.
doi:10.3233/SSW200019

Explanations in Predictive Analytics:
Case Studies

Jiewen WU [a], Minh NGUYEN [c], Gia H. NGO [d], and Nancy F. CHEN [b]

[a] *Huawei Technologies Co., Ltd., China*
[b] *Institute for Infocomm Research, Agency for Science, Technology and Research (A*STAR), Singapore*
[c] *University of California, Davis, USA*
[d] *Cornell University, USA*

Abstract. Predictive analytic tasks identify likely future outcomes based on historical and current data. Predictions alone, however, are usually insufficient for users to make sound decisions, due to reasons such as regulatory requirements, distrust towards black box technology. To this end, explanations have been used as one way to enable adoption of predictive analytics. In particular, semantics-rich explanations that leverage knowledge graphs are explored by both academics and practitioners. This chapter presents three case studies: predictive analytics for identifying abnormal expense claims, mitigating project risks, and predicting pronunciations and learning the language model of Chinese characters. In addition to predictions, explanations play an important part in these cases. They could impact decision making, e.g., by showing that a project is risky likely because of the incompetent delivery centers, or they can enhance users' trust in the predictive models, e.g., by presenting the dependencies exist between the pronunciation of a Chinese character and that of its substructures. Regardless of the size or the form of the knowledge graphs, the three case studies show that explanations built on domain knowledge add invaluable insights to predictive analytics.

Keywords. Predictive Analytics, Explanations, Machine Learning, Deep Learning, Classification, eXplainable AI

1. Introduction

Data analytics presents an opportunity for medical doctors to improve their diagnosis accuracy, for financial professionals to optimize their operations, among others. In these situations, analytics starts from descriptive tasks, i.e., to understand what has happened in the past. Thanks to descriptive analytics, doctors can, for example, tell if they had frequently provided incorrect diagnosis of a particular diseases, while asset managers can find out what was the best diversification strategy in the past year. Descriptive analytics provides insightful information on historical and current events, but people or organizations need to anticipate what is likely to happen next, rather than reacting to what has already happened. Moving beyond descriptive analytics, predictive analytics provides a means to expect what might happen in the future. For instance, doctors in ICU want to quickly and accurately examine a patient's conditions in the next hour or two based on his/her current conditions. Asset managers instead need to estimate the future risk of changing the current portfolio. In many similar scenarios, predictive analytics is beneficial for humans to effectively assess complicated and time-sensitive matters.

As we move towards more advanced and complicated analytics methods, the explainability of analytic insights and models will become critical due to a combination of factors, e.g., users' trust, compliance to regulations, brand reputation management, and so on. When users ask for explanations, they may be looking for ways to describe a predictive model, to highlight the strengths and weaknesses of a model, or to identify any potential biases. So, explanations can come in different styles with diverse details. Nevertheless, explanations must possess the ability to articulate the decisions of a predictive model, addressing one or more the following aspect of predictive analytics: transparency, accuracy, fairness, accountability, and robustness.

In the business world, explainability receives more attention than ever due to the wide adoption of Artificial Intelligence (a.k.a. AI) in enterprise applications. There have been several commercial solutions to explanations. As an example, Causality Link shared in [3] about their AI platform, which uses text-mined, linked knowledge for business insights. In September, 2019, Moody's downgraded Ford. For investors, a single rating is a nuance as it does not provide rich information to understand how such a downgrade was derived. Causality Link's platform applies contextual sentiment analysis across millions of relevant articles to suggest the early warning signs for this downgrade. Such aggregated information, organized in the form of linked knowledge, are typical knowledge graph supported explanations. Another vendor in the finance industry, Quantexa, use its proprietary knowledge graph for use cases based on financial crimes and risk assessment [30]. In particular, users can leverage the knowledge graph to identify causal effects among events: another example of explanations.

The need of explanations is not only for the financial industry. We have also seen research in explaining the results from sophisticated modeling approaches in general domains [8, 19, 22, 37]. In this chapter, we present a few case studies where predictive analytics was applied and explanations were necessary. In particular, we highlight the role of knowledge graphs for generating explanations in these solutions.

2. Predicting and Explaining Abnormal Expenses

Every organization has to deal with expenses claims by its employees. One major concern in expense management is to single out abnormal expense claims. In this case study, the prediction problem is, based on the historical claims, to find out potentially abnormal expenses among the newly filed claims. In the business context in [15], predictive modeling alone does not fully solve the business problem. Business owners are indeed interested in the abnormal claims, but they, particularly, the auditors, also require the solutions to provide the nature and causes of identified claims. We show how [15] addresses this problem with explainability using underlying knowledge graphs.

2.1. Predictions

In [15], the system, AI for Finance System (AIFS), is presented to identify and predict abnormal expenses by the employees of Accenture. AIFS takes as input the following types of data:

- Expenses and demographics data of Accenture employees in 2015. This dataset contains 190,000+ unique travelers' records in over 500 cities worldwide. There are around 2,500 to 24,800 records per city.
- Public datasets on planned events, e.g., music performances, concerts, political demonstrations, etc. The sources of such data include Eventbrite (`https://www.eventbrite.com`), Eventful (`http://api.eventful.com`), and EventRegistry (`http://eventregistry.org`).
- Spatial GPS data over the world map (`https://www.openstreetmap.org/`).
- Public, open-domain knowledge graphs. Two popular knowledge graphs are used: DBpedia (`http://wiki.dbpedia.org`) and Wikidata (`https://www.wikidata.org`).
- Proprietary knowledge graph developed by Accenture. This small knowledge graph consists of 25 resources structured in a taxonomy for event types.

How does AIFS identify abnormal expenses? It performs semantic integration of heterogeneous and exogenous raw data such as events, employee expenses and their profile (among others). All data sources are semantically aligned with knowledge graphs shown above. Once data is semantically linked, they provide the foundations for associating the context of expenses with their degree of abnormality. To illustrate, an expense can be understood better when the dimensions about travel trip, business justification, city destination or travel duration are known.

AIFS uses the following algorithm to decide if an expense is abnormal or not. We briefly describe the algorithm here, while more details are available in Algorithm 1 in [15]. The detection algorithm first retrieves all similar expenses to the target expense e using some predefined similarity function. It then learns rules from similar expenses through association rule mining [18] between expenses and city context, and retrieves relevant semantic context for e. Specifically, rules are selected depending on minimal threshold of support and confidence. Finally, the algorithm fires all rules to derive abnormality.

As an example, one sample rule represented by description logics is given below.

$$HighlyAbnormalExpense(e) \leftarrow inCity(e,c) \wedge expensedBy(e,p)$$

$$\wedge (Manager \sqcap \exists careerLevel.\exists greaterThan.Level7)(p)$$

$$\wedge (EuropeanCity \sqcap CityOver1MillionPopulation)(c)$$

$$\wedge (\exists amount \exists greaterThan.90\%ContextExpenses)(e)$$

This rule stipulates that *an expense claim by a manager with career level over 7, who travels to an European city with over 1 million population, and who spends more than 90% of other expense claims in the context, is considered to be a highly abnormal expense claim.*

Once a set of highly confident rules are learnt, they can be used to predict the level abnormality of a new expense claim. Moreover, AIFS deals with another type of predictions, i.e., for a planned trip, the system projects the cost of the trip. This projection is useful for planning expenses budget, as well as for avoiding unnecessary spending. For this type of prediction, AIFS auto-correlates data on a time basis for retrieving all similar past events. Then it mines association rules between past events and abnormal expenses over time. The prediction results are obtained by extending the rule on the temporal dimension and validated using semantic consistency. An example of failed consistency checking is that the number of overpriced nights is more than 20% of the duration of the multiple-day event in a city.

2.2. Explanations on Prediction Results

Identifying abnormal expenses is helpful, but business owners in this context demands that the nature and possible causes of such expenses can be captured. Business owners want to establish new policy through the insights over the abnormal expenses, and corporate auditors expect evidences of abnormal expenses to better communicate with employees.

2.2.1. Explanation Generation

To learn to generate explanations, a dataset of 106,809 North America and Europe travel related expense items was partly annotated by domain experts. This results in a dataset of 8,324 abnormal expense items with explanations. The annotated dataset forms a finite state machine, in which a state contains some contextual information and a transition means a specific piece of information can be thought of as a possible explanation towards one abnormal expense. A transition, connecting abnormal expenses to any similar context and potential explanations, embeds a conditional probability of explaining the expense with this explanation given a specific context.

When a new abnormal expenses arrives, AIFS inspects the state machine to retrieve similar contexts i.e., expenses type, cities and events, among others. Here, the similarity computation is analogous to the approach in [20]. Explanations of the new expense are then derived from similar expenses and contexts. The assumption is that similar context leads to similar explanations.

Figure 1 shows a sample explanation page of the AIFS for some expense claim. The explanations, as explained in the figure, are presented in two categories, major contributing factors and detailed causes. The two categories are essentially the hierarchical representation of explanations in the AIFS system. In the next section, we delve into this hierarchy.

2.2.2. Explanation Details

As shown in Figure 1, explanations are described in two categories, the main type and the more specific details. For instance, the first category can be *external events* and the second can be *music festival*. According to the data definitions in Section 2.1, each category has a predetermined number of class, validated by domain experts.

The 5 main types are:

- behavioral causes for individual frauds by examining recurring patterns;
- social dynamic events capture external and general events occurring in a city, e.g., sport or music events;
- business dynamics refer to internal events inside employees' company;
- spatial dimension emphasizes city capacity, e.g., number of accommodation types, rooms, population density;
- temporal dimension defines seasonal causes.

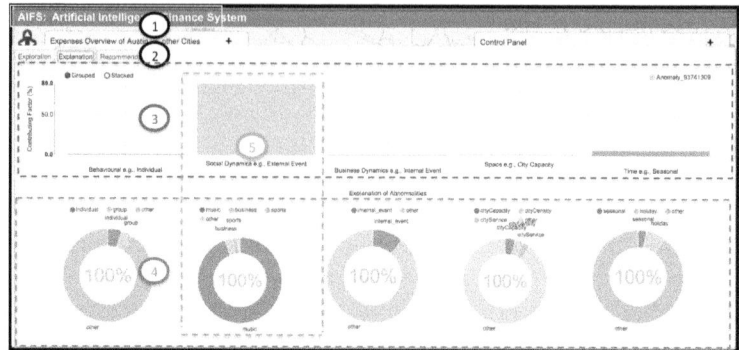

Figure 1. An example page of the AIFS system for expenses related to the city Austin. (1) the geographic location of the expenses. (2) Different tabs show explorations, predictions and explanations. (3) 5 contributing factors in the range [0,100]. (4) Detailed explanations of each contributing factor. (5) Illustration of the top contributing factor of a specific expense.

Considering Figure 1, these five types are the top-panel, contributing factors of the abnormality, summing up to 100. In the example of Figure 1 (item 5), social dynamics is the dominating factor, far more than the rest 4 types.

Lower level of explanation cases, represented as pie charts in Figure 1, provides more specific types for each contributing factor, e.g., various type of events for external events, or city services and density for spatial dimension. In the example of Figure 1, the majority of similar abnormal expenses (and context) were caused by similar type of external events (item 4). Furthermore, the main lower level causes are festive music event (item 5) in Austin.

2.3. Discussions

The AIFS system combines a number of techniques to explore, explain, and predict expenses in large enterprises. Focusing on the explanations, we found that this particular setup has met several challenges, as stated in [15].

- The choice of knowledge representation has great impact on the computational performance as it affects both consistency checking and similarity computation. Fortunately, in AIFS, the light profile OWL 2 EL [24] was chosen to trade off expressivity (and accuracy) for scalability.
- Existing prediction algorithms may need to be adapted to accommodate for explanations and other required features in specific use cases. In AIFS, the version of association rule mining is a semantic extension of the Apriori algorithm [1], which supports subsumption tests for determining association rules. Also, the association is mined between data descriptions, e.g., type of events, expenses, context, not between data instances.

3. Project Risk Management

In enterprises, managing risks is one of the most important operation tasks. Project risk management has long been studied in a variety of aspects, e.g., risk identification, estimation, and control [4]. A business needs to identify, externalize, and mitigate risks, rather than eliminating risks.

In large organizations, such as Accenture, project risk management has been a vital part of the company's operation; though the process entails intensive manual operations, from data collection to risk prediction. Here is a short overview of project risk management in the company. When a project is started (from sales phase), data about the project is collected and sent to a risk officer for risk scoring. The risk officer follows a set of business rules and assign a risk tier to the project. Based on the computed risk tier, a project will be assigned a corresponding Quality Assurance Director (QAD), who oversees the project to identify and mitigate its risks. One challenge is the lack of qualified QADs to oversee all the projects. Thus, a new risk management tool is required.

The intelligent risk management tool [36] in this context needs to predict project risks automatically. The sources of the risk can be manifold, such as the dependencies of the clients, the terms and conditions stipulated in the contract, or the capability of the company to staff the project with the right people, among others. So, the intelligent risk management tool should deal with multiple, heterogeneous data sources to make predictions.

3.1. Datasets

There are two categories of datasets used for predicting the risk tier of a project: enterprise, private data and external, public data.

- Accenture Enterprise Datasets. (1) Accenture Business Schema, an enterprise knowledge graph that describes the organization structure of Accenture entities and metadata of several types of artifacts in the Enterprise data, e.g., such as employees, contracts, among others. In particular, there is a taxonomy describing the company's risk model, i.e., the set of risk factors for Accenture projects. (2) Accenture Data Lake is the internal hub for accessing key business data sourced from a variety of systems, ranging from SAP to MS SQL Server to documents. There is data about human resources (e.g., employees), financial outcomes (e.g., contract economics), and risk assessment (e.g., review meeting minutes and notes).
- External Datasets. Apart from the internal datasets, some external datasets were also used and integrated with the internal datasets. The primary data concerns about Accenture's clients, including online financial reports, search trends, news reports about the clients, and so on. To help integrate data from various data sources, DBpedia was used as the open-domain knowledge graph.

3.2. Predicting and Explaining the Risk Tier of a Project

With all the data available, the first task is to gather, clean, understand, link all data for feature engineering, which is then used by predictive modeling for risk predictions [36]. For the purpose of predicting project risks, features in the following aspects are collected/derived from the aforementioned datasets.

- Client demographics. This includes the internal classification of the client involved in the project, the nature of its business, its financial stability, its recent news coverage and sentiment from the general public, search trends in commercial search engines, and so on.

- Project demographics, which includes the nature of the project, the size of the revenue, the projected revenue at completion (done by sales experts), business units for the project, and so on.
- Capability. This category of features consists of the number and the hierarchy of the employees assigned to carry out the project, the necessary skills required for the project, the demographics of the delivery centers, and so on.

To obtain the ground truth, the QADs, as domain experts, suggested a few risk tiers for historical projects based on the financial target of a project. The risk tiers range from *no risk* to *high risk*. For instance, if a project has a target revenue much higher than the contract revenue, the project is considered to be of low risk. The problem is how to determine the risk tier for a project at the early stages (e.g., sales phase). Thus, the task of assessing project risk is reduced to this classification task.

Many classifiers can be used to predict the risk tier of a project. The final choice was random forests [14]. First of all, random forest delivers superior performance than logistic regression or support vector machine, among others. However, a deep neural network (DNN) based classifier can slightly outperform the random forest solution. It would be natural to select the best performing algorithm as the predictive model. Nevertheless, the QADs demand that the underlying predictive model must be able to explain how a risk tier is obtained by the algorithm [17]. Since random forests have decision trees in the internal representation, they are more amenable to explanations than the black-box neural networks.

Explaining Random Forest Classification Predictions   The most straightforward approach to interpret random forests is to use important factors [14]. However, QADs expressed two concerns about this approach. First, the important factors are on the model level, meaning all projects will get the same weights of the factors (features). QADs specifies that each project should receive different weights on the same set of factors. Second, the features are either directly drawn from or derived from the raw data sources, and they are difficult to understand by end users, i.e., QADs.

To deal with the first concern, we implement an effective method on top of random forests to identify *important* features for a single testing project [17]. The set of important features varies according to the input features of the given project. The method consists of the following steps:

1 For each tree in the random forests, record the count of the splitting features at each node along the path to the final prediction leaf.
2 For all trees, sum up all the counts of each feature, grouped by the final predictions. Note that a tree/path can reach non-majority classes.
3 Normalize the counts into percentage of each features in the paths/trees that lead to the majority class.

Observe that at step 3 in the above method, the counts of features leading to non-majority classes are simply discarded. From an explanation point of view, such negative, when presented with positive evidences, can be more convincing, as proposed in [16].

To handle the second concern on feature understanding, Accenture business schema is used. This enterprise knowledge graph is compact and concise. Inside this knowledge graph, there is a mapping between risk factors and the associated data sources of each risk factor. By cleaning and mapping low-level features to high-level risk factors, our

QADs can understand the impact of each business factor, because the sum of all features' percentage in step 3 above is the contributing percentage of the corresponding factor.

3.3. Explaining Actions in Context

Once the risk tier of a project is identified, the next and essential task of the risk management team is to determine what is actionable. In general, a QAD works with the project team to determine on the right actions to mitigate the risk. In this process, a QAD needs an efficient way to read the relevant meeting documents, e.g., to identify the list of actions. She may also want to understand the context of each action accurately if she is new to a project or business.

We leave out the details of action recommendation as it is not relevant for the topic of concern in this chapter. Instead, we show that how to contextualize the actions in this business setting to help the QADs [36]. This is, again, a form of explanations, i.e., *why* a specific action is recommended and how is it *relevant* to the reader [16]. To recap the details of action contextualization presented in [36], we highlight the three core steps below:

3.3.1. Markup

This step identifies the salient terms in an action through part-of-speech (POS) tagging and named entity recognition (NER), e.g., resources, capability, delivery center, and so on. For instance, the action that reads "schedule the next MLR" has two key terms: "schedule" and "MLR" (for management level review).

3.3.2. Semantic Embedding

This step puts an action in its global context. The terms from the action will be mapped to concepts in the enterprise and public knowledge graphs. Furthermore, more relevant concepts through graph traversal will be gathered to serve as the larger, richer global context of this action. For example, this step can find out that "MLR" is a subclass of "ProjectReview" with additional attributes, e.g., the minimum number of attendees.

3.3.3. Scoping

Information overloading is detrimental to effective explanations. Thus, the scoping steps aims to reduce the potentially large knowledge graph obtained from semantic embedding. Specifically, the reduction is to retain user-centric context. Roughly, the profile of a user is used to filter the content of the knowledge graph, e.g., entities known to the user can be discarded. Details are available in [36].

We summarize this section with Figure 2. In this figure, we can see concrete examples of contextualized actions, and how all the relevant information is organized and visualized to enhance the explanation power.

3.4. Discussions

Predicting the risk tier of a project is a straightforward classification problem, however, explaining the classification results is not quite so. We have seen in this use case that decision makers rather compromise some degree of accuracy to have explanations of pre-

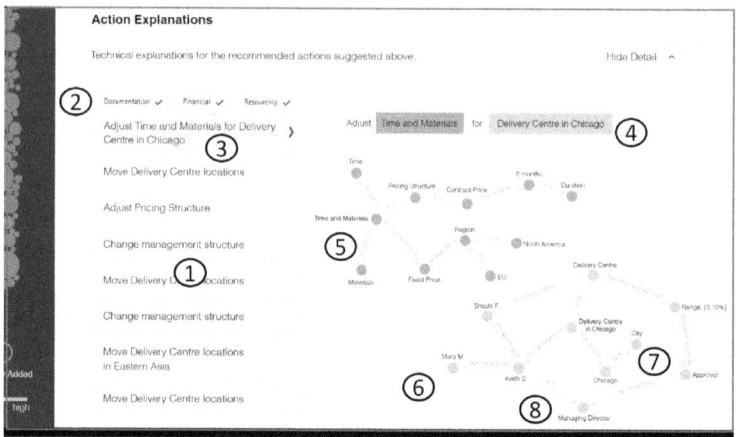

Figure 2. An example page of contextualized actions with graphic explanations. On the left, items 1-3 are the recommended actions. Item 4 is the selected action, in which two terms are identified. Items 5-8 are the sub-knowledge graphs as the context for the two actions, respectively.

dictive models/results. The explanations of random forest classification results are also dependent on the availability of a compact knowledge graph to generate effective explanations for end users, who might not understand implementation details of predictive modeling, such as data representation, feature selection, or algorithmic complexity.

4. Pronunciation Prediction and Language Modeling for Chinese Characters

In languages with logographic origin like Mandarin, Japanese or Cantonese, logographs are characters and there are thousands of characters. In contrast, alphabetic languages usually have far fewer characters (e.g. 26 characters for English). Although the characters are numerous, they are not invented arbitrarily. The characters have systematic structures that encode phonological and semantic information [11]. Language learners usually exploit these (logographic) structures to learn characters' pronunciation [9]. The structures are hierarchical and they play a key role in arranging characters into a taxonomy.

Character	Onset	Nucleus	Coda
蒸 - to steam (verb)	z	i	ng
烝 - steam (noun)	z	i	ng
丞 - to assist	s	i	ng
永 - name of a river	c	i	ng
一 - one	j	a	t

Figure 3. *An example of logographic structure. The left panel shows a binary tree representing the logograph 蒸. The leaf nodes (position 2, 5, 6, 7) are sub-units forming the logograph (analogous to letters forming English words). The inner nodes (position 1, 3, 4) are composition operators (such as vertical stacking) applied to children nodes. The logograph 蒸 is formed by composing all the nodes in the tree in a bottom-up fashion. The sub-trees rooted at positions 3, 4, 5, 6, 7 also form logographs (烝, 丞, 永, 火, 一). The right table shows the logographs' meanings and their pronunciation in Cantonese.*

Figure 3 shows how logographic structures encode phonological and semantic information. The 永 sub-unit (position 6) hints at the nucleus and coda in the logographs' pronunciation. In addition, the 火 sub-unit[1] (position 5) suggests that the logographs containing this sub-unit must be related to fire. For the four logographs 蒸, 烝, 丞, 氶, the structure of one logograph is nested within that of the preceding logograph. For example, 烝 is nested within 蒸. Being able to focus on relevant sub-units of logographs might explain how humans can remember the pronunciation and meanings of thousands of distinct characters.

In machine learning, there are many work exploiting structures to achieve better task performance [2, 6, 12, 25, 26, 33, 39]. For logographs in particular, logographic structures can be leveraged to construct representation of characters (character embeddings) that better captures semantic [34, 38] or phonological information [27]. The models used in these work are often neural networks which perform well but are hard to interpret. However, for logographic structures, it is possible to have a neural network model of character embeddings that are both accurate and interpretable. This is because it is relatively straightforward to attribute prediction accuracy to specific components within the logographic structures. For example, predicting the pronunciation of 蒸, 烝, 丞, 氶 accurately should be the result of focusing on the 氶 sub-unit. On the other hand, extracting the semantic of 蒸 and 烝 accurately should be by looking at the 火 sub-unit. Thus, by using a model that forms a character embeddings from sub-units in the logographic structures in a bottom-up fashion, we could verify whether the model is working soundly by looking at how the sub-units contribute to the character embeddings.

4.1. Pronunciation Prediction

In this task, models have to predict the pronunciation (onset, nucleus, and coda) of logographs (characters) given the logographs themselves. The prediction requires the models to locate the phonological information residing within the logographic structures. This task is a good case study for models' interpretability, since it is relatively straightforward for humans to determine where phonological information originates within the logographic structures and therefore to determine if the model is working correctly.

4.1.1. Model

In order to predict, the model needs to obtain the logographic structures from the characters. Figure 4 shows how the logographic structure (represented as a binary tree) is constructed for the character 仕.

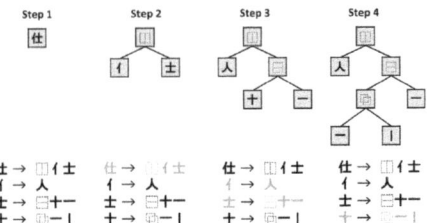

Figure 4. *Construction of recursive logographic structure using a rule-based parser.*

---

[1] 火 is written as ⺣ when is it at the bottom position.

To construct character embeddings from tree structures, one can use bag-of-words models, sequence models, or tree-structured models. Since the order of sub-units within characters partly determines the characters' pronunciation and meaning, models that ignore order such as bag-of-words models are sub-optimal for constructing character embeddings.

Sequence models such as recurrent neural networks [7] (RNNs) are order-sensitive but the order used by RNN makes it hard to visualize the contribution of sub-units or sub-trees to the character embeddings. In contrast, recursive neural networks, such as treeLSTM [35, 40], construct character embeddings following bottom-up order, and are easier to visualize the contribution of the sub-trees.

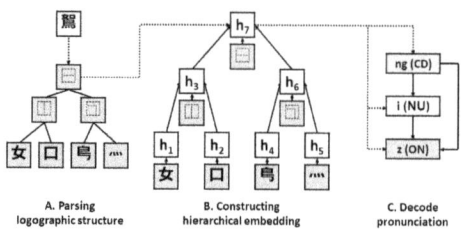

A. Parsing logographic structure   B. Constructing hierarchical embedding   C. Decode pronunciation

Figure 5. *Phonological prediction model using logographic structure. (A) The input logograph is decomposed into the logographic structure using a rule-based parser. (B) treeLSTM constructs embedding from the structure. (C) The embedding is then used to predict the pronunciation.*

Figure 5 shows how the treeLSTM is used to predict the pronunciation of a character. First the logographic structure is obtained for the character. Then, treeLSTM constructs the character embedding from the structure. Finally, the character embedding is used by a classifier to to predict the pronunciation.

The hidden state of the root node, h_7, is the representation of the entire tree and is also the embedding of the character 鴽 (meaning *quail* in English). The hidden state h_3, is the representation of the left sub-tree and is also the embedding of character 如 (meaning *resembling* in English). The hidden state h_6, is the representation of the right sub-tree and is also the embedding of character 鳥 (meaning *bird* in English).

In the final step, h_7 is fed into a classifier to predict the character pronunciation. However, for diagnostic purpose, h_3 and h_6 can also be fed into the same classifier to predict the pronunciation from the left and right sub-trees. If sub-units in the left sub-tree hints at the character pronunciation, then the pronunciation obtained from h_3 and h_7 should be the same (or very similar). Likewise, if sub-units in the right sub-tree hints at the character pronunciation, then the pronunciation obtained from h_4 and h_7 should be the same. Thus, it is possible to verify that the model uses the correct sub-units to arrive at the pronunciation.

4.1.2. Finding Explanations in Model Prediction

Essentially, the model weights the sub-units in the logographic structure and uses the most relevant sub-units for prediction. The working of the model can be explained by how it weights the sub-units. By looking at a particular subset of characters that are well-understood, one can assess whether the model's working is logical. In particular, the semantic-phonetic compounds can be used for this assessment.

The semantic-phonetic compounds account for more than 80% of frequently used Chinese characters [21]. These compounds consist of sub-units that might contain phonetic or semantic information [11]. Pronunciation of these compounds could conceivably be predicted from the phonetic sub-units. Amongst semantic-phonetic compounds, characters with the left-right arrangement (in which the semantic sub-unit is on the left and the phonetic sub-unit is on the right) are the most common. For characters with the left-right arrangement, a good pronunciation prediction model should weight the right child (the likely phonetic sub-unit) of a root node more than the left child. In fact, the model prefers the right child almost 100% of the time [28]. Thus, the model considers the right sub-units to be more relevant for pronunciation prediction for the majority of compound characters with the left-right arrangement. As the model working is consistent with human intuition, it can be trusted to perform as well as humans.

However, this is not sufficient to trust the model since it is common for machine learning models to perform well on average cases but fail unexpectedly at more difficult cases [13]. Being able to explain the model prediction for these more difficult cases would ascertain that the model would work on unseen cases.

Figure 6 and 7 show two difficult examples and how the model predicts. The Figures can be used to explain the prediction of the model. In the figures, the central panel shows the hidden states of the model. The last hidden state is the character embedding while the preceding hidden states are embeddings of the sub-trees. Sub-trees that contributes significant weight to the character embeddings would have hidden states that are similar (in term of color and intensity) to the last hidden state. For example, in Figure 6, the third hidden state $\mathbf{h}_3$ contributes more than the sixth hidden state $\mathbf{h}_6$ to the last hidden state. Therefore, the sub-tree corresponding to the third hidden state (left sub-tree) is more relevant than the sub-tree corresponding to the sixth hidden state (right sub-tree). The left column shows the input sub-units. The right column shows the predicted pronunciations by applying the classifier to all the hidden states.

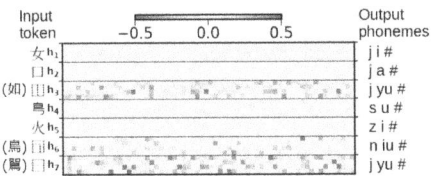

Figure 6. *Visualizing the construction of the character embedding for* 鴽 *(quail). The central panel shows the hidden states. The left column shows the input sub-units. The right column shows the predicted pronunciations using the hidden states. The bottom rows of the right columns are the predicted pronunciations for the logographs ("j yu #"). Ground-truth pronunciation is "j yu #".*

Figure 6 is a hard example because the phonetic sub-units are not on the right sub-tree but are on the left sub-tree. The model predicted the pronunciation correctly by seemingly focusing on the more relevant sub-tree (left sub-tree). In addition, the pronunciation of the left sub-tree (which corresponds to the third row from the top) is the same as the pronunciation of the character (which corresponds the bottom row). Thus, this shows that the model can generalize to hard examples as well.

Figure 7 shows how the models predict the pronunciation of the character 賄 (bribery). This is a hard case because of the complexity of the logographic structure. The pattern of the hidden states' magnitude is consistent with the logographic structure

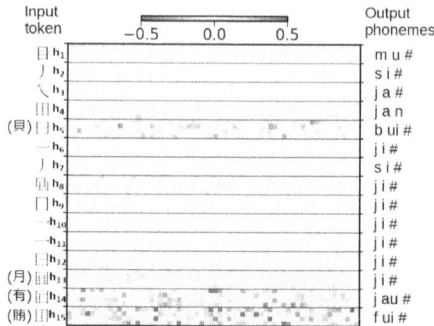

Figure 7. *Visualizing the construction of the character embedding for* 賄 *(bribery). The central panel shows the hidden states* h_i. *The left column shows the input sub-units. The right column shows the predicted pronunciations using the hidden states* h_i. *The bottom row of the right column is the predicted pronunciations for the logographs ("f ui #"). Ground-truth pronunciation is "f ui #".*

of the input character with two sub-trees 貝 and 有. Specifically, not only was the final pronunciation prediction of 賄 correct ("f ui #"), but pronunciation of the sub-trees (貝 and 有) were also correct ("b ui #" and "j au #" respectively).

4.2. Language Modeling

Language modeling is a useful auxiliary task, as it characterizes many aspects of language beyond semantics (including syntactic structure and discourse processing), and language modeling can be used to pre-train many other tasks [5,10,29,31,32], thus, it has a lot of down-stream applications. However, due to the multifaceted nature of language modeling tasks, it is hard to analyze the results qualitatively. Nevertheless, since language modeling requires the character embeddings to contain semantic information, the learned embeddings can be interpreted by looking at the relationship between characters.

Given enough data, standard embeddings [23] can learn character representation well. In practice, there is never enough data, especially for low-frequency characters. Thus, it is a common practice to only include the most common characters and convert the rest of the characters to a dummy token (UNK). Exploiting logographic structure, a language model can learn better representations of low-frequency Chinese characters.

Figure 8b and 8a show language models with hierarchical and standard embeddings as input respectively. The hierarchical embeddings are constructed by utilizing the logographic structures in the similar manner described in Section 4.1.1. Thus hierarchical embeddings are imbued with semantic information from the sub-units without requiring any training data while standard embeddings are not. This difference can be visualized by looking at the nearest-neighbors of low-frequency characters after training the language models.

4.2.1. Explaining the Embedding Models

For an embedding model, like the standard embedding model or the hierarchical embedding model, each character is represented as a vector of numbers which can be considered as a point in space. By looking at how the characters are positioned in space, one can explain how the model represents attributes of characters. The closer in space the two

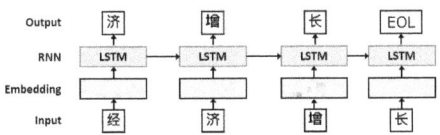

(a) *Standard embeddings as input*

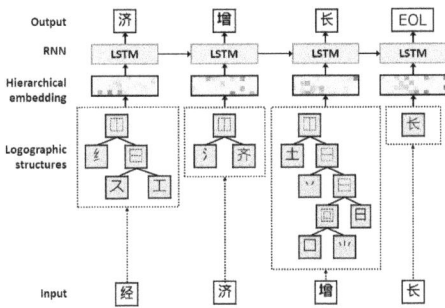

(b) *Hierarchical embeddings as input*

Figure 8. *Language model*

characters, the more attributes they share. The attributes can be semantic or phonological. Ideally, characters that are close in this space should describe similar things or concepts or should have similar pronunciations. If the neighbors are semantically or phonologically close then it is more certain that the embedding model is sensible.

Similar to Section 4.1, most machine learning models usually perform equally well for the average cases, which in the case of language modeling are the frequent characters. Learning the representations of the rare or infrequent characters is more challenging. Examples of infrequent characters and their nearest neighbors (characters that are most similar to the infrequent characters in the embedding space) are presented in Table 1. Table 1 shows that the infrequent characters and their nearest neighbors are relatively close in meaning when using hierarchical embeddings. Hierarchical embeddings could learn better representations of infrequent characters than standard embeddings could since the latter ignores the morphology within characters.

For standard embeddings, infrequent characters and their neighbors are generally unrelated. For example, *spider* is unrelated to *a plant*, *drawer*, or *scold*. It is possible that with little training data, the infrequent characters' embedding stay close to the original random initialized values and hence are far away from related characters in the embedding space. For hierarchical embeddings, infrequent characters are more related to their neighbors. The relatedness between infrequent characters and their neighbors can be semantic or phonological. For example, the first row in Table 1 shows characters (蛛,蛐,蚶,蚜) that share the same semantic sub-units (shown in red). Accordingly, *spider* is semantically related to *cricket*, *ark clam*, and *louse* since they are all insects. The second row in Table 1 shows another example in which characters (蛛,蛐,蚶,蚜) have the same phonetic sub-units (shown in blue). Correspondingly, "zh ai #" is phonologically related (having similar pronunciation) to "ch ai #", "z i #", and "c i #".

Character	Standard Embedding	Hierarchical Embedding
蛛, spider, "zh u #"	苌, *a plant*, "ch a ng" 屉, *drawer*, "t i #" 叱, *scold*, "ch i #"	蛐, *cricket*, "q u #" 蚶, *ark clam*, "q u #" 蚜, *louse*, "y a #"
砦, fort, "zh ai #"	省, *omit*, "sh e ng" 南, *south*, "n a n" 被, *blanket*, "b ei #"	柴, *firewood*, "ch ai #" 紫, *purple*, "z i #" 雌, *female*, "c i #"
珮, jade belt, "p ei #"	此, *this*, "c i #" 军, *army*, "j u n" 门, *gate*, "m e n"	佩, *pendant*, "p ei #" 玑, *imperfect pearl*, "j i #" 罐, *watering can*, "g ua n"

Table 1. *Nearest neighbors in embedding space of infrequent words. The meaning and Mandarin pronunciation are shown next to the characters. The common sub-units between the characters and their neighbors in the embedding space are color-coded. Red sub-units carry semantic information. Blue sub-units carry phonetic information.*

4.3. Discussion

Logographs (Chinese characters) have recursive structures that contain phonological and semantic information. Developmental psychology literature suggests that native speakers leverage on logographic structures to learn how to read. Exploiting recursive logographic structures to build character embeddings can lead to embeddings that yield both better results and interpretability. Through the pronunciation prediction experiment, it is clear that treeLSTM conceivably resembles how humans perform reading tasks, suggesting that exploiting structures not only improves performance, but might also help us develop more interpretable models. Diagnostic analysis also suggests that the embeddings can capture the phonological information of not only structurally simple characters but also complex characters. In addition, in language modeling, constructing embeddings using logographic structures improved the representation of infrequent characters which can be seen by more related groupings of characters in the embedding space.

5. Conclusions

This chapter presents three case studies for predictive analytics. Although they are different on various fronts, we have seen that explanations are necessary to enhance the acceptance of predictions. However, we also note that the need for explanations is seldom associated with the complexity of the analytic techniques. Whether the predictions are inferred by random forests or the more complicated LSTMs, explanations are necessary because the human users rely on them to make sound judgement about leveraging predictive models. For explanations, the generation is ad-hoc, depending on the data availability, the requirement from users, among others. In all case studies, structures such as knowledge graphs are used. It is interesting to see that explanations do not necessarily require complex knowledge graphs. Rich, domain-specific and general knowledge graph can be combined to explain abnormal expenses, while the structural composition taxonomy of Chinese characters can also work well for explaining how a pronunciation is correctly learnt.

References

[1] Rakesh Agrawal and Ramakrishnan Srikant. Fast algorithms for mining association rules in large databases. In *Proceedings of the 20th International Conference on Very Large Data Bases*, 1994.

[2] Samuel R Bowman, Jon Gauthier, Abhinav Rastogi, Raghav Gupta, Christopher Manning, and Christopher Potts. A fast unified model for parsing and sentence understanding. In *Proceedings of ACL*, 2016.

[3] Causality Link. Whitepaper: Anticipating the ford downgrade – example application of contextual sentiment analysis. `http://causalitylink.com/2019/09/26/wp-ford-downgrade/`. Accessed in December, 2019.

[4] Chris Chapman. Project risk analysis and management—pram the generic process. *International Journal of Project Management*, 15(5):273 – 281, 1997.

[5] Jacob Devlin, Ming-Wei Chang, Kenton Lee, and Kristina Toutanova. BERT: Pre-training of deep bidirectional transformers for language understanding. In *Proceedings of NAACL-HLT*, pages 4171–4186, 2019.

[6] Akiko Eriguchi, Kazuma Hashimoto, and Yoshimasa Tsuruoka. Tree-to-sequence attentional neural machine translation. In *Proceedings of ACL*, 2016.

[7] Alex Graves. Generating Sequences With Recurrent Neural Networks. *CoRR*, abs/1308.0850, 2013.

[8] Lisa Anne Hendricks, Zeynep Akata, Marcus Rohrbach, Jeff Donahue, Bernt Schiele, and Trevor Darrell. Generating visual explanations. In Bastian Leibe, Jiri Matas, Nicu Sebe, and Max Welling, editors, *Computer Vision – ECCV 2016*, pages 3–19, Cham, 2016. Springer International Publishing.

[9] Connie Suk-Han Ho and Peter Bryant. Phonological skills are important in learning to read Chinese. *Developmental psychology*, 33(6), 1997.

[10] Jeremy Howard and Sebastian Ruder. Universal language model fine-tuning for text classification. In *Proceedings of ACL*, 2018.

[11] Janet Hui-wen Hsiao and Richard Shillcock. Analysis of a Chinese phonetic compound database: Implications for orthographic processing. *Journal of psycholinguistic research*, 35(5), 2006.

[12] Ozan Irsoy and Claire Cardie. Deep recursive neural networks for compositionality in language. In *Proceedings of NIPS*, pages 2096–2104, 2014.

[13] Robin Jia and Percy Liang. Adversarial examples for evaluating reading comprehension systems. In *Proceedings of EMNLP*, pages 2021–2031, 2017.

[14] Breiman L. Random forests. *Machine Learning*, 45(1):5–32, 2001.

[15] Freddy Lécué and Jiewen Wu. Explaining and predicting abnormal expenses at large scale using knowledge graph based reasoning. *J. Web Semant.*, 44:89–103, 2017.

[16] Freddy Lécué and Jiewen Wu. Semantic explanations of predictions. *CoRR*, abs/1805.10587, 2018.

[17] Freddy Lécué, Jiewen Wu, and Ian Harris. Interpretation of predictive models using semantic grouping. U.S. Patent Application 15/445282.

[18] Freddy Lécuée and Jeff Z. Pan. Predicting knowledge in an ontology stream. In *Proceedings of the Twenty-Third International Joint Conference on Artificial Intelligence*, 2014.

[19] Tao Lei, Regina Barzilay, and Tommi S. Jaakkola. Rationalizing neural predictions. In *EMNLP 16'*, 2016.

[20] Lei Li and Ian Horrocks. A software framework for matchmaking based on semantic web technology. In *Proceedings of the 12th International Conference on World Wide Web*, WWW '03, page 331–339, New York, NY, USA, 2003. Association for Computing Machinery.

[21] Y Li and JS Kang. Analysis of phonetics of the ideophonetic characters in Modern Chinese. *Information analysis of usage of characters in modern Chinese*, pages 84–98, 1993.

[22] David Martens and Foster Provost. Explaining data-driven document classifications. *MIS Q.*, 38(1):73–100, March 2014.

[23] Tomas Mikolov, Ilya Sutskever, Kai Chen, Greg S Corrado, and Jeff Dean. Distributed representations of words and phrases and their compositionality. In *Proceedings of NIPS*, 2013.

[24]   Boris Motik, Bernardo Cuenca Grau, Ian Horrocks, Zhe Wu, Achille Fokoue, and Carsten Lutz. Owl 2 web ontology language profiles (second edition). `https://www.w3.org/TR/2012/REC-owl2-profiles-20121211/`. Accessed in December, 2019.

[25]   Hoang Gia Ngo, Nancy F Chen, Binh Minh Nguyen, Bin Ma, and Haizhou Li. Phonology-augmented statistical transliteration for low-resource languages. In *Sixteenth Annual Conference of the International Speech Communication Association*, 2015.

[26]   Hoang Gia Ngo, Minh Nguyen, and Nancy F Chen. Phonology-augmented statistical framework for machine transliteration using limited linguistic resources. *IEEE/ACM Transactions on Audio, Speech and Language Processing (TASLP)*, 27(1), 2019.

[27]   Minh Nguyen, Hoang Gia Ngo, and Nancy F Chen. Multimodal neural pronunciation modeling for spoken languages with logographic origin. In *Proceedings of EMNLP*, 2018.

[28]   Minh Nguyen, Hoang Gia Ngo, and Nancy F Chen. Hierarchical character embeddings: Learning phonological and semantic representations in languages of logographic origin using recursive neural networks. *IEEE/ACM Transactions on Audio, Speech, and Language Processing*, 2019.

[29]   Matthew Peters, Mark Neumann, Mohit Iyyer, Matt Gardner, Christopher Clark, Kenton Lee, and Luke Zettlemoyer. Deep contextualized word representations. In *Proceedings of NAACL-HLT*, pages 2227–2237, 2018.

[30]   Quantexa. The state of ai in finance services: Survey report. `https://www.quantexa.com/the-state-of-ai-in-financial-services-survey-report/`. Accessed in December, 2019.

[31]   Alec Radford, Karthik Narasimhan, Tim Salimans, and Ilya Sutskever. Improving language understanding by generative pre-training. 2018.

[32]   Prajit Ramachandran, Peter Liu, and Quoc Le. Unsupervised pretraining for sequence to sequence learning. In *Proceedings of EMNLP*, 2017.

[33]   Richard Socher, Alex Perelygin, Jean Wu, Jason Chuang, Christopher Manning, Andrew Ng, and Christopher Potts. Recursive deep models for semantic compositionality over a sentiment treebank. In *Proceedings of EMNLP*, 2013.

[34]   Tzu-Ray Su and Hung-Yi Lee. Learning Chinese word representations from glyphs of characters. In *Proceedings of EMNLP*, 2017.

[35]   Kai Sheng Tai, Richard Socher, and Christopher Manning. Improved semantic representations from tree-structured long short-term memory networks. In *Proceedings of ACL*, 2015.

[36]   Jiewen Wu, Freddy Lécué, Christophe Gueret, Jer Hayes, Sara Van De Moosdijk, Gemma Gallagher, Peter Mccanney, and Eugene Eichelberger. Personalizing actions in context for risk management using semantic web technologies. In *Proceedings of International Semantic Web Conference, 2017*, 2017.

[37]   Kelvin Xu, Jimmy Ba, Ryan Kiros, Kyunghyun Cho, Aaron Courville, Ruslan Salakhudinov, Rich Zemel, and Yoshua Bengio. Show, attend and tell: Neural image caption generation with visual attention. In *International conference on machine learning*, pages 2048–2057, 2015.

[38]   Song Yan, Shi Shuming, and Li Jing. Joint learning embeddings for Chinese words and their components via ladder structured networks. In *Proceedings of IJCAI*, 2018.

[39]   Dani Yogatama, Phil Blunsom, Chris Dyer, Edward Grefenstette, and Ling Wang. Learning to compose words into sentences with reinforcement learning. In *Proceedings of ICLR*, 2017.

[40]   Xiaodan Zhu, Parinaz Sobihani, and Hongyu Guo. Long short-term memory over recursive structures. In *Proceedings of ICML*, 2015.

Knowledge Graphs for eXplainable Artificial Intelligence: Foundations, Applications and Challenges 213
I. Tiddi et al. (Eds.)
IOS Press, 2020
doi:10.3233/SSW200020

Generating Explanations in Natural Language from Knowledge Graphs

Diego MOUSSALLEM [a], René SPECK [b,c], and Axel-Cyrille NGONGA NGOMO [a]

[a] *DICE Group, Department of Computer Science, Paderborn University, Germany*
[b] *Scalable Data Management, University Computing Centre, Leipzig University, Germany*
[c] *Institute for Applied Informatics, Leipzig, Germany*

Abstract. With the ever-growing adoption of Artificial Inteligence (AI) models comes an increasing demand for making their output actions understandable. With this aim, it is crucial to generate natural language explanations of their models. One way of achieving this goal is to translate the languages of the Semantic Web (SW) into natural language. In this chapter, we give an overview of how SW languages can be used to generate texts and consequently explanations. We begin by presenting LD2NL, a framework for verbalizing the three key languages of the Semantic Web, i.e., RDF, OWL, and SPARQL. Afterward, we talk about the generation of texts by relying on Neural Network (NN) models. We hence present NeuralREG, an approach for generating referring expression of Knowledge Graph (KG) entities while generating texts. Both frameworks are evaluated in open surveys with 150 persons. The results suggest that although generating explanations from KGs is in its infancy, both LD2NL and NeuralREG can generate verbalizations that are close to natural languages, and non-experts can easily understand that. In addition to that, it enables non-domain experts to interpret AI actions with more than 91% of the accuracy of domain experts.

Keywords. Knowledge Graphs, Natural Language Generation, Semantic Web, OWL, Explanations, eXplainable AI

1. Introduction

Obtaining an explainable AI system demands the capability of automatically generating explanations in coherent natural language texts from non-linguistic data, in our case, from KGs. This process of automatically generating texts is named as Natural Language Generation (NLG) [52]. Conforming to [42], NLG approaches range from (i) rule based approaches (ii) modular statistical approaches which divide the process into three phases (planning, selection and surface realization) and use data driven approaches for one or more of these phases (iii) hybrid approaches which rely on a combination of handcrafted rules and corpus statistics and (iv) the more recent neural network based models.

Recently, an interest in the development of NLG systems focusing on verbalizing KGs has been increased [1, 18, 25, 44]. KGs are usually composed by description languages which rely on the SW vision such as, Resource Description Framework (RDF), SPARQL Protocol and RDF Query Language (SPARQL) and Web Ontology Language (OWL), and store factual knowledge in structured data with relationships between resources. They are rather difficult to understand for non-expert users. For example, while the meaning of the OWL class expression `Class: Professor SubClassOf: worksAt SOME University` is obvious to every SW expert, this expression ("Every professor works at a university") is rather difficult to fathom for lay persons.

In this chapter, we begin by presenting an open-source holistic NLG framework for the SW, named LD2NL, which facilitates the verbalization of the three key languages of the SW, i.e., RDF, OWL, and SPARQL into Natural Language (NL). This framework is based on a bottom-up paradigm for verbalizing SW data. Additionally, LD2NL builds upon *SPARQL2NL* as it is open-source and the paradigm it follows can be reused and ported to RDF and OWL. Thus, LD2NL is capable of generating either a single sentence (explanation) or a summary of a given KG resource, rule, or query. LD2NL is evaluated using 66 experts in Natural Language Processing (NLP) and SW as well as 20 non-experts who were lay users or non-users of SW. The results suggest that LD2NL generates texts which can be easily understood by humans.

Besides its use in traditional pipeline NLG systems [52], KG has also become relevant in modern "end-to-end" NLG approaches, which perform the task in a more integrated manner [26, 35]. Therefore, we present NeuralREG, an approach which relies on deep neural networks for making decisions about the entities form and content in one go without explicit feature extraction from RDF KGs. Referring Expression Generation (REG) concentrates on the creation of referring expressions that identify and describe specific entities. Some of these approaches have recently focused on inputs which references to entities are delexicalized to general tags (e.g., ENTITY-1, ENTITY-2) in order to decrease data sparsity. Based on the delexicalized input, the model generates outputs which may be liked to templates in which references to the discourse entities are not realized (as in "The ground of ENTITY-1 is located in ENTITY-2."). While NeuralREG is compatible with different applications of REG models, it focuses on the last one, i.e., relying on a specifically constructed set of 78,901 referring expressions to 1,501 entities in the context of the RDF KG, derived from a (delexicalized) version of the WebNLG corpus [25, 26].

In the following, we give a brief background regarding SW technologies in the context of NLG task. Afterwards, we present some of the core insights and algorithms underlying LD2NL and NeuralREG. Finally, we report their evaluation results. Due to space limitation, we cannot present all algorithms in detail.[1]

2. Background

2.1. OWL

OWL[2] [47] is the de-facto standard for machine processable and interoperable ontologies on the SW. In its second version, OWL is equivalent to the description logic $\mathcal{SROIQ}(D)$. Such expressiveness has a higher computational cost but allows the development of interesting applications such as automated reasoning [7]. OWL 2 ontologies consist of the following three different syntactic categories:

---

[1]We refer the reader to the papers for a complete explanation of the algorithms implemented in LD2NL and NeuralREG.

[2]`www.w3.org/TR/owl2-overview/`

Entities, such as *classes*, *properties*, and *individuals*, are identified by IRIs. They form the primitive terms and constitute the basic elements of an ontology. Classes denote sets of individuals and properties link two individuals or an individual and a data value along a property. For example, a class `:Animal` can be used to represent the set of all animals. Similarly, the object property `:childOf` can be used to represent the parent-child relationship and the data property `:birthDate` assigns a particular birth date to an individual. Finally, the individual `:Alice` can be used to represent a particular person called "Alice".

Expressions represent complex notions in the domain being described. For example, a *class expression* describes a set of individuals in terms of the restrictions on the individuals' characteristics. OWL offers existential (**SOME**) or universal (**ONLY**) qualifiers and a variety of typical logical constructs, such as negation (**NOT**), other Boolean operators (**OR, AND**), and more constructs such as cardinality restriction (**MIN, MAX, EXACTLY**) and value restriction (**VALUE**), to create class expressions. Such constructs can be combined in arbitrarily complex class expressions CE according to the following grammar

```
CE = A | C AND D | C OR D | NOT C | R SOME C | R ONLY C | R
     MIN n | R MAX n | R EXACTLY n | R VALUE a | {a₁,...,aₘ}
```

where A is an atomic class, C and D are class expressions, R is an object property, a as well as a_1 to a_m with $m \geq 1$ are individuals, and $n \geq 0$ is an integer.

Axioms are statements that are asserted to be true in the domain being described. Usually, one distinguish between (1) *terminological* and (2) *assertional* axioms. (1) terminological axioms are used to describe the structure of the domain, i.e., the relationships between classes resp. class expressions. For example, using a subclass axiom (**SubClassOf:**), one can state that the class `:Koala` is a subclass of the class `:Animal`. Classes can be subclasses of other classes, thus creating a taxonomy. In addition, axioms can arrange properties in hierarchies (**SubPropertyOf:**) and can assign various characteristics (**Characteristics:**) such as transitivity or reflexivity to them. (2) Assertional axioms formulate facts about individuals, especially the classes they belong to and their mutual relationships. OWL can be expressed in various syntaxes with the most common computer readable syntax being RDF/XMLA more human-readable format is the Manchester OWL Syntax (MOS) [32]. For example, the class expression that models people who work at a university that is located in Spain could be as follows in MOS:

```
Person AND worksAt SOME (University AND locatedIn VALUE Spain)
```

Likewise, expressing that every professor works at a university would read as

```
Class: Professor
  SubClassOf: worksAt SOME University
```

In the same way, saying that there is only one birth date for each individual in the domain can be done with

```
ObjectProperty: birthDate
  Characteristics: functional
```

Moreover, the facts that Albert Einstein is a person and was born in Ulm might be expressed by

```
Individual: Albert_Einstein
  Types: Person
  Facts: birthPlace Ulm
```

2.2. RDF

RDF [51] uses a graph-based data model for representing knowledge. Statements in RDF are expressed as so-called triples of the form (subject, predicate, object). RDF subjects and predicates are Internationalized Resource Identifierss (IRIs) and objects are either IRIs or literals.[3] RDF literals always have a datatype that defines its possible values. A predicate denotes a *property* and can also be seen as a binary relation taking subject and object as arguments. For example, the following triple expresses that Albert Einstein was born in Ulm:

```
:Albert_Einstein :birthPlace :Ulm .
```

and the statement that Einstein's birth date was on March 14, 1879 can be done by

```
:Albert_Einstein :birthDate "1879-03-14"^^xsd:date .
```

The RDF vocabulary comprises some built-in properties, the most common one being rdf:type, which states that a resource denoted by the subject is an instance of the class specified by the object of the triple. For example, the following triples states that Albert Einstein is a scientist:

```
:Albert_Einstein rdf:type :Scientist .
```

2.3. SPARQL

Commonly, the selection of subsets of RDF is performed using the SPARQL query language[4]. SPARQL can be used to express queries across diverse data sources. *Query forms* contain variables that appear in a solution result. They can be used to select all or a subset of the variables bound in a pattern match. They exist in four different instantiations, i.e., *SELECT, CONSTRUCT, ASK* and *DESCRIBE*. The *SELECT* query form is the most commonly used and is used to return rows of variable bindings. Therefore, we use this type of query in our explanation. *CONSTRUCT* allows to create a new RDF graph or modify the existing one through substituting variables in a graph templates for each solution. *ASK* returns a Boolean value indicating whether the graph contains a match or not. Finally, *DESCRIBE* is used to return all triples about the resources matching the query. For example, 1 represents the following query "Return all scientists who were born in Ulm".

---

[3]For simplicity, we omit RDF blank nodes in subject or object position.
[4]http://www.w3.org/TR/sparql11-query

```
SELECT ?person
WHERE {
    ?person a dbo:Scientist;
        dbo:birthPlace dbr:Ulm.
}
```

Listing 1: All scientists who were born in Ulm

3. Rule and Template-based NLG Approaches

Rule and template-based NLG approaches comprise choosing the correct rules and templates for the current task. Those approaches are limited to the number of cases they can handle but perform well so that many industry solutions rely on these approaches. Thus, those approaches cannot scale or adapt.

According to [6, 27, 57], there has been plenty of work done that investigated the generation of NL text from SW data. However, the subject of research has only recently gained significant momentum. This interest comes from the great number of published works such as [5, 12, 19, 20] which used RDF as an input data and achieved promising results. RDF has also been showing promising benefits in the generation of benchmarks for NLG systems [25, 30, 41, 49, 54, 58].

Despite the plethora of recent works written on handling RDF data, only a few have exploited the generation of NL from OWL and SPARQL. For instance, [1] generates sentences in English and Greek from OWL ontologies. Also, SPARQL2NL [44] uses rules to verbalize atomic constructs and combine their verbalization into sentences.

3.1. LD2NL Framework

The goal of LD2NL is to provide an integrated system which generates a complete and correct NL representation for the most common used SW modeling languages RDF and OWL. In terms of the standard model of NL generation proposed by Reiter & Dale [52], our steps mainly play the role of the micro-planner, with focus on aggregation, lexicalization, referring expressions and linguistic realization. In the following, we present our approach to formalizing NL sentences for each of the supported languages.

3.1.1. From RDF to NL

Lexicalization. The lexicalization of RDF triples must be able to deal with resources, classes, properties and literals.

Classes and resources The lexicalization of classes and resources is carried out as follows: Given a URI u we ask for the English label of u using a SPARQL query.[5] If such a label does not exist, we use either the fragment of u (the string after #) if it exists, else the string after the last occurrence of /. Finally this NL representation is realized as a noun phrase, and in the case of classes is also pluralized. As an example, `:Person` is realized as `people` (its label).

---

[5] Note that it could be any property which returns a NL representation of the given URI, see [21].

Properties The lexicalization of properties relies on the insight that most property labels are either nouns or verbs. While the mapping of a particular property p can be unambiguous, (e.g., if p is labeled country, the possessive clause realization is clearly to prefer), some property labels are not as easy to categorize. For examples, the label crosses can either be the plural form of the noun cross or the third person singular present form of the verb to cross. To automatically determine which realization to use, we relied on the insight that the first and last word of a property label are often the key to determining the type of the property: properties whose label begins with a verb (resp. noun or gerund) are most to be realized as verbs (resp. nouns). We devised a set of rules to capture this behavior, which we omit due to space restrictions. In some cases (such as crosses) none of the rules applied. In these cases, we compare the probability of $P(p|\text{noun})$ and $P(p|\text{verb})$ by measuring

$$P(p|X) = \frac{\sum\limits_{t \in synset(p|X)} \log_2(f(t))}{\sum\limits_{t' \in synset(p)} \log_2(f(t'))}, \tag{1}$$

where $synset(p)$ is the set of all synsets of p, $synset(p|X)$ is the set of all synsets of p that are of the syntactic class $X \in \{\text{noun}, \text{verb}\}$ and $f(t)$ is the frequency of use of p in the sense of the synset t according to WordNet. For

$$\frac{P(p|\text{verb})}{P(p|\text{noun})} \geq \theta, \tag{2}$$

we choose to realize p as a noun; else we realized it as a verb. For $\theta = 1$, for example, dbo:crosses is realized as a verb.

Literals Literals in an RDF graph usually consist of a *lexical form* LF and a *datatype IRI* DT, represented as "LF"^^<DT>. Optionally, if the datatype is rdf:langString, a non-empty *language tag* is specified and the literal is denoted as *language-tagged string*[6]. The realization of language-tagged strings is done by using simply the lexical form, while omitting the language tag. For example, "Albert Einstein"@en is realized as Albert Einstein. For other types of literals, we further differentiate between built-in and user-defined datatypes. For the former, we also use the lexical form, e.g. "123"^^xsd:int ⇒ 123, while the latter are processed by using the literal value with its representation of the datatype IRI, e.g., "123"^^dt:squareKilometre as 123 square kilometers.

Realizing A Single RDF Triple. The realization ρ of a triple (s p o) depends mostly on the verbalization of the predicate p. If p can be realized as a noun phrase, then a possessive clause can be used to express the semantics of (s p o), more formally

1. ρ(s p o) ⇒ poss(ρ(p),ρ(s)) ∧ subj(BE,ρ(p))
   ∧ dobj(BE,ρ(o))

For example, if ρ(p) is a relational noun like birth place e.g. in the triple (:Albert_Einstein :birthPlace :Ulm), then the verbalization is Albert Einstein's birth place is Ulm. Note that BE stands for the verb "to be". In case p's realization is a verb, then the triple can be verbalized as follows:

2. ρ(s p o) ⇒ subj(ρ(p),ρ(s)) ∧ dobj(ρ(p),ρ(o))

---

[6]In RDF 1.0 literals have been divided into "plain" literals with no type and optional language tags, and typed literals.

For example, in (`:Albert_Einstein :influenced :Nathan_Rosen`) $\rho(p)$ is the verb `influenced`, thus, the verbalization is Albert Einstein influenced Nathan Rosen.

Realizing RDF Triples to NL.   The same procedure of generating a single triple can be applied for the generation of each triple in a set of triples. However, the NL output would contain redundant information and consequently sound very artificial. Thus, the goal is to transform the generated description to sound more natural. To this end, we focus on two types of transformation rules (cf. [16]): *ordering and clustering* and *grouping*. In the following, we describe the transformation rules we employ in more detail. Note that clustering and ordering is applied before grouping.

Clustering and ordering rules   We process the input trees in descending order with respect to the frequency of the variables they contain, starting with the projection variables and only after that turning to other variables. As an example, consider the following triples about two of the most known people in the world:

```
:William_Shakespeare rdf:type :Writer .
:Albert_Einstein :birthPlace :Ulm .
:Albert_Einstein :deathPlace :Princeton
:Albert_Einstein rdf:type :Scientist .
:William_Shakespeare :deathDate
"1616-04-23"^^xsd:date .
```

The five triples are verbalized as given in 3a–3e. Clustering and ordering first take all sentences containing the subject `:Albert_Einstein`, i.e. 3b –3d, which are ordered such that copulative sentences (such as Albert Einstein is a scientist) come before other sentences, and then takes all sentences containing the remaining subject `:William_Shakespeare` in 3a and 3e resulting in a sequence of sentences as in 4.

3. (a) William Shakespeare is a writer.
    (b) Albert Einstein's birth place is Ulm.
    (c) Albert Einstein's death place is Princeton.
    (d) Albert Einstein is a scientist.
    (e) William Shakespeare's death date is 23 April 1616.
  4. Albert Einstein is a scientist. Albert Einstein's birth place is Ulm. Albert Einstein's death place is Princeton. William Shakespeare's is a writer. William Shakespeare's death date is 23 April 1616.

Grouping   [16] describes grouping as a process "collecting clauses with common elements and then collapsing the common elements". The common elements are usually subject noun phrases and verb phrases (verbs together with object noun phrases), leading to *subject grouping* and *object grouping*. To maximize the grouping effects, we collapse common prefixes and suffixes of sentences, irrespective of whether they are full subject noun phrases or complete verb phrases. In the following we use $X_1, X_2, \ldots X_N$ as variables for the root nodes of the input sentences and Y as variable for the root node of the output sentence. Furthermore, we abbreviate a subject $\texttt{subj}(X_i, s_i)$ as s_i, an object $\texttt{dobj}(X_i, o_i)$ as o_i, and a verb $\texttt{root}(ROOT_i, v_i)$ as v_i.

Subject grouping* collapses the predicates (i.e. verb and object) of two sentences if their subjects are the same, as specified in 5 (abbreviations as above).

5. $\rho(s_1) = \rho(s_2) \wedge \texttt{cc}(v_1, coord)$
    $\Rightarrow \texttt{root}(Y, \texttt{coord}(v_1, v_2)) \wedge \texttt{subj}(v_1, s_1) \wedge \texttt{dobj}(v_1, o_1) \wedge \texttt{subj}(v_2, s_1) \wedge \texttt{dobj}(v_1, o_2)$

```
subj verb dobj₁ . subj verb dobj₂.
▷ subj verb dobj₁ and dobj₂.
```

An example are the sentences given in 6, which share the subject Albert Einstein and thus can be collapsed into a single sentence.

  6. Albert Einstein is a scientist and Albert Einstein is known for general relativity.
     ⇒ Albert Einstein is a scientist and known for general relativity.

Object grouping* collapses the subjects of two sentences if the realizations of the verbs and objects of the sentences are the same, where the *coord* ∈ {and, or} is the coordination combining the input sentences X_1 and X_2, and coord ∈ {conj, disj} is the corresponding coordination combining the subjects.

  7. $\rho(o_1) = \rho(o_2) \wedge \rho(v_1) = \rho(v_2) \wedge cc(v_1, coord)$
     $\Rightarrow root(Y, PLURAL(v_1)) \wedge subj(v_1, coord(s_1, s_2)) \wedge dobj(v_1, o_1)$

For example, the sentences in 8 share their verb and object, thus they can be collapsed into a single sentence. Note that to this end the singular auxiliary was needs to be transformed into its plural form were. In case the subjects themselves share common elements, the subjects are collapsed as well, as in 9.

  8. Benjamin Franklin was born in Boston. Leonard Nimoy was born in Boston. ⇒ Benjamin Franklin and Leonard Nimoy were born in Boston.
  9. Abraham Lincoln's birth place is Washington or Abraham Lincoln's death place is Washington. ⇒ Abraham Lincoln's birth place or death place is Washington.

3.1.2. Multilingual Natural Language Generation - The Case of Brazilian Portuguese

Presently, the generation of natural language from RDF KG has gained substantial attention [6, 57]. However, English is the only language which has been widely targeted, even though there are studies which explore the generation of content in languages other than English. Here, we describe RDF2PT, an approach which generates texts in Brazilian Portuguese from RDF KGs[18]. RDF2PT is a rule-based approach and while the exciting avenue of using deep learning techniques in NLG approaches [27] is open to this task and deep learning has already shown promising results for RDF data [56], the morphological richness of Portuguese led to develop first a rule-based approach in order to identify the challenges imposed by this language from the KG perspective before applying Machine Learning (ML) algorithms.

RDF2PT approach is akin to the approach LD2NL [45] described in subsection 3.1. As seen, a generic NLG pipeline is composed by three tasks which are *Document Planning*, *Micro Planning* and *Realization*. RDF2PT operates mostly at the level of the first two and to the *Realization* task, RDF2PT uses an adaption of SimpleNLG to Brazilian Portuguese [17].

In the following sections, the RDF2PT steps according to an NLG system pipeline [27] are described. The Portuguese version of DBpedia is used as a Knowledge Base (KB) [2, 38] and as source for our examples.

Micro Planning - Lexicalization. This step comprises the main contribution of RDF2PT for verbalizing the triples in Brazilian Portuguese. In contrast to English, Brazilian Portuguese is a morphologically rich language which contains the grammatical gender of words. Grammatical gender plays a key role because it affects the generation of determiners and pronouns. It also influences the inflection of nouns and verbs. For instance, the passive expression of the verb `nascer` (en: "be born") is `nascida` if the subject is feminine or `nascido` if masculine. Thus, the gender of words is essential for comprehending the semantics of a given Portuguese text. Also, Brazilian Portuguese has different possibilities in the expression of subject possessives. Hence, RDF2PT has to deal with the following phenomena while lexicalizing:

- **Grammatical gender** - In Portuguese, the gender varies between masculine and feminine. This variation leads to supplementary challenges when lexicalizing words automatically. For example, a gender may be represented by articles "um" and "o" (masculine) or "uma" and "a" (feminine). However, the gender also affects the inflection of words. For instance, for the word "cantor" (en: "singer"), if the subject is feminine, the word becomes "cantora". However, there are words which do not inflect, e.g., the word "gerente" (en: "manager"). If the subject is a woman, we only refer to it by using the article "a", i.e., "a gerente". Therefore, there are some challenges to tackle for recognizing the gender and assigning it correctly. A tricky example to solve automatically is "O Rio de Janeiro é uma cidade" (en: Rio de Janeiro is a city). In this case, the subject is masculine but its complement is feminine. Devising handcrafted rules to handle these phenomena can become a hard task. To address this challenge, we use a Part-Of-Speech tagger (TreeTagger in our case) as it retrieves the gender along with the parts of speech.[7] All the obtained genders are attached along with the lexicalizations for supporting the realization step.

- **Classes and resources** - The lexicalizaton of classes and resources is carried by using a SPARQL query to get their Portuguese labels through the `rdfs:label` predicate[8]. In case such a label does not exist, we use either the fragment of their URI (the string after the # character) if it exists, or the string after the last occurrence of "/". Finally, this natural language representation is lexicalized as a noun phrase. Afterwards, RDF2PT recognizes the gender. In case the resource is recognized as a person, RDF2PT applies a string similarity measure (0.8 threshold) between the lexicalized word with a list of names provided by SemWeb2NL. This list is divided by masculine and feminine which in turn results in the gender. If the resource is not a person, we use Tree-tagger.

- **Properties** - The lexicalization of properties relies on one of the results of [44], i.e., that most property labels are either nouns or verbs. To determine which lexicalization to use automatically, we rely on the insight that the first and last words of a property label in Portuguese are commonly the key to determining the type of property. We then use the Tree-Tagger to get the part of speech of predicates. Properties whose label begins with a verb are lexicalized as verbs. For example, the predicate `dbo:knownFor`, which Portuguese label is "conhecido por", has the

---

[7]see the POS tags `http://www.cis.uni-muenchen.de/~schmid/tools/TreeTagger/data/Portuguese-Tagset.html`

[8]Note that it could be any property which returns a natural language representation of the given URI, see [21].

first word identified as an inflection of the verb "conhecer" (en:know). Therefore, RDF2PT lexicalizes and sets it as a verb. We devised a set of rules to capture this behavior, which we omit due to space restrictions.[9] Moreover, RDF2PT uses some pre-defined templates for improving the quality of lexicalization. For example, the predicate `dbo:birthPlace`, RDF2PT uses the verb "nascer" (eng: be born) along with the predicate "em" (en: "in"), so this predicate can be lexicalized as "nasceu em" (en: was born in).

For predicates which are recognized as nouns, RDF2PT relies on labels. For instance, `dbo:birthDate` is labeled as "data de nascimento" and recognized as a noun phrase because of its first word "data". RDF2PT also uses the first word of predicates to set the gender. For example, `dbo:deathPlace` is transliterated as "local de falecimento". "local" is masculine. Hence, the determiner to be used in front of this predicate needs to be "o". In contrast to `dbo:birthDate` ("data de nascimento"), the word "data" is feminine, thus the determiner must be "a".

- **Literals** - In an RDF graph, literals usually consist of a *lexical form* LF and a *datatype IRI* DT. If the datatype is `rdf:langString`, a non-empty *language tag* is specified and the literal is denoted as a *language-tagged string*.[10] Accordingly, the lexicalization of strings with language tags is carried by using simply the lexical form, while omitting the language tag. For example, `''Albert Einstein"@pt` is lexicalized as "Albert Einstein" or `"Alemanha"@pt` ("Germany"@en) is lexicalized as "Alemanha". For other types of literals, we differentiate between built-in[11] and user-defined datatypes. For built-in literals, we use the lexical form, e.g., `"123"^^xsd:int` $\Rightarrow$ "123". User-defined types are processed by using the literal value together with the (pluralized) natural language representation of the datatype IRI. Thus, we lexicalize `"123"^^dt:squareKilometre` as "123 quilômetros quadrados" (en: "123 square kilometers").

Referring expression generation.   In this step, RDF2PT relies on the number of subjects contained by the RDF statements and only uses other expressions to refer to a given subject in case there is more than one mention of it. RDF2PT replaces the subject by possessive or personal pronouns with the corresponding gender depending on the predicates. For instance, given a triple `dbr: Albert_Einstein dbo:birthPlace dbr:Ulm`, the predicate is a noun phrase then the subject is replaced by a possessive form which is "seu" (en:"his"). However, Brazilian Portuguese has two different ways to express possession and this variation exists due to the necessity of handling complex syntaxes in some sentences and also because the gender of pronouns agrees with objects instead of subjects. For example, "A professora proibiu que o aluno utilizasse seu dicionário." (eng: "The teacher forbade the student to use `his/her` dictionary"). The possessive pronoun `seu` in this sentence does not indicate explicitly to whom the dictionary belongs, if it belongs to the `professora` (eng:teacher) or `aluno` (eng:student). Thus, we have explicitly to define the possessive pronoun in order to decrease the ambiguity in texts and it is obviously important when generating text from data. If this sentence was translated into English, we would have indicated to whom the dictionary belonged, `her` or `his`. To this end, we

---

[9]All rules can be found in our code.

[10]In RDF 1.0 literals have been divided into "plain" literals with no type and optional language tags, and typed literals.

[11]List of data types: `https://www.w3.org/TR/rdf11-concepts/#xsd-datatypes`

handle the ambiguity of possessive pronouns by interspersing the alternative forms, e.g., dele (eng:his) or dela (eng: her)" which agrees with the subject. However, it is used just in case more than one subject exists in the same description.

In case the predicate is recognized as a verb (e.g, dbr: Albert_Einstein dbo:knownFor dbr:General_relativity), the subject is replaced by its respective personal pronoun ele (eng: "he"). While setting the pronouns, RDF2PT recognizes the gender's subject. The dbo:knownFor is a verb phrase, thus the subject is replaced by the personal pronoun ":ele"(see Table 1).

Triples before co-reference
1 - (Albert Einstein, ser, cientista)
2 - (Albert Einstein, local de nascimento, Ulm)
3 - (Albert Einstein, ser conhecido por, teoria da relatividade.)

Triples after co-reference
1 - (Albert Einstein, ser, cientista)
2 - (**seu**, local de nascimento, Ulm.)
3 - (**ele**, ser conhecido por, teoria da relatividade).

Table 1. Example of triples in the coreference generation task.

Linguistic realization.   This last step is responsible for mapping the obtained descriptions of sentences from the aforementioned tasks and verbalizing them syntactically, morphologically and orthographically into a correct natural language text. To this end, we perform this step by relying on a Brazilian adaptation of SimpleNLG [17] and [44].

3.1.3. From OWL to NL

OWL 2 ontologies consist of Entities, Expressions and Axioms as introduced in subsection 2.1. While both expressions and axioms can be mapped to RDF[12], i.e. into a set of RDF triples, using this mapping and applying the triple-based verbalization on it would lead to a non-human understandable text in many cases. For example, the intersection of two classes :A and :B can be represented in RDF by the six triples

```
_:x rdf:type owl:Class .
_:x owl:intersectionOf _:y1 .
_:y1 rdf:first :A .
_:y1 rdf:rest _:y2 .
_:y2 rdf:first :B .
_:y2 rdf:rest rdf:nil .
```

The verbalization of these triples would result in Something that is a class and the intersection of something whose first is A and whose rest is something whose first is B and whose rest is nil., which is obviously far away from how a human would express it in NL. Therefore, generating NL from OWL requires a different procedure based on its syntactic categories, OWL expressions and OWL axioms.

---

[12]https://www.w3.org/TR/owl2-mapping-to-rdf

While handling OWL entities is similar to the verbalization of RDF resources and literals (Section 3.1.1), OWL expressions and OWL axioms are much more complex. We show general rules for each of them in the following.

OWL Entities   The verbalization of OWL entities is similar to the verbalization of their RDF counterparts (Section 3.1.1): OWL classes are handled like RDF classes, individuals are processed like RDF resources, OWL object and data properties are verbalized like RDF properties, and OWL literals are converted to NL like it's done for literals in RDF.

OWL Class Expressions   In theory, class expressions can be arbitrarily complex, but as it turned out in some previous analysis [50], in practice they seldom arise and can be seen as some corner cases. For example, an ontology could contain the following class expression about people and their birth place:

```
Person AND birthPlace SOME (City AND locatedIn VALUE France)
```

Class expressions do have a tree-like structure and can simply be parsed into a tree by means of the binary OWL class expressions constructors contained in it. For our example, this would result in the following tree:

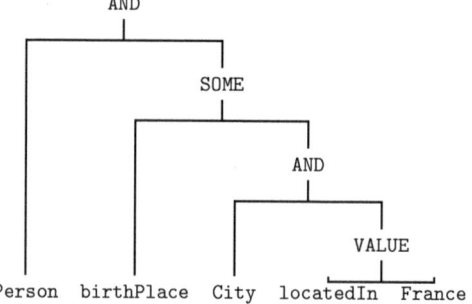

Such a tree can be traversed in post-order, i.e. sub-trees are processed before their parent nodes recursively. For the sake of simplicity, we only process sub-trees that represent proper class expression in our example, i.e. we omit `birthPlace`, `locatedIn`, and `France`. Moreover and again for simplicity, we'll explain the transformation process by starting from the right-hand side of the tree. Thus, in our example we begin with the class expression `City` which is transformed to `everything that is a city` and `locatedIn VALUE France` resulting in `everything that is located in France` by application of a rule.

Both class expressions are used in the conjunction `City AND locatedIn VALUE France`. Thus, the next step would be to merge both phrases. An easy way is to use the coordinating conjunction and, i.e. `everything that is a city and everything that is located in France`. Although the output of this transformation is correct, it still contains unnecessarily redundant information. Therefore, we apply the aggregation procedure described in Section 3.1.1, i.e. we get `everything that is a city and located in France`. Yet, the aggregation can still be improved: if there is any atomic class in the conjunction, we know that this is more specific than the placeholder `everything`. Thus, we can replace it by the plural form of the class, finally resulting in `cities that are located in France`. The same procedure is applied for its parent class expression being the existential restriction

```
birthPlace SOME (City AND locatedIn VALUE France)
```

This will be transformed to everything whose birth place is a city that is located in France. Note, that we used the singular form here, assuming that the property birthPlace is supposed to be functional in the ontology. In the last step, we process the class expression Person, which gives us everything that is a person. Again, due to the conjunction we merge this result with with the previous one, such that in the end we get people whose birth place is a city that is located in France.

OWL Axioms   As we described in Section 3.1.3, OWL axioms can roughly be categorized into terminological and assertional axioms. Therefore, we have different procedures for processing each category:

Assertional Axioms (ABox Axioms) - Most assertional axioms assert individuals to atomic classes or relate individuals to another individual resp. literal value. For example, axioms about the type as well as birth place and birth date of Albert Einstein can be expressed by

```
Individual: Albert_Einstein
   Types: Person
   Facts: birthPlace Ulm, birthDate "1879-03-14"^^xsd:date
```

Those axioms can simply be rewritten as triples, thus, we can use the same procedure as we do for triples (Section 3.1.1). Converting them into NL gives us Albert Einstein is a person whose birth place is Ulm and whose birth date is 14 March 1879. OWL also allows for assigning an individual to a complex class expression. In that case we'll use our conversion of OWL class expressions as described in Section 3.1.3.

Terminological Axioms (TBox Axioms) - According to [50], most of the terminological axioms used in ontologies are subclass axioms. By definition, subclass and superclass can be arbitrarily complex class expressions CE_1 and CE_2, i.e. CE_1 SubClassOf CE_2, but in praxis it is quite often only used with atomic classes as subclass or even more simple with the superclass also being an atomic class. Nevertheless, we support any kind of subclass axiom and all other logical OWL axioms in LD2NL. For simplicity, we outline here how we verbalize subclass axioms in LD2NL. The semantics of a subclass axiom denotes that every individual of the subclass also belongs to the superclass. Thus, the verbalization seems to be relatively straightforward, i.e. we verbalize both class expressions and follow the template : every $\rho(CE_1)$ is a $\rho(CE_2)$. Obviously, this works pretty well for subclass axioms with atomic classes only. For example, the axiom about the person class and its subclass is verbalized as every scientist is a person.

```
Class: Scientist
   SubClassOf: Person
```

If the subclass is a complex class expressions, we have to distinguish between those that contain an atomic class on the top level, e.g. $CE_1 = $ (A AND CE), and others. In the former case, we can still use every ... As an example, the subclass Person AND worksAt SOME University leads to every person that works at a university ... In the latter case, we can simply use the result of the verbalization of CE_1, i.e. either everything that ... or everything whose .... The same distinction has to be done for the superclass. If there is any atomic class on the top level, we can stick to the template, i.e. ... is a $\rho(CE_2)$. Otherwise, e.g. if $CE_2 = $ (R SOME CE), we verbalize it to The semantics of a subclass axiom denotes

3.2. From SPARQL to NL

A SPARQL SELECT query can be regarded as consisting of three parts: (1) a *body section* B, which describes all data that has to be retrieved, (2) an *optional section* O, which describes the data items that can be retrieved by the query if they exist, and (3) a *modifier section* M, which describes all solution sequences, modifiers and aggregates that are to be applied to the result of the previous two sections of the query. Let *Var* be the set of all variables that can be used in a SPARQL query. In addition, let R be the set of all resources, P the set of all properties and L the set of all literals contained in the target knowledge base of the SPARQL queries at hand. We call $x \in Var \cup R \cup P \cup L$ an *atom*. The basic components of the body of a SPARQL query are triple patterns $(s,p,o) \in (Var \cup R) \times (Var \cup P) \times (Var \cup R \cup L)$. Let W be the set of all words in the dictionary of our target language. We define the realization function $\rho : Var \cup R \cup P \cup L \rightarrow W^*$ as the function which maps each atom to a word or sequence of words from the dictionary. The extension of ρ to all SPARQL constructs maps all atoms x to their realization $\rho(x)$ and defines how these atomic realizations are to be combined. We denote the extension of ρ by the same label ρ for the sake of simplicity. We adopt a rule-based approach to achieve this goal, where the rules extending ρ to all valid SPARQL constructs are expressed in a conjunctive manner. This means that for premises $P_1, \ldots, P_n$ and consequences $K_1, \ldots, K_m$ we write $P_1 \wedge \ldots \wedge P_n \Rightarrow K_1 \wedge \ldots \wedge K_m$. The premises and consequences are explicated by using an extension of the Stanford dependencies[13].

We rely especially on the constructs explained in Table 2.

For example, a possessive dependency between two phrase elements e_1 and e_2 is represented as $poss(e_1,e_2)$. For the sake of simplicity, we slightly deviate from the Stanford vocabulary by not treating the copula to be as an auxiliary, but denoting it as BE. Moreover, we extend the vocabulary by the constructs conj and disj which denote the conjunction resp. disjunction of two phrase elements. In addition, we sometimes reduce the construct subj$(y,x) \wedge$ dobj(y,z) to the triple $(x,y,z) \in W^3$.

3.2.1. English evaluation

LD2NL is evaluated in three different experiments based on human ratings. We divided the volunteers into two groups—domain experts and non-experts. The group of domain experts comprised 66 persons while there were 20 non-experts forming the second group. In the first experiment, an OWL axiom and its verbalization were shown to the experts who were asked to rate the verbalization regarding the two following measures according to [25]: (1) Adequacy: Does the text contain only and all the information from the data? (2) Fluency: Does the text sound fluent and natural?. For both measures the volunteers were asked to rate on a scale from 1 (Very Bad) to 5 (Very Good). The experiment was

---

[13]For a complete description of the vocabulary, see https://stanford.io/2EzMjmo.

Table 2. Dependencies used by LD2NL.

Dependency	Explanation
`amod`	Represents the *adjectival modifier* dependency. For example `amod(ROSE,WHITE)` stands for white rose.
`cc`	Stands for the relation between a conjunct and a given conjunction (in most cases and or or). For example in the sentence John eats an apple and a pear, `cc(PEAR,AND)` holds. We mainly use this construct to specify reduction and replacement rules.
`conj`*	Used to build the *conjunction* of two phrase elements, e.g. `conj(subj(EAT,JOHN), subj(DRINK,MARY))` stands for John eats and Mary drinks.
	`conj` is not to be confused with the logical conjunction ∧, which we use to state that two dependencies hold in the same sentence. For example `subj(EAT,JOHN)` ∧ `dobj(EAT,FISH)` is to be read as John eats fish.
`disj`*	Used to build the *disjunction* of two phrase elements, similarly to `conj`.
`dobj`	Dependency between a verb and its *direct object*, for example `dobj(EAT,APPLE)` expresses to eat an/the apple.
`nn`	The *noun compound modifier* is used to modify a head noun by the means of another noun. For instance `nn(FARMER,JOHN)` stands for farmer John.
`poss`	Expresses a possessive dependency between two lexical items, for example `poss(JOHN,DOG)` expresses John's dog.
`prep_X`	Stands for the preposition X, where X can be any preposition, such as via, of, in and between.
`prepc_X`	Clausal modifier, used to modify verb or noun phrases by a clause introduced by some preposition X, e.g. `prepc_suchthat(PEOPLE,c)` represents people such that c, where c is some clause, e.g. their year of birth is 1950.
`root`	Marks the root of a sentence, e.g. the verb. For example `ROOT(EAT)` ∧ `subj(EAT,JOHN)` means John eats. The root of the sentence will not always be stated explicitly in our formalization.
`subj`	Relation between *subject* and verb, for example `subj(BE,JOHN)` expresses John is.

carried out using 41 axioms of the Koala ontology.[14] Because of the complexity of OWL axioms, only domain experts were asked to perform this experiment.

In the second experiment, a set of triples describing a single resource and their verbalization were shown to the volunteers. The experts were asked to rate the verbalization regarding adequacy, fluency and *completeness*, i.e., whether all triples have been covered. The non-experts were only asked to rate the fluency. The experiment was carried out using 6 DBpedia resources. In the third experiment, the verbalization of an OWL class and 5 resources were shown to the human raters. For non-experts, the resources have been verbalized as well, while for domain experts the resources were presented as triples. The task of the raters was to identify the resource that fits the class description and, thus, is

---

[14]https://github.com/pezra/pretty-printer/blob/master/Jenna-2.6.3/testing/ontology/bugs/koala.owl

an instance of the class. We used 4 different OWL axioms and measured the amount of correctly identified class instances.

Results. In our first series of experiments, the verbalization of OWL axioms, we achieved an average adequacy of 4.4 while the fluency reached 4.38. In addition, more than 77% of the verbalizations were assigned the maximal adequacy (i.e., were assigned a score of 5, see Fig. 1). The maximal score for fluency was achieved in more than 69% of the cases (see Fig. 1). This clearly indicates that the verbalization of axioms generated by LD2NL can be easily understood by domain experts and contains all the information necessary to access the input OWL class expression.

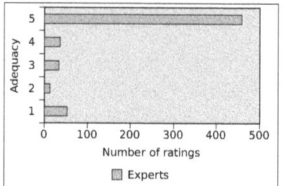 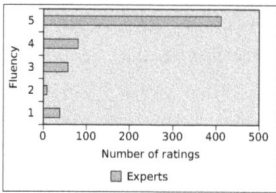

Figure 1. Experiment I: adequacy (left) and fluency (right) ratings

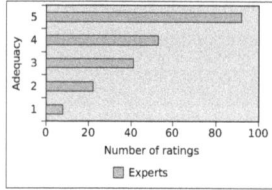 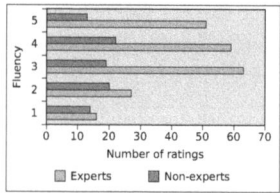 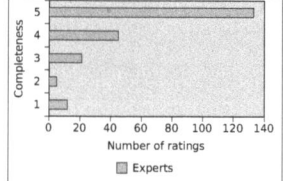

Figure 2. Experiment II: adequacy (left), fluency (middle) and completeness (left) results

Experiments on the verbalization of summaries for RDF resources revealed that verbalizing resource summaries is a more difficult task. While the adequacy of the verbalization was assigned an average score of 3.92 by experts (see Fig. 2), the fluency was assigned an average score of 3.47 by experts and 3.0 by non-experts (see Fig. 2). What these results suggest is that (1) our framework generates sentences that are close to that which a domain expert would also generate (adequacy). However (2) while the sentence is grammatically sufficient for the experts, it is regarded by non-domain experts (which were mostly linguists) as being grammatically passably good but still worthy of improvement. The completeness rating achieves a score of 4.31 on average (see Fig. 2). This was to be expected as we introduced a rule to shorten the description of resources that contain more than 5 triples which share a common subject and predicate. Finally, we measured how well the users and experts were able to understand the meaning of the text generated by our approach. As expected, the domain experts outperform the non-expert users by being able to find the answers to 87.2% of the questions. The score achieved by non-domain experts, i.e., 80%, still suggest that our framework is able to bridge the gap pertaining to understand RDF and OWL for non-experts from 0% to 80%, which is more than 91.8% of the performance of experts.

This result clearly suggests that overall, our framework can be used by non-experts, who will achieve close to expert performance on RDF and OWL without any prior

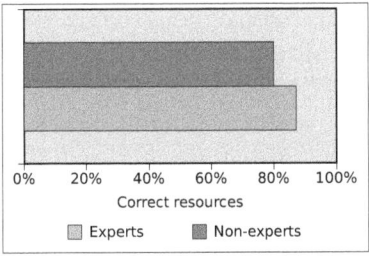

Figure 3. Experiment III: amount of correct triples

knowledge of these languages. These results are in line with the results reported in papers on SPARQL2NL.

3.2.2. Portuguese Evaluation

RDF2PT evaluation methodology is based on [25] and [22]. Its main goal was to evaluate how well RDF2PT represents the information obtained from the data. The evaluation set is divided into expert and non-expert users. Both sets were made up of native speakers of Brazilian Portuguese. Afterward, six DBpedia categories like [25] for selecting the topic of texts are chosen. The categories were Astronaut, Scientist, Building, WrittenWork, City, and University. The details of both evaluation sets are described below.

Experts - The aim was to evaluate the adequacy and fluency of the generated texts from the perspective of experts. All experts hold at least a master degree in the fields NLP or SW. In the questionnaire, two questions as [25] were used: (1) Adequacy: Does the text contain only and all the information from the data? (2) Fluency: Does the text sound fluent and natural? Then 10 experts were asked to evaluate 12 texts distributed across the aforementioned DBpedia categories, with two pieces of text from each category. All texts were generated automatically by the RDF2PT approach. The answers were on a scale from 1 to 5.

Non-experts - the goal was to evaluate the clarity and fluency of the generated texts. To this end, three types of texts were created. First, the texts were generated using a baseline of RDF2PT approach, which removes the functional words and also does not apply coreference rules. This version served as baseline as there is no other work pertaining to generating Brazilian Portuguese from RDF. Second, the texts generated using the RDF2PT approach were used. The third type of texts were created manually by three different human annotators.

In total, three versions of 18 texts (one text per resource) were selected randomly from the aforementioned DBpedia categories (total: 54 texts). These texts were distributed over three lists, such that each list contained one variant of each text, and there was an equal number of texts from the three types (Baseline, RDF2PT, Human). The experiment was run on CrowdFlower and is publicly available.[15]

The experiment was performed by 30 participants (10 per list). They were asked to rate each text considering the clarity and fluency based on two questions from [22] on a scale from 1 (Very Bad) to 5 (Very Good). The questions were: (1) Fluency: Does the text present a consistent, logical flow? (2) Clarity: Is the text easy to understand?

---

[15]https://ilk.uvt.nl/~tcastrof/semPT/evaluation/

Portuguese Results.   Figure 4 displays the average fluency and clarity of the texts among Experts. The results suggest that RDF2PT is able to capture and represent the information from data adequately. Also, the generated texts are fluent enough to be understood by humans.

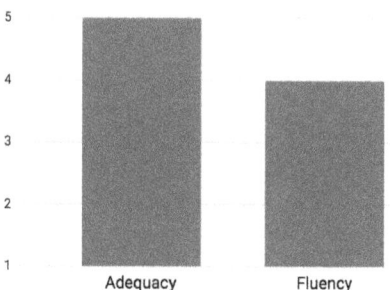

Figure 4. RDF2PT results in experts survey

Figure 5 depicts the average fluency and clarity of the texts from Non-experts, where their topics are described by *Baseline*, *RDF2PT* and *Human* approaches respectively. Inspection of this figure clearly shows that *Baseline* texts are rated lower than both the *RDF2PT* and *Human* texts, in fact, *RDF2PT* is superior to *Baseline* and close to *Human*.

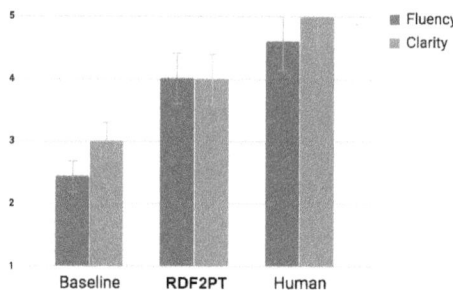

Figure 5. Results in non-experts experiment

A statistical analysis was performed to measure the significance of the difference between the types (Baseline, RDF2PT, Human). First, a Friedman test [24] was carried out which resulted in a significant difference in the fluency ($x^2 = 193.61$, $\rho <0.0001$) and clarity ($x^2 = 180.9$, $\rho <0.0001$) for the three kinds of texts. Afterward, a post-hoc analysis was conducted with Wilcoxon signed-rank test corrected for multiple comparisons using the Bonferroni method, resulting in a significance level set at $\rho <0.017$. Texts of the Baseline are hence significantly less statistically understandable (Z=525 and $\rho <0.017$.) and fluent (Z=275.5 and $\rho <0.017$.) than those generated by the RDF2PT approach. However, RDF2PT also generates texts less comprehensible (Z=1617.5 and $\rho <0.017$.) and fluent (Z=1640.0 and $\rho <0.017$.) than those generated by humans. Clearly, humans were superior to Baseline in terms of comprehensibility (Z=234.5 and $\rho <0.017$.) and fluency (Z=264.0.0 and $\rho <0.017$.), as we expected. Therefore, there is a significant difference among all models, being baseline < model < human.

Rule- and Template-based approaches are still widely used for domain-specific NLG systems due to the lack of training data for ML models. For example, the automatic generation of medical records requires specific vocabulary on diseases, more specifically, the aspects of each disease according to its code. Therefore, Rule- and Template-based approaches are still relevant and should be combined with ML models in which we give an overview in the following section.

4. Statistical and Neural-based NLG Approaches

Statistical and neural-based NLG approaches have been gaining interest, and targeting to overcome the disadvantages of rule and template-based approaches (Section 3). The problem can be seen as a three-phase paradigm by breaking the problem down to (i) content planning, (ii) content selection and (iii) surface realization. In recent years, we have seen a surge of interest in using (deep) neural networks for a wide range of NLG-related tasks following encode-decoder paradigm, as the generation of (first sentences of) Wikipedia entries [37], poetry [62], and texts from abstract meaning representations [9, 35, e.g.,]. Also applications for controlling the style of generated outputs [23, e.g.,] and the generation of image descriptions [4, e.g.,] have generated a lot of interest.

Those approaches are in need of large training datasets and archive unsatisfying performance on test datasets with unknown domains.

4.1. Improving Entities in Text Generation

Since the KG input data often consists of entities and their relations, generating references for these entities is a core task in many NLG systems [15, 36]. REG, the task responsible for generating these references, is typically presented as a two-step procedure. First, the referential form needs to be decided, asking whether a reference at a given point in the text should assume the form of, for example, a proper name ("Frida Kahlo"), a pronoun ("she") or description ("the Mexican painter"). In addition, the REG model must account for the different ways in which a particular referential form can be realized. For example, both "Frida" and "Kahlo" are name-variants that may occur in a text, and she can alternatively also be described as, say, "the famous female painter".

Most of the earlier REG approaches focus either on selecting referential form [10, 46], or on selecting referential content, typically zooming in on one specific kind of reference such as a pronoun [8, 29], definite description [14, 15] or proper name generation [11, 55, 59]. Instead, NeuralREG: an end-to-end approach proposes addressing the full REG task, which given a number of entities in a text, produces corresponding referring expressions, simultaneously selecting both form and content. NeuralREG is based on neural networks which generate referring expressions to discourse entities relying on the surrounding linguistic context, without the use of any feature extraction technique. In the next section, we show how NeuralREG models the problem of generating a referring expression to a discourse entity.

4.1.1. NeuralREG

NeuralREG aims to generate a referring expression $y = \{y_1, y_2, ..., y_T\}$ with T tokens to refer to a target entity token $x^{(wiki)}$ given a discourse pre-context $X^{(pre)} =$

$\{x_1^{(pre)}, x_2^{(pre)}, ..., x_m^{(pre)}\}$ and pos-context $X^{(pos)} = \{x_1^{(pos)}, x_2^{(pos)}, ..., x_l^{(pos)}\}$ with m and l tokens, respectively. The model is implemented as a multi-encoder, attention-decoder network with bidirectional [53] Long Short-Term Memory (LSTM) [31] sharing the same input word-embedding matrix V, as explained further.

Context encoders.   NeuralREG model starts by encoding the pre- and pos-contexts with two separate bidirectional LSTM encoders [31, 53]. These modules learn feature representations of the text surrounding the target entity $x^{(wiki)}$, which are used for the referring expression generation. The pre-context $X^{(pre)} = \{x_1^{(pre)}, x_2^{(pre)}, ..., x_m^{(pre)}\}$ is represented by forward and backward hidden-state vectors $(\overrightarrow{h}_1^{(pre)}, \cdots, \overrightarrow{h}_m^{(pre)})$ and $(\overleftarrow{h}_1^{(pre)}, \cdots, \overleftarrow{h}_m^{(pre)})$. The final annotation vector for each encoding timestep t is obtained by the concatenation of the forward and backward representations $h_t^{(pre)} = [\overrightarrow{h}_t^{(pre)}, \overleftarrow{h}_t^{(pre)}]$. The same process is repeated for the pos-context resulting in representations $(\overrightarrow{h}_1^{(pos)}, \cdots, \overrightarrow{h}_l^{(pos)})$ and $(\overleftarrow{h}_1^{(pos)}, \cdots, \overleftarrow{h}_l^{(pos)})$ and annotation vectors $h_t^{(pos)} = [\overrightarrow{h}_t^{(pos)}, \overleftarrow{h}_t^{(pos)}]$. Finally, the encoding of target entity $x^{(wiki)}$ is simply its entry in the shared input word-embedding matrix V_{wiki}.

Decoder.   The referring expression generation module is an LSTM decoder implemented in 3 different versions: `Seq2Seq`, `CAtt` and `HierAtt`. All decoders at each timestep i of the generation process take as input features their previous state s_{i-1}, the target entity-embedding V_{wiki}, the embedding of the previous word of the referring expression $V_{y_{i-1}}$ and finally the summary vector of the pre- and pos-contexts c_i. The difference between the decoder variations is the method to compute c_i.

Seq2Seq   models the context vector c_i at each timestep i concatenating the pre- and pos-context annotation vectors averaged over time:

$$\hat{h}^{(pre)} = \frac{1}{N} \sum_i^N h_i^{(pre)} \tag{3}$$

$$\hat{h}^{(pos)} = \frac{1}{N} \sum_i^N h_i^{(pos)} \tag{4}$$

$$c_i = [\hat{h}^{(pre)}, \hat{h}^{(pos)}] \tag{5}$$

CAtt   is an LSTM decoder augmented with an attention mechanism [3] over the pre- and pos-context encodings, which is used to compute c_i at each timestep. NeuralREG computes energies $e_{ij}^{(pre)}$ and $e_{ij}^{(pos)}$ between encoder states $h_i^{(pre)}$ and $h_i^{(post)}$ and decoder state s_{i-1}. These scores are normalized through the application of the softmax function to obtain the final attention probability $\alpha_{ij}^{(pre)}$ and $\alpha_{ij}^{(post)}$. Equations 6 and 7 summarize the process with k ranging over the two encoders ($k \in [pre, pos]$), being the projection matrices $W_a^{(k)}$ and $U_a^{(k)}$ and attention vectors $v_a^{(k)}$ trained parameters.

$$e_{ij}^{(k)} = v_a^{(k)T} \tanh(W_a^{(k)} s_{i-1} + U_a^{(k)} h_j^{(k)}) \tag{6}$$

$$\alpha_{ij}^{(k)} = \frac{\exp(e_{ij}^{(k)})}{\sum_{n=1}^N \exp(e_{in}^{(k)})} \tag{7}$$

In general, the attention probability $\alpha_{ij}^{(k)}$ determines the amount of contribution of the jth token of k-context in the generation of the ith token of the referring expression. In each decoding step i, a final summary-vector for each context $c_i^{(k)}$ is computed by summing the encoder states $h_j^{(k)}$ weighted by the attention probabilities $\alpha_i^{(k)}$:

$$c_i^{(k)} = \sum_{j=1}^{N} \alpha_{ij}^{(k)} h_j^{(k)} \tag{8}$$

To combine $c_i^{(pre)}$ and $c_i^{(pos)}$ into a single representation, this model simply concatenate the pre- and pos-context summary vectors $c_i = [c_i^{(pre)}, c_i^{(pos)}]$.

HierAtt implements a second attention mechanism inspired by [40] in order to generate attention weights for the pre- and pos-context summary-vectors $c_i^{(pre)}$ and $c_i^{(pos)}$ instead of concatenate them. Equations 9, 10 and 11 depict the process, being the projection matrices $W_b^{(k)}$ and $U_b^{(k)}$ as well as attention vectors $v_b^{(k)}$ trained parameters ($k \in [pre, pos]$).

$$e_i^{(k)} = v_b^{(k)T} \tanh(W_b^{(k)} s_{i-1} + U_b^{(k)} c_i^{(k)}) \tag{9}$$

$$\beta_i^{(k)} = \frac{\exp(e_i^{(k)})}{\sum_n \exp(e_i^{(n)})} \tag{10}$$

$$c_i = \sum_k \beta_i^{(k)} U_b^{(k)} c_i^{(k)} \tag{11}$$

Decoding.   Given the summary-vector c_i, the embedding of the previous referring expression token $V_{y_{i-1}}$, the previous decoder state s_{i-1} and the entity-embedding V_{wiki}, the decoders predict their next state which later is used to compute a probability distribution over the tokens in the output vocabulary for the next timestep as Equations 12 and 13 show.

$$s_i = \Phi_{dec}(s_{i-1}, [c_i, V_{y_{i-1}}, V_{wiki}]) \tag{12}$$

$$p(y_i|y_{<i}, X^{(pre)}, x^{(wiki)}, X^{(pos)}) = \tag{13}$$
$$\text{softmax}(W_c s_i + b)$$

In Equation 12, s_0 and c_0 are zero-initialized vectors. In order to find the referring expression y that maximizes the likelihood in Equation 13, a beam search with length normalization with $\alpha = 0.6$ [60] is applied:

$$lp(y) = \frac{(5 + |y|)^\alpha}{(5 + 1)^\alpha} \tag{14}$$

The decoder is trained to minimize the negative log likelihood of the next token in the target referring expression:

$$J(\theta) = -\sum_i \log p(y_i|y_{<i}, X^{(pre)}, x^{(wiki)}, X^{(pos)}) \tag{15}$$

4.1.2. Automatic evaluation

The performance of NeuralREG against two baselines are compared: *OnlyNames* and a model based on the choice of referential form method of [10], dubbed *Ferreira*. The models are created by relying on the training, development and test referring expression sets of WebNLG corpus.

Metrics   The referring expressions produced by the evaluated models are compared with the gold-standards ones using accuracy and String Edit Distance [39]. Since pronouns are highlighted as the most likely referential form to be used when a referent is salient in the discourse, as argued in the introduction it is also computed pronoun accuracy, precision, recall and F1-score in order to evaluate the performance of the models for capturing discourse salience. Finally, the original templates are lexicalized with the referring expressions produced by the models and compared them with the original texts in the corpus using accuracy and BLEU score [48] as a measure of fluency. Since NeuralREG does not handle referring expressions for constants (dates and numbers), they are copied from their source version into the template.

Post-hoc McNemar's and Wilcoxon signed ranked tests adjusted by the Bonferroni method were used to test the statistical significance of the models in terms of accuracy and string edit distance, respectively. To test the statistical significance of the BLEU scores of the models, a bootstrap resampling together with an approximate randomization method is used [13][16].

Settings   NeuralREG was implemented using Dynet [43]. Source and target word embeddings were 300D each and trained jointly with the model, whereas hidden units were 512D for each direction, totaling 1024D in the bidirectional layers. All non-recurrent matrices were initialized following the method of [28]. Models were trained using stochastic gradient descent with Adadelta [61] and mini-batches of size 40. Each model ran for 60 epochs, applying early stopping for model selection based on accuracy on the development set with patience of 20 epochs. For each decoding version (Seq2Seq, CAtt and HierAtt), the best combination of drop-out probability was found 0.2 or 0.3 in both the encoding and decoding layers, using beam search with a size of 1 or 5 with predictions up to 30 tokens or until 2 ending tokens were predicted (*EOS*). The results described in the next section were obtained on the test set by the NeuralREG version with the highest accuracy on the development set over the epochs.

Results.   Table 3 summarizes the results for all models on all metrics on the test set and Table 4 depicts a text example lexicalized by each model. The first thing to note in the results of the first table is that the baselines in the top two rows performed quite strong on this task, generating more than half of the referring expressions exactly as in the gold-standard. The method based on [10] performed statistically better than *OnlyNames* on all metrics due to its capability, albeit to a limited extent, to predict pronominal references (which *OnlyNames* obviously cannot).

The results are reported on the test set for NeuralREG+Seq2Seq and Neural-REG+CAtt using dropout probability 0.3 and beam size 5, and NeuralREG+HierAtt with dropout probability of 0.3 and beam size of 1 selected based on the highest accuracy on the development set. Importantly, the three NeuralREG variant models statistically

---

[16]https://github.com/jhclark/multeval

	All References		Pronouns				Text	
	Acc.	SED	Acc.	Prec.	Rec.	F-Score	Acc.	BLEU
OnlyNames	0.53^D	4.05^D	-	-	-	-	0.15^D	69.03^D
Ferreira	0.61^C	3.18^C	0.43^B	0.57	0.54	0.55	0.19^C	72.78^C
NeuralREG+Seq2Seq	$0.74^{A,B}$	$2.32^{A,B}$	0.75^A	0.77	0.78	0.78	0.28^B	$79.27^{A,B}$
NeuralREG+CAtt	0.74^A	2.25^A	0.75^A	0.73	0.78	0.75	0.30^A	79.39^A
NeuralREG+HierAtt	0.73^B	2.36^B	0.73^A	0.74	0.77	0.75	$0.28^{A,B}$	79.01^B

Table 3. (1) Accuracy (Acc.) and String Edit Distance (SED) results in the prediction of all referring expressions; (2) Accuracy (Acc.), Precision (Prec.), Recall (Rec.) and F-Score results in the prediction of pronominal forms; and (3) Accuracy (Acc.) and BLEU score results of the texts with the generated referring expressions. Rankings were determined by statistical significance.

outperformed the two baseline systems. They achieved BLEU scores, text and referential accuracies as well as string edit distances in the range of 79.01-79.39, 28%-30%, 73%-74% and 2.25-2.36, respectively. This means that NeuralREG predicted 3 out of 4 references completely correct, whereas the incorrect ones needed an average of 2 post-edition operations in character level to be equal to the gold-standard. When considering the texts lexicalized with the referring expressions produced by NeuralREG, at least 28% of them are similar to the original texts. Especially noteworthy was the score on pronoun accuracy, indicating that the model was well capable of predicting when to generate a pronominal reference in our dataset.

The results for the different decoding methods for NeuralREG were similar, with the NeuralREG+CAtt performing slightly better in terms of the BLEU score, text accuracy and String Edit Distance. The more complex NeuralREG+HierAtt yielded the lowest results, even though the differences with the other two models were small and not even statistically significant in many of the cases.

4.1.3. Human Evaluation

Complementary to the automatic evaluation, we also compared the performance of NeuralREG against two aforementioned baselines. An evaluation with human judges is performed, comparing the quality judgments of the original texts to the versions generated by our various models. The experiment had a latin-square design, distributing the 144 trials over 6 different lists such that each participant rated 24 trials, one for each of the 24 corpus instances, making sure that participants saw equal numbers of triple set sizes and generated versions. Once introduced to a trial, the participants were asked to rate the fluency ("does the text flow in a natural, easy to read manner?"), grammaticality ("is the text grammatical (no spelling or grammatical errors)?") and clarity ("does the text clearly express the data?") of each target text on a 7-Likert scale, focussing on the highlighted referring expressions. The experiment is available on the website of the author.[17] 60 participants were recruited, 10 per list, via Mechanical Turk. Their average age was 36 years and 27 of them were females. The majority declared themselves native speakers of English (44), while 14 and 2 self-reported as fluent or having a basic proficiency, respectively.

---

[17]https://ilk.uvt.nl/~tcastrof/acl2018/evaluation/

Model	Text
OnlyNames	**alan shepard** was born in **new hampshire** on **1923-11-18** . before **alan shepard** death in **california** **alan shepard** had been awarded **distinguished service medal (united states navy)** an award higher than **department of commerce gold medal** .
Ferreira	**alan shepard** was born in **new hampshire** on **1923-11-18** . before **alan shepard** death in **california** **him** had been awarded **distinguished service medal** an award higher than **department of commerce gold medal** .
Seq2Seq	**alan shepard** was born in **new hampshire** on **1923-11-18** . before **his** death in **california** **him** had been awarded **the distinguished service medal by the united states navy** an award higher than **the department of commerce gold medal** .
CAtt	**alan shepard** was born in **new hampshire** on **1923-11-18** . before **his** death in **california** **he** had been awarded **the distinguished service medal by the us navy** an award higher than **the department of commerce gold medal** .
HierAtt	**alan shephard** was born in **new hampshire** on **1923-11-18** . before **his** death in **california** **he** had been awarded **the distinguished service medal** an award higher than **the department of commerce gold medal** .
Original	**alan shepard** was born in **new hampshire** on **18 November 1923** . before **his** death in **california** **he** had been awarded **the distinguished service medal by the us navy** an award higher than **the department of commerce gold medal** .

Table 4. Example of text with references lexicalized by each model.

	Fluency	Grammar	Clarity
OnlyNames	4.74^C	4.68^B	4.90^B
Ferreira	4.74^C	4.58^B	4.93^B
NeuralREG+Seq2Seq	$4.95^{B,C}$	$4.82^{A,B}$	4.97^B
NeuralREG+CAtt	$5.23^{A,B}$	$4.95^{A,B}$	$5.26^{A,B}$
NeuralREG+HierAtt	$5.07^{B,C}$	$4.90^{A,B}$	$5.13^{A,B}$
Original	5.41^A	5.17^A	5.42^A

Table 5. Fluency, Grammaticality and Clarity results obtained in the human evaluation. Rankings were determined by statistical significance.

Results.   Table 5 summarizes the results. Inspection of this table reveals a clear pattern: all three neural models scored higher than the baselines on all metrics, with especially NeuralREG+CAtt approaching the ratings for the original sentences, although – again – differences between the neural models were small. Concerning the size of the triple sets, we did not find any clear pattern. To test the statistical significance of the pairwise comparisons, we used the Wilcoxon signed-rank test corrected for multiple comparisons using the Bonferroni method. Different from the automatic evaluation, the results of both baselines were not statistically significant for the three metrics. In comparison with the neural models, NeuralREG+CAtt significantly outperformed the baselines in terms of fluency, whereas the other comparisons between baselines and neural models were not statistically significant. The results for the 3 different decoding methods of NeuralREG also did not reveal a significant difference. Finally, the original texts were rated significantly higher than both baselines in terms of the three metrics, also than NeuralREG+Seq2Seq and NeuralREG+`HierAtt` in terms of fluency, and than NeuralREG+`Seq2Seq` in terms of clarity.

5. Conclusion

Our overall evaluation results, which comprising rule-based and statistical approaches, suggest that the verbalization of the considered SW languages is a non-trivial task that can be approached by using a bottom-up approach. As expected, the verbalization of short expressions leads to sentences that read as created by humans. However, due to the complexity of the semantics that can be expressed by those languages at hand, long expressions can sound mildly artificial. Our results suggest that although the generated text can sound artificial, it is still clear enough to enable non-expert users to achieve results that are comparable to those achieved by experts. Hence, our first conclusion is that the approaches, as mentioned earlier, NeuralREG and LD2NL, clearly serve their purpose. Still, potential improvements can be derived from the results achieved during the experiments. In particular, we will consider the used of attention-based encoder-decoder networks to improve the fluency of complex sentences. Moreover, while the OWL verbalization was close to NL, the RDF was less natural, but still sufficient to convey the meaning expressed by the corresponding set of triples.

Both frameworks for verbalizing SW languages clearly support the explanation of AI models. Especially AI approaches that rely on RDF, OWL, and SPARQL (for automatically generating queries). Generating explanations from KGs is in its infancy, and this chapter gives an overview of how to develop these systems to make ML models understandable for lay users. We envision the extensions of RDF-to-Text to verbalize the languages SWRL [33] and SHACL [34].

References

[1] Ion Androutsopoulos, Gerasimos Lampouras, and Dimitrios Galanis. Generating natural language descriptions from OWL ontologies: The natural owl system. *J. Artif. Int. Res.*, 48(1):671–715, October 2013.

[2] Sören Auer, Christian Bizer, Georgi Kobilarov, Jens Lehmann, Richard Cyganiak, and Zachary Ives. Dbpedia: A nucleus for a web of open data. *The semantic web*, pages 722–735, 2007.

[3] Dzmitry Bahdanau, Kyunghyun Cho, and Yoshua Bengio. Neural machine translation by jointly learning to align and translate. *arXiv preprint arXiv:1409.0473*, 2014.

[4] Raffaella Bernardi, Ruket Cakici, Desmond Elliott, Aykut Erdem, Erkut Erdem, Nazli Ikizler-Cinbis, Frank Keller, Adrian Muscat, and Barbara Plank. Automatic Description Generation from Images: A Survey of Models, Datasets, and Evaluation Measures. *Journal of Artificial Intelligence Research*, 55:409–442, 2016.

[5] Or Biran and Kathleen McKeown. Discourse planning with an n-gram model of relations. In *EMNLP*, pages 1973–1977, 2015.

[6] Nadjet Bouayad-Agha, Gerard Casamayor, and Leo Wanner. Natural language generation in the context of the semantic web. *Semantic Web*, 5(6):493–513, 2014.

[7] Lorenz Bühmann, Jens Lehmann, and Patrick Westphal. Dl-learner—a framework for inductive learning on the semantic web. *Journal of Web Semantics*, 39:15–24, 2016.

[8] Charles B. Callaway and James C. Lester. Pronominalization in generated discourse and dialogue. In *Proceedings of the 40th Annual Meeting on Association for Computational Linguistics*, ACL '02, pages 88–95, Stroudsburg, PA, USA, 2002. Association for Computational Linguistics.

[9] Thiago Castro Ferreira, Iacer Calixto, Sander Wubben, and Emiel Krahmer. Linguistic realisation as machine translation: Comparing different mt models for amr-to-text generation. pages 1–10. Association for Computational Linguistics, 2017.

[10] Thiago Castro Ferreira, Emiel Krahmer, and Sander Wubben. Towards more variation in text generation: Developing and evaluating variation models for choice of referential form. In *Proceedings of the 54th Annual Meeting of the Association for Computational Linguistics (Volume 1: Long Papers)*, pages 568–577. Association for Computational Linguistics, 2016.

[11] Thiago Castro Ferreira, Emiel Krahmer, and Sander Wubben. Generating flexible proper name references in text: Data, models and evaluation. In *Proceedings of the 15th Conference of the European Chapter of the Association for Computational Linguistics: Volume 1, Long Papers*, pages 655–664. Association for Computational Linguistics, 2017.

[12] Philipp Cimiano, Janna Lüker, David Nagel, and Christina Unger. Exploiting ontology lexica for generating natural language texts from rdf data. In *Proceedings of the 14th European Workshop on Natural Language Generation*, pages 10–19, Sofia, Bulgaria, August 2013. ACL.

[13] Jonathan H. Clark, Chris Dyer, Alon Lavie, and Noah A. Smith. Better Hypothesis Testing for Statistical Machine Translation: Controlling for Optimizer Instability. In *Proceedings of the 49th Annual Meeting of the Association for Computational Linguistics: Human Language Technologies: Short Papers - Volume 2*, ACL'11, pages 176–181, Portland, Oregon, 2011.

[14] Robert Dale and Nicholas Haddock. Generating referring expressions involving relations. In *Proceedings of the fifth conference on European chapter of the Association for Computational Linguistics*, EACL '91, pages 161–166, Stroudsburg, PA, USA, 1991. Association for Computational Linguistics.

[15] Robert Dale and Ehud Reiter. Computational interpretations of the gricean maxims in the generation of referring expressions. *Cognitive science*, 19(2):233–263, 1995.

[16] H. Dalianis and E.H. Hovy. Aggregation in natural language generation. In G. Adorni and M. Zock, editors, *Trends in natural language generation: an artificial intelligence perspective*, volume 1036 of *Lecture Notes in Artificial Intelligence*, pages 88–105. Springer, 1996.

[17] Rodrigo De Oliveira and Somayajulu Sripada. Adapting simplenlg for brazilian portuguese realisation. In *INLG*, pages 93–94, 2014.

[18] Diego Moussallem, Thiago Castro Ferreira, Marcos Zampieri, Maria Claudia Cavalcanti, Geraldo Xexéo, Mariana Neves, and Axel-Cyrille Ngonga Ngomo. RDF2PT: Generating Brazilian Portuguese Texts from RDF Data. In *The 11th edition of the Language Resources and Evaluation Conference, 7-12 May 2018, Miyazaki (Japan)*, 2018.

[19] Daniel Duma and Ewan Klein. Generating natural language from linked data: Unsupervised template extraction. In *IWCS*, pages 83–94, 2013.

[20] Basil Ell and Andreas Harth. A language-independent method for the extraction of rdf verbalization templates. In *INLG*, pages 26–34, 2014.

[21] Basil Ell, Denny Vrandecic, and Elena Paslaru Bontas Simperl. Labels in the web of data. In *Proceedings of ISWC*, volume 7031, pages 162–176. Springer, 2011.

[22] Thiago Castro Ferreira, Emiel Krahmer, and Sander Wubben. Towards more variation in text generation: Developing and evaluating variation models for choice of referential form. In *ACL (1)*, 2016.

[23] J. Ficler and Y. Goldberg. Controlling Linguistic Style Aspects in Neural Language Generation. *ArXiv e-prints*, July 2017.

[24] Milton Friedman. The use of ranks to avoid the assumption of normality implicit in the analysis of variance. *Journal of the american statistical association*, 32(200):675–701, 1937.

[25] Claire Gardent, Anastasia Shimorina, Shashi Narayan, and Laura Perez-Beltrachini. Creating training corpora for nlg micro-planners. In *Proceedings of the 55th Annual Meeting of the Association for Computational Linguistics (Volume 1: Long Papers)*, pages 179–188. Association for Computational Linguistics, 2017.

[26] Claire Gardent, Anastasia Shimorina, Shashi Narayan, and Laura Perez-Beltrachini. The webnlg challenge: Generating text from rdf data. pages 124–133. Association for Computational Linguistics, 2017.

[27] Albert Gatt and Emiel Krahmer. Survey of the state of the art in natural language generation: Core tasks, applications and evaluation. *arXiv preprint arXiv:1703.09902*, 2017.

[28] Xavier Glorot and Yoshua Bengio. Understanding the difficulty of training deep feedforward neural networks. In Yee Whye Teh and Mike Titterington, editors, *Proceedings of the Thirteenth International Conference on Artificial Intelligence and Statistics*, volume 9 of *Proceedings of Machine Learning Research*, pages 249–256, Chia Laguna Resort, Sardinia, Italy, 13–15 May 2010. PMLR.

[29] Renate Henschel, Hua Cheng, and Massimo Poesio. Pronominalization revisited. In *Proceedings of the 18th conference on Computational linguistics-Volume 1*, pages 306–312. Association for Computational Linguistics, 2000.

[30] Daniel Hewlett, Aditya Kalyanpur, Vladimir Kolovski, and Christian Halaschek-Wiener. Effective nl paraphrasing of ontologies on the semantic web. In *Workshop on end-user semantic web interaction, 4th int. semantic web conference, galway, ireland*, 2005.

[31] Sepp Hochreiter and Jürgen Schmidhuber. Long short-term memory. *Neural computation*, 9(8):1735–1780, 1997.

[32] Matthew Horridge, Nick Drummond, John Goodwin, Alan L Rector, Robert Stevens, and Hai Wang. The Manchester OWL syntax. In *OWLed*, volume 216, 2006.

[33] Ian Horrocks, Peter F. Patel-Schneider, Harold Boley, Said Tabet, Benjamin Grosofand, and Mike Dean. SWRL: A semantic web rule language combining OWL and RuleML. W3C Member Submission, May 2004.

[34] Holger Knublauch and Dimitris Kontokostas. Shapes constraint language (shacl). *W3C Candidate Recommendation*, 11(8), 2017.

[35] I. Konstas, S. Iyer, M. Yatskar, Y. Choi, and L. Zettlemoyer. Neural AMR: Sequence-to-Sequence Models for Parsing and Generation. *ArXiv e-prints*, April 2017.

[36] Emiel Krahmer and Kees van Deemter. Computational generation of referring expressions: A survey. *Computational Linguistics*, 38(1):173–218, 2012.

[37] Rémi Lebret, David Grangier, and Michael Auli. Neural text generation from structured data with application to the biography domain. In *Proceedings of the 2016 Conference on Empirical Methods in Natural Language Processing*, pages 1203–1213. Association for Computational Linguistics, 2016.

[38] Jens Lehmann, Robert Isele, Max Jakob, Anja Jentzsch, Dimitris Kontokostas, Pablo N Mendes, Sebastian Hellmann, Mohamed Morsey, Patrick Van Kleef, Sören Auer, et al. Dbpedia–a large-scale, multilingual knowledge base extracted from wikipedia. *Semantic Web*, 6(2):167–195, 2015.

[39] V. I. Levenshtein. Binary Codes Capable of Correcting Deletions, Insertions and Reversals. *Soviet Physics Doklady*, 10:707, February 1966.

[40] Jindřich Libovický and Jindřich Helcl. Attention strategies for multi-source sequence-to-sequence learning. *arXiv preprint arXiv:1704.06567*, 2017.

[41] Rania Mohammed, Laura Perez-Beltrachini, and Claire Gardent. Category-driven content selection. In *Proceedings of the 9th International Natural Language Generation conference*, pages 94–98, 2016.

[42] Preksha Nema, Shreyas Shetty, Parag Jain, Anirban Laha, Karthik Sankaranarayanan, and Mitesh M. Khapra. Generating descriptions from structured data using a bifocal attention mechanism and gated orthogonalization. In *Proceedings of the 2018 Conference of the North American Chapter of the Association for Computational Linguistics: Human Language Technologies, Volume 1 (Long Papers)*, pages 1539–1550, New Orleans, Louisiana, June 2018. Association for Computational Linguistics.

[43] G. Neubig, C. Dyer, Y. Goldberg, A. Matthews, W. Ammar, A. Anastasopoulos, M. Ballesteros, D. Chiang, D. Clothiaux, T. Cohn, K. Duh, M. Faruqui, C. Gan, D. Garrette, Y. Ji, L. Kong, A. Kuncoro, G. Kumar, C. Malaviya, P. Michel, Y. Oda, M. Richardson, N. Saphra, S. Swayamdipta, and P. Yin. DyNet: The Dynamic Neural Network Toolkit. *ArXiv e-prints*, January 2017.

[44] Axel-Cyrille Ngonga Ngomo, Lorenz Bühmann, Christina Unger, Jens Lehmann, and Daniel Gerber. Sorry, i don't speak sparql: translating sparql queries into natural language. In *Proceedings of the 22nd international conference on World Wide Web*, pages 977–988. ACM, 2013.

[45] Axel-Cyrille Ngonga Ngomo, Diego Moussallem, and Lorenz Bühman. A Holistic Natural Language Generation Framework for the Semantic Web. In *Proceedings of the International Conference Recent Advances in Natural Language Processing*, page 8. ACL (Association for Computational Linguistics), 2019.

[46] Naho Orita, Eliana Vornov, Naomi Feldman, and Hal Daumé III. Why discourse affects speakers' choice of referring expressions. In *Proceedings of the 53rd Annual Meeting of the Association for Computational Linguistics and the 7th International Joint Conference on Natural Language Processing (Volume 1: Long Papers)*, pages 1639–1649. Association for Computational Linguistics, 2015.

[47] W3C OWL Working Group. *OWL 2 Web Ontology Language: Document Overview*. W3C Recommendation, 2009.

[48] Kishore Papineni, Salim Roukos, Todd Ward, and Wei-Jing Zhu. Bleu: a method for automatic evaluation of machine translation. In *Proceedings of 40th Annual Meeting of the Association for Computational Linguistics*, pages 311–318, Philadelphia, Pennsylvania, USA, July 2002. Association for Computational Linguistics.

[49] Laura Perez-Beltrachini, Rania Sayed, and Claire Gardent. Building rdf content for data-to-text generation. In *COLING*, pages 1493–1502, 2016.

[50] Richard Power and Allan Third. Expressing OWL Axioms by English Sentences: Dubious in Theory, Feasible in Practice. In *Proceedings of the 23rd International Conference on Computational Linguistics: Posters*, pages 1006–1013, Stroudsburg, PA, USA, 2010. ACL.

[51] W3C RDF Working Group. *RDF 1.1 Concepts and Abstract Syntax*. W3C Recommendation, 2014.

[52] Ehud Reiter and Robert Dale. *Building natural language generation systems*. Cambridge University Press, New York, NY, USA, 2000.

[53] Mike Schuster and Kuldip K Paliwal. Bidirectional recurrent neural networks. *IEEE Transactions on Signal Processing*, 45(11):2673–2681, 1997.

[54] Rolf Schwitter, Marc Tilbrook, et al. Controlled natural language meets the semantic web. In *Proceedings of the Australasian Language Technology Workshop*, volume 2, pages 55–62, 2004.

[55] Advaith Siddharthan, Ani Nenkova, and Kathleen McKeown. Information status distinctions and referring expressions: An empirical study of references to people in news summaries. *Computational Linguistics*, 37(4):811–842, 2011.

[56] Amin Sleimi and Claire Gardent. Generating paraphrases from dbpedia using deep learning. *WebNLG 2016*, page 54, 2016.

[57] Kamenka Staykova. Natural language generation and semantic technologies. *Cybernetics and Information Technologies*, 14(2):3–23, 2014.

[58] Xiantang Sun and Chris Mellish. Domain independent sentence generation from rdf representations for the semantic web. In *Combined Workshop on Language-Enabled Educational Technology and Development and Evaluation of Robust Spoken Dialogue Systems, European Conference on AI, Riva del Garda, Italy*, 2006.

[59] Kees van Deemter. Designing algorithms for referring with proper names. pages 31–35. Association for Computational Linguistics, 2016.

[60] Yonghui Wu, Mike Schuster, Zhifeng Chen, Quoc V. Le, Mohammad Norouzi, Wolfgang Macherey, Maxim Krikun, Yuan Cao, Qin Gao, Klaus Macherey, Jeff Klingner, Apurva Shah, Melvin Johnson, Xiaobing Liu, Łukasz Kaiser, Stephan Gouws, Yoshikiyo Kato, Taku Kudo, Hideto Kazawa, Keith Stevens, George Kurian, Nishant Patil, Wei Wang, Cliff Young, Jason Smith, Jason Riesa, Alex Rudnick, Oriol Vinyals, Greg Corrado, Macduff Hughes, and Jeffrey Dean. Google's neural machine translation system: Bridging the gap between human and machine translation. *CoRR*, abs/1609.08144, 2016.

[61] Matthew D. Zeiler. ADADELTA: An Adaptive Learning Rate Method. *CoRR*, abs/1212.5701, 2012.

[62] Xingxing Zhang and Mirella Lapata. Chinese poetry generation with recurrent neural networks. In *Proceedings of the 2014 Conference on Empirical Methods in Natural Language Processing (EMNLP)*, pages 670–680. Association for Computational Linguistics, 2014.

Part 3

Challenges for Knowledge-Based eXplainable Systems

Knowledge Graphs for eXplainable Artificial Intelligence: Foundations, Applications and Challenges   245
I. Tiddi et al. (Eds.)
IOS Press, 2020
© 2020 Akademische Verlagsgesellschaft AKA GmbH, Berlin. All rights reserved.
doi:10.3233/SSW200022

Directions for Explainable Knowledge-Enabled Systems

Shruthi CHARI [a], Daniel M. GRUEN [b], Oshani SENEVIRATNE [a], and
Deborah L. MCGUINNESS [a]

[a] *Rensselaer Polytechnic Institute, Troy, NY, USA*
[b] *IBM Research, Cambridge, MA, USA*

Abstract. Interest in the field of Explainable Artificial Intelligence has been growing for decades, and has accelerated recently. As Artificial Intelligence models have
become more complex, and often more opaque, with the incorporation of complex
machine learning techniques, explainability has become more critical. Recently,
researchers have been investigating and tackling explainability with a user-centric
focus, looking for explanations to consider trustworthiness, comprehensibility, explicit provenance, and context-awareness. In this chapter, we leverage our survey
of explanation literature in Artificial Intelligence and closely related fields and use
these past efforts to generate a set of explanation types that we feel reflect the expanded needs of explanation for today's artificial intelligence applications. We define each type and provide an example question that would motivate the need for
this style of explanation. We believe this set of explanation types will help future
system designers in their generation and prioritization of requirements and further
help generate explanations that are better aligned to users' and situational needs.

Keywords. KG4XAI, Knowledge Graphs, eXplainable AI, Explainable Knowledge-
Enabled Systems, Current Focus, Future Game-Changers

1. Introduction

The field of Artificial Intelligence (AI) has evolved from solely symbolic- and logic-
based expert systems to hybrid systems that employ both statistical and logical reasoning techniques. This shift and a greater incorporation of AI capabilities in systems
across industries and consumer applications, including those that have significant, even
life-or-death, implications have led to an increased demand for explainability. Advances
in explainable AI have been tightly coupled with the development of AI approaches,
such as the categories we covered in our earlier chapter, "Foundations of Explainable
Knowledge-enabled Systems," spanning expert systems, semantic web approaches, cognitive assistants, and machine learning methods. We note that these approaches tackle
specific aspects of explainability. For example, explanations generated by expert systems
and semantic applications primarily served the purposes for providing reasoning traces,
provenance, and justifications. Those provided by cognitive assistants were capable of
adapting their form to suit the users' needs, and, in the ML and expert systems domains,
explanations provided an intuition for the model's functioning.

However, with the increased complexity of AI models, researchers have realized
that the mechanistic explanation of the system's working alone might be insufficient

for the end-users' needs. In a recent essay, Paez [43] reasons that explanations need to convey a "pragmatic and naturalistic account of understanding in AI." This idea of greater comprehensibility and user-focus is supported by several recent survey papers [7,17, 32] and position statements [14,38]. In our earlier chapter, "Foundations of Explainable Knowledge-enabled Systems", we presented definitions that we synthesized from the literature for explanations and explainable knowledge-enabled systems.

1.1. Definitions

1.1.1. Explanation

"An account of the system, its workings, the *implicit and explicit* knowledge it uses to arrive at conclusions in general and the specific decision at hand, that is *sensitive* to the end-user's *understanding, context, and current needs.*"

1.1.2. Explainable Knowledge-enabled systems

"AI systems that include a representation of the domain knowledge in the field of application, have mechanisms to incorporate the *users' context*, are *interpretable*, and host *explanation facilities* that generate *user-comprehensible, context-aware, and provenance-enabled* explanations of the mechanistic functioning of the AI system and the knowledge used."

1.2. Overview

In this chapter, we identify directions for research that could be instrumental in contributing to improving user aspects of explainable AI, providing explanations conducive "to the end user's *understanding, context, and current needs,*" as previously described. Additionally, we survey different explanation types that possess components, and exhibit presentation styles, tailored and variably suited for different contexts and situations. In Section 2, we present a detailed overview of the explanation types that we have identified from the literature while focusing on their strengths and suitability to different AI scenarios. Further, in Section 3, we provide descriptions of directions for research that we believe will help generate various aspects of explainability, such as those related to causality and trustworthiness. In the same section, we also review methods that will help us better understand the explainability space, such as semantic representations and neuro-symbolic techniques. Ultimately, through our reviews in this chapter, we would like to highlight the idea that explanations are diverse, but always contain knowledge (model-specific, background, scientific, everyday, etc.) that can be variably presented in different presentation styles, and with different granularities, to suit the users' contexts, situations, preferences, and needs.

2. Hybrid Explanations

As we discussed, explanations have evolved through shifts in the computing era. As we suggested earlier in Section 1 and from our review of foundational approaches in our earlier chapter, we find that the generation of explanations have primarily been driven by capabilities of AI systems, and not by the demands of end-users. We identify that this is an issue, as consumers of AI systems, users reserve the right to understand and utilize results presented by the system they are using. Researchers [7,14,38] have noted that the users might not benefit from a mechanistic explanation of the system, and providing interpretable results alone is not sufficient for users to act on the conclusions produced by AI systems. Mittelstadt et al. [38] and Biran and Cotton [7] suggest that we need to look beyond the explanation types being generated by current AI systems and borrow from adjacent explanation sciences, such as social sciences and psychology.

In our quest to develop explainable health assistants, as part of the Health Empowerment by Analytics, Learning, and Semantics (HEALS) project,[1] we conducted a literature review to catalog the different explanation types. In Table 1, we present our definitions of the nine explanation types that we researched in the form of a taxonomy. While our cataloging will eventually help us build a semantic understanding of the explanation space, it also helps us understand that each explanation type tackles different aspects of explainability, and we need to design hybrid explanations to meet the diverse needs of users, contexts, and situations.

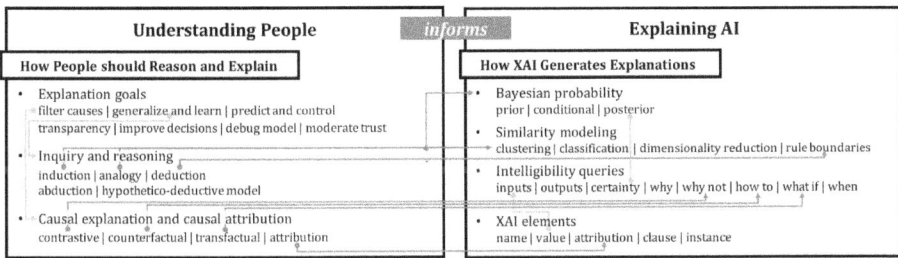

Figure 1. A partial conceptual framework mapping explanation types capable of being generated by explainable AI methods to the reasoning employed by users [Image taken from Lim et al. [31] and Wang et al. [57]]. For the full framework see Wang et al. [57].

Similarly, a recent paper by Lim et al. [31] investigates the link between user reasoning strategies and the reasoning strategies used by AI methods. This paper begins to connect how people reason and how AI methods can generate components that would satisfy the "explanation goals"[2] (e.g., improving decision-making, transparency, model debugging, etc.) that users desire. From an implementation standpoint, the authors build on an earlier taxonomy of intelligibility types proposed by Lim and Dey [30], and link intelligibility queries, including 'Inputs,' 'Outputs,' 'Certainty,' 'Why,' 'Why Not,' 'What If,' and 'When,' to the associated explanation type being explored/generated by explainable AI models. Such a conceptual framework, as seen in Figure 1, is interesting, since they are beginning to think of the implementation of AI explainability from a user perspective. Additionally, the questions addressed by our identified explanation types, presented in Table 1, are aligned with the intelligibility queries proposed in this paper, reiterating that each explanation type tackles different aspects of explainability. Efforts, such as this paper, that explore the diverse, explainable AI landscape, in conjunction with an

---

[1]HEALS press release: `https://science.rpi.edu/biology/news/ibm-and-rensselaer-team-research-chronic-diseases-cognitive-computing`

[2]The full list of explanation goals adapted from Nunes and Jannach [42] will be presented in Section 3.3

understanding of the different explanation types, can help us generate explanations more suited to the users' needs.

In the rest of this section, we will present a review of the survey and position papers that we used as guides to present the explanation types.

2.1. Findings from Review and Position papers

A recent position paper [38] presents links to explanations from the social sciences domain to the explanation needs in the explainable AI community. While this paper posits that their ideas are focused on how to better communicate the explanations of interpretability of black-box, deep learning models, the principles discussed apply to a broader class of AI models. The authors suggest that *everyday* and *scientific* explanations used in domains such as psychology and social sciences, are also applicable to explaining AI models because they are able to present abstract information at different granularities. Further, they draw a parallel between *scientific* explanations and *trace-based* explanations, in that both of these might not be understandable to all users. Hence, they present a case that, when explanations are delivered to humans who are selective and social in their processes, the explanations need to be *contrastive* and *communicative*. They conclude that the explainable AI community needs to provide explanations that are directly targeted and tailored to the needs of the users. We note that, in our taxonomy of explanation types (Table 1), we don't account for implementation challenges, and we include certain explanations, such as *everyday* explanations, that require common-sense knowledge that may be difficult to gather and operationalize.

Furthermore, another survey paper [7] motivates the need to leverage explanation science literature from related fields, such as constraint programming, forensic sciences, context-aware systems, case-based reasoning, causal discovery, etc. The authors present a brief description of the usage of explanations in these domains, and use these related fields to motivate their plausible adoption in the explanation of the interpretability of ML models. In addition, the DARPA XAI report [19] also lists desirable explanation types, focusing on their form of delivery (explanation modalities), including visualizations, analytical statements, alternate choices, and case-based presentations.

2.2. Summary

Research in different explanation types is influenced by research from interdisciplinary fields, spanning social sciences and philosophy. While generating our catalog of definitions for different explanation types (Table 1), we identified that certain explanation types, such as *contrastive, counterfactual, case-based, and trace-based* explanations, are well-documented in the computer science literature. However, for some other explanation types, such as *statistical, everyday, and scientific* explanations, we had to refer to literature from other domains, such as philosophy. We believe that explanations presented to users include components from different explanation types. For example, users require causal justifications to trust AI systems [13], statistical evidence for future exploration, scientific summaries to comprehend the system [12], and everyday explanations conducive to their understanding [38]. Hence, we believe that there is a need to expand the explanation types our AI systems can currently support and build explanation facilities to generate hybrid and user-centric explanations. In Section 3, we present technologies that,

Table 1. A catalog of different explanation types (ordered alphabetically), their definitions, and a motivating explanation question that a healthcare provider may ask.

Explanation Type	Example Provider Question and Literature-Derived Definition
Case-based	**"To what other situations has this recommendation been applied?"** Case-based explanations contain results that "are based on actual prior cases that can be presented to the user to provide compelling support for the system's conclusions" [9]. Borrowing from [29] and [1], we opine that an AI system generating case-based explanations needs to remember and adapt explanations of similar prior cases [29], or needs to reason "from experiences (old cases) in an effort to solve problems, critique solutions and explain anomalous situations" [1]. Case-based explanations can involve analogical reasoning, relying on similarities between features of the case and of the current situation.
Contextual	**"What broader information about the current situation prompted you to suggest this recommendation now?"** Contextual explanations are those that refer to information about items other than the explicit inputs and output, such as information about the user, situation, and broader environment that affected the computation. Providing such information requires that a system be "context-aware," and can include information about a "user's tasks, significant user attributes, organizational environment, and technical and physical environments" [16].
Contrastive	**"Why administer this new drug over the one I would typically prescribe?"** As described by [55] and [37], contrastive explanations define an output of interest and present contrasts between the fact (the event that did occur), the given output, and the foil (the event that did not occur), the output of interest.
Counterfactual	**"What if the patient had a high risk for cardiovascular disease? Would you still recommend the same treatment plan?"** Counterfactual explanations address the question of what results would have been obtained with a different set of inputs than those used. Paraphrasing [59], counterfactual explanations are causal in nature and are generated by tracing patterns of a special kind of causal dependence.
Everyday	**"Why are gloves recommended when dealing with high-risk patients?"** Everyday explanations are accounts of the real world that appeal to the user based on their general understanding and knowledge [36] of how the world works, and that help them understand why particular facts (events, properties, decisions, etc.) occurred [37]. There is evidence that users prefer everyday explanations that are causal in nature [60].
Scientific	**"What is the biological basis for this recommendation?"** Scientific explanations reference the results of rigorous scientific methods, such as observations and measurements, to explain something we see in the natural world [40]. Adapting from [37], we add that scientific explanations usually contain different components of interacting knowledge, including theories or mechanisms such as physiological ones, which are sets of principles that form building blocks for models; models which represent the relationships between entities and their attributes informed by taxonomies and other classification schemes; and data (e.g. measurements, observations).
Simulation-based	**"What would happen if this recommendation is followed?"** Simulation-based explanations are those based on an imagined or implemented imitation of a system or process and the results that emerge from similar inputs. As simulations can often be run numerous times (e.g. Monte Carlo simulations), and the mechanisms in the simulation can often be observed and traced directly, simulation-based explanations can have elements of statistical and trace-based explanations. Heal suggests that these explanations [21] contain facts that humans would use to determine an outcome in a specified case, and these explanations are intended to "replace and amplify real experiences with guided ones, often "immersive" in nature, that evoke or replicate substantial aspects of the real world in a fully interactive fashion" [28].
Statistical	**"What percentage of similar patients who received this treatment recovered?"** Statistical explanations present an account of the outcome based on data about the occurrence of events under specified (e.g., experimental) conditions. Statistical explanations refer to numerical evidence on the likelihood of factors or processes influencing the result. [22] add that a particularly high probability allows the outcome to be expected with practical certainty in any one case where the specified conditions occur.
Trace-based	**"What steps were taken by the system to generate this recommendation?"** Trace-based explanations describe the underlying sequence of steps used by the system to arrive at a specific result. They reveal "the line of reasoning per case" [30], and "addresses the question of why and how the application did something" [30].

in our opinion, will be instrumental in contributing to aspects of the various explanation components required to generate the explanation types shown in Table 1.

3. Directions

Today more than ever, there is a need to present *personalized, trustworthy, and context-aware* explanations to users of AI systems [38,7]. While defining explanations (Section 1), we suggest that explanations should be generated with a user focus. This idea of keeping the end-user in mind while building explanation facilities is corroborated in [38], wherein they recommend that explanations should "facilitate informed dialogue between users, developers, algorithmic systems, and other stakeholders." In this section, we seek to provide a review of approaches that we believe will be instrumental in increasing the user's trust in explanations and enabling more adaptive and user-centric explanations. The approaches that, in our opinion, will serve as the directions for research in explainable AI include Causal Methods, Neuro-Symbolic AI systems, and representation techniques to model the explainability space and to enable trustworthy data sharing that includes nascent approaches, such as Distributed Ledgers Technology (DLT). We posit that causal methods that provide causal justifications for decisions will help in building the users' trust in the system [32]. On the other hand, Neuro-Symbolic approaches will improve the intelligibility issue[3] aspect of ML models. Semantic representations of the explainability space will aid in systematically understanding and identifying aspects of explanations. Such organizations will then further help in building AI systems that will assist users via a "Distributed Cognition" approach [25] where the system generates explanations aligned with the users' requirements. Furthermore, as a technology that champions trustworthy interactions between mutually distrusting parties, DLTs are emerging as one of the many solutions to tackle trust issues in AI "black-box" models, and address the lack of explainability by providing data and AI model provenance that cannot be repudiated.

3.1. Causal Methods

Causality has been explored as a critical component of explanations since at least the 1990s [45,58]. Causality and causal reasoning have been pursued as research domains often independently of ML and Semantic Web efforts. However, AI researchers are now realizing and starting to suggest that causality is vital for presenting explanations to end users [13,49,17]. Doshi and Kim [13] cite causality as a desired property for explainability. They state [13] that causal reasoning can be used to explain when a "predicted change in output due to a perturbation will occur in the real system." This idea that the system should respond to a causal dependence also suggests that the system should encode causal knowledge, which as per Pearl [46], is missing from association based AI methods.

---

[3]Our definition of intelligibility is very similar to the description proposed by Lipton [32] and Lou et al. [33], in that intelligible models are interpretable wherein the contribution of model features to a decision can be deciphered.

[4]Judea Pearl (judea@cs.ucla.edu) is a professor of computer science and statistics and director of the Cognitive Systems Laboratory at the University of California, Los Angeles, USA.

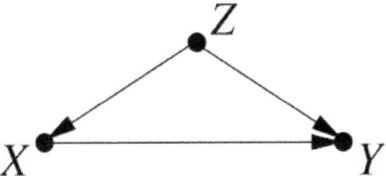

Figure 2. A representation of Pearl's cause-effect model [44,46] where $Q = P(Y|do(X))$, where X has an effect on Y and both depend on Z. Hence, he formulated the overall problem as a Bayesian equation in that $E_z = \sum_z P(Y|X,Z)P(Z)$. Pearl provides an intuitive example [46] of gender (Z) being a confounder on the effect that taking a drug (X) will have on recovery (Y). [Image is taken from [46] with permission from the author, Prof. Judea Pearl. [4]]

A representation of causal models has been presented by [48] and may be most simply presented as the well-known three-step Bayesian, cause-effect model proposed by Pearl [44]. Read [48], positioned his knowledge structure on Schank and Abelson's [52] findings that humans cognitively inferred their next set of actions or exhibited a behavior based on a cause from an event. However, Pearl took his representation of causality a step further in introducing counterfactuals as a component. He noted that counterfactuals played a significant role in scientific and legal thinking, where the "what if" and "but if not for" type of questions are asked to identify the cause of a problem. Pearl has made significant contributions to the field of causality [45,46,44], and in our review of causal methods, we will summarize some of his most relevant contributions. Through our review of causal methods, we will show the need to more fully integrate them into future, hybrid AI approaches to address user-centric questions.

Level (Symbol)	Typical Activity	Typical Questions	Examples
1. Association $P(y|x)$	Seeing	What is? How would seeing X change my belief in Y?	What does a symptom tell me about a disease? What does a survey tell us about the election results?
2. Intervention $P(y|do(x),z)$	Doing Intervening	What if? What if I do X?	What if I take aspirin, will my headache be cured? What if we ban cigarettes?
3. Counterfactuals $P(y_x|x',y')$	Imagining, Retrospection	Why? Was it X that caused Y? What if I had acted differently?	Was it the aspirin that stopped my headache? Would Kennedy be alive had Oswald not shot him? What if I had not been smoking the past 2 years?

Figure 3. An organization of the typical questions and examples tackled by each level in the three-level causal hierarchy proposed by Pearl [Image is taken from Pearl [46] with permission from the author, Prof. Judea Pearl.]

In his widely-cited book [44], Pearl introduced a causal model for representing cause-effect relationships (Figure 2). This mathematical formulation of causality enabled researchers in fields, such as epidemiology and life sciences, to express causal structures [47]. In addition, one of his recent technical reports [46] abstracts his cause-effect model and presents an overview of the three-step knowledge hierarchy (Figure 3) of causality that is comprised of Association, Intervention, and Counterfactual knowledge [46]. Pearl notes that current ML techniques can address questions on *Association* knowledge (i.e., Why am I being shown this answer? What else can I buy in addition to toothpaste?). In other words, *Association* knowledge contains correlations learned from associations. However, he adds that questions on *Intervention* knowledge require the system to understand and encode knowledge about the world besides just the data it is inferring a decision on. Finally, he states that *Counterfactual* questions that address the "but why not" question would need the system to be aware or understand the cause-effect relationships. We believe that this clear separation and identification of knowledge, in a hierarchical fashion, would allow AI systems to identify the components that would be necessary to generate explanations for these broad knowledge categories. While causal structures are desirable, it is generally hard to discover these models due to their dependence on human cognition. However, there have been approaches that mimic human reasoning and identify causal relationships from text [3,6,18,26][5] through the leveraging of the semantics of causal mentions. These techniques look for words such as the ones listed in Pearl's report [46], including "cause," "allow," "preventing," "attributed to," "discriminating" and "should I". Further, in the same report [46], Pearl presents seven tools in which causal methods are required:

1. Encoding Causal Assumptions – Transparency and Testability
2. Do-calculus and the control of confounding
3. The Algorithmization of Counterfactuals
4. Mediation Analysis and the Assessment of Direct and Indirect Effects
5. Adaptability, External Validity, and Sample Selection Bias
6. Recovering from Missing Data
7. Causal Discovery

We believe that some of these tools, like Algorithmization of Counterfactuals, Causal Discovery, and Assessment of Direct and Indirect Effects, will be particularly useful to include in explanations that provide the users' causal justifications for the conclusions being recommended to them by the AI system.

In conclusion, we believe that causal representations will enable the ability of AI systems to address a broader class of explanations beyond the traditional "Why, What, and How" [10] questions. Additionally, with a concrete, cause-effect graphical model, such as the one proposed by Pearl [44,47], the field has moved closer to a semantic representation of causality that may be used in a wide range of implemented systems. Such a semantic representation of causal structures in KGs would lend to the development of causal, neuro-symbolic integrations.

3.2. Neuro-Symbolic AI Methods

Neuro-Symbolic integration is a hybrid field that marries inductive and statistical learning capabilities of ML methods with the symbolic and conceptual representation capabilities of knowledge representation disciplines. Neuro-Symbolic Integration is not a new field [5,39], however, there has been a resurgence in interest due to its connection to ex-

---

[5]We list cause-effect words from Pearl's report [46], but more can be found in the citations we have linked.

plainable AI. In this section, we discuss some opinions from the literature to demonstrate the capabilities of Neuro-Symbolic Integration.

In their position paper Hitzler et al. [24], present distinctions between neural and Symbolic AI techniques to suggest that, with their contrasting strengths and applications, each of these two systems can assist each other to build a comprehensive solution. They point out that neural ML methods with their "connectionist approach"[6] are robust, noise-tolerant, and have the ability to identify patterns that even humans find hard to identify without prior training. On the other hand, the authors state that the semantic representation of knowledge allows symbolic AI methods to derive deeper relationships and provide high-confidence, provenance-aware results. However, they point out that the considerable reliance of symbolic AI methods on logical encoding makes them *brittle* and less-tolerant towards data flaws and noise. Conversely, in-line with the position from other interpretable AI papers [32,49], they state that ML methods suffer from being unintelligible and have non-transparency issues. Hence, through presenting the strengths and weaknesses of neural and symbolic AI techniques, they affirm the need for Neuro-Symbolic Integration.

Further, Hitzler et al. [24], identify tasks that will benefit from a Neuro-Symbolic Integration, including *knowledge acquisition, fuzzy reasoning, and interpreting deep learning methods*. An illustration of a typical Neuro-Symbolic AI system where neural approaches aid symbolic systems in knowledge generation, and where symbolic systems provide the knowledge encoding to explain the functioning and results of neural methods, is seen in Figure 4. We believe each of the tasks identified in [24] will play a key role in the development of the hybrid knowledge-enabled systems (definition under Section 1). More specifically, a strong, scalable encoding of user and domain knowledge can help ML methods be "transparent, understandable, verifiable, and trustworthy" [24].

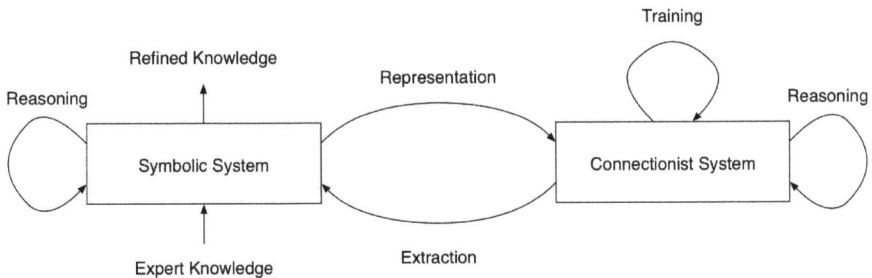

Figure 4. A schematic overview of a Neuro-Symbolic integration where connectionist approaches, such as ML methods and symbolic AI methods, help each other. [Image is taken from Bader and Hitzler [5]]

A knowledge acquisition use case is demonstrated by Alshahrani et al. [2] in a biomedical setting, where they use neural methods to learn enriched KG embeddings of RDF and OWL representations of biomedical data and knowledge. The authors combine data from widely-used biomedical ontologies and knowledge bases, including the Gene Ontology [4], the Human Phenotype Ontology [50], the Side Effect Resource (SIDER)

---

[6]In the literature [5,39], connectionist approaches have been associated with neural networks that connect layers and nodes within layers.

[27], etc.[7] In this effort, they use a random walk algorithm to learn the local representations of KG nodes in such a manner so that deep learning models can utilize the semantic node rich content present in KGs. Through embeddings that allow for the combination of data and information, they find that traditional ML methods are capable of finding more drug-drug and drug-disease interactions. More recently, researchers from the University of Massachusetts, Amherst are working on Box embeddings of KGs [56] to represent rich and fine-grained concepts present in KGs, such as transitive relations, definitions of negative properties, etc. Further, the authors allow for the representation of probabilistic scores in the Box embeddings to model uncertain knowledge. The KG embedding efforts are not only allowing neural approaches to leverage knowledge in their predictions, but are enriching semantic methods by allowing for the ability to draw inferences without relying solely on crafted inference rules.

In summary, while the role of Neuro-Symbolic Integration might not be directly observable in explanations produced by explainable AI, the capabilities enabled by this integration will allow for the inclusion of knowledge in ML methods. This combination of data and knowledge will help ML methods provide provenance-aware and grounded results. Additionally, this integration will help symbolic systems be probabilistic and fuzzy, allowing them to be dynamic to user requests. Hence, we believe that Neuro-Symbolic Integration is desirable for the development of knowledge-enabled systems.

3.3. Semantic Representation of the Explainability space

Since the emergence of Semantic Web [23] technologies and the renewed interest in explainability since the late 2000s, there have been few noteworthy efforts [42,53] to represent explanations and their dependencies in the AI world. These representation efforts have begun to result in the development of information artifacts, such as explanation taxonomies [31,42], general-purpose knowledge graphs [54], and ontologies [53]. As we stated in Section 2, building a semantic understanding of explanations will help us identify components that contribute to them, and will enable the development of hybrid AI models that are adept at generating them. In this section, we review a taxonomical structuring of explanations [42], a knowledge graph framework [54] and ontology design pattern for explanations [53]. The taxonomy and ontology design pattern for explanations generates a knowledge representation of explanations (with different granularities) upon the analysis of its dependencies, usage in different fields, and the goals that they support. Additionally, Dedalo, the knowledge graph framework [54], provides a method to identify background knowledge for information clusters generated by AI models.

Tiddi et al. developed a design pattern for explanations upon surveying the role of explanations in various fields, spanning Linguistics, Computer Science, Neuroscience, and Sociology [53]. While they found that the components of explanations vary in each field, they identified that certain components could minimally represent explanations. These components included the associated 'event(s),' [8] underlying 'theory(ies),' 'situation(s)' the explanations are applied to, and 'condition(s)' the explanations utilize. Additionally, in their ontology design pattern the authors incorporated standard nomenclature such as 'explanandum' ("that which is explained") and 'explanans' ("that which does

---

[7]We only list a few of the knowledge bases used in Alsaharani et al. [2], find the complete list in their paper

[8]Ontology classes labels are referred to in single quotes, and are in-line with the terminology used in the original paper [53]

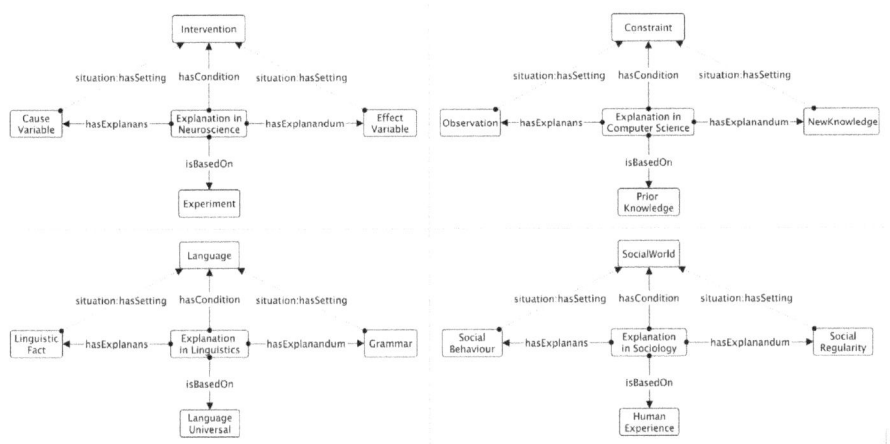

Figure 5. Conceptualization of explanations in different fields based on the ontology design pattern proposed by Tiddi et al.[53]. It is interesting to note that the authors have used the same property set to model explanations and their components in different fields. Such an encoding highlights that, while explanations serve diverse purposes and are instantiated by different components across fields, the structural composition remains the same in that explanations have 'setting,' 'condition,' and are based on some 'theory' [Image is taken from Tiddi et al. [53]].

the explaining") to associate explanations with the accounts of the premise that they are linked to and the strategies that are used to generate these accounts, respectively. With the explanation components and nomenclature in place, the authors solidified the representation of explanations as a quad, expressible as $E = \{A, P, T, C\}$, "where A stands for the antecedent event/explanans, P for the posterior event/explanandum, C for the situational context they are happening in and T for the theory governing those events." [53] They used this backbone notation of $E = \{A, P, T, C\}$ to represent explanations in different fields (see Figure 5). An example would be in the Neuroscience domain where explanations are based on results from experiment (T), have a pre-event in a cause variable (A), and output a posterior result in the form of an effect variable (P).

In a related effort, Tiddi et al. developed the knowledge graph framework, Dedalo [54], to extract background knowledge from Linked Data that can be used to populate explanations of clusters irrespective of the field of application. For this purpose, the authors used an Inductive Logic Programming (ILP) approach in conjunction with a heuristically driven method to identify background knowledge clauses to explain/interpret the results of AI models. A sample of an output fact from Dedalo could be "Enrico Motta is associated with the Semantic Web." While Dedalo is a useful, general-purpose fact identifier, it might not be sufficient to entirely extract or identify knowledge necessary to generate all of the explanation types that we identified in Table 1. Furthermore, neither Dedalo, nor the ontology design pattern for explanations, account for the different purposes that the explanations serve. However, this gap is somewhat addressed by the taxonomy of explanations developed by Nunes and Jannach [42].

More recently, Nunes and Jannach [42] conducted a systematic review of papers in explainable AI, making several analyses of the explanation space on the basis of their following research questions:

1. What are the characteristics of explanations provided to users, in terms of content and presentation?
2. How are explanations generated?
3. How are explanations evaluated?
4. What are the conclusions of evaluation or foundational studies of explanations?

Their analyses of the various papers considered in their review resulted in interesting findings, including a catalog of explanation goals, and the categorization of different forms of knowledge that constitute the explanation components. The explanation goals spanned properties such as *Transparency, Effectiveness, Trust, Persuasiveness, Satisfaction, Education, Scrutability, Efficiency*, and *Debugging*. Furthermore, they grouped the knowledge into broad- and low-level categories, of which the broad-level categories were comprised of *preferences and inputs, decision inference process, background information*, and *alternative information*. Finally, the authors used their findings to construct a taxonomical organization of the explainability space, [9] associating with explanations and components such as their *level of detail, objectives* (purpose, stakeholder goals, user-perceived factors), *generality, user interface components* (presentation and content), etc. While the ontology design pattern for explanations simplifies the model of explanations based on its content dependencies, the taxonomy of explanations provides a comprehensive view of explanations with factors, such as the goals they address, the content they contain, the user purpose they serve, etc.

In summary, the semantic representations of explanations, such as the ones we reviewed, can not only help provide a more precise understanding and organization of the explainable AI space but can also improve the flexibility of constructing AI models that serve the users' needs for explainability. Specifically, we believe that these semantic representations, that are being actively explored as a by-product to meet the growing needs of explainable AI [14,32,38], are a step towards generating hybrid explanations (such as the ones mentioned in Section 2) with various strengths and capabilities. Further, while these representations might not contribute to techniques that generate explanations, they can aid in ensuring that the explanations generated are in-line with our definition of the explainable knowledge-enabled system, i.e., to generate explanations that are "user-comprehensible, context-aware and provenance-enabled explanations of the mechanistic functioning of the AI system and the knowledge used."

3.4. Distributed Ledger Technology for Knowledge-enabled AI

In recent decades, one key priority in AI research has been pursuing optimal performance, often at the expense of interpretability [19]. However, the crucial questions, driven by a social reluctance to accept AI-based decisions, may lead to entirely new dynamics and technologies, fostering explainability, and authenticity. Distributed Ledger Technology (DLT) is emerging as one of the many solutions to tackle trust issues in AI models, and addresses the lack of explainability by providing data and cryptographically verifiable AI model provenance. DLTs provide the following four key features that are desirable for explainable AI:

1. Transparency and visibility of the data and AI algorithms

---

[9]For the full taxonomy of explanations diagram refer to Figure 11 in [42]

2. Immutability of the input data and parameters
3. Traceability and nonrepudiation of the output
4. Automatic execution of logic through smart contracts

In cases where the data provider is concerned about data misuse, the DLT will inherently preserve the provenance of the data records cryptographically, making it impossible to deny the misuse of the data. There are already proposals for programmable DLT platforms that enable smart, contract-based programming models for decentralized AI applications, which ensure the self-execution of AI agents based on predefined terms and conditions that will ultimately lead to innovations in systems suited for explainable AI [35].

Undoubtedly, it is desirable to have an immutable trail to track the development of the data flow and complex behaviors of AI-based systems for model debugging purposes. DLTs can do precisely that, tracking every step in the data processing and decision-making chain. Through tracking behaviors of AI-based systems across different data input and application scenarios, we gain more understanding of and confidence in the decisions made by those systems. Furthermore, it provides insights into tuning those "black boxes" to balance performance and prediction accuracy with the explainability of the system. In case of unfortunate and/or unforeseen incidents that arise due to the application of the AI models, these DLT-based trails will be essential to determine whether humans (and who precisely) or machines are at fault [11]. If it is later discovered that a dataset is corrupted long after the model is trained, it may be hard to figure out which estimated parameters have been corrupted as well, and the influence of the corrupted data on the model output. However, according to Marechaux et al. [34], if AI training is treated as a DLT transaction, then the ledger will store valuable traceability information. During model training, a transaction record is created to store contextual information in the ledger, such as the training model type, the dataset used, and the value of the parameters, both before and after the training. Therefore, DLTs can be leveraged to improve dataset traceability and consistency of ML models.

There are several notable applications of DLT in AI to provide explainability. Salah et al. identify that DLTs can help in designing trustworthy and interpretable transparent AI algorithms to know why the algorithm is reaching a specific decision by tracing executions in many application areas, including healthcare, military, and autonomous vehicles [51]. Nassar et al. propose a model in which AI and explainable AI nodes or predictors that act as trusted oracles, perform computation, and interact with smart contracts deployed on DLT-systems which record and log execution outcomes and decisions in the immutable ledger [41]. Ferrer et al. have explored a future in which untrusting devices, for example, swarm robotics, Internet of Thing (IoT) devices, or cell phones, will coordinate and make joint decisions [15], and the ledger will be used to explain the decisions of the collective AI agents, after-the-fact.

Recently deep fake images and videos have seen an uptick in contributing to misinformation on the Web. In order to address this problem Hassan et al. propose a DLT-based solution for proof of authenticity of digital videos in which a secure and trusted traceability to the original video creator or source can be established, in a decentralized manner. Their solution makes use of a decentralized storage system called the Inter-Planetary File System (IPFS), Ethereum name service, and a decentralized reputation system. Their premise is that if a video or piece of digital content is not traceable, then the digital content cannot be trusted [20]. The digital trace, or the lack of a digital trace, provides the explanation for the deep fake content. Calvaresi et al. describe a system that combines explainable AI, with DLT to ensure trust in domains where, due to environmental constraints or to some characteristics of the users/agents in the system, the effectiveness of the explanation may drop dramatically [8]. They draw an example from Unmanned Aerial Vehicles (UAVs) working in a multi-agent autonomous system.

4. Conclusion

We have reviewed and summarized approaches from research that we believe will serve as directions for explainable AI. With the increasing focus on explainable AI, we are at the cusp of a new era of AI, where explainability plays a pivotal role in the adoption of AI systems. This renewed interest has resulted in review papers and position statements that call for greater user-centric explainability. From our literature review and our resulting set of synthesized definitions of explanations and explainable knowledge-enabled systems, we have identified current directions for research, in addition to building a catalog of hybrid explanations, that will contribute in different ways to provide "user-comprehensible, context-aware, and provenance-enabled" explanations.

In our previous review ("Foundations of Explainable Knowledge-enabled Systems") of AI systems, we showed how different AI domains (i.e., expert systems, Semantic Web, cognitive assistants, and ML domains) and varying methodologies are suited to different aspects of explanations. In this chapter, we have built on this review and have identified AI methods that will aid in improving particular aspects of explainability, such as trust, comprehensibility, adaptiveness and causality. The next-generation hybrid AI systems would benefit from these identified strengths, utilizing a (potentially carefully chosen) collection of these techniques in combination to provide more complete and satisfying explanations. More specifically, we have shown that causal and neuro-symbolic methods, semantic representations of explainability, and mechanisms for trustworthy knowledge sharing through DLTs may play important roles in the future.

Further, we noted that different situations, contexts, and user requirements demand explanations of varying complexities, granularities, levels of evidence, presentations, etc. We presented a catalog of the nine explanation types that we synthesized from our literature review and our work on explaining complex and customized health assistants. We believe these explanation descriptions may support an explanation methodology style and even a technical selection approach when designing customized explanation components.

In conclusion, we believe that the increased adoption of AI systems and the need not only to understand the rationale behind their decisions, but also to make the results more useful in context and helpful in furthering joint human/computer reasoning, will lend to the development of new, explainable AI techniques. Furthermore, we opine that these explainable AI techniques will leverage different knowledge silos and sources, utilize a combination of explanation types, and incorporate mechanisms to improve the interpretability of AI models. We believe that current research and future research in explainable knowledge-enabled systems will serve as a means to build a more comprehensive and user-centric understanding of explainability.

5. Acknowledgments

This work is partially supported by IBM Research AI through the AI Horizons Network. We thank our colleagues from IBM Research, Amar Das, Morgan Foreman and Ching-Hua Chen, and from RPI, James P. McCusker, and Rebecca Cowan, who greatly assisted the research and document preparation.

References

[1] Ibrahim M Ahmed, Marco Alfonse, Mostafa Aref, and Abdel-Badeeh M Salem. Reasoning techniques for diabetics expert systems. *Procedia Computer Sci.*, 65:813–820, 2015.

[2] Mona Alshahrani, Mohammad Asif Khan, Omar Maddouri, Akira R Kinjo, Núria Queralt-Rosinach, and Robert Hoehndorf. Neuro-symbolic representation learning on biological knowledge graphs. *Bioinformatics*, 33(17):2723–2730, 2017.

[3] Nabiha Asghar. Automatic extraction of causal relations from natural language texts: a comprehensive survey. *arXiv preprint arXiv:1605.07895*, 2016.

[4] Michael Ashburner, Catherine A Ball, Judith A Blake, David Botstein, Heather Butler, J Michael Cherry, Allan P Davis, Kara Dolinski, Selina S Dwight, Janan T Eppig, et al. Gene ontology: tool for the unification of biology. *Nature genetics*, 25(1):25–29, 2000.

[5] Sebastian Bader and Pascal Hitzler. Dimensions of neural-symbolic integration-a structured survey. *arXiv preprint cs/0511042*, 2005.

[6] Aron K Barbey and Philip Wolff. Learning causal structure from reasoning. In *Proc. of the Annual Meeting of the Cognitive Sci. Society*, volume 29, 2007.

[7] Or Biran and Courtenay Cotton. Explanation and justification in machine learning: A survey. In *IJCAI-17 workshop on explainable AI (XAI)*, volume 8, page 1, 2017.

[8] Davide Calvaresi, Yazan Mualla, Amro Najjar, Stéphane Galland, and Michael Schumacher. Explainable multi-agent systems through blockchain technology. In *Proc. of the 1st Int. Workshop on eXplanable TRansparent Autonomous Agents and Multi-Agent Systems (EXTRAAMAS 2019)*, 2019.

[9] Pádraig Cunningham, Dónal Doyle, and John Loughrey. An evaluation of the usefulness of case-based explanation. In *Int. Conf. on Case-Based Reasoning*, pages 122–130. Springer, 2003.

[10] Jasbir S Dhaliwal and Izak Benbasat. The use and effects of knowledge-based system explanations: theoretical foundations and a framework for empirical evaluation. *Information systems research*, 7(3):342–362, 1996.

[11] T. N. Dinh and M. T. Thai. Ai and blockchain: A disruptive integration. *Computer*, 51(9):48–53, Sep. 2018.

[12] Derek Doran, Sarah Schulz, and Tarek R Besold. What does explainable ai really mean? a new conceptualization of perspectives. *arXiv preprint arXiv:1710.00794*, 2017.

[13] Finale Doshi-Velez and Been Kim. Towards a rigorous science of interpretable machine learning. *arXiv preprint arXiv:1702.08608*, 2017.

[14] Finale Doshi-Velez, Mason Kortz, Ryan Budish, Chris Bavitz, Sam Gershman, David O'Brien, Stuart Schieber, James Waldo, David Weinberger, and Alexandra Wood. Accountability of ai under the law: The role of explanation. *arXiv preprint arXiv:1711.01134*, 2017.

[15] Eduardo Castelló Ferrer. The blockchain: a new framework for robotic swarm systems. In *Proc. of the Future Technologies Conf.*, pages 1037–1058. Springer, 2018.

[16] Int. Organization for Standardization. *Human-centred design processes for interactive systems*. Int. Organization for Standardization, 1999.

[17] Leilani H Gilpin, David Bau, Ben Z Yuan, Ayesha Bajwa, Michael Specter, and Lalana Kagal. Explaining explanations: An approach to evaluating interpretability of machine learning. *arXiv preprint arXiv:1806.00069*, 2018.

[18] Roxana Girju, Dan I Moldovan, et al. Text mining for causal relations. In *Florida Artificial Intelligence Research Society (FLAIRS) Conf.*, pages 360–364, 2002.

[19] David Gunning. Explainable artificial intelligence (xai). *Defense Advanced Research Projects Agency (DARPA), nd Web*, 2, 2017.

[20] Haya R Hasan and Khaled Salah. Combating deepfake videos using blockchain and smart contracts. *IEEE Access*, 7:41596–41606, 2019.

[21]   Jane Heal. Simulation, theory, and content. *Theories of theories of mind*, pages 75–89, 1996.
[22]   Carl G Hempel. Deductive-nomological vs. statistical explanation. *University of Minnesota Press, Minneapolis*, 1962.
[23]   James Hendler and Eric Miller. Integrating applications on the semantic web. *J. of the Institute of Electrical Engineers of Japan*, Vol 122(10):676–680, October 2002.
[24]   Pascal Hitzler, Federico Bianchi, Monireh Ebrahimi, and Md Kamruzzaman Sarker. Neural-symbolic integration and the semantic web. *Semantic Web*, (Preprint):1–9, 2019.
[25]   James Hollan, Edwin Hutchins, and David Kirsh. Distributed cognition: toward a new foundation for human-computer interaction research. *ACM Transactions on Computer-Human Interaction (TOCHI)*, 7(2):174–196, 2000.
[26]   Randy M Kaplan and Genevieve Berry-Rogghe. Knowledge-based acquisition of causal relationships in text. *Knowledge Acquisition*, 3(3):317–337, 1991.
[27]   Michael Kuhn, Ivica Letunic, Lars Juhl Jensen, and Peer Bork. The sider database of drugs and side effects. *Nucleic acids research*, 44(D1):D1075–D1079, 2016.
[28]   Fatimah Lateef. Simulation-based learning: Just like the real thing. *J. of Emergencies, Trauma and Shock*, 3(4):348, 2010.
[29]   David B Leake. Evaluating explanations. In *AAAI*, pages 251–255, 1988.
[30]   Brian Y Lim, Anind K Dey, and Daniel Avrahami. Why and why not explanations improve the intelligibility of context-aware intelligent systems. In *Proc. of the SIGCHI Conf. on Human Factors in Computing Systems*, pages 2119–2128. ACM, 2009.
[31]   Brian Y Lim, Qian Yang, Ashraf M Abdul, and Danding Wang. Why these explanations? selecting intelligibility types for explanation goals. In *IUI Workshops*, 2019.
[32]   Zachary C Lipton. The mythos of model interpretability. *Queue*, 16(3):31–57, 2018.
[33]   Yin Lou, Rich Caruana, and Johannes Gehrke. Intelligible models for classification and regression. In *Proc. of the 18th ACM SIGKDD Int. Conf. on Knowledge discovery and data mining*, pages 150–158. ACM, 2012.
[34]   Jean-Louis Marechaux. Towards advanced artificial intelligence using blockchain technologies. *IEEE Blockchain Technical Briefs*, 2019.
[35]   Tshilidzi Marwala and Bo Xing.   Blockchain and artificial intelligence.   *arXiv preprint arXiv:1802.04451*, 2018.
[36]   Katherine L McNeill and Joseph Krajcik. Inquiry and scientific explanations: Helping students use evidence and reasoning. *Sci. as inquiry in the secondary setting*, pages 121–134, 2008.
[37]   Tim Miller. Explanation in artificial intelligence: Insights from the social sciences. *Artificial Intelligence*, 267:1–38, 2019.
[38]   Brent Mittelstadt, Chris Russell, and Sandra Wachter. Explaining explanations in ai. In *Proc. of the Conf. on fairness, accountability, and transparency*, pages 279–288. ACM, 2019.
[39]   Raymond Mooney, Jude Shavlik, Geoffrey Towell, and Alan Gove. An experimental comparison of symbolic and connectionist learning algorithms. *Readings in machine learning*, pages 171–176, 1990.
[40]   J Moore. Varieties of scientific explanation. *The Behavior Analyst*, 23(2):173–190, 2000.
[41]   Mohamed Nassar, Khaled Salah, Muhammad Habib ur Rehman, and Davor Svetinovic. Blockchain for explainable and trustworthy artificial intelligence. *Wiley Interdisciplinary Reviews: Data Mining and Knowledge Discovery*, 2019.
[42]   Ingrid Nunes and Dietmar Jannach. A systematic review and taxonomy of explanations in decision support and recommender systems. *User Modeling and User-Adapted Interaction*, 27(3-5):393–444, 2017.
[43]   Andrés Páez. The pragmatic turn in explainable artificial intelligence (xai). *Minds and Machines*, 29(3):441–459, 2019.
[44]   Judea Pearl. *Causality*. Cambridge university press, 2009.
[45]   Judea Pearl. Theoretical impediments to machine learning, 2017.
[46]   Judea Pearl. The seven tools of causal inference, with reflections on machine learning. *Commun. ACM*, 62(3):54–60, 2019.
[47]   Judea Pearl and Dana Mackenzie. *The book of why: the new science of cause and effect*. Basic Books, 2018.
[48]   Stephen J Read. Constructing causal scenarios: A knowledge structure approach to causal reasoning. *J. of Personality and Social Psychology*, 52(2):288, 1987.
[49]   Marco Tulio Ribeiro, Sameer Singh, and Carlos Guestrin. Why should i trust you?: Explaining the

predictions of any classifier. In *Proc. of the 22nd ACM SIGKDD Int. Conf. on knowledge discovery and data mining*, pages 1135–1144. ACM, 2016.

[50] Peter N Robinson, Sebastian Köhler, Sebastian Bauer, Dominik Seelow, Denise Horn, and Stefan Mundlos. The human phenotype ontology: a tool for annotating and analyzing human hereditary disease. *The American J. of Human Genetics*, 83(5):610–615, 2008.

[51] K. Salah, M. H. U. Rehman, N. Nizamuddin, and A. Al-Fuqaha. Blockchain for ai: Review and open research challenges. *IEEE Access*, 7:10127–10149, 2019.

[52] Roger C Schank and Robert P Abelson. Scripts, plans, and knowledge. In *IJCAI*, pages 151–157, 1975.

[53] Ilaria Tiddi, Mathieu d'Aquin, and Enrico Motta. An ontology design pattern to define explanations. In *Proceedings of the 8th International Conf. on Knowledge Capture*, pages 1–8, 2015.

[54] Ilaria Tiddi, Mathieu d'Aquin, and Enrico Motta. Dedalo: Looking for clusters explanations in a labyrinth of linked data. In *European Semantic Web Conf.*, pages 333–348. Springer, 2014.

[55] Jasper van der Waa, Marcel Robeer, Jurriaan van Diggelen, Matthieu Brinkhuis, and Mark Neerincx. Contrastive explanations with local foil trees. *arXiv preprint arXiv:1806.07470*, 2018.

[56] Luke Vilnis, Xiang Li, Shikhar Murty, and Andrew McCallum. Probabilistic embedding of knowledge graphs with box lattice measures. *arXiv preprint arXiv:1805.06627*, 2018.

[57] Danding Wang, Qian Yang, Ashraf Abdul, and Brian Y Lim. Designing theory-driven user-centric explainable ai. In *Proceedings of the 2019 CHI Conference on Human Factors in Computing Systems*, pages 1–15, 2019.

[58] James Woodward. *Making things happen: A theory of causal explanation*. Oxford university press, 2005.

[59] Jim Woodward. Explanation, invariance, and intervention. *Philosophy of Sci.*, 64:S26–S41, 1997.

[60] Jeffrey C Zemla, Steven Sloman, Christos Bechlivanidis, and David A Lagnado. Evaluating everyday explanations. *Psychonomic bulletin & review*, 24(5):1488–1500, 2017.

262   *Knowledge Graphs for eXplainable Artificial Intelligence: Foundations, Applications and Challenges*
I. Tiddi et al. (Eds.)
IOS Press, 2020
© 2020 Akademische Verlagsgesellschaft AKA GmbH, Berlin. All rights reserved.
doi:10.3233/SSW200023

The Data Ethics Challenges of Explainable AI and Their Knowledge-Based Solutions

Mathieu D'AQUIN

Data Science Institute
Insight SFI Research Centre for Data Analytics
NUI Galway, Ireland

Abstract. Explainable AI has recently gained momentum as an approach to overcome some of the more obvious ethical implications of the increasingly widespread application of AI (mostly machine learning). It is however not always completely evident whether providing explanations actually achieves to overcome those ethical issues, or rather create a false sense of control and transparency. This and other possible misuses of Explainable AI leads to the need to consider the possibility that providing explanations might itself represent a risk with respect to ethical implications at several levels. In this chapter, we explore through a series of scenarios how explanations in certain circumstances might affect negatively specific ethical values, from human agency to fairness. Through those scenarios, we discuss the need to consider ethical implications in the design and deployment of Explainable AI systems, focusing on how knowledge-based approaches can offer elements of solutions to the issues raised. We conclude on the requirements for ethical explanations, and on how hybrid-systems, combining machine learning with background knowledge, offer a way towards achieving those requirements.

Keywords. Ethics, Explanations, Scenarios, Ethics-by-Design, Knowledge Graphs, Knowledge-Based Systems, eXplainable AI

1. Introduction, background and related work

Explainable Artificial Intelligence (AI) is a current trend which aims at making the results of AI systems more interpretable by providing "explanations" to justify them. The need for such explanations is more prominently justified in systems used for the purpose of decision making, and has at least been partially driven by recent European regulation requiring automatic decisions to be explained and interpretable [5]. While AI could refer to a wide variety of approaches, we assume here that, in the context of Explainable AI, the technique which results are explained falls in the general category of "data centric" approaches, such as machine learning or data mining, both because they are the ones for which the need for explanation is more obvious, and because they have received a lot of attention in the last few years from academia and industry. This still covers a large number of the applications of AI such as recommendation, prediction and classification, which have been considered within a large number of application domains, including healthcare, finance, retail, media, etc.

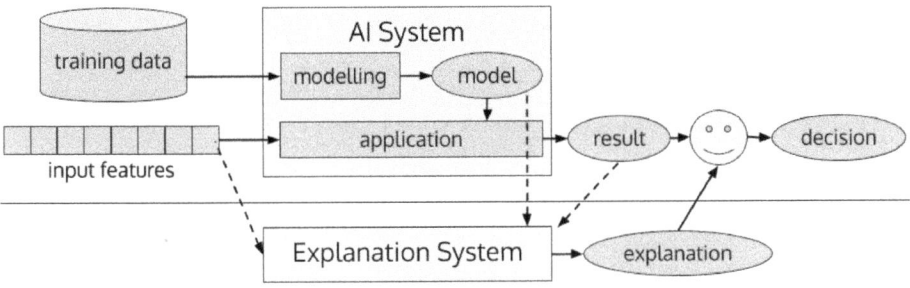

Figure 1. Simplified view of the (data-centric) AI process and the place of explanations.

As depicted in Figure 1, in such an AI process, as considered here, the main role of the human user (besides the parts that are directly related to designing and implementing the process, such as selecting the training data, the model, etc.) is in using the results of the process in order to make a decision. A base definition of Explainable AI is therefore, as also depicted, an extension of this process where the result comes with an explanation enabling the user to make a better decision. We will discuss later in this section what such an explanation can, and should, be, but we start here by looking at the general categories of approaches that exist in the literature to produce them.

Based for example on [10], we distinguish three main types of approaches to producing explanations:

- Using explainable models (e.g. decision trees, or recommendation by explanation [9]): These are approaches where the explanation is generated out of showing directly the inner working of the AI system, which uses interpretable models or has been designed to be inherently explainable.
- Reverse engineering the result (e.g. Deep Explainer [7]): These are approaches that extract from the model and its application salient features that were used to generate the result, as a way to justify this result.
- Reconnecting input and results (path-based explanations and/or sensitivity analysis): In those approaches, the model used by the AI system itself is not used to generate an explanation, but an explanation is generated out of finding credible connections between the input features and the output of the system, or through perturbing the input of the system to show where results might change (i.e. sensitivity analysis [4]).

Other chapters in this book describe techniques that exploit knowledge graphs to provide explanations and which mostly fall under one of those categories. Here however, we focus on the ethics implications of explanations. There has been much discussion, including in relation to regulation, concerning the ethical aspects of not providing explanations. Here, we therefore rather focus on cases where ethical implications might emerge from providing such explanations. To do so, we rely on the approach advocated in [3,13,12], in particular with respect to the use of anticipatory scenarios to analysis possible outcomes of the deployment of technologies. We devise such scenarios to explore some of the possible ethical implications of deploying explainable AI, and see what role knowledge-based approaches [1] can take in alleviating negative consequences in such scenarios. To do so, we consider scenarios according to four different dimensions:

- The kind of technique used for producing explanations (i.e. the above categories).
- The level of deployment/control (i.e. whether the technology is available to/under control of a selected few, or used by millions).
- Whether the technology is used and operating in the way intended, or is subject to abuses, incorrect or misleading results.
- The particular category of ethical values that the technology might be affecting.

The first dimension was explained already earlier, and the second is self-explanatory. To understand the possible effect of varying the third dimension, it is first important to clarify what explanations are expected to deliver, and therefore what they are. According to [1], the objective of an explanation is to provide the human user, the person or group of persons making a decision, with the ability to assess the correctness, accuracy and adequacy of the result. Looking at it from a more conceptual level, [11] studied the use of the term "explanation" in various disciplines, to provide an ontological view of the fundamental components of an explanation, reproduced in Figure 2. This is relevant since, as will be discussed later in this chapter, several ways in which explanations might not be adequate, including through being misleading, is in situations where some of those components are missing or do not play their expected roles.

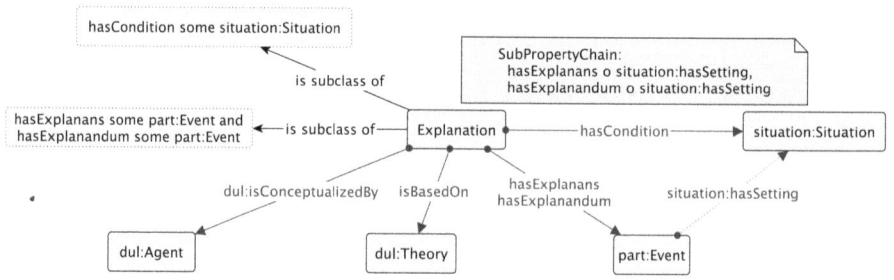

Figure 2. Conceptual model of explanations (from [11]).

Also, as mentioned earlier, to understand ethics implication of a process or technology, we need to look at the specific values that are being affected by the technology deployed, i.e. the fourth dimension in the list above. There are a number of values that can be considered, and that have been used to analyze ethics aspects in a number of domains (see for example [2]). Here, we look at the values represented in the "Trustworthy AI assessment list" (pilot phase) of the "Ethics Guidelines for Trustworthy AI" published by the High-Level Expert Group on Artificial Intelligence of the European Commission [6]: Human agency and oversight; technical robustness and safety; privacy and data governance; transparency; diversity, non-discrimination and fairness; societal well-being; and accountability. Those have been chosen specifically to assess ethics aspects of AI technology, and are therefore appropriate to our goal. Each of the following sections looks into scenarios specifically considering the impact of Explainable AI on a particular value in this list. In each section, we present a scenario that illustrates possible ethical issues according to the considered value, extend the discussion to aspects beyond the scenario, and envision possible knowledge-based solutions to the issues raised. While this cannot be considered an exhaustive approach to uncovering possible ethical issues from Explainable AI, it provides a framework for designers, developers and users of such systems to explore such issues, which is consistent with the Trustworthy AI assessment list and guidelines cited above.

2. Human agency and oversight

As every morning, Dr. Laplace, oncologist, receives the results from the previous day's analyses of his patients' data, together with recommendations for treatment. Each recommendation comes with a justification, based on the genetic profile of the patient, the tumor, as well as results from the latest literature and clinical trials. As always, most of them are quite straightforward and Dr. Laplace just taps "approved" so the treatment can go forward. As always too, a few of them seem, sometimes more than slightly, unexpected. Each justification shows to Dr. Laplace that the recommendation is valid according to latest research, of which she was not aware. She spends a bit more time on those anyway, for good conscience, before approving them.

Human agency is the capacity of a human being, actor in a process, to act upon and within the environment of this process. The scenario described provides a sense of how explanations, in this case the justifications for the treatment recommendations, can reduce human agency, namely, the capacity of Dr. Laplace to act upon the decision of treatment.

The process in which Dr. Laplace engages can be seen as science fiction, but is far from implausible, even within the next few years. Precision medicine has made much progress, and many researchers are working on establishing (often knowledge graph-based) approaches to achieve exactly what is described (see for example [8]). In this process, explanations have been introduced as a way to provide transparency, and to integrate the human expert in the decision process, being the ultimate decision maker. Those explanations are however based on much more information than the expert user can integrate. They are not questionable, as the human expert would have to spend enormous efforts to explore all the ramifications of the recommendation and of the associated explanation. We can expect this process to have been put in place as an attempt to reduce the effort, and time, required by the practitioner to decide on a treatment. Spending the same effort in tracing back the reasoning from its automated "assistant" would therefore be counter-productive. In addition, going against the recommendation of the tool would represent a risk for Dr. Laplace. In case of a serious problem with the treatment, justifying the decision as having followed the advise of the tool, which appeared well justified, would be much easier than justifying going against it. Dr. Laplace therefore ends up simply ticking the box, with her involvement being reduced to maintaining the presence of oversight in a decision which was really made algorithmically.

The kind of technique used to produce the explanation here is not made explicit. It is however obvious that techniques that produce explanations independently from the process that produces the result would create additional issues. Namely, as there is no necessary alignment between the explanation and the inference performed by the AI process, tracing back this process would be immensely more difficult.

The presented scenario is a typical case of a system deployed and used by and for a select group of people. In this case, it seems reasonable, as the decision requires medical knowledge to be properly made/validated. The issue of the ability to question the explanation provided would therefore be even more significant if the process involved users without the required knowledge to understand them (as discussed in Section 6).

Finally, the scenario assumes that the system works in the way intended. There are, of course, many potential issues associated with the possibility that the system could be "hacked", but those are similar to the ones associated with more or less any medical system dealing with patient treatments. Of course, the issues regarding human agency would be even more prominent if the explanations made were inaccurate, or based on false premises, and no AI system can be considered entirely immune from such problems.

Regarding possible solutions, the main issue here might be seen as coming from the fact that only one recommendation per case is provided, with only one explanation that cannot reflect the whole of the system's inference, but only the positive indicators that have led to this result. In such cases, a solution commonly proposed is for the system to also give indicators of the level of confidence in its recommendation. In order to be effective however, such confidence indicators would have to be interpretable. An approach here would therefore be to provide, instead of one recommendation/explanation/confidence indicator, a network of possible recommendations, together with the positive and negative indicators that provide evidence in favor or against a particular course of treatment. In other words, the explanation in this case is replaced by a specific knowledge graph of the treatment options, genetic markers and research results for the practitioner to explore, in order to make an informed decision.

3. Technical robustness and safety

Joining the prestigious Nisachausette Institute of Technology (NIT) has always been a challenge, and many have found the selection process to be unfair and to lack in transparency. Surprisingly, to its administrators, setting up an automated selection process which not only explains the reasons for the result, but also publicly shares those explanations (anonymized) for all candidates, has not made people more confident. Jeff already tried three years ago. He got rejected because the "pattern of interactions generated from his use of the online assessment tool did not match the ones of successful NIT students". He spent those three years collecting explanations from all others, analyzing the features used, comparing negative cases to positive cases, figuring out what behavior, engagement, attitude would increase his chances of acceptance. He learned how to fake successful patterns and finally got accepted. He got a great degree, as did all the other "fakers" he met at NIT (they had a secret club).

Technical robustness and safety include a number of different aspects, including whether the system or process in place can be exploited to achieve something other than intended, as well as, according to [6], whether the system is accurate.

In this scenario, the underlying AI system relies on invalid or irrelevant signals to make a decision, which already shows a lack of robustness. The focus here however is on how the explanations add to the issue by emphasizing the inaccuracy and the use of spurious signals in the decision making process, and on how the availability of large amounts of explanations can help individuals with the right understanding and skillset to exploit those inaccuracies to their advantage. Of course, the scenario has a happy ending, with Jeff and others getting their degree at NIT. We could even imagine the head of NIT knowing about the practice and relying on a principle that if someone is clever enough to game the system, they deserve a place. This however remains an issue as it amounts to pretending that the profound lack of robustness of the system is a feature, the "real test", even though other candidates would be reluctant to use the same approach as Jeff, considering it cheating.

While this scenario might appear quite specific, it is easy to imagine others where explanations, especially the availability of multiple explanations, enable users to reverse-engineer the model used to make a decision, so to exploit its weaknesses. This, of course, can only be applied in cases where the explanation is directly related to the inner-working of the model, by being based on the model's actual inference or on extracting the most salient features used in the decision.

This scenario also expects a system available to a large number of people, where there is a way to collect information about the inner working of the model, through having access to multiple explanations. This can be achieved either through accessing explanations from multiple users (as in the scenario) or in cases where the user is not limited in the number of inputs they can enter, by systematically exploring the space of inputs, to analyze and map both the space of outputs and the space of explanations.

Finally, the case of Jeff and NIT assumes that the AI system is inaccurate and that the explanation system is being exploited in a way different from the one intended. It therefore goes against robustness and (in a very broad sense) safety at two levels. We could easily imagine however a way in which the explanation system could be used in exactly the right way, but through explaining results based on irrelevant, biased data, would end-up strengthening those results, and therefore justifying the biases embedded in the data.

A key part of the reason why the explanation system fails in this and similar scenarios is that it provides an incomplete explanation. Indeed, it explains the link between the input of the AI system (the explanans, see Figure 2) and its output (the explanandum), but without providing grounding for it (the theory). There is no valid relationship between the two components as the model relies on spurious signals learned from historical data. In other words, the explanation amounts to nothing more than saying "you got those results because the system used those features". A solution to this would be to not only construct explanations from tracing back the behavior of the systems, but by also integrating external knowledge that can justify this behavior and ground the signals on which the system relies. In other words, the explanation should rather be "you got those results because the system used those features and there is a known, causal relationship between those features and what the system is trying to predict" (in our case, whether the candidate will succeed in their studies at NIT). A knowledge-based solution to integrating those "known relationships" would consist of building a knowledge-graph of existing empirical results in the considered field from the scientific literature (in our case, robust studies of the abilities and characteristics of candidates that are more conducive to success as a student). Of course, a consequence of this would be an increased ability of the explanation system to discard spurious, ungrounded results from the AI system (as in the case of Jeff), by recognizing explanations that are not justified by knowledge of the domain.

4. Privacy and data governance

Jane didn't really know what to watch when starting Webflux. She really enjoyed the last movie she watched, "The 12 Zebras", as did her friend Nat. Nat seems to be the only one to share her tastes around here. Nobody else they talked to in their small village had seen that movie. Most of them don't even have Webflux. But then, the first recommendation it comes up with now is a movie called "Fifty nuances of Purple". Jane checks the explanation provided and it says "This movie was watched and highly rated by someone who also watched "The 12 Zebras" in your neighborhood." That would have to be Nat then, but Jane wonders why she didn't mention that movie when they talked about what to watch next.

Privacy and data governance relate mostly, in the context of this chapter, to the protection of personal data from unintended disclosure.

In this scenario, it appears that Nat, Jane's friend, did not want her to know that she watched and enjoyed a particular movie, or at least, the movie streaming service should not be revealing it without her knowledge and consent. This case might seem trivial, especially compared to scenarios in healthcare, education or finance, but it simply illustrates how explanations, by revealing more information about the inner working of AI systems, increase the risk of disclosure in cases when personal data is being used by those systems. We therefore expect the issue to be applicable to many other scenarios, especially in collaborative-filtering, hyperlocal and/or highly personalized recommendations.

Interestingly, the issue with disclosure of personal information might appear whether or not the information is actually used by the AI system. Indeed, the issue here is that the explanation system uses specific information that might lead to accidental disclosure. In other words, the explanation system can be treated entirely separately from the AI system as one that manipulates personal data, and which outputs, even though aggregated (at least in the case of our scenario), could reveal more information than intended.

The scenario relies on a case where a large number of people use and have access to the AI system and the explanations. This is necessary in this case for the personal information being disclosed to actually be available in the system, and for the expectation of anonymity brought by aggregation to be present. We could however also imagine other scenarios where explainable AI systems trained on large amounts of personal data from many individuals are used by only a few selected people (because of addressing highly specialized tasks) and still lead to similar accidental disclosures.

Also, whether the explanation system works as expected or not appears irrelevant here since the issue of accidental personal data disclosure is independent of the objectives of both the AI system and the explanation system. One could argue that, if considering anonymity and data protection as requirements, then the explanation system is not operating adequately, which leads to the main difficulty in addressing the issue –contradictory requirements– as discussed below.

While the scenario and the issue might appear trivial, finding a solution may be surprisingly complicated. Indeed, one could simply treat the personal data in input of the explanation system through any existing anonymity filter. Obfuscating the data about Nat's rating or location using k-anonymity for example would resolve the issue in our scenario. However, it would also have rendered the explanation inaccurate. According to European regulation, directly or indirectly identifiable information provided to a system cannot be disclosed to a third party without explicit, direct consent from the data subject, and without justification of purpose. The same regulation also states that individuals have a right to be given an explanation for the output of an algorithm. Those requirements could end-up contradicting each other when the only way not to indirectly disclose identifiable information would be to produce an explanation that does not actually reflect the inference made by the AI system[1]. Balancing those two aspects, anonymity and accuracy, might end-up being a complex challenge that could involve nuanced notions of user preferences, information sensitivity, user prior knowledge, etc. This forms a complex network of varied elements which knowledge-based approaches can help manage, enabling potentially complex reasoning.

5. Transparency

It is the third time Claire submitted her research grant proposal to the Wakandian Science Foundation (WSF), and the third time it gets rejected by the automated proposal pre-selection process. This AI system was trained on hundreds of accepted and rejected grant proposals, relying on all aspects of the applications, from the text of the research plan to the proposed budget, so to predict the likelihood of a given proposal being accepted. Proposals that fall below a certain threshold are automatically rejected, without a human being reviewing them. The objective was to reduce the ever-increasing workload associated with assessing the ever-increasing number of proposals submitted. Short feedback is provided on the rejected proposals, justifying the rejection, based on reverse-engineering the complex model making the prediction to extract salient features and connect them with feedback provided to past rejected proposals from the training set. The first one Claire got was "Budget too high", so she reduced the budget. The second one was "Insufficient community engagement", so she added workshops with community stakeholders. The third piece of explanation Claire received was "Insufficient resources to carry out workplan". She is now lost and gives up on what would have been a very impactful project.

Transparency, as a characteristic of a system, corresponds to the system being open and clearly communicating on the processes it carries out. To a large extent, explanations in AI are assumed to support increasing transparency.

In the scenario above however, it is less than clear that this is the case. We can assume that, to function, the AI system put in place by the WSF would rely on a large number of rich features. It would include basic numeric features, such as the amount of funding requested, the duration of the proposed project, the number of tasks and workpackages, the number of partners and the size of teams. It would likely also include structured

---

[1]We would of course assume that, in our case, data protection would take priority over the right to explanation.

information about the workplan and the applicants, as well as embeddings of texts and other media included in the different sections. As a result, the outcome of the prediction would be based on inferences using evidence from thousands of those features. Actually accounting for the entirety of such inferences would require an explanation almost as complex as the model itself, and therefore entirely unusable. The approach taken here, which is common in current explainable AI research, is to reduce the explanation to the most prominent (i.e. salient) features. While this can work well in cases where specific features have a significantly stronger contribution to the result than others, we can expect that for Claire's proposal, it was not the case. In other words, while budget, engagement and workload could have been marginally more salient than others, the aggregation of potentially thousands of other, slightly less salient features was actually the main driver for the outcome. The explanation system is an algorithm that outputs an estimate of the likely explanation, and is itself a black-box. It only gives the illusion of transparency, while actually further obfuscating an algorithmic decision.

This scenario is based on the assumption that the explanation system uses a method based on reverse-engineering the process captured by the model used by the AI system, to extract salient features that can be used to come up with realistic "feedback" according to past proposal review reports. Since this is done to avoid actually describing the inner-working of the AI system, it could easily be imagined that the explanation is constructed entirely independently from the AI system, i.e. that the feedback would be lifted from similar rejected proposals, without even attempting to connect this to features used by the AI system. The same issue would obviously appear in this case. Using an explainable model would, on the other hand, avoid the issue of transparency. The scenario however assumes that the problem is so complex that explainable models are not applicable. Applying sensitivity analysis could also help giving a more straightforward explanation, but again, the complexity of the model/problem would likely mean that too many features are needed to be considered. Assuming it was feasible however, sensitivity analysis would transform the explanation into something that could be interpreted as "your proposal would have been accepted if you had done X, Y and Z." Besides the list of features to change and the list of possible alternative explanations being potentially very large, this would open up to issues such as the ones illustrated in the scenario of Section 3.

The particular issue described here, explanations giving a false sense of transparency for a process that is too complex to be transparent, can appear whether the system is used by millions, or only by a few people. Also, the issue appears whether or not the explanation system works as designed. It is clear however that it is an issue related to the fact that the explanation system is not designed to achieve what an explanation system should deliver: A valid, accurate representation of the process leading to the AI system's result.

It is not clear whether the problems described above can really have a solution. However, understanding the relative importance of features used to build more nuanced explanations, as well as their connection with the actual output (i.e. addressing the "theory" component of the explanation) can help alleviating those problems. In other words, as with the human agency scenario (Section 2), providing more knowledge about the aspects, entities and indicators contributing to the result, and about their connections, while not removing the issue entirely, can support the human user making the final decision in taking into account the known incompleteness of the explanation. That is however if, unlike in our scenario, a human indeed takes the final decision.

6. Fairness, societal well-being and accountability

Robert's company was going well. His platform combining Internet of Things technology with robotics and community engagement had been deployed and was now working for several associations and local councils to support communities in some of the least favored areas of the city, helping them overcome some of the key reasons for the issues they were facing. Also, he had just found the perfect property where to move his family: A nicely sized 4 bedroom house in one of the areas his company had helped turn around. He believed it was going to work. Obtaining the mortgage was not supposed to be an issue: Even if he was not very rich, his status of CEO of a successful company should make him a great candidate for the bank. His application was nevertheless rejected. The explanation that came with it was rather unclear about the reasons. It talked about the projected value of the property at short term, based on extrapolating over historical data, being expected to continue declining, and that features of the profile of the applicant (occupation, career prospect) and of the property (history of occupation) leading to a low confidence in a successful relocation. Despite his principles and beliefs, Robert follows the recommendation of his bank advisor to move to a "more suitable" part of the city.

In this scenario, we consider three interrelated aspects. First, on "Diversity, non-discrimination and fairness", which relates to the system gathering equally for all users, and not favoring some users over irrelevant features, the most evident issue is that the explanation in the scenario requires mastering a vocabulary and understanding a domain which only a few of the users would really know. This appears unavoidable, since the decision itself is based on features in this specialized domain (finance, the property market, etc.) on which the system cannot expect all users to be experts. While the explanation is supposed to provide a way for the user to question the reasons for the decision, it instead leads to even more confusion. The user is left with no ability to question the explanation itself. There is no opportunity for disagreeing.

Second, this scenario also strongly relates to "societal well-being". Indeed, digging a bit deeper, Robert might have noticed that both explanations provided are based on assumptions that relate to the way the area has been considered in the past and to the way people sharing his profile have acted in the past. More explicitly, the system has rejected his application because, not being aware of the interventions from Robert's company, it considered the area of the property as a risky place for investment and unlikely to be suited, as a long term home, to someone with a CEO profile. Those represents systematic biases: Unfair assessments based on generalizing over aggregated, past data, not taking sufficiently into account specific circumstances and additional variables affecting future prospects. While this is unrelated to the presence of an explanation, since those biases would be there anyway, the explanation fails to uncover them. Instead of clearly demonstrating to Robert how the decision was based on wrong assumptions, enabling him to question it, it justifies the biases in a way that make them appear more valid than they are. Since they drive investment and relocation decisions, those biases in this specific scenario would actively contribute to slowing down improvements in the considered area of the city.

Third, the scenario also relates to issues of "accountability". Indeed, as discussed above, it appears here that the decision is based on reasons that do not apply well. We can imagine that, reviewing those kinds of decisions later, the bank might realize that a mistake was made, and that properties in the area considered by Robert were being wrongly assessed. Ideally, we would assume that decisions are not made entirely automatically and that a human expert validates them before presenting them to the user. Indeed, in the scenario, Robert deals with an advisor who is supposedly there to help him with his decision. However, the advisor in this case instead takes the role of supporting Robert in finding an alternative that would be more suitable to the system, rather than in understanding the decision in a way that can make it questionable. Similarly to what is described in Section 2, while the advisor should be accountable for the decision, the presence of a "categorical" explanation for the decision makes it even less possible to go against it. In the event of a review, it appears easier for the "accountable" advisor to justify his decision based on the explanation of the system, rather than taking the risk of contradicting it.

The particular technique used to come up with an explanation here is not very relevant to the issues themselves. The scenario makes assumptions about the explanations being strongly related to the actual features used by the AI system, suggesting a "reverse engineering-style" explanation, which can be seen to be at the origin of its lack of clarity. The issue of explanations masking implicit biases on which the decision relies is however even more likely to happen when explanations are not directly based on analyzing the process and features applied by the AI system.

The aspect of whether the system is used and controlled by many is interesting here. The particular scenario presented is one of a system used by many, but controlled by a few. It is easy to imagine many others configurations where societal well-being and/or fairness are affected by the aspect of who controls the system, and by how it is expected, and failing, to cater for a wide variety of users.

Finally, it is clear that in this scenario, as in Section 5, while the explanation system does what it is designed to do, it is not designed to truly achieve the purpose of explanations. Instead of providing a way to understand the decision, see when they might be misguided, and question them, they achieve making them more obscure and less questionable.

As mentioned above, the decision here is not entirely automatic, and is partly handled by a human advisor who should be able to interpret the explanation based on their own background knowledge. This represents an obvious element of solution: In cases like this one where the features and decisions cannot easily be explained without referring to specialized background knowledge, the introduction of background knowledge is required. An explanation could indeed be made more accessible to the final user, and possibly help them understand it enough to detect biases and invalid assumptions, if reconnected to background knowledge that is accessible to them. The issue is that explanations are, in this kind of cases, framed within a particular area of background knowledge that requires a certain amount of expertise (finance, property market). Making such specialized background knowledge explicit, also explicitly encoding relevant background knowledge from the user (i.e. for Robert, what his company has been doing, his objectives, etc.) and aligning those two related but differently framed knowledge domains could help formulating explanations produced based on the features of the former in a way that is meaningful to the later.

7. Conclusion: Towards a more ethical, knowledge-based Explainable AI

There is a lot of expectations associated with Explainable AI, which are strongly related to the current trend that applications of AI rely on complex, fundamentally hard to interpret models, based on picking and extrapolating from sometimes counterintuitive signals from large amounts of data. The scenarios presented above however illustrate some cases in which, if not considered carefully, the application of explanations with those models could have unintended consequences, often counter to the original purpose of explanations. There are, naturally, many other scenarios that could be considered, addressing the same or other, possibly more precise values. It is obvious already from the scenarios presented and the associated discussions that those issues are interrelated, and that problems with respect to specific values are often strongly connected to problems regarding others. For example, the scenario for human agency could be similarly used to discuss inclusion, societal well-being, accountability, etc.

In relation to this, while the objective of this chapter is to raise awareness of the need to consider the potential impact of explanations and not to assume that the mere presence of explanations is sufficient to achieve transparency and human agency, the scenarios above also show some common traits with respect to the way issues come about in the application of Explainable AI. In particular, several of the issues come from the explanations not being sufficient to provide a complete, questionable view of the decision made, or are not sufficiently interpretable themselves to truly enable informed decisions.

For this reason, we extract two main conclusions from this exercise in looking at Explainable AI from the point of view of ethics values. First, there are a number of properties that explanations need to have in order to be effective and to reduce the risk of unintended consequences. Namely, explanations should be:

Complete: As discussed in [11] (see Figure 2), an explanation requires to include not only some form of correlation between what is being explained (the decision) and what explains it (in many cases, the features used). It needs to explicitate what relates those (the theory), i.e. by which mechanism or principle those features actually impact on the decision.

Complete again: In several of our scenarios, a part of the issue is that alternatives to the decisions are not presented, and the reasons for them being discarded are not explained. In other words, the results are only positively explained, and do not present the whole background for the decision. In some cases of course, the reason for this is that the whole justification for the decision is simply too complex to be of any use as an explanation (see Section 5).

Honest: In order to serve their purpose, explanations should accurately capture the way in which the AI system has produced its results. As shown in several scenarios, oversimplifications or indirect explanations can, paradoxically, end up being more misleading than the absence of explanation.

Understandable: While this might appear obvious, the purpose of explanations being to make a complex result interpretable, as illustrated by several scenarios, it is not trivially achieved. Indeed, to be honest, explanations might have to be complex, and by being complex and referring to processes and entities with which the user cannot relate, fail in providing any added value.

The second level of conclusion we reach is that, in many cases, to move towards achieving the properties above, it is required to integrate some elements of a knowledge-based approach. Indeed, the main issue of Explainable AI, as applied to machine learning, is that there is a wide gap between the numerical, complex, connected methods implemented by those approaches and the knowledge of the user. Interpretability is fundamentally the ability to integrate new information (the result of the AI system) within an existing knowledge framework (the one of the user). As discussed in the sections above, possible solutions to improving the interpretability of the results of AI systems beyond "basic" explanations therefore involve mapping such explanations, the entities and the processes to which they relate, with knowledge represented in a way that makes it manipulable and integrable by the user. This could provide a layer above the low level features on which explanations rely, bridging the gap between the elementary, numerical operations of machine learning and the understanding of the results produced, so to support informed, intelligent decision making.

Acknowledgement

This work has been partly funded by Science Foundation Ireland (SFI) under Grant Number SFI/12/RC/2289_P2, Insight SFI Research Centre for Data Analytics.

References

[1]   Rajendra Akerkar and Priti Sajja. *Knowledge-based systems*. Jones & Bartlett Publishers, 2010.
[2]   Sally Bean. Navigating the murky intersection between clinical and organizational ethics: A hybrid case taxonomy. *Bioethics*, 25(6):320–325, 2011.
[3]   Mathieu d'Aquin, Pinelopi Troullinou, Noel E O'Connor, Aindrias Cullen, Gráinne Faller, and Louise Holden. Towards an ethics by design methodology for ai research projects. In *Proceedings of the 2018 AAAI/ACM Conference on AI, Ethics, and Society*, pages 54–59. ACM, 2018.
[4]   Andries Petrus Engelbrecht, Ian Cloete, and Jacek M Zurada. Determining the significance of input parameters using sensitivity analysis. In *International Workshop on Artificial Neural Networks*, pages 382–388. Springer, 1995.
[5]   Bryce Goodman and Seth Flaxman. European union regulations on algorithmic decision-making and a "right to explanation". *AI Magazine*, 38(3):50–57, 2017.
[6]   High Level Expert Group on AI, European Commission. Ethics guidelines for trustworthy ai, 2019.
[7]   Grégoire Montavon, Sebastian Lapuschkin, Alexander Binder, Wojciech Samek, and Klaus-Robert Müller. Explaining nonlinear classification decisions with deep taylor decomposition. *Pattern Recognition*, 65:211–222, 2017.
[8]   Peipei Ping, Karol Watson, Jiawei Han, and Alex Bui. Individualized knowledge graph: a viable informatics path to precision medicine. *Circulation research*, 120(7):1078–1080, 2017.
[9]   Arpit Rana and Derek Bridge. Explanations that are intrinsic to recommendations. In *Proceedings of the 26th Conference on User Modeling, Adaptation and Personalization*, pages 187–195. ACM, 2018.
[10] Wojciech Samek, Thomas Wiegand, and Klaus-Robert Müller. Explainable artificial intelligence: Understanding, visualizing and interpreting deep learning models. *arXiv preprint arXiv:1708.08296*, 2017.

[11] Ilaria Tiddi, Mathieu d'Aquin, and Enrico Motta. An ontology design pattern to define explanations. In *Proceedings of the 8th International Conference on Knowledge Capture*, page 3. ACM, 2015.

[12] Pinelopi Troullinou, Mathieu d'Aquin, and Ilaria Tiddi. Re-coding black mirror chairs' welcome & organization. In *Companion Proceedings of the The Web Conference 2018*, pages 1527–1528. International World Wide Web Conferences Steering Committee, 2018.

[13] Pinelopi Troullinou and Mathieu d'Aquin. Using futuristic scenarios for an interdisciplinary discussion on the feasibility and implications of technology. *Black Mirror and Critical Media Theory*, page 69, 2018.

I. Tiddi et al. (Eds.)
IOS Press, 2020
doi:10.3233/SSW200024

Who Is This Explanation for?
Human Intelligence and Knowledge
Graphs for eXplainable AI

Irene CELINO

Cefriel – Politecnico di Milano
Viale Sarca 226, 20126 Milano – Italy

Abstract. eXplainable AI focuses on generating explanations for the output of an AI algorithm to a user, usually a decision-maker. Such user needs to interpret the AI system in order to decide whether to trust the machine outcome. When addressing this challenge, therefore, proper attention should be given to produce explanations that are *interpretable* by the target community of users.

In this chapter, we claim for the need to better investigate what constitutes a *human explanation*, i.e. a justification of the machine behavior that is interpretable and actionable by the human decision makers. In particular, we focus on the contributions that *Human Intelligence* can bring to eXplainable AI, especially in conjunction with the exploitation of Knowledge Graphs.

Indeed, we call for a better interplay between Knowledge Representation and Reasoning, Social Sciences, Human Computation and Human-Machine Cooperation research – as already explored in other AI branches – in order to support the goal of eXplainable AI with the adoption of a *Human-in-the-Loop* approach.

Keywords. Explainability, Human Intelligence, Human Computation, Human-in-the-Loop, Human-Machine Cooperation, Knowledge Graphs

1. Introduction

The recent renaissance of Machine Learning and Artificial Intelligence approaches brought a new wave of interest in such methods and technologies. Autonomous agents and automatic systems are now available and more affordable than before, but, if we relied only on popular news and communication, we would tend to think that they completely got rid of human intervention both in their setup and in their operation. Any practitioner, however, knows very well that human contributions are indispensable in order to set up, train, optimize and operate such systems.

Referring to the AI systems that more strongly rely on data and in particular to predictive Machine Learning, human knowledge is still required in all phases to answer relevant questions that are not necessarily targeted to the AI experts:

- *before creating a model*: during training set creation ("what data can I use to build a model?")
- at *model building time*: during model validation ("is my model correct?", "is my model good enough?") and during model refinement ("what additional training data/features would improve my model performance?")

- *using the model in production*: to ensure algorithmic transparency ("should I trust the way my model gave such a prediction?") and to provide explainability ("why did my model give such an outcome/prediction?")

In this chapter, we focus on the role that Human Intelligence and (human-generated) Knowledge Graphs play to answer the above questions. We also claim that, with special reference to explainability, humans are only partially considered in eXplainable AI research, while they should, because the required explanations should be useful for human comprehension.

The remainder of the chapter is structured as follows: related work is illustrated in Section 2, and Section 3 clarifies what we mean by explanation and why humans are needed in their generation; opportunities for (human) eXplainable AI coming from the employment of Human Intelligence and Knowledge Graphs are outlined in Section 4, and Section 5 presents some conclusions and traces some possible future work.

2. Related Work

In the context of Artificial Intelligence and Machine Learning, several research trends investigate the role and interplay between humans and machines.

A new emerging process of scientific inquiry is shown in [1]: different people beyond scientists are now involved in such a process, because laymen participate both in the creation/collection of information (via user-generated content) and in the coding/labelling/validation phases (e.g. through Crowdsourcing or Citizen Science); the authors call for a new data analytics paradigm with user involvement, and demonstrate experimental results to show the effect of interface design on how users transform information.

Indeed, the power of the "crowd" is often leveraged to create large-scale training sets for Machine Learning, by adopting Crowdsourcing [2], Human Computation [3] and Citizen Science [4] approaches. Moreover, knowledge in human cognitive processes may assist the design and implementation of Machine Learning, as claimed in [5]; however, the current popularity of black-box models hinders an effective human intervention because those approaches negatively impact on trustworthiness, interpretability and the discovery of hidden rules.

User trust is indeed an important indicator because it correlates with system accuracy: humans are able to dynamically adjust their reliance based on a system perceived accuracy and they even show acceptance thresholds [6]: this implies the need to correctly design an AI system to sustain the desired level of user trust. The validation phase of Machine Learning algorithms also benefits from the integration of user-centered evaluation: the authors of [7] advocate adopting user-centered design (iterative) approaches for Machine Learning, in model optimization, selection and validation.

Different families of methods explicitly aim to improve learned models based on human knowledge. Active Learning [8] is based on the idea that a Machine Learning algorithm can achieve greater accuracy with fewer labeled training instances if it is allowed to "choose" the data from which it learns, by asking queries to an "oracle" which usually is a human annotator. Transfer Learning [9] emerged to fulfill the need to build real world applications in which it is expensive or impossible to re-collect the training data required and rebuild the models; in such cases knowledge transfer is attempted by adapting a model already trained on some domain (with the help of human annotators) to a different domain.

Human-Machine Cooperation is at the heart of Interactive Machine Learning [10], in which a human operator and a machine collaborate to achieve a task; while coupling algorithm-centered analysis with human-centered evaluation seems to yield better results than a fully automated or fully manual approach, research is still needed to explore to what extent this mix can provide benefits [11]: participatory design with end-users could help incorporating human expertise in algorithms and models; visualization techniques could facilitate user feedback; creativity, lateral thinking and exploration can also support, if suitable tools and objective and subjective metrics are developed.

In general, in order to improve and optimize the interaction between humans and machines, a perspective shift should be adopted, for example by walking away from a purely technical optimization and embracing a designer mindset, like the one proposed in [12], in which the author invites to stop seeing technologies as a collection of tools and gadgets and instead start seeing them as an evolutionary flow around human problems, whose parts ultimately integrate to create a new category of things named agentive technologies or "AI that works for people".

3. What is an explanation for humans

The rationale behind eXplainable AI research is that Artificial Intelligence systems should not only display an intelligent behavior, but they also should be able to explain such behavior. The naturally raising question is what an explanation is and how to generate it. In this section, we attempt at illustrating the characteristics of explanations and we justify the need for "Human Intelligence" and "Human-in-the-Loop" approaches also in relation to eXplainable AI.

3.1. A working definition of explanation

Let us consider the simple example of email categorization between spam and non-spam. Here the task is binary classification (i.e., the output of a Machine Learning classifier is the labeling of each mail as spam or non-spam).

An explanation consists in a set of hints to understand the relationship between the characteristics of an individual (e.g. an email) and the model prediction on that individual (e.g. this email is spam). The explanation is used by a human decision-maker, who should decide whether to trust the system (e.g. accept or reject the prediction of the spam classifier) [13].

User trust can happen at different levels: on the individual prediction, when the user requires an explanation about a specific instance (e.g. why *this* mail is spam) or on an entire model, when the user needs to decide whether to trust the system altogether. In the latter case, an explanation could require selecting a representative sample of individuals (e.g. a set of spam/non-spam emails) and explaining each individual in the sample.

The main characteristics that an explanation should display (again according to [13]) are fidelity, model-independence and interpretability. *Local fidelity* or local faithfulness means that a prediction should be valid in the vicinity of the individual; global fidelity would of course be desirable, but it could be challenging for complex models. The explanation should also be *model-agnostic*, in that it should be independent on the specific type of AI model. Finally, *interpretability* is the qualitative understanding of the relationship between the input variables and the response (e.g. the relation between the words contained in an email and the email categorization as spam/non-spam).

Interpretability is the key aspect for an explanation to be accepted by a user; in our example of an email classifier, an interpretable explanation could rely on a list of words (e.g. the system thinks this email is spam because it contains the following words) rather that be based on opaque clues (e.g. word embeddings) which are not easily understandable by a human. The level of interpretability of an explanation of course depends on the audience, because humans use their previous knowledge about the application domain to interpret an explanation and accept/reject a prediction based on their understanding.

3.2. Explanation from a human point of view

The latest point on interpretability clarifies that proper attention should be given to the different kinds of explanations that could be generated, in particular by distinguishing "machine" explanations from "human" explanations.

Indeed, most XAI research has been focusing on generating *machine explanations*, i.e. justifications of what/how the machine "thinks". In other words, machine explanations try to explain the scientific theory behind a model, to allow for phenomena comprehension. In case of interpretable models (like linear regression or decision trees), the machine explanation consists in making explicit the mathematical/logical relation between inputs and outputs (e.g. tree model of decisions). In case of black-box models, especially for deep learning and other complex approaches, the machine explanation may be based on "compressed" models or other approximation techniques that still use an explicit representation of the relation between inputs and outputs.

Instead, *human explanations* focus on what a human user wants to know in order to interpret a model and make subsequent decisions. The user may be uninterested in the internal functioning of an algorithm, as she may even be unable to understand a potentially complex mathematical formulation of the function that transforms the input parameters in the output prediction. On the contrary, the user is interested in getting useful clues on why a specific output is given, in order to evaluate if such output is "reliable" from a human understanding point of view.

As a consequence, in order to be useful, a human explanation needs to display some specific characteristics [14]. An explanation should be *selective*: it should not provide all possible reasons, but convey only the "relevant" causes; indeed, people usually do not expect an explanation to consist of a complete cause of an event, also to let the explanation itself being reduced to a cognitively manageable size; moreover, an explanation should not contain useless information, like presuppositions or beliefs that the user already holds. Humans psychologically prefer *contrastive* explanations, in that they are used to reason according to counter-factual causality (i.e. people do not ask why an event A happened, but rather why an event A happened instead of some other event B), especially in case of an anomaly or an abnormal event. Another characteristic of human explanations is that they are usually *social*, involving the interaction between (multiple) explainers and explainees; also with respect to eXplainable AI, explanations should be seen as an interactive process, including interaction and dialogue with a mix of human and machine participants.

From all the above considerations, it is apparent that eXplainable AI research should go well beyond automatic methods to generate explanations; it is of utmost importance to keep the *Human-in-the-Loop*. There are at least two main reasons to advocate for the active involvement of people in eXplainable AI [15]: on the one hand, if explanation formulation is delegated to "computer scientists", the risk is that such explanations are too close to the model and too far from human understanding, especially that of domain/business users who need to interpret such information; on the other hand, there is a large body of knowledge about explanations from the social sciences (philosophy, psychology, cognitive science), which could bring tangible benefits to eXplainable AI research in terms of getting to a "good" explanation from a human point of view [16].

4. Human Intelligence and Knowledge Graphs to support eXplainable AI

The Semantic Web has always relied on humans, since most of its tasks are knowledge-intensive and context-specific and, as such, they require user engagement for their solution (e.g., conceptual modeling, multi-language resource labelling, content annotation with ontologies, concept/entity similarity recognition). With the rise of Knowledge Graphs and their popularity, new opportunities have emerged to exploit them for AI in general and specifically for eXplainable AI [17].

Without the claim of being exhaustive, in the following we illustrate a set of approaches that can bring Human Intelligence and Knowledge Graphs to the benefit of eXplainable AI, with specific reference to Machine Learning. We distinguish between two main types of opportunities, those related to the exploitation of (human-generated) Knowledge Graphs and those that capitalize on the direct involvement of people; we depict them in Figure 1 along two axes, representing whether Human Intelligence is employed in data/knowledge representation or for explanations.

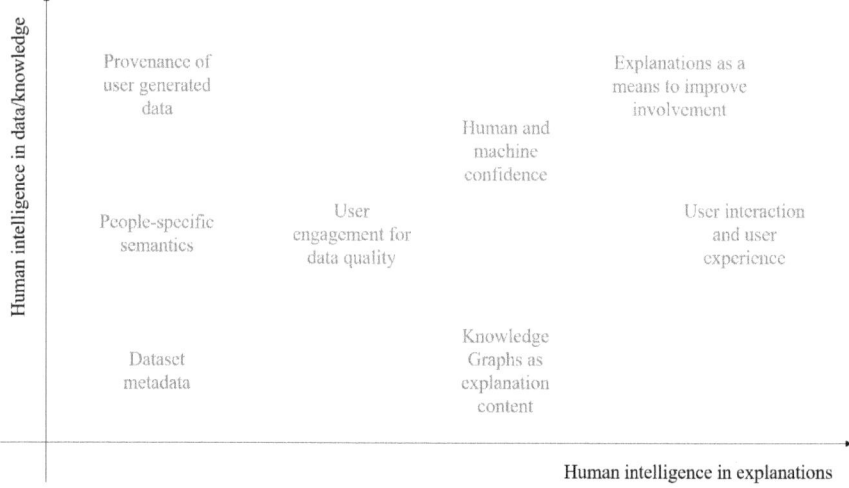

Figure 1. Graphical representation of Human Intelligence approaches.

4.1. (Human) Knowledge Graphs for XAI

The first set of approaches exploits Knowledge Graphs to support explanation generation. We specifically focus on the role of human-generated information to directly and indirectly support XAI.

4.1.1. Dataset metadata

Structured data represents an invaluable input for any Machine Learning approach. Consequently, linked data and Knowledge Graphs represent as such a rich and priceless contribution. An important role can even be played by simple metadata: descriptive metadata about datasets, in the form of DCAT [18] and related vocabularies, can be exploited to improve data sourcing. The information about where some data comes from can also be re-used for explanations: users can better judge the reliability or the meaningfulness of a machine output if they are given also the detail about the original sources.

For example, the opportunities to facilitate dataset reuse in the development of chatbots are illustrated by the BotDCAT-AP vocabulary [19], an extension of the Data Catalogue (DCAT) Application Profile. BotDCAT-AP enables the description of intents (i.e., the actions users want to accomplish by interacting with a chatbot) and entities (i.e., individual information units associated to an intent) supported by a dataset and the method to access it; as such, it enables and fosters reusability of datasets (including Knowledge Graphs) across chatbot systems. It could also be exploited further to support the generation of explanations for the chatbot "replies" in terms of recognized intents/entities and used datasets.

4.1.2. People-specific semantics

Different users may have different interests or skills and, as a consequence, they may need different explanations. User-generated data often implicitly contains hints on *what people care about*; this can be an opportunity to exploit when providing explanations on systems trained on such data.

For example, spatial data analytics of OpenStreetMap manual tagging showed to be beneficial for geo-ontology engineering, by surfacing latent semantic differences in concepts by different communities [20]: the same "concept" of spatial object (e.g., a pub) may have slightly diverging meanings in different places (e.g., a place to dine in UK, a bar to have a drink in Italy). This implicit semantics, when extracted and made explicit, can be exploited also for explanation generation, because it can contribute to convey the right "semantics" to the right community.

4.1.3. Provenance of user-generated data

Providing better data for training in turn leads to better models, as well as to more interpretable explanations. When data is user-generated, quality assurance is an important step, for example to aggregate inputs from multiple contributors (cf. "truth inference" in Crowdsourcing [21]). Provenance metadata about human contributions often contain important clues that can be exploited both for quality improvement and for generating explanations.

For example, in the case of the Human Computation-powered volunteered geographic information (VGI) illustrated in [22], the involvement of a crowd of volunteers, potentially untrained or non-experts, implies that VGI can be of varying quality; tracing VGI provenance enables the recording of the collection activity: the information about who gathered what, where and when is then employed to compute and judge the VGI quality. The same provenance information can be offered to users of systems trained on such user-generated data, to explain where some prediction comes from.

4.1.4. Knowledge graphs as explanation content

Structured knowledge and Knowledge Graphs can be used as basis for explanations, because they may already contain the rationale behind the relationship between inputs and outputs of a system. Whenever a predictive system is based on a knowledge base, the relevant part of it that motivates a system output can be directly used as explanation.

For example, graph traversal information is used to explain the suggestions of a knowledge-based recommender system in [23]: the logical path connecting a user (e.g., John loves hard rock music) and a recommended item (e.g., X is a Web-radio broadcasting rock music) provides a digestible account of the reasons behind the recommendation (e.g., John is recommended to listen to X, because John *loves* hard rock music, hard rock *is a kind of* rock music, X *broadcasts* rock music). The chain of relevant connected resources/properties (i.e., the set of triples composing a path between the user and the recommended item) already constitutes a human explanation for the recommendation.

4.2. Human Intelligence for XAI

The second set of approaches directly focuses on the active involvement of people to the benefit of XAI.

4.2.1. User engagement for data quality

As claimed in Section 3, in order to provide human explanations, we should turn to social sciences, which may help in the involvement and engagement of people also during the phase of explanation generation for AI systems. Engaging humans is a challenge by itself, therefore eXplainable AI could reuse the research results in relation to designing and exploiting behaviors, personal motivations and incentive mechanisms.

For example, the evaluation and improvement of data quality can be achieved through an analysis of contributions: user behavior influences data quality and should be taken into account, to evaluate the reliability of user-generated information, to better design data collection systems and to generate explanations. As demonstrated in [24], the presence of tangible rewards, leveraging extrinsic motivation, affects quantity and quality of collected data; moreover, an analysis of accuracy and participation of contributors highlights different engagement profiles, which should be taken into account when aggregating user-generated data and should be capitalized for explainability.

4.2.2. User interaction and user experience

Lessons learned and best practices from user experience design can also inform human-powered explanation generation, because they can help in designing suitable tools and data value chains that involve and engage people to bring benefit to AI in general and eXplainable AI specifically.

Indeed, a carefully designed user interaction with digital tools proves to be key in raising attention and improving data quality, as shown in [25] with respect to survey data collection: an improvement on user experience, making questionnaire compilation more enjoyable, leads also to higher-quality information, because it reduces the satisfying effect and increases response quality. Therefore, involving users for the generation or validation of explanations, for example by adopting a social and interactive pattern guided by a design thinking approach, can maximize user attention and ease user experience, thus making sure that the result is a *good* explanation from a human point of view.

4.2.3. Human and machine confidence

Predictive Machine Learning modeling aims at building a trustworthy system able to provide prediction on unknown cases; to evaluate model confidence, different metrics are usually employed to give quantitative estimates of a prediction reliability. Reporting confidence metrics to support prediction explanation is a means to increase user trust, but again those quantitative hints should be interpretable from a human point of view.

Human intervention can be also employed to support a model evaluation and, consequently, a model explanation through confidence metrics. Indeed, it can happen that what is "difficult" to predict for an algorithm (i.e. predictions with low confidence metrics) is also difficult for humans to judge; the case of questionable image classification is illustrated in [26], where the correspondence exists between low-confidence machine classifications and user disagreement. The correlation between human and machine predictions and their respective confidence/reliability can be exploited to understand the reasons behind a model and can therefore improve both the modeling phase (by incorporating additional human knowledge in training) and the generation of explanations (which can be closer to human understanding).

4.2.4. Explanation as a means to improve user involvement

The most challenging aspect of Human-Machine Cooperation is the effective involvement of people in the various phases of modeling. While users are already employed in data collection and model validation, further opportunities lie in a more interwoven interaction between human steps and automatic steps. Therefore, explanations are not only an objective as such, but they can be an instrument to further involve and motivate human participants in the AI system life-cycle.

For example, in order to identify and reduce bias in knowledge representation and modeling, the involved users should not only be exposed to potential biased information, but should also be given an explanation for such an identified bias, to understand the reasons behind a questionable piece of information or prediction. A Human-in-the-Loop approach to identify and resolve implicit bias in Knowledge Graphs is illustrated in [27]: users are involved not only to accept/reject an identified bias, but they are also engaged as decision-makers to evaluate if further actions should be taken to solve such bias.

5. Conclusions

eXplainable AI aims at generating explanations to justify the output of an algorithm to a user, usually a decision-maker. Those explanations need to be interpretable by the intended target users and, therefore, cannot be restricted to the "scientific modeling" (i.e., the explanation of the scientific/mathematical law or theory behind an artificial model), but should be focused on addressing the needs of the decision makers, which exploit such explanations and decide whether to trust an AI system.

Therefore, a better understanding of *Human Intelligence* is needed to make sure that the generated explanations are "good enough" to be used in practice: a certain help can come from social sciences, but even within the ICT community, we identify several opportunities. On the one hand, Knowledge Representation and Reasoning (KRR) research has always been addressing the open issue of human knowledge formalization; in this context, therefore, eXplainable AI can leverage all the experience related to the involvement of human annotators and crowdsourced knowledge bases and Knowledge Graphs (e.g. DBpedia [28] and Wikidata [29]): indeed, the same Human Intelligence that supports KRR tasks can be similarly exploited for eXplainable AI.

On the other hand, Human Computer Interaction (HCI) research has been focusing on improving and optimizing user experience with digital tools; in this context, eXplainable AI can leverage the approaches and methods to support the "interaction" between a human user and a digital explanation, improving interpretability and promote trust. AI system should be designed to allow and facilitate the exchange with the relevant user communities: while people are already heavily involved in data collection, their engagement in other steps of the AI life-cycle is still to be fully explored, especially with respect to explainability.

The big challenge is to define flexible and complex human-computer cooperative systems, able to guide in the preparation, building and production of data processing pipelines involving Artificial Intelligence technologies. Human Intelligence and Knowledge Graphs should become first-order citizens of such data value chains, not only to improve the performance of such artificial systems, but also – and foremost – to assure that AI outcomes are relevant and usable by human decision makers.

Acknowledgments

The presented research was partially supported by the ACTION project (grant agreement number 824603), co-funded by the European Commission under the Horizon 2020 Framework Programme. We would like to thank Gloria Re Calegari and Ilaria Tiddi for their feedback and revision on this chapter.

References

[1]   P.C. Shih, Beyond Human-in-the-Loop: Empowering End-Users with Transparent Machine Learning, in: *Human and Machine Learning*, Springer, 2018, pp. 37–54.
[2]   J. Howe, *Crowdsourcing: How the power of the crowd is driving the future of business*, Random House, 2008.
[3]   E. Law and L.v. Ahn, *Human computation*, Vol. 5, Morgan & Claypool Publishers, 2011, pp. 1–121.
[4]   A. Irwin, *Citizen science: A study of people, expertise and sustainable development*, Routledge, 2002.
[5]   R. Zheng and K. Greenberg, Effective Design in Human and Machine Learning: A Cognitive Perspective, in: *Human and Machine Learning*, Springer, 2018, pp. 55–74.
[6]   K. Yu, S. Berkovsky, D. Conway, R. Taib, J. Zhou and F. Chen, Do I trust a machine? Differences in user trust based on system performance, in: *Human and Machine Learning*, Springer, 2018, pp. 245–264.

[7] S.A. Cambo and D. Gergle, User-Centred Evaluation for Machine Learning, in: *Human and Machine Learning*, Springer, 2018, pp. 315–339.

[8] B. Settles, Active learning literature survey, Technical Report, University of Wisconsin-Madison Department of Computer Sciences, 2009.

[9] S.J. Pan and Q. Yang, A survey on transfer learning, *IEEE Transactions on knowledge and data engineering* **22**(10) (2009), 1345–1359.

[10] S. Amershi, J. Fogarty and D. Weld, Interactive Machine Learning for On-Demand Group Creation in Social Networks', in: *Proceedings of the SIGCHI Conference on Human Factors in Computing Systems*, 2012, pp. 21–30.

[11] N. Boukhelifa, A. Bezerianos and E. Lutton, Evaluation of interactive machine learning systems, in: *Human and Machine Learning*, Springer, 2018, pp. 341–360.

[12] C. Noessel, *Designing agentive technology: AI that works for people*, Rosenfeld Media, 2017.

[13] M.T. Ribeiro, S. Singh and C. Guestrin, " Why should i trust you?" Explaining the predictions of any classifier, in: *Proceedings of the 22nd ACM SIGKDD international conference on knowledge discovery and data mining*, 2016, pp. 1135–1144.

[14] B. Mittelstadt, C. Russell and S. Wachter, Explaining explanations in AI, in: *Proceedings of the conference on fairness, accountability, and transparency*, 2019, pp. 279–288.

[15] T. Miller, P. Howe and L. Sonenberg, Explainable AI: Beware of inmates running the asylum or: How I learnt to stop worrying and love the social and behavioural sciences, *arXiv preprint arXiv:1712.00547* (2017).

[16] T. Miller, Explanation in artificial intelligence: Insights from the social sciences, *Artificial Intelligence* **267** (2019), 1–38.

[17] F. Lecue, On the role of knowledge graphs in explainable AI, *Semantic Web* **11**(1) (2020), 41–51. doi:10.3233/SW-190374.

[18] R. Albertoni, D. Browning, S. Cox, A. Gonzalez Beltran, A. Perego and P. Winstanley, Data Catalog Vocabulary (DCAT) - Version 2, Technical Report, W3C, 2020.

[19] P. Cappello, M. Comerio and I. Celino, BotDCAT-AP: An Extension of the DCAT Application Profile for Describing Datasets for Chatbot Systems., in: *PROFILES at ISWC*, 2017.

[20] G. Re Calegari, E. Carlino, I. Celino and D. Peroni, Supporting geo-ontology engineering through spatial data analytics, in: *European Semantic Web Conference*, Springer, 2016, pp. 556–571.

[21] Y. Zheng, G. Li, Y. Li, C. Shan and R. Cheng, Truth inference in crowdsourcing: Is the problem solved?, *Proceedings of the VLDB Endowment* **10**(5) (2017), 541–552.

[22] I. Celino, Human computation VGI provenance: Semantic web-based representation and publishing, *IEEE Transactions on Geoscience and Remote Sensing* **51**(11) (2013), 5137–5144.

[23] D. Dell'Aglio, I. Celino and D. Cerizza, Anatomy of a semantic web-enabled recommender system, in: *Proceedings of the 4th International Workshop Semantic Matchmaking and Resource Retrieval in the Semantic Web, 9th International Semantic Web Conference, Shanghai*, 2010.

[24] G. Re Calegari and I. Celino, Interplay of Game Incentives, Player Profiles and Task Difficulty in Games with a Purpose, in: *European Knowledge Acquisition Workshop*, Springer, 2018, pp. 306–321.

[25] I. Celino and G. Re Calegari, Submitting surveys via a conversational interface: an evaluation of user acceptance and approach effectiveness, *International Journal of Human Computer Studies* **139** (2020). doi:10.1016/j.ijhcs.2020.102410.

[26] G. Re Calegari, G. Nasi and I. Celino, Human computation vs. machine learning: an experimental comparison for image classification, *Human Computation* **5**(1) (2018), 13–30.

[27] A. Morales Tirado, A. Oelen, V. Pasqual, M. Shi, A. Umbrico, W. Xu and I. Celino, A human-in-the-loop framework to handle implicit bias in crowdsourced KGs, Knowledge Graphs evolution and preservation – Technical Report from the International Semantic Web Research Summer School (ISWS 2019), 2019.

[28] S. Auer, C. Bizer, G. Kobilarov, J. Lehmann, R. Cyganiak and Z. Ives, Dbpedia: A nucleus for a web of open data, in: *The semantic web*, Springer, 2007, pp. 722–735.

[29] S. Malyshev, M. Krötzsch, L. González, J. Gonsior and A. Bielefeldt, Getting the most out of Wikidata: semantic technology usage in Wikipedia's knowledge graph, in: *International Semantic Web Conference*, Springer, 2018, pp. 376–394.

IOS Press, 2020
© *2020 Akademische Verlagsgesellschaft AKA GmbH, Berlin. All rights reserved.*
doi:10.3233/SSW200025

Managing Identity in Knowledge-Based Explainable Systems

Ilaria TIDDI, and Joe RAAD

Dept. of Computer Science, Vrije Universiteit Amsterdam, The Netherlands

Abstract. In this chapter, we focus on the role of identity links in knowledge-based explainable systems, i.e. systems that rely on background knowledge from knowledge graphs to build explanations. With the rise of explainable transparent methods in the area of eXplainable AI, systems integrating multiple sources of aligned knowledge will become more and more common. We hypothesize that the interpretability and results of these systems could be affected by the discrepancy and misalignment between knowledge sources – a widely known problem in the Knowledge Representation community. We therefore study the role of identity in knowledge-based explainable systems, i.e. if and how explainable systems do rely on multiple knowledge graphs, then show examples of the impact of misusing identity on the interpretability of a system. Finally, we describe methods that can promote the correct alignment of knowledge sources. Our hope is to provide support to improving current knowledge-based explainable methods and, more in general, foster a better integration of knowledge representation and explainable AI.

Keywords. Identity Management, owl:sameAs, Entity Linking, Explainability, eXplainable AI

1. Introduction

A number of knowledge sources and related applications rely nowadays on the use of owl:sameAs, allowing to link entities of one dataset to the ones represented in other existing knowledge sources. Originally defined by [1], owl:sameAs relationships (also called *identity links*) have a very strict semantics: "an owl:sameAs statement indicates that two IRI references refer to the same thing", meaning that the statement $\langle e_1$, owl:sameAs $e_2 \rangle$ indicates that every property asserted for e_1 should be inferred for e_2, and vice versa. By allowing the reuse of resource identifiers and explicitly stating their equivalences, owl:sameAs statements have therefore helped creating a huge Web of Data, with hundreds of thousands of linked datasets [5].

Identity links can be extremely useful for developing intelligent knowledge-based systems, enabling the serendipitous discovery of new, unrevealed knowledge. Throughout the years, a number of applications using identity links to obtain more information and improve their results for a better user experience have been developed, such as exploratory search systems [16,36,40], recommender systems [15,25,47], and virtual assistants [44,48,50]. While these applications show the power of identity links within the Web of (Linked) Data, they have also raised a number of questions about their misuse [23]. Dataset modifications have resulted in broken/inaccessible IRI, information redundancy and incorrect declaration of identity, which, in turn, can have wide-ranging effects, including rendering applications largely unusable. This need of better understanding the role of `owl:sameAs` links across datasets has resulted in a large body of studies in the area of Knowledge Representation, that focused on empirically analyzing the use of identity links in knowledge-based applications [3,26,46,52].

In this chapter, we study the role and the use of identity links in knowledge-based explainable (KBX-) systems. Explanations in Artificial Intelligence have re-gained momentum due to the newest machine (deep) learning techniques, that are able to achieve human-like performance but are still largely inscrutable. The newly born eXplainable AI field [22] focuses on making these methods explainable, interpretable, and consequently more transparent. We hypothesize that the misuse of identity links could affect the interpretability of explainable systems, that do not tolerate data uncertainty caused by discrepancy and misalignment between knowledge sources. This could result in the systems being unable to integrate multiple, heterogeneous datasets, which instead could greatly benefit their explainability and a more transparent reasoning. Our goal is to investigate how to promote the correct use of identity links across knowledge sources and how this can improve the current methods for knowledge-based eXplainable AI systems. To the best of our knowledge, the misuse of identity links in XAI is yet to be explored.

In order to do so, we will first analyze how identity is being managed in knowledge-based eXplainable systems, and specifically if multiple knowledge sources are being used to generate explanations, which, and how. We then show two examples of how the misuse of identity links can affect interpretability of a knowledge-based system. We further investigate which methods we investigate which methods can be used to verify the correctness of asserted identity links. Finally, we discuss additional open challenges and future directions to improve current knowledge-based explainable methods and, more in general, promote a better integration of knowledge representation and eXplainable AI methods.

2. Background on Identity

Identity is an old and thorny topic. Classically speaking, entities that are identical are considered to share the same properties. With N denoting the set of all names, and Ψ the set of all properties, this "Indiscernibility of Identicals" (1) is attributed to Leibniz and its converse, the "Identity of Indiscernibles" (2) states that entities that share the same properties are identical. It also follows from Leibniz's Law that identity is reflexive, symmetrical and transitive.

$$a = b \rightarrow (\forall_{\psi \in \Psi})(\psi(a) = \psi(b)) \tag{1}$$

$$(\forall_{\psi \in \Psi})(\psi(a) = \psi(b)) \rightarrow a = b \tag{2}$$

The identity relation induces a partitioning of N into a collection of non-empty and mutually disjoint *equivalence classes* $N_k \subseteq N$. From the premises $\psi(a)$, and $a, b \in N_k$, it follows that $\psi(b)$ is also the case. In fact, this deduction is central to the Web of Data as it allows complementary descriptions of the same resource to be maintained locally, yet interchanged globally, merely by interlinking the names that are used in those respective descriptions. However, there are also problems with it, and – consequently – criticisms have been leveled against it.

While these problems are not new in the field of Knowledge Representation [20,41], they are however specifically visible in the context of the Web of Data due to its unprecedented size, the heterogeneity of its content and users, and the absence of a central naming authority. This section briefly presents some of the well-known issues with this notion of identity.

Philosophical Problems. From a philosophical point of view, two major issues arise with the notion of identity. Firstly, identity poses problems over time, as a ship[1] may still be considered the same ship even though some, or even all, of its original components (i.e. properties) have been replaced by new ones [31]. In addition, identity is context-dependent [18], allowing two medicines having the same chemical structure to be considered the same in a medical context, but different in other contexts (e.g. because they are produced by different companies). These issues in the classical identity definition have led to various philosophical theories, such as the distinction between *accidental properties* (i.e. traits that could be taken away from an object without making it a different thing), and *essential properties* (core elements needed for a thing to be the thing that it is) [28].

Practical Problems. The notion of identity is also standardized as part of the Web Ontology Language, and the innate issues related to identity are naturally found also in knowledge-based applications. In fact, and due to the Open World Assumption and the continuous increase of properties belonging to Ψ, identity statements in the Web of Data are becoming more and more controversial.

Firstly, unless two things are explicitly said to be different (e.g. using `owl:differentFrom`), the absence of an identity statement between them does not mean that they are not identical. Compared to the 558M `owl:sameAs` present in a 2015's crawl of the Web of Data [17], `owl:differentFrom` statements were barely present (i.e. only 3.6K statements found in the same dataset).

Additionally, `owl:sameAs` links are generally automatically generated through heuristic entity resolution techniques, that employ practical, *brute force* strategies and often do not guarantee accuracy. For example, the precision of such tools ranged between 67% and 86% in the 2017 and 2018 Ontology Alignment Evaluation Initiative (OAEI)[2].

Finally, studies have shown that data modelers have different opinions about whether two objects are the same or not. In [24] for instance, three KR experts were asked to judge 250 `owl:sameAs` links collected from the Web. The evaluation shows high disagreements, with one judge confirming the correctness of only 73 `owl:sameAs` statements, whilst the two other experts judging up to 132 and 181 links as true statements. While in some cases this may be due to differences in modeling competence, there is also the problem that two modelers may consider different parts of the same knowledge graph within different contexts.

3. Identity Management in current KBX-systems

After introducing some of the known issues with the notion of identity standardized in the `owl:sameAs` predicate, our first step is to understand if and how identity links are

---

[1]Reference to the ship of Theseus or Theseus's paradox, cfr: `https://en.wikipedia.org/wiki/Ship_of_Theseus`.

[2]`http://oaei.ontologymatching.org/2018/results/conference/index.html`

being used and managed in knowledge-based systems. We therefore look at methods that allow to reason over multiple, connected knowledge sources to generate explanations. While the use of multiple knowledge graphs in the XAI landscape is at its early stage, we identified three types of works:

1. *Mapping-based methods.* The first area includes works that integrates knowledge from sources that provide direct mappings, i.e. alignments between entities of different nature. For instance, the Visual Genome [29] maps scene descriptions to Word-Net's object synsets; while ImageNet provides mappings of the images to both Word-Net and ConceptNet. These works are mostly focused on explanations in multi-classification problems, such as images or text, and reasoning if mostly performed on common-sense knowledge (as opposed to fact-based knowledge). For example, [33] uses WordNet-Visual Genome mappings to explain and augment the description of a given scene, where objects have been identified using a CNN. In [58], mappings between DBpedia, WebChild and ConceptNet are used to allow a RNN-LSTM model to extract facts (in the form sets of of triples) that can explain the answers to a given visual question given as an input. Authors of [35] integrate both ConceptNet and Word-Net in an attention-based model for reading comprehension, explaining the answer for any given document by reasoning on the information retrieved from these external knowledge sources.

2. *Schema-based methods.* In the second area we find works that align resources using TBoxes, i.e. declaring identical entities if belonging to equivalent between classes. These works mostly focus on binary predictions, and equivalence is often manually declared. For example, [30] uses RDFS ontologies to enhance input data points of a binary classifier, abstracting them into concepts that be used to derive human-understandable explanations. These concepts are extracted from the DBpedia and the Microsoft Concept Graph and then manually mapped to a domain ontology. A knowledge graph-based transfer learning approach is proposed in [9] to explain predictions of delayed flights. The idea is to first learn the predictions based on the dataset and a local OWL ontology, then use DBpedia entities to explain positive and negative transfers from one domain to another. Finally, [10] combined ontological knowledge and reasoning capabilities of existing lexical knowledge bases (BabelNet, NASARI, and ConceptNet) to build explanations accompanying scores predicting entity similarity.

3. *Query-based methods.* These works integrate datasources using either SPARQL queries or follow-your-nose strategies for forward-only querying. For example, [42] exploits WordNet as a pivot to build links between Wikidata and ImageNet, and then explains an scene using a pre-trained CNN using OpenCV's outputs, WordNet's synsets and Wikidata properties. [59] uses the Linked Data Cloud to extend a QA-system that retrieves answers and additional information from the graph. An inference model relying on is used to map variables to SPARQL queries, infer `owl:sameAs` links, retrieve answers from the graph, and extend the information with the additional relevant knowledge. In [32], a large-scale knowledge graph integrating DBpedia, schema.org and YAGO is exploited to automatically build explanations for travel recommendations in natural language. In [14], Freebase and Wikidata are used to visually explain unexpected price changes of stock trends using a Temporal Convolutional Network. The graphs are used as external background knowledge, to derive embeddings for events and price values extracted from a dataset of financial news. A QA-based

conversational agent for storytelling using knowledge of FrameNet, WordNet and the Open Mind Common-sense dataset is used in [53]. The authors exploit WordNet's verbal causal relationships `cs(Cause, Effect)` and `ent(Action,Consequence)` to generate sentences answering *why* questions about a story.

These works show that identity can be used in a variety of contexts (e.g. images, text, speech) to extract additional information from heterogeneous, connected knowledge graphs, mainly bringing forward the idea that the graphs' topology (i.e. semantic edges, paths between nodes) are the key to provide context to a system's output, and consequently to generate explanations. The following question arising is therefore how the misuse of identity could, in practice, affect these systems? In the following, we answer this question by providing two case scenarios.

4. Limitations of `owl:sameAs` in Knowledge-Based eXplainable systems

This section shows two practical examples of how the misuse of identity can affect knowledge-based explainable systems that rely on links across data sources. In particular, we show how results of a knowledge-based explainable system can be biased by (1) the *incompleteness* (i.e. uneven representation of identities in a dataset) and (2) the incorrectness (wrong attribution of identity across datasets) of `owl:sameAs` links.

4.1. Data Incompleteness : Knowledge-Based eXplanations

In 2014, the system Dedalo was introduced as a framework to automatically explain the similarity of unsupervised learning outputs using knowledge extracted from the Web of Data [55]. Dedalo was based on two main assumptions:

1. if items happen to be in the same group (better defined as cluster), there is an underlying common characteristics that makes them belonging together, which can go beyond the way items were grouped;
2. the Web of Data consists in a graph of IRI entities connected through RDF properties, that can be blindly navigated in order to serendipitously discover knowledge across different data sources using link traversal, and these can be exploited to find the characteristics that items within a group have in common;

and two consequently derived observations:

1. resources (nodes) in the graph of the Web of Data can have a common walk, expressed in the form of a chain of contiguous RDF properties (i.e. a graph *path*), to a specific, more distant, resource;
2. if items of a cluster, represented as resources in the graph, share the same path to a specific entity, then the path and the found entity can be used as an explanation to their grouping.

Based on the above, Dedalo then applies a greedy graph search strategy [54], aiming at finding the least-cost path from the set of initial nodes (the entities within the cluster to be explain) to a distant goal node, i.e. an entity that the initial nodes might have in common somewhere in the graph, and uses an adaptation of Entropy [51] to estimate this cost. Because the Web of Data can be traversed by IRI dereferencing, Dedalo explores the graph by trying to improve the accuracy of the explanations, defined in terms of F-Measure, by iteratively deepening the exploration of the graph.

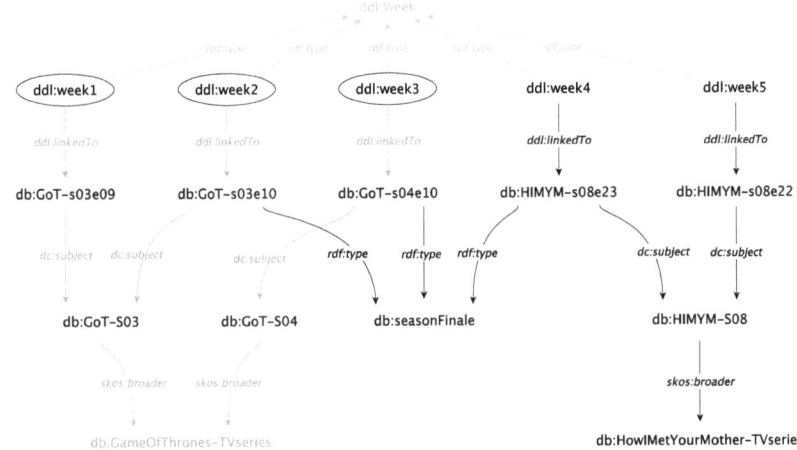

Figure 1. Example of automatic generation of explanations using knowledge from the Web of Data.

Let us take the example of the term "A Song of Ice and Fire", whose popularity varies depending on the time the year according to Google Trends, a well-known website to analyses the top searches on Google[3]. In Figure 1, G is a RDF graph that includes a set E of 5 entities, each of which represents a week time frame where some TV series episodes have been broadcasted. Links from a week to a broadcasted event are labelled `ddl:linkedTo`. From the Google Trend data, we know that the first three entities $E_1 = \{$`ddl:week1, ddl:week2, ddl:week3`$\}$ (with $E_1 \subset E$) are the ones where more people searched for the term "A Song of Ice and Fire", and we are looking at explain why the term is particularly popular in these specific weeks. In order to do this, Dedalo iteratively builds the graph starting from the 5 initial entities in E by dereferencing them, revealing the IRIs they link to, and gradually detecting that the most interesting explanation for E_1 is that all entities are linked to `db:GameOfThrones-TVseries`. This is expressed in the graph as a chain of RDF properties and one final IRI resource, $\langle$`ddl:linkedTo-dc:subject-skos:broader · db:GameOfThrones-TVseries`$\rangle$, explaining that during the weeks belonging to E_1, an episode related to the TV series "Games of Thrones" has been broadcasted, resulting in an increase of searches for the book that inspired the series.

In a real-world scenario, we have a dataset of university students clustered according to the UK district they come from. The unsupervised learning reveals that there might be a correlation between faculties and geographical regions: for instance, Figure 2 shows that students enrolling to the Health and Social Care Faculty are concentrated around the Glasgow and Manchester areas (2a), while the Business and Law Faculty attracts students the districts around London (2b). The assumption is that there should be an eco-

---

[3]https://trends.google.com/trends/explore?hl=en-US&tz=-60&geo=US&q=A+Song+of+Ice+and+Fire&sni=3.

demographic explanation to this, and that Dedalo can use the socio-geographic information contained in DBpedia, GeoNames or Freebase, to detect the knowledge needed to build such explanation.

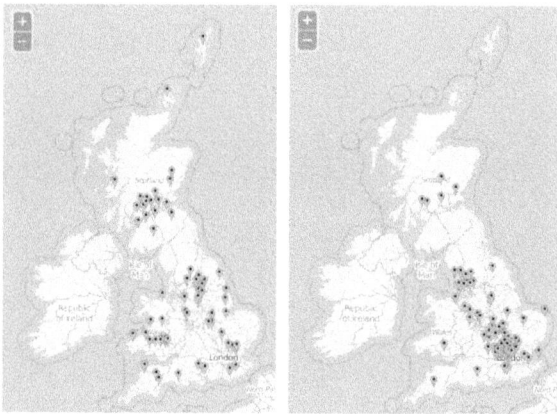

(a) Enrollment in the Faculty of   (b) Enrollment in the Faculty of
Health and Social Care.   Business and Law.

Figure 2. Example of explaining complex phenomena (student enrolment).

By introducing `owl:sameAs` links to the initial resource set to allow Dedalo's search to span across external data sources, the best explanation obtained for the Health and Social Care group was as follows: ⟨`owl:sameAs -cyc:broaderTerm · cyc:TheNorthernHe-misphere`⟩ with a F1 score of $F = 48,9\%$. Indeed, here more elements of the cluster appear to be located in the Northern Hemisphere, with an F-Measure of 48,9%. If we are talking about districts from the United Kingdom, what happened to the rest of the elements in the cluster? And how is it possible that such an explanation is the most representative for that one cluster, while other clusters also include only UK districts? A step back and a look at the graph processed by Dedalo while following links between IRI resources revealed that data links were incomplete, i.e. out of the 380 UK districts in Linked Data, only 137 were connected to an entity in graph through the walk ⟨`owl:sameAs, cyc:broaderTerm`⟩. This resulted in an even distribution of the values computed by Dedalo's process, affecting recall and precision, and consequently, the final explanations to be generated.

4.2. Data Incorrectness : Knowledge-Based Question Answering

Another example where the misuse of `owl:sameAs` can affect the interpretability of knowledge-based systems is question answering (QA). Knowledge-based QA-systems use the structure and semantics of KGs as a form of explicit reasoning, i.e. by considering answers an indicative explanations of a given question. This consequently enables end-users to access and validate information provenance, validity and context through transparent reasoning.

A wrong misuse of `owl:sameAs` links in the Web, however, can have an impact on the performance of these systems. Let us take the example of [7], presenting a QA system asking the question "Who are the band members of ABBA?" as the following SPARQL query:

```
select distinct ?member ?label {
    ?member
        skos:subject dbc:ABBA_members;
        rdfs:label ?label.
    filter(lang(?label) = "en") }
```

As of 2020, the above query ran against DBpedia endpoint returns no results, likely due to the use of the property `skos:subject`, which is no longer used to represent the ABBA members URI resources. `owl:sameAs` links represent an opportunity here, as links in the Web of Data could be followed to retrieve results from external datasets. The query can be changed as:

```
select distinct ?member ?label {
    ?member
        owl:sameAs*/skos:subject/owl:sameAs* dbc:ABBA_members;
        rdfs:label/owl:sameAs* ?label.
    filter(lang(?label) = "en") }
```

Table 1 shows the 92 returned results for this query. These results include the four correct answers, offering many alternative names/IRIs from DBpedia, Wikidata, OpenCyc, the New York Times, and other datasets, as well as many other that can be considered incorrect – ABBA's drummer, their manager, and a stalker of one of the band members.

Result	Correct Answer	Number of `owl:sameAs` entities
Björn Ulvaeus (band member)	✔	28
Agnetha Fältskog (band member)	✔	26
Anni-Frid Lyngstad (band member)	✔	9
Stig Andersson (band manager)	✗	9
Benny Andersson (band member)	✔	6
Benny Anderssons Orkester (new band)	✗	5
Ola Brukert (drummer)	✗	3
Agnetha Ulvaeus (Agnetha F. married name)	✗	2
Gert van der Graaf (stalker of Agnetha Fältskog)	✗	2
Stig Andersson (sportsman)	✗	2

Table 1. The 92 results of the ABBA band member query.

This problem is well known and mostly due to the erroneous declaration of `owl:sameAs` statements often resulting in equivalence sets of entities much larger than what they should be (e.g. Bolivia, Dublin, Coca-Cola and Albert Einstein resulting the same concepts, cfr. [46]).

The examples above show practical issues arising when misusing identity links. In the following, we overview the current approaches on identity management, in order to identify and provide solutions for knowledge-based explainable systems on how to exploit linked data sets in the most efficient way.

5. Current solutions to the Identity Problem

The identity problem in the Web of Data has led to a number of complementary solutions over the years, tackling various aspects of this problem. We identify three families of approaches: a first family focused on reuse of `owl:sameAs`, encouraging and facilitating a more responsible use of identity links through centralized management; a second family of observatories, approaches allowing to detect and find the explicitly and implicitly asserted identity links; finally, a last family of identity validators, focused on assessing the quality of the existing `owl:sameAs` links. Next, we will give an overview over these solutions.

5.1. Centralized Identity Management

In the early days of the Web, it was originally conceived that resource identifiers would fall into two classes: locators (URLs) to identify resources by their locations in the context of a particular access protocol such as HTTP or FTP, and names (URNs). URNs [34], were supposed to be the standard for assigning location-independent, globally unique, and persistent identifiers to arbitrary subjects. Each identifier has a defined namespace that is registered with the Internet Assigned Numbers Authority (IANA). For instance, ISBN is a registered namespace that unambiguously identifies any edition of a text-based monographic publication that is available to the public. For example, *urn:isbn:0451450523* is a URN that identifies the book "The Last Unicorn", using the ISBN namespace. Because of the lack of a well-defined resolution mechanism, and the organizational hurdle of requiring registration with IANA, URNs are hardly used (a total of 47K URNs in the 2015 copy of the Web of Data, with only 73 registered[4] URN namespaces with IANA at the time of writing). Since 2005, the use of the terms URNs and URLs has been deprecated in technical standards in favor of the term Uniform Resource Identifier (IRI), which encompasses both, and the term Internationalized Resource Identifier (IRI) which extends the IRI character set that only supports ASCI encoding.

A more recent proposal for a centrally managed naming service was proposed by [6]. This public entity name service (ENS), named Okkam[5], intends to establish a global digital space for publishing and managing information about entities. Every entity is uniquely identified with an unambiguous universal IRI known as an OKKAM ID, with the idea of encouraging people to reuse these identifiers instead of creating new ones. Each OKKAM ID is matched to a set of existing identifiers (e.g. DBpedia and Wikidata IRIs), using several data linking algorithms that are available in the public entity name service hosted at `http://okkam.org`. For instance, the company Apple has a profile with an Okkam ID[6], which is linked to other non-centrally managed IDs (e.g. `dbpedia/resource/Apple_Inc`). For each OKKAM entity, a set of attributes are collected and stored in the service for the purpose of finding and distinguishing entities from another. This centralized solution did not receive uptake in the wider Semantic Web community. This is not entirely unexpected, since the introduction of a centralized naming authority amounts to a strong departure from the original (Semantic) Web ideology, while at the same time requiring significant changes to the use and interchange of information from the Web of Linked Data in practice.

---

[4]https://www.iana.org/assignments/urn-namespaces/urn-namespaces.xhtml
[5]As a variation of Occam's razor: "entities are not to be multiplied without necessity"
[6]eid-9bc2b9fd-cb41-4401-8204-6c8933010acf

5.2. Identity Observatories

Other approaches tried to limit the identity problem in the Web of Data by providing centralized access to identity statements that are published in a decentralized way. Such identity observatories allow data consumers to make an informed decision regarding the quality of identity statements they encounter. In recent years, three identity observatories were introduced [3,19,37]. These web services allow users to find for a given IRI, the list of identifiers that belong to the same equivalence class. Whilst in [3] and [37] these equivalence classes are based solely on the transitive closure of owl:sameAs triples, the Consistent Reference Service (CRS) [19] incorporates a mix of identity and similarity relationships (such as owl:sameAs, umbel:isLike, skos:closeMatch, and vocab:similarTo). This service is based on 346M triples harvested from multiple RDF dumps and SPARQL endpoints, and hosted at http://sameas.org. Since its introduction in 2009, this large collection of triples linking over 203M IRIs, and resulting in 62.6M identity bundles, has been the basis for many subsequent approaches aiming to detect erroneous identity links (e.g. [12,13,56]). In 2016, the authors of [37,38] introduced LODsyndesis, a co-reference service hosted at http://www.ics.forth.gr/isl/LODsyndesis. This service is based on the transitive closure of 44M owl:sameAs triples, in which the data is harvested from existing data dumps (cfr. [49], datahub.io, and linklion.org), and subsets of DBpedia, Wikidata, Yago, and Freebase. This closure results in 24M equivalence classes, that covers more than 65M terms. Finally, a recent identity observatory was introduced by [3], and hosted at https://www.sameas.cc/. This service provides the largest collection of owl:sameAs statements that has been gathered from the LOD Cloud to date. This collection of 558.9M distinct owl:sameAs is based on the 2015 LOD Laundromat corpus [4], and contains 179M unique IRIs. It also contains the largest owl:sameAs equivalence closure, which consists of 49M equivalence classes.

5.3. Identity Validation

Various approaches have been proposed for detecting erroneous identity statements, based on different aspects:

1. *Source Trustworthiness*. An early approach for detecting erroneous identity statements in the Web of Data is idMesh [11], a probabilistic and decentralized framework for entity disambiguation. idMesh hypothesizes that links published by trusted sources (e.g., OpenID-based) are more likely to be correct. The approach detects conflicts between owl:sameAs and owl:differentFrom assertions by using a graph-based constraint satisfaction solver that exploits the symmetric and transitive nature of the owl:sameAs relation. The detected conflicts are resolved based on the iteratively refined trustworthiness of the sources from which the assertions originate.
2. *UNA Violations*. Several approaches have made use of the hypothesis that individual datasets apply the Unique Name Assumption (UNA) [13,56], and that violations of the UNA that are caused by cross-dataset linking are indicative of erroneous identity links. De Melo [13] applies a linear programming relaxation algorithm that seeks to delete the minimal number of owl:sameAs statements such that the UNA is no longer violated. Valdestilhas et al. [56] detect the resources that share the same equivalence

class and that belong to the same dataset, and ranks erroneous candidates based on the number of UNA violations.

3. *Content-based approaches.* Paulheim [45] represents each identity link as a feature vector in a high dimensional vector space, using direct types and in- and/or outgoing properties. They have tested different outlier detection methods in order to assign a score to each link, indicating the likeliness of being an outlier. Cuzzola et al. [12] propose to calculate a similarity score between the names that are involved in a given `owl:sameAs` link, by using the textual descriptions that are associated to these names (e.g., through the `rdfs:comment` property).

4. *Ontology Axiom Violations.* Hogan et al. [27] exploit ten OWL 2 RL rules in order to express the semantics of axioms such as `owl:differentFrom` and `owl:complementOf` in order to detect inconsistencies. Whenever an inconsistent equality set is detected, the erroneous links are identified by incrementally rebuilding the equality set in a manner that preserves consistency. Papaleo et al. [43] exploit class disjointness, (inverse) functional properties, locally complete properties, and property mappings in order to detect inconsistencies in an RDF graph made of the subparts of the two RDF descriptions involved in conflicting statements.

5. *Network Metrics.* Finally, a last category of approaches used network metrics for evaluating the quality of `owl:sameAs` links. Whilst in [46], the exploited identity network solely contains `owl:sameAs` statements, in [21] the local network considers all properties and names related to the two names linked by an `owl:sameAs`. Specifically, this approach aims at measuring the impact that a given `owl:sameAs` has on this local network, using three classic network metrics (clustering coefficient, betweenness centrality, and degree) and two metric specific to the Web of Data (description richness and `owl:sameAs` chains). In the latter work, the hypothesis is that a correct `owl:sameAs` will contribute in closing an open `owl:sameAs` chain. In [46], the approach brings forward the hypothesis that the more densely a group of names is interlinked, the higher the likelihood of those names to be identical. The approach firstly partitions the identity network into different connected components and then detects the community structure in each of these components. Finally, it assigns an error degree to each `owl:sameAs` based on the density of the community(ies) in which the two interlinked names belong and the reciprocity of the link.

6. Identity in Knowledge-Based eXplainable systems : Open Challenges

Although methods exist, that cope with erroneous identity statements in the Web of Data, we argue that additional effort is needed in order to provide solutions to guarantee robust, interpretable systems. Here, we discuss open challenges and ideas for future directions.

Uptake of Erroneous Link Detectors. Erroneous link detection approaches are often useful for specific datasets and/or in specific applications, but are not yet widely used by clients in practice. The reason for this is that existing identity resolution approaches are relatively complex to implement, computationally expensive to use, make assumptions that are valid for some but not all datasets, and rely on properties like text labels and/or ontological axioms that are present in some, but not all datasets. As such, existing identity resolution approaches are inherently at odds with graph-based navigation clients, which are generally light-weight, run on commodity hardware (e.g. within a web browser), and

Result	≤ 1.0	≤ 0.8	≤ 0.6	≤ 0.4	≤ 0.2	≤ 0.0
Björn Ulvaeus (band member)	28	8	8	3	2	2
Agnetha Fältskog (band member)	26	4	4	2	1	1
Anni-Frid Lyngstad (band member)	9	3	3	2	1	1
Benny Andersson (band member)	6	2	2	1	1	1
Ola Brukert (drummer)	3	2	2	1	1	1
Agnetha Ulvaeus (Agnetha F. married name)	2	0	0	0	0	0
Stig Andersson (band manager)	9	4	4	1	1	1
Gert van der Graaf (stalker of Agnetha Fältskog)	2	0	0	0	0	0
Benny Anderssons Orkester (new band)	5	3	3	0	0	0
Stig Andersson (sportsman)	2	2	2	0	0	0

Table 2. Results of the ABBA band member query using different error degrees.

are expected to be so generic as to be able to navigate the Web of Data, or at least a significant subset of it.

Solutions such as MetaLink [2] are needed to enable KBX-systems to make informed decisions about whether or not to follow specific links in the Web. MetaLink is a resource containing *metadata* for a very large set of Web-crawled `owl:sameAs` links, describing the degree of trustworthiness as defined using the error metrics of [46]. Taking back the examples Section 4, a resource as such can help increase the quality of the returned results. For example, Table 2 shows the number of results for different error degrees in MetaLink. The column under ≤ 1.0 shows the results when all available links are followed, i.e., without distinguishing between high and low error degrees. The subsequent columns lower the error degree, resulting in more trustworthy links. While the use of such a resource is inconclusive for this query, we can nevertheless see that the number of incorrect results have decreased when only links with a low error degree are followed (e.g. error degree ≤ 0.4).

Similarly, Dedalo's could enquire with MetaLink on the trustworthiness of the links discovered during the graph traversal, and improve on the quality and accuracy explanations generated.

Increase Semantics of `owl:sameAs` links. In Section 5, several alternative identity predicates were presented. A big downside of these alternatives is their lack of formal semantics. For instance, in `skos:exactMatch` whether a degree of confidence is high (enough) is subjective, and the meaning of this relation even changes over time, because information is always evolving over time. Also, some proposed alternative properties do not denote equivalence relations, which means that they are of limited use in reasoning and linking. Another downside of these approaches is that they require data publishers to change their modeling practice. A lot of momentum is needed in order to create new knowledge graphs, or to change existing ones in order to make use of these alternative properties. As a result, most of these proposals lack uptake and are only used in a handful of datasets.

Integrate Distributed Knowledge. As seen, the use of multiple knowledge graphs in KBX-application is increasing. Indeed, it is unrealistic to assume that the available knowledge is stored in a single collection or dataset. Moreover, each different organization or user, represents and stores their data in different places and with different ways (different conceptualizations, models and formats). There are two main challenges related to this topic. First, the different representations of the data used makes the task of aggregation, interlinking and integration very difficult (e.g. see [39] for a recent survey). Second, the selection of the appropriate dataset to exploit, between the wide range of the available sources, is not a trivial task, and dataset search is an open problem [8].

Exploit Multilinguality. One advantage of certain knowledge graphs such as Wikidata and BabelNet is their multilingual nature. Multilinguality is still an open challenge in many systems, but could support explainability and transparency as knowledge sources could be used for training across languages (i.e. there are plenty of datasets for some natural languages, and very few for others). This idea has been advanced by [57], but further research is needed in this direction to explore their applicability in the field of eXplainable AI.

Tackle KGs Scalability. While KBX-systems make use of aligned knowledge sources, they make a limited use of the information extracted from the graphs – mostly, restricted to nodes and their closest neighborhood. This is likely due to a scalability problem, i.e. the computational costs that are related to reason over large-scale knowledge graphs, preventing a KBX-system to perform more advanced inference. More scalable techniques are needed in this direction.

7. Conclusions

The chapter focuses on the role and the usage of identity links in explainable systems that rely on knowledge graphs to build their explanations. First, we showed that the use of multiple knowledge graphs is becoming more and more common in explainable systems. We then showed examples of the impact that a misuse of identity can have on the systems' results and interpretability. Finally, we identified and described methods that can promote the correct management of identity links across knowledge sources. Our hope is to provide support to improving current knowledge-based explainable methods and, more in general, foster a more solid integration of knowledge representation frameworks with eXplainable AI systems.

References

[1]   S. Bechhofer, F. Van Harmelen, J. Hendler, I. Horrocks, D. L. McGuinness, P. F. Patel-Schneider, L. A. Stein, et al. Owl web ontology language reference. *W3C recommendation*, 10(02), 2004.

[2]   W. Beek, J. Raad, E. Acar, and F. van Harmelen. Metalink: A travel guide to the lod cloud. In *ESWC*. Springer, 2020.

[3]   W. Beek, J. Raad, J. Wielemaker, and F. van Harmelen. sameas. cc: The closure of 500m owl: sameas statements. In *ESWC*, pages 65–80. Springer, 2018.

[4]   W. Beek, L. Rietveld, H. R. Bazoobandi, J. Wielemaker, and S. Schlobach. Lod laundromat: a uniform way of publishing other people's dirty data. In *ISWC*, pages 213–228. Springer, 2014.

[5]   C. Bizer, T. Heath, and T. Berners-Lee. Linked data: The story so far. In *Semantic services, interoperability and web applications: emerging concepts*, pages 205–227. IGI Global, 2011.

[6]   P. Bouquet, H. Stoermer, and D. Giacomuzzi. OKKAM: enabling a web of entities. In *I3*, volume 249 of *CEUR Workshop Proceedings*, 2007.

[7]   A. Buikstra, H. Neth, L. Schooler, A. t. Teije, and F. v. Harmelen. Ranking query results from linked open data using a simple cognitive heuristic. In *IJCAI-11*, 2011.

[8]   A. Chapman, E. Simperl, L. Koesten, G. Konstantinidis, L.-D. Ibáñez, E. Kacprzak, and P. Groth. Dataset search: a survey. *The VLDB Journal*, pages 1–22, 2019.

[9]   J. Chen, F. Lecue, J. Z. Pan, I. Horrocks, and H. Chen. Knowledge-based transfer learning explanation. In *Sixteenth International Conference on Principles of Knowledge Representation and Reasoning*, 2018.

[10] D. Colla, E. Mensa, D. P. Radicioni, and A. Lieto. Tell me why: Computational explanation of conceptual similarity judgments. In *International Conference on Information Processing and Management of Uncertainty in Knowledge-Based Systems*, pages 74–85. Springer, 2018.

[11] P. CudreMauroux, P. Haghani, M. Jost, K. Aberer, and H. De Meer. idmesh: graph-based disambiguation of linked data. In *WWW*, pages 591–600. ACM, 2009.

[12] J. Cuzzola, E. Bagheri, and J. Jovanovic. Filtering inaccurate entity co-references on the linked open data. In *DEXA*, pages 128–143. Springer, 2015.

[13] G. de Melo. Not quite the same: Identity constraints for the web of linked data. In *Twenty-Seventh AAAI Conference on Artificial Intelligence*, 2013.

[14] S. Deng, N. Zhang, W. Zhang, J. Chen, J. Z. Pan, and H. Chen. Knowledge-driven stock trend prediction and explanation via temporal convolutional network. 2019.

[15] T. Di Noia, R. Mirizzi, V. C. Ostuni, and D. Romito. Exploiting the web of data in model-based recommender systems. In *Proceedings of the sixth ACM conference on Recommender systems*, pages 253–256. ACM, 2012.

[16] V. Dimitrova, L. Lau, D. Thakker, F. Yang-Turner, and D. Despotakis. Exploring exploratory search: a user study with linked semantic data. In *Proceedings of the 2nd international workshop on intelligent exploration of semantic data*, page 2. ACM, 2013.

[17] J. Fernández, W. Beek, M. Martínez-Prieto, and M. Arias. Lod-a-lot. In *ISWC*, pages 75–83. Springer, 2017.

[18] P. Geach. Identity. *Review of Metaphysics*, 21:3–12, 1967.

[19] H. Glaser, A. Jaffri, and I. Millard. Managing co-reference on the semantic web. In *WWW Workshop on Linked Data on the Web*, 2009.

[20] J. Grant and V. S. Subrahmanian. Reasoning in inconsistent knowledge bases. *IEEE Trans. Knowl. Data Eng.*, 7(1):177–189, 1995.

[21] C. Guéret, P. Groth, C. Stadler, and J. Lehmann. Assessing linked data mappings using network measures. In *ESWC*, pages 87–102. Springer, 2012.

[22] D. Gunning. Explainable artificial intelligence (xai). *Defense Advanced Research Projects Agency (DARPA), nd Web*, 2, 2017.

[23] A. Haller, J. D. Fernández, M. R. Kamdar, and A. Polleres. What are links in linked open data? a characterization and evaluation of links between knowledge graphs on the web. *Working Papers on Information Systems, Information Business and Operations*, (2/2019), 2019.

[24] H. Halpin, P. J. Hayes, J. McCusker, D. McGuinness, and H. Thompson. When owl:sameAs isn't the same: An analysis of identity in Linked Data. In *ISWC*, pages 305–320. Springer, 2010.

[25] B. Heitmann and C. Hayes. Using linked data to build open, collaborative recommender systems. In *2010 AAAI Spring Symposium Series*, 2010.

[26] A. Hogan, J. Umbrich, A. Harth, R. Cyganiak, A. Polleres, and S. Decker. An empirical survey of linked data conformance. *Web Semantics: Science, Services and Agents on the World Wide Web*, 14:14–44, 2012.

[27] A. Hogan, A. Zimmermann, J. Umbrich, A. Polleres, and S. Decker. Scalable and distributed methods for entity matching, consolidation and disambiguation over linked data corpora. *Web Semantics Journal*, 10:76–110, 2012.

[28] S. Kripke. Naming and necessity. In *Semantics of natural language*, pages 253–355. Springer, 1972.

[29] R. Krishna, Y. Zhu, O. Groth, J. Johnson, K. Hata, J. Kravitz, S. Chen, Y. Kalantidis, L.-J. Li, D. A. Shamma, et al. Visual genome: Connecting language and vision using crowdsourced dense image annotations. *International Journal of Computer Vision*, 123(1):32–73, 2017.

[30] F. Lécué and J. Wu. Semantic explanations of predictions. *arXiv preprint arXiv:1805.10587*, 2018.

[31] D. Lewis. On the plurality of worlds. *Oxford*, 14:43, 1986.

[32] V. Lully, P. Laublet, M. Stankovic, and F. Radulovic. Enhancing explanations in recommender systems with knowledge graphs. *Procedia Computer Science*, 137:211–222, 2018.

[33] K. Marino, R. Salakhutdinov, and A. Gupta. The more you know: Using knowledge graphs for image

classification. *arXiv preprint arXiv:1612.04844*, 2016.

[34] M. Mealling and R. Daniel. Uri resolution services necessary for urn resolution (rfc 2483), 1999.

[35] T. Mihaylov and A. Frank. Knowledgeable reader: Enhancing cloze-style reading comprehension with external commonsense knowledge. *arXiv preprint arXiv:1805.07858*, 2018.

[36] R. Mirizzi, A. Ragone, T. Di Noia, and E. Di Sciascio. Semantic wonder cloud: exploratory search in dbpedia. In *International Conference on Web Engineering*, pages 138–149. Springer, 2010.

[37] M. Mountantonakis and Y. Tzitzikas. On measuring the lattice of commonalities among several linked datasets. *Proceedings of the VLDB Endowment*, 9(12):1101–1112, 2016.

[38] M. Mountantonakis and Y. Tzitzikas. Scalable methods for measuring the connectivity and quality of large numbers of linked datasets. *Journal of Data and Information Quality (JDIQ)*, 9(3):15, 2018.

[39] M. Mountantonakis and Y. Tzitzikas. Large-scale semantic integration of linked data: A survey. *ACM Computing Surveys (CSUR)*, 52(5):1–40, 2019.

[40] A. Musetti, A. G. Nuzzolese, F. Draicchio, V. Presutti, E. Blomqvist, A. Gangemi, and P. Ciancarini. Ae-moo: Exploratory search based on knowledge patterns over the semantic web. *Semantic Web Challenge*, 136, 2012.

[41] N. Nguyen. *Advanced methods for inconsistent knowledge management*. Springer Science & Business Media, Secaucus, NJ, USA, 2007.

[42] F. Å. Nielsen. Linking imagenet wordnet synsets with wikidata. *arXiv preprint arXiv:1803.04349*, 2018.

[43] L. Papaleo, N. Pernelle, F. Saïs, and C. Dumont. Logical detection of invalid sameas statements in rdf data. In *EKAW*, pages 373–384. Springer, 2014.

[44] A. Papangelis, P. Papadakos, M. Kotti, Y. Stylianou, Y. Tzitzikas, and D. Plexousakis. Ld-sds: Towards an expressive spoken dialogue system based on linked-data. *arXiv preprint arXiv:1710.02973*, 2017.

[45] H. Paulheim. Identifying wrong links between datasets by multi-dimensional outlier detection. In *WoDOOM*, pages 27–38, 2014.

[46] J. Raad, W. Beek, F. van Harmelen, N. Pernelle, and F. Saïs. Detecting erroneous identity links on the web using network metrics. In *ISWC*, pages 391–407. Springer, 2018.

[47] Y. Raimond, C. Sutton, and M. Sandler. Interlinking music-related data on the web. *IEEE MultiMedia*, 16(2):52–63, 2009.

[48] J. F. Sánchez-Rada and C. A. Iglesias. Onyx: A linked data approach to emotion representation. *Information Processing & Management*, 52(1):99–114, 2016.

[49] M. Schmachtenberg, C. Bizer, and H. Paulheim. Adoption of the linked data best practices in different topical domains. In *ISWC*, pages 245–260. Springer, 2014.

[50] F. J. Serón and C. Bobed. Vox system: a semantic embodied conversational agent exploiting linked data. *Multimedia Tools and Applications*, 75(1):381–404, 2016.

[51] C. E. Shannon. A mathematical theory of communication. *Bell system technical journal*, 27(3):379–423, 1948.

[52] B. Spahiu, C. Xie, A. Rula, A. Maurino, and H. Cai. Profiling similarity links in linked open data. In *2016 IEEE 32nd International Conference on Data Engineering Workshops (ICDEW)*, pages 103–108. IEEE, 2016.

[53] P. Tarau and E. Figa. Knowledge-based conversational agents and virtual storytelling. In *Proceedings of the 2004 ACM symposium on Applied computing*, pages 39–44. ACM, 2004.

[54] I. Tiddi, M. d'Aquin, and E. Motta. Walking linked data: a graph traversal approach to explain clusters. In *Proceedings of the 5th International Conference on Consuming Linked Data-Volume 1264*, pages 73–84. CEUR-WS. org, 2014.

[55] I. Tiddi, M. d'Aquin, and E. Motta. Dedalo: Looking for clusters explanations in a labyrinth of linked data. In *European Semantic Web Conference*, pages 333–348. Springer, 2014.

[56] A. Valdestilhas, T. Soru, and A. Ngonga Ngomo. Cedal: time-efficient detection of erroneous links in large-scale link repositories. In *ICWI*, pages 106–113. ACM, 2017.

[57] D. Vrandecic, M. Ortiz, and T. Schneider. Toward an abstract wikipedia. In *Description Logics*, 2018.

[58] P. Wang, Q. Wu, C. Shen, A. Dick, and A. van den Hengel. Fvqa: Fact-based visual question answering. *IEEE transactions on pattern analysis and machine intelligence*, 40(10):2413–2427, 2018.

[59] Y. Zhang, S. He, K. Liu, and J. Zhao. A joint model for question answering over multiple knowledge bases. In *Thirtieth AAAI Conference on Artificial Intelligence*, 2016.

IOS Press, 2020

Subject Index

Knowledge Graphs for eXplainable Artificial Intelligence: Foundations, Applications and Challenges   303
I. Tiddi et al. (Eds.)
IOS Press, 2020

Author Index